TCP/IP

FOR

DUMMIES®

6TH EDITION

by Candace Leiden and Marshall Wilensky

Foreword by Scott Bradner
University Technology Security Officer, Harvard University

WILEY

Wiley Publishing, Inc.

TCP/IP For Dummies, 6th Edition

Published by
Wiley Publishing, Inc.
111 River Street
Hoboken, NJ 07030-5774
www.wiley.com

WILEY

About the Authors

Forced to learn about computers because she was afraid of slide rules, **Candace Leiden** has worked as a software developer, system administrator, and database designer and administrator. Formerly the president of Cardinal Consulting, Inc., Candace is now a systems and database performance consultant and instructional design consultant for international courseware in those areas. Her customers have included Cardinal Consulting, Compaq Computer, Digital Equipment Corporation, the United Nations, several major pharmaceutical corporations, Oracle Corporation, and Hewlett-Packard. Candace is an internationally recognized speaker on relational databases and the Linux and Unix operating systems. Candace is also the author of *Linux Bible* (Wiley Publishing). Candace met Marshall Wilensky in 1981, when they worked at the same company. She taught him everything he knows.

Marshall Wilensky has been wrangling computers and networks for more than 30 years (and still has fewer wrinkles than Candace and less gray hair). In corporate life, he has had the privilege of working for companies ranging from 25 people (who are 25 years old) to more than 300,000 worldwide. He has been a consultant, a programmer, a system administrator, and a network manager for large multivendor and multiprotocol networks, including those at the Harvard University Graduate School of Business Administration.

Marshall met Candace Leiden in 1981 when they worked at the same company. He taught her everything she knows. They are also, most importantly, married (to each other).

Candace and Marshall are both members-at-large of ICANN (Internet Corporation for Assigned Names and Numbers).

Dedication

Candace dedicates this book to Marshall Wilensky (no one knows the meaning of the phrase "in sickness and in health" better than Marshall) and to Emily Duncan, who is wise beyond her years. Even though she has been through some tough times, Emily rules!

Marshall dedicates this edition of the book to his late parents, Leo and Estelle Wilensky, and to Roxcy Platte and the people who help him with the toughest subject he has ever tackled.

In memory of:

Helen Louise Duncan

Christine Evans Staley

They are missed every day.

Authors' Acknowledgments

Thanks to everyone at Wiley who worked on this book. We continue to be surprised at how many people it takes to create a book. We'd like to thank the team at Wiley for putting up with us. Thanks also go to Katie Mohr, for her patience and diplomacy. So many people worked hard to turn our manuscript into a real book. Thanks also to our project editor, Kim Darosett, who never once had a discouraging word. When we finish a manuscript, Kim still has a lot of hard work to do. We're grateful to Kim, Rebecca Whitney, Jen Riggs, and Barry Childs-Helton for their hard work. Their edits make this a better book in many ways. We appreciate the work the Composition Services department did in drawing tidy figures from our rough, hand-drawn sketches and in making our screen shots and text files look nice.

Finally, thank you to Cynthia Woods, a gifted and inspiring musician, who allowed us to use her beautiful Web page as one of our examples.

Publisher's Acknowledgments

We're proud of this book; please send us your comments through our online registration form located at `http://dummies.custhelp.com`. For other comments, please contact our Customer Care Department within the U.S. at 877-762-2974, outside the U.S. at 317-572-3993, or fax 317-572-4002.

Some of the people who helped bring this book to market include the following:

Acquisitions and Editorial

Project Editor: Kim Darosett

Acquisitions Editor: Katie Mohr

Copy Editors: Barry Childs-Helton, Heidi Unger, Rebecca Whitney

Technical Editor: Allen Wyatt

Editorial Manager: Leah P. Cameron

Sr. Editorial Assistant: Cherie Case

Cartoons: Rich Tennant
(`www.the5thwave.com`)

Composition Services

Project Coordinator: Patrick Redmond

Layout and Graphics: Reuben W. Davis, Timothy C. Detrick, Melissa K. Smith, Christine Williams

Proofreaders: David Faust, Jessica Kramer, Lisa Young Stiers

Indexer: Estalita Slivoskey

Publishing and Editorial for Technology Dummies

    Richard Swadley, Vice President and Executive Group Publisher

    Andy Cummings, Vice President and Publisher

    Mary Bednarek, Executive Acquisitions Director

    Mary C. Corder, Editorial Director

Publishing for Consumer Dummies

    Diane Graves Steele, Vice President and Publisher

Composition Services

    Debbie Stailey, Director of Composition Services

Table of Contents

Foreword

For both good and ill, modern society around the world has been transformed by the Internet. But the Internet was not the first data communications network, not by a long shot. So what was it about the Internet that enabled the revolution? In a very basic way, it was the use of TCP/IP. TCP/IP enabled the Internet to be the first data network where the use could be driven by the users and not controlled by the carriers. TCP/IP is an end-to-end protocol. The network is there to carry the bits from any device at the edge of the network to any other device. This stands in stark contrast to X.25, frame relay, ATM, and other carrier-managed data networks, where the carrier determined who you could talk to, and in an even starker contrast to the phone network, where the carrier determined what you could do.

This end-to-end architecture has resulted in an amazing proliferation of applications because the network does not get in the way of individual entrepreneurs developing the next great thing and running it over the Internet. It also did not get in the way of millions of people putting up their own Web pages, or, with somewhat more controversy, swapping music and movie files. Even if you take into account the Internet boom and subsequent bust, the Internet, and TCP/IP, are here to stay. And, while here, they will continue to radically change the way we interact with employers, service providers, each other, and the world at large.

You can easily go through life without having to understand how this Internet thing works because it will continue to work even if you do not understand it. I do not have any meaningful understanding of the Theory of Relativity yet make use of its implications every day.

TCP/IP For Dummies, 6th Edition, is for those of you who aren't just curious about how things work, but who want to actually understand what's behind the curtain. (Hint: It's not the Wizard of Oz.)

Scott Bradner
University Technology Security Officer, Harvard University

Introduction

TCP/IP is the glue that holds together the Internet and the World Wide Web. To be well connected (network-wise, that is), sooner or later you have to become familiar with TCP/IP applications and services. If you want to understand what TCP/IP is, what it's for, why you need it, and what to do with it, and you just don't know where to start — this book is for you.

If you're on a network, whether you know it or not, odds are, you're working with TCP/IP and its many pieces and parts. We help you understand how it all fits together. We also give you plenty of hands-on tips so that you can get all those pieces and parts set up and running.

We take the mystery out of TCP/IP by giving you down-to-earth explanations for all the buzzwords and technical jargon that TCP/IP loves.

This isn't a formal tutorial; skip around and taste TCP/IP in little bites. If you need to impress your boss and colleagues with buzzwords, you can find out just enough to toss them around intelligently with the technocrats at meetings and parties. Or, you can go further and discover how to set up and use the most important features and tools. If you want the full TCP/IP banquet, you can explore the technical tasks that take place behind the scenes to make the Internet and the Web work. It's right here in your hands.

About This Book

We hope you find *TCP/IP For Dummies,* 6th Edition, to be a fun and fast way to dive into the guts of the Internet. The book is both an introduction to the basics and a reference to help you work with Internet applications and tools on all kinds of connected computers. We added and updated the latest Internetworking protocols and servers — with examples from Microsoft Windows Server 2008, Windows 7, Windows Vista, Windows XP, Linux, Unix, and Mac OS X. Here are just a few of the subjects we describe:

- Uncover the relationships among TCP/IP, the Net, and the Web.

- Get up and running and *keep* running on the Internet, whether you have a small network or a big enterprise network and whether it's wired or wireless.

✔ Install and configure TCP/IP client and server applications and services.

✔ Phone home without the phone or the bill, thanks to VoIP.

✔ Build and enforce security everywhere on your network.

✔ Get in on all the newest Internet security protocols and trends.

✔ Boldly go to the next generation: IPv6.

This book is loaded with information. But don't try to read it from cover to cover in one sitting — you may hurt yourself. If your head explodes and bits and bytes go flying, please don't blame us.

Conventions Used in This Book

All commands that you need to enter yourself appear either in bold, **like this**, or on a separate line, like this:

```
COMMAND to type
```

To enter this command, you type **COMMAND to type** exactly as you see it here and then press Enter.

When you type commands, be careful to use the same upper- and lowercase letters that we show you. (Some computer systems are fussy about this issue.)

When we want you to move through a series of menus or buttons, we say "Click" once and then point to the next place with a command arrow (⇨).

Whenever we show you something that's displayed onscreen (such as an error message or a response to your input), it looks like this:

```
A TCP/IP message on your screen
```

Foolish Assumptions

In writing this book, we tried not to make too many assumptions about you. We figure that you've done a little Web browsing and e-mailing. Our only assumption is that you're not really a dummy — you're just trying something new. Good for you!

How This Book Is Organized

This book contains five parts, each of which contains several chapters. We don't expect you to read the whole book from cover to cover, but please feel free to do so. Instead, you can glance at the table of contents for the topic you're interested in and go from there. The layout of the book is easy to follow. Here's a quick look at what you can find in each major part.

Part I: TCP/IP from Names to Addresses

Part I starts at the beginning with the buzzwords and how TCP/IP and the Internet are joined at the hip. You also find out that, contrary to its name, TCP/IP is so much more than just two protocols. We give you a quick look at the most important protocols, and you get to see all the lingo that should take you far through this century.

You'll find that as much as people like names, computers like numbers even more. After you get some of the buzzwords under your belt, the chapters in Part I explain what an Internet protocol (IP) address is, how to build one, how to use it, and how to be frugal and save enough Internet addresses for someone else. We clue you in on different ways to make IP addresses go further. No worries — the Internet won't get full.

Part II: Getting Connected

After you know how IP addresses are constructed, we move on to setting up your TCP/IP network, both wired and wireless, to connect to the world (the Internet). In this part of the book, we show you how hardware and software work together to make a network. We discuss just the minimum hardware you need to understand.

Then we throw in IPv6, which puts you ahead of most people in understanding the next generation of Internet addresses. If you're not ready to go where no one (well, hardly anyone) has gone before, don't worry — you can skip Chapter 9 entirely.

Part III: Configuring Clients and Servers: Web, E-Mail, and Chat

TCP/IP is a big set of protocols, services, and applications. Whether you're aware of it or not, you use TCP/IP applications and services to do everything from reading news to exchanging e-mail and online conversations with your friends to copying good stuff like games, technical articles, and even TCP/IP itself. This section explains how these applications and services work behind the scenes with client/server technology. The numerous hands-on sections help you configure popular applications and services for both clients and servers.

Security is one of the stars of Part III. Hackers love to try to break into your Web, e-mail, and chat applications, and we love to show you how to thwart their every move. We throw in a quick-start security guide to get you going. If you're interested in online shopping or banking, we walk you through a secure Internet credit card transaction.

Part IV: Even More TCP/IP Applications and Services

"How could there possibly be more?" you might ask. Well, we told you that TCP/IP consists of much more than just a couple of protocols — for example, there's Mobile IP, for when you take your laptop to your favorite café rather than to your office. If you have a smartphone or organizer, such as a Palm or BlackBerry, you need to know this stuff. But wait! There's more. How about saving big bucks on phone calls? With or without a phone? Voice over Internet Protocol, or just VoIP, lets you make calls, even international ones, for free. Finally, Part IV covers remote access applications, from sharing files to working on someone else's computer when you're 5,000 miles away.

Part V: Network Troubleshooting and Security

Part V delves into some advanced topics. If you're a system or network administrator, you may need to know more than just the basics about network hardware. We hope that after you install and configure TCP/IP and your network applications, nothing ever goes wrong for you, but stuff happens. Part V steps you through a basic troubleshooting procedure so that you can figure out what went wrong and where. Then you can fix it.

The rest of Part V is devoted to security. You find practical security tips, and you can delve deeper, to see how to use encryption, authentication, digital certificates, and signatures. You get hands-on advice for setting up a software firewall and the Kerberos authentication server.

Part VI: The Part of Tens

You may already know that every *For Dummies* book has one of these parts. In it, you can find security tips, Internet traffic factoids, advice about places to go and things to do (even if you never leave your computer), and more security pointers. And all this happens in, roughly, sets of ten.

Icons Used in This Book

Signals nerdy technofacts that you can easily skip without hurting your TCP/IP education. But if you're even a part-time techie, you probably love this stuff.

Indicates nifty shortcuts that make your life easier.

Lets you know that a loaded gun is pointed directly at your foot. Watch out!

Marks information that's important to commit to memory. To siphon off the most important information in each chapter, just skim through these icons.

Marks important TCP/IP security issues. *Lots* of security icons are in this book.

Where to Go from Here

Check out the table of contents or the index and decide where you want to start. If you're an information technology manager, you're probably interested in buzzwords and you know why everyone is on the TCP/IP bandwagon. If you're a system or network administrator, start with Chapter 2 or 4, where we describe the major protocols and what they do. Chapters 12, 14, 20, and 21 talk about Internet security — a topic that's for everyone concerned that their personal data is at risk.

Or, you can just turn the pages one by one. We don't mind. Really.

Part I
TCP/IP from Names to Addresses

The 5th Wave   By Rich Tennant

"This part of the test tells us whether you are personally suited to the job of network administrator."

In this part . . .

Y ou can't play the game if you don't know the rules. And TCP/IP is the set of rules, or *protocols,* for networks. TCP/IP is the software underpinning of the Internet and its World Wide Web. TCP/IP also includes services and applications that work with the protocols. Before we get into the hairy details of the protocols themselves, we give you some background on the people and committees who decide the direction of TCP/IP's growth. Did you know that you can be part of these groups? We tell you how. You also become familiar with TCP/IP and Internet buzzwords.

Part I then delves into the ingredients of the TCP/IP suite: the protocols and services themselves and IP addressing. You see how the protocols fit into the layers of the TCP/IP network model, and you take a look at the most important ones. TCP/IP is a *suite* because it consists of more protocols than the two it's named for, plus a set of services and applications. The TCP/IP protocols, services, and applications in the suite work together just like the rooms in a hotel suite or the pieces in a furniture suite work together. The set of protocols is also referred to as a *stack.*

From there, we go into Internet addressing.

People love names. Computers love numbers. You'll hear this in each part of this book.

If your computer is named Woodstock, for example, the Internet may think of it as 198.162.1.4. You get to see how to build and understand these numeric addresses. Also, if you're worried because you think that the Internet is running low on addresses, Part I eases your worries by cluing you in to a couple of different ways to make IP addresses go further: subnetting and NAT (Network Address Translation).

Bear in mind that TCP/IP stays alive by morphing regularly — at times, daily. So, the list of protocols we describe here — the Internet's rules — will be even longer by the time you read this book.

Chapter 1

Understanding TCP/IP Basics

In This Chapter

▶ Protocols in this chapter: IP, TCP, IPSec, PPTP, L2TP

▶ Introducing TCP/IP

▶ Defining a protocol

▶ Understanding RFCs — the protocol documentation

▶ Differentiating between intranets, extranets, and Virtual Private Networks (VPNs)

▶ Figuring out who's in charge of TCP/IP and the Internet

▶ Investigating different types of networks that rely on TCP/IP software

*Y*ou bought or borrowed this book, or maybe you're just flipping through it to pick up some information and tips about TCP/IP and its pieces and parts. Transmission Control Protocol/Internet Protocol, or TCP/IP, is the internationally accepted software for networking in general and, specifically, for making the Internet's services possible.

As you read this book, you get a behind-the-scenes look at how TCP/IP makes the Internet work. You also see how to use TCP/IP to set up your own home, office, or even international network. This chapter gets started by defining a protocol in general and TCP/IP protocols specifically. Proposals known as Requests for Comment, or *RFCs,* document how TCP/IP should function. You may wonder who's in charge of defining these protocols that rule the Internet. The answer is: lots of people who join international committees. This chapter describes the main Internet governing committees and what they do.

The Internet is one giant worldwide network that consists of tens of thousands of other networks. We give you an idea in this chapter of the different kinds of networks that connect via TCP/IP into the Internet.

The TCP/IP pronunciation guide

Pronouncing TCP/IP is easy — you just say the name of each letter and ignore the slash (/). Ready? It sounds like this:

"Tee cee pee eye pee"

Skip the silly jokes, please. We've made them all. By the way, some people find five letters too much to pronounce, so they just say "IP" to refer to the whole thing.

Following Rules for the Internet: TCP/IP Protocols

A *protocol* is a set of behavior-related rules that people follow. Some protocols are formally defined. For example, when people meet and greet each other, they might say, "Enchante de faire votre conaissance" or "How do you do"? We also hear our niece, Emily, and her friends saying "Hey, dude!" All these examples are widely accepted behaviors for people to start communicating — they are protocols. The more formal greetings are written down in etiquette books. "Hey, dude" has become accepted (at least by people much younger than we are) because of its wide use. Common ways of connecting aren't enough, though. After you meet, you need a common language in order to communicate. Just as people connect and communicate in accepted ways, computers connect and communicate with each other and with you. In the world of computers and networks, TCP/IP is a common language used for both connection and communication.

Although TCP/IP sounds like it consists of just two protocols, it's a whole set of protocols for connecting computers to the Internet. This set of protocols is the TCP/IP *stack,* or *protocol suite.* We describe in Chapter 2 the most well-known protocols in the TCP/IP stack. Before we get to the protocols themselves, the following sections look at who's in charge of the Internet and who decides what gets to be a standard part of the TCP/IP protocol suite. You also get familiar with Requests for Comments (RFCs), the documents that describe TCP/IP standards.

Who's in charge of the Internet and TCP/IP?

You're in charge. Or, you might say that everyone is, and no one is, in charge of the Internet and TCP/IP. No one person, organization, corporation, or government owns or controls the TCP/IP protocols or the Internet. Moreover, no one person, organization, corporation, or government finances the TCP/IP protocols or the Internet. To say that no one controls TCP/IP and the Internet doesn't mean, however, that protocols magically appear with no control or that the Internet just does whatever it wants.

This list describes some of the important organizations and committees that *steer* TCP/IP and Internet policies:

- **Internet Society (ISOC):** The Internet Society (`www.isoc.org`) guides the future of the Internet by overseeing Internet standards, public policy, education, and training. ISOC members include corporations, international and governmental organizations, and individuals. The Internet Activities Board (refer to third bullet), the Internet Engineering Task Force (refer to fourth bullet), and the Internet Research Task Force are all part of the ISOC.

- **Internet Corporation for Assigned Names and Numbers (ICANN):** The nonprofit corporation ICANN, at `www.icann.org`, is in charge of assigning Internet addresses. ICANN, pronounced "eye can," is run by an international board of directors and funded by the Internet community.

- **Internet Activities Board (IAB):** IAB, at `www.iab.org`, defines the architecture for the Internet. The IAB — just say its letters, "i-a-b" — also oversees the Internet's protocols (TCP/IP). The IAB contains subcommittees of volunteers who set standards and work on new solutions to Internet growth problems.

- **Internet Engineering Task Force (IETF):** IETF, at `www.ietf.org`, is a community of more than 70 informal committees responsible for keeping the Internet up and running every day. The IAB supervises the IETF, which is pronounced simply "i-e-t-f." You can join the IETF working groups to help draft and develop standards for TCP/IP protocols.

Figure 1-1 shows how these Internet management groups are organized.

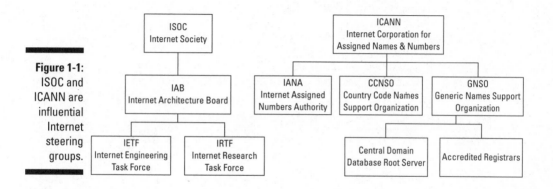

Figure 1-1: ISOC and ICANN are influential Internet steering groups.

Checking out RFCs: The written rules

TCP/IP protocols are written down in special Request for Comments (RFC) documents. An RFC (pronounced "r-f-c") document is available for everyone to read and comment on — it's part of the democracy of the Internet.

Toasting the RFC Editor

Surprise! The RFC Editor isn't just one person. It consists of a small group of people who work for the Internet Society. The RFC Editor Web site, at www. rfc-editor.org, keeps the official index of all RFCs ever written. You can find any RFC there. We find this site to be one of the most useful when we want information about what's going on with TCP/IP. You can search RFCs by number, author, title, or keyword. For example, click the link Search for an RFC and Its Meta-Data and then search for the keyword **security**. Notice how many pages it takes to display the results. And the list of results only grows — an RFC is never removed. It may be declared obsolete, but it stays available.

Knowing who writes RFCs

If you come up with an idea for a new or an improved capability for TCP/IP, you write your proposal as an RFC and submit it to an Internet committee for review. Working groups from various committees collaborate on most RFCs. You can join these working groups if you want to help but don't want to write a whole RFC on your own. For example, to join an IETF working group, send an e-mail to Iptel-request@ietf.org.

Understanding RFC categories

Three categories of RFCs are on the standards track:

- **Standard (STD):** An approved technical standard
- **Draft standard:** On its way to being adopted as a standard
- **Proposed standard:** On its way to being adopted as a draft standard

Here are some other RFC categories:

- **Best current practices (BCP):** Guidelines and recommendations, such as RFC 4107, "Guidelines for Cryptographic Key Management"
- **Experimental (EXP):** Part of a research or development project, such as RFC 5335, "Internationalized Email Headers"
- **Historic:** Refers to the fact that most historic RFCs are former standards that are now obsolete and have been replaced by more current RFCs
- **Informational (FYI):** Provides general information, such as RFC 4677, "The Tao of IETF — A Novice's Guide to the Internet Engineering Task Force"

If you have time and a sense of humor, check out the RFCs written on April 1, but *do not* take them seriously!

Examining Other Standards Organizations That Add to the Rules

Although the Internet corporations, committees, and groups listed in the preceding section specify the rules for using TCP/IP, other groups set standards for related technologies, as described in this list:

- **Institute of Electrical and Electronics Engineers (IEEE):** The IEEE (pronounce it "eye-triple-e") sets hardware standards, such as the hardware that connects Local Area Networks (LANs) and Wireless Local Area Networks (WLANs).

- **World Wide Web Consortium (W3C):** Although the Web is part of the Internet and follows TCP/IP standards, the W3C (say the letters and number "w-c-3") sets standards related to Web services.

- **International Organization for Standardization (ISO):** ISO ("eye-so") sets all kinds of standards, not just for networks. One of its standards indicates how the computers that run your car should interconnect.

- **Open Systems Interconnection (OSI):** The OSI ("o-s-i") sets networking protocol standards similar to TCP/IP, but different. At one time, OSI thought that its protocols would replace TCP/IP, but as hard as its members worked, it didn't happen.

- **Free Software Foundation (FSF) General Public License (GPL):** The FSF set up the GNU (pronounced "guh-new") project to create and distribute free software. GNU software, licensed under the GPL, is the reason that the Linux operating system is available for free or for a very low cost. GNU also provides lots of network tools and utilities as well as complete TCP/IP stacks.

Distinguishing Between the Internet, an Internet, and an Intranet

Yes, we realize that you already know what the Internet is. But just so that we're all using the same definition, the *Internet* is the worldwide collection of interconnected computer networks that use the TCP/IP protocol. These networks reach every continent — even Antarctica — and nearly every country.

The Internet also consists of much more than its network connections. It's all the individual computers connected to those individual networks, plus all the users of those computers, all the information accessible to those users, and all the knowledge those people possess. The Internet is just as much about people and information as it is about computers and computer networks.

Although the Internet is public, many organizations (companies and universities, for example) have their own, private internets that may connect to it. *An* internet is built the same way as *the* Internet, except that an internet is private. You might even have *an* internet in your home.

REMEMBER

Both the Internet and internets run on TCP/IP protocol software. In this book, we distinguish *the* Internet from *an* internet by capitalizing *the* Internet.

The difference between *an* internet and an intranet is just terminology. The term *intranet* is fairly recent. Old-timers (such as the authors of this book) grew up with "*an* internet" and now we use both terms. The important concept is that all kinds of "nets" run with TCP/IP.

Extending Intranets to Extranets

Intranets are the building blocks of extranets. If part of your intranet is available to people outside your organization, such as customers and suppliers, the part you share with the outside world is an *extranet*. An extranet has these characteristics:

- ✔ It consists of multiple, interconnected intranets/internets.
- ✔ An organization's extended family of partners work together electronically.
- ✔ It might not exist physically — it's a *virtual* network.

Because an *intranet* is a private network within an organization or a department, you might find a few different intranets in a large institution. A university on the east coast, for example, might have one intranet for its medical school, another intranet for its college of liberal arts, and a third intranet for its business school. That university may also network those intranets into an even bigger intranet. Then, so that the university community can reach the rest of the world, the university intranet needs to be connected to the (capital *I*) Internet.

When that university needs to share data with a different university on the west coast, the two universities can link their respective intranets to create an *extranet*. Figure 1-2 shows how the east and west coast universities form an extranet.

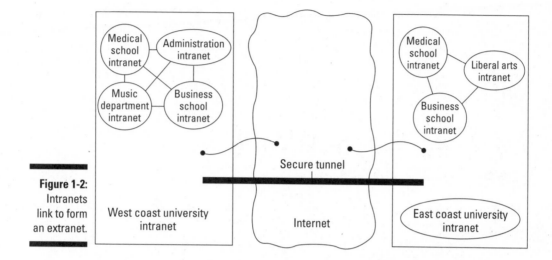

Figure 1-2:
Intranets
link to form
an extranet.

An extranet consists of as many intranets as you need in order to communicate with your partners.

Introducing Virtual Private Networks

A *Virtual Private Network,* or *VPN* ("v-p-n"), is a private network that runs over public facilities, such as the Internet. Although it may seem like a contradiction to run a private network over the (very) public Internet, it works. In the olden days of computers (which is often six months ago, but we're talking as long as five years ago), if you wanted to work away from your office, you usually used a very slow modem to dial in across your phone line to the office computer. This method was slow and not secure because bad people could steal the data you were sending and receiving across the telephone lines.

Nowadays, most telecommuters connect to their offices through VPNs. They let you work as though you're on-site when you're not. You run VPN client software to establish a secure connection over the Internet to your organization's network. It's just like being in the office.

A VPN

✔ Is safe and secure because it scrambles *(encrypts)* data before sending it over the public lines

✔ Uses special tunneling and security protocols on the public network

See the section about the IPSec, PPTP, and L2TP protocols in Chapter 22 for more information.

> ✔ Saves money for a large organization's networks because sharing the public Internet is cheaper than leasing private telecommunication lines
>
> ✔ Connects both intranets and extranets

The extranet shown earlier, in Figure 1-2, is also a VPN.

Exploring Geographically Based Networks

Whether you're sending e-mail or browsing the Web, your data gets broken up into small pieces called packets. In other words, your data is "packetized" before it goes onto a network. Packets of data travel over many different kinds of geographical distances, ranging from local to global and beyond to space. TCP/IP doesn't care about earthly distance — just that your data gets where it's going. In this section, get ready for a lot of jargon-y terms that look a lot alike. If you aren't interested in network architecture, feel free to skip this section and save your brain from getting muddled.

Networks connected by wires and cables

Networks come in different shapes and sizes. Two main architectures for networks — LANs (Local Area Networks) and WANs (Wide Area Networks) — are usually based on these factors:

> ✔ The distance the network covers
>
> ✔ Architecture and connection media
>
> ✔ Speed
>
> ✔ Purpose
>
> (For example, does the network connect a city, a campus, or just a bunch of storage devices?)

Exploring LANs

Pronounce LAN as a word — "lan" (rhymes with "pan"). The computers and other devices in a LAN communicate over small geographical areas, such as these:

> ✔ Your home office — or even the whole house
>
> ✔ One wing of one floor in a building

- ✔ Maybe the entire floor, if it's a small building
- ✔ Several buildings on a small campus

Incorporating WANs

Imagine a company that has several buildings in different towns and provinces, or even in different countries. Does that mean that all the people who work in the company can't be on the same network because a LAN is limited by distance? Of course not. The Internet is worldwide and beyond, so you can even bounce data off satellites in outer space, to create a WAN.

A WAN ("wan") spans geographical distances that are too large for LANs. Figure 1-3 shows two LANs connected to form a WAN.

Wireless networks

You don't need cables and wires to connect the computers that comprise a network. You can go wireless, and cables can be expensive. (Air, a wireless connection media, is free — at least for now.) Just as cabled LANs and WANs exist, wireless LANs (WLANs) and wireless WANs (WWANS) also exist.

You pronounce WLAN as the letter *w* followed by the word *LAN:* "double-you-lan." Pronounce WWAN as the letter *w* followed by the word *WAN:* ("double-you wan").

Although the following network technologies differ, your packets of data can fly through the air faster than Superwoman:

- ✔ **WLAN:** Uses radio waves to connect computers and networks. It shows up in homes, cafés, malls — even whole cities.

- ✔ **WWAN:** WWANs are based on telecommunications (mobile cellular networks) and use Worldwide Interoperability for Microwave Access (WiMAX) technology. A WWAN lets anyone with a computer work anywhere within a mobile phone network.

The geography of TCP/IP

TCP/IP fits everywhere. Regardless of your geographical network technology, in the end it's TCP/IP that carries your data, such as e-mail or Web pages, to you.

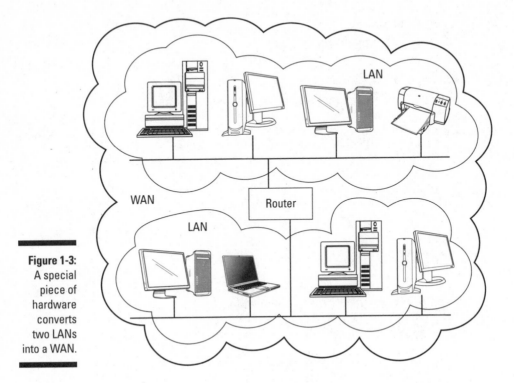

Figure 1-3:
A special
piece of
hardware
converts
two LANs
into a WAN.

Chapter 2

Layering TCP/IP Protocols

*1*f you already read Chapter 1, you know that a *protocol* is the set of agreed-on practices, policies, and procedures used for communication. In this book, we look at TCP/IP as the protocol set for communication between two or more computers. Remember that TCP/IP is a large suite of components that work together. In this chapter, we first describe the layered TCP/IP organization and then the protocols themselves.

TCP/IP technology is designed to allow all parts of your network to work together, regardless of which suppliers you bought them from. To make your network parts cooperate, TCP/IP divides network functions (for example, sending data or connecting different computer hardware) into layers and defines how those layers should interact.

Taking a Timeout for Hardware

There's no point in having software if you have no hardware on which to run it. Although TCP/IP protocols are software, we need to discuss network connection media and Ethernet — the most widely used local-area network (LAN) technology on the Internet. Talking about software without occasionally mentioning hardware is almost impossible, so we mention Ethernet in the following sections of this chapter and in other chapters in this book.

Starting with network connection media

Suppose that you want to connect all your networked devices — computers, printers, mobile phone, television, and game system — on your home network. Connection media and devices include much more than cables and wires. You can connect devices by using wireless access points, fiber optics, microwaves, infrared signals, and signals beamed to and from satellites.

The most important connection device is the *network interface card* (or *NIC*, also known as a *network adapter* or a *network card*). This computer circuit board (or *card,* for short) lets your computer be connected to a network by cables or air. The NIC converts data into electrical signals. Most computers come with a NIC, either wireless or wired or both, already installed inside the case. The NIC's manufacturer hardcodes on every NIC a unique hardware address known as the Media Access Control (MAC). Some protocols access this address. Figure 2-1 shows an example of a NIC with its MAC highlighted. Your card may look a little different, but all NICs function exactly the same.

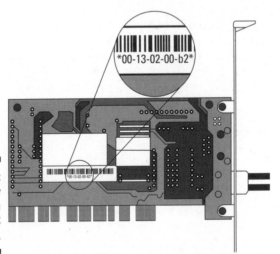

Figure 2-1: Every NIC has a unique MAC address.

Colliding with Ethernet

Ethernet is by far the most widely used LAN technology. (See the nearby sidebar, "How fast can Ethernet go?") Ethernet hardware ranges from fat, orange cables to plain old air. Ethernet allows any device on a network, from a giant corporate database server to the cash register in the local delicatessen, to send and receive packetized data.

How fast can Ethernet go?

The IEEE defines different kinds of Ethernet, depending on the connection media and the speed at which Ethernet moves the network data. In an Ethernet LAN, devices connect to the bus, not to each other. When the first edition of this book was written, Ethernet transmitted 1 gigabit (1 billion bits) of data across the network per second. That's equal to 125 megabytes. Fast, huh? Ethernet can now move data at 10 gigabits per second. If you do the math, you see lots of zeros. Wait — there's more! An IEEE group working on faster Ethernet is developing standards for 40 gigabits per second and 100 gigabits per second.

Ethernet uses the Carrier Sense Multiple Access/Collision Detection (CSMA/CD) technique. This very long name has a simple meaning: When a network device realizes that a packet collision has occurred, it knows when to wait and retry. With Ethernet, the data from the small deli's cash register is just as important as anything that the headquarters' big server has to send. All devices on the network are equal. You see in Figure 2-2 a basic LAN connected by Ethernet. Each device on the network, including the printer, has a NIC and TCP/IP software running.

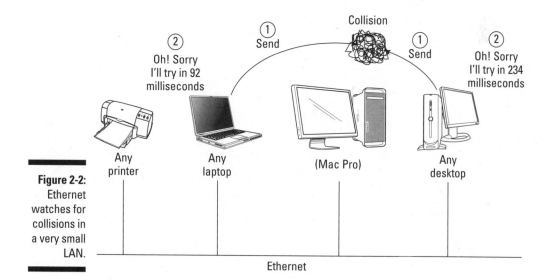

Figure 2-2: Ethernet watches for collisions in a very small LAN.

Stacking the TCP/IP Layers

TCP/IP software organizes the protocols in layers so that five layers are stacked up in the TCP/IP model. We love desserts and snacks, so we like to describe TCP/IP as a five-layer cake. Figure 2-3 gives you an idea of how the layers are structured.

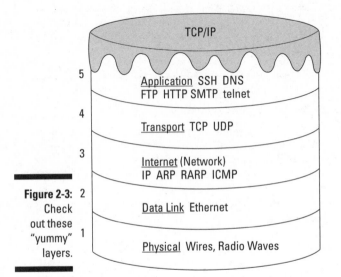

Figure 2-3: Check out these "yummy" layers.

Technically, the five layers in the "cake" comprise a *stack,* and the protocols that sit in these layers comprise a *protocol stack.*

Each layer of the stack depends on the layers below it; that is, each layer *services* the layer above or below it. When two computers communicate, each computer has its own set of layers. When you send a message to another computer on the network, your information starts at the top layer of your computer, travels down all the layers to the bottom of the stack, and then jumps to the other computer. When your information arrives on the other computer, it starts at the bottom layer and moves up the stack to the application in the top layer.

Each layer has a special function: The lower layers are hardware oriented, and the highest layer provides user services, such as e-mail, file transfers, and general network monitoring. Look at Figure 2-4 to see how data moves through these layers.

In the following sections, we examine each layer, starting with Layer 1, at the bottom of the cake.

How many TCP/IP stacks exist?

The answer is "only one, yet many." Or, "It depends." Only one set of standards exists for a TCP/IP stack. Those standards come from RFCs, described in Chapter 1. On the other hand, the protocols, services, and applications are software programs. *Somebody* has to write the programs to implement TCP/IP software. And — oh, boy! — are there ever a lot of somebodies. A TCP/IP stack usually is supplied with your computer. If you buy a computer that runs a version of Microsoft Windows, a team of Microsoft programmers most likely wrote the programs that make your computer's stack run. If your computer is a Mac, Apple Computer programmers wrote the stack. It doesn't matter

who wrote the TCP/IP stack. What's important is that the programs work the way they're supposed to, according to the RFCs.

Most Linux and Unix operating systems (and there are *so* many) have built-in TCP/IP protocol stacks.

If you don't like the way your stack is programmed, you can swap in another stack. Even better, you can download and swap in a free stack, or just part of a stack, from the Internet. If you search for the phrase **free software TCP/IP** at www.google.com, you see a long list of TCP/IP programs.

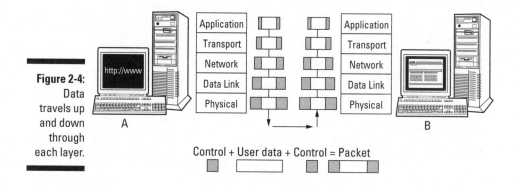

Figure 2-4:
Data travels up and down through each layer.

Control + User data + Control = Packet

Layer 1: The physical layer

The physical layer at the bottom of the stack is pure hardware, including the cable or satellite (or other) connection medium and the network interface card. This layer is where electrical signals move around (and we try not to think too hard about how it works). Protocols in the two bottom hardware layers aren't part of the TCP/IP stack. The physical layer transforms data into bits that move across the network media. The protocols in the physical layer include protocols related to cables, or to air, in the case of wireless. The physical layer also has protocols for connection methods.

Layer 2: The data link layer

This layer is another one that we don't want to strain our brains trying to figure out — again, hardware is involved. This layer splits data into packets to be sent across the connection medium, and then wiring, such as Ethernet or token ring, gets involved. The data link layer moves data up through the higher layers for transportation across networks and through tunnels to Virtual Private Networks (VPNs).

The data link layer also includes protocols that work with your Media Access Control (MAC) address and your network interface card (NIC).

A MAC address is a hardwired special address on your NIC. Every NIC has a unique MAC address.

For example, after the information is on the wire (or in the air, in the case of wireless), the data link layer handles any interference. If heavy sunspot activity occurs, the data link layer works hard to ensure that the interference doesn't garble the electric signals.

Layer 3: The internet layer

The bottom two layers are hardware related, whereas TCP/IP is software. Layer 3 (sometimes called the *network layer*) is the first place where a TCP/IP protocol fits into the networking equation: IP is this TCP/IP protocol. This layer receives packets from the data link layer (Layer 2) and sends them to the correct network address. If more than one possible route (or *path*) is available for the data to travel, the internet layer works out the best route. Without it, the data couldn't reach the correct location. We explain the IP protocol, and others, in the later section "Internet layer protocols."

Layer 4: The transport layer

Although the internet layer routes your information to its destination, it can't guarantee that the packets holding your data will arrive in the correct order or won't pick up any errors during transmission. That's one of the transport layer's jobs. TCP works at the transport layer to ensure that the packets have no errors and that all packets arrive and are reassembled in the correct order. Without this layer, you couldn't trust your network. UDP also works at the transport layer and shares one function with TCP: to move your data up to the next layer. However, sometimes network services would rather be fast than correct, so UDP does no error checking on your packets, saving transport time. (We explain in more detail what TCP and UDP do in the section "Transport layer protocols," later in this chapter.)

Layer 5: The application layer

The TCP/IP protocols that sit on Layer 5 receive packets from the lower protocols, de-packetize them back into their original form, and let the various TCP/IP applications and services manage the data according to the original user request, such as, "Please browse the Web." Layer 5

- **Establishes and coordinates a *session*, which is a connection between two computers:** Before two computers can transmit data between themselves, they must establish a session. The session announces that a transmission is about to occur and, at the end of it, determines whether the transmission was successful.

- **Works with operating systems to convert files from one format to another, if the server and client use different formats:** Without file format conversion, file transfers could happen only between computers that have the same file format.

- **Sets up the environment so that applications can communicate with each other and with users:** Requests for service and data start at the application layer and move down through the remaining four layers before going out across a network. The application layer is also where secure protocols for specific applications, such as Web browsing and e-mail, reside.

Chewing through Network Layers: A Packet's Journey

TCP/IP slices your network message into *packets* (little bites) and sends them out to the network. When the packets arrive at their destination, TCP/IP reassembles them into your original message. We use the life span of a packet to explain the layers in the network model.

A packet's life begins when an application creates it. Each packet then travels down the layers of the sending *host* (computer), across the network cables, up the layers of the destination host, and into the appropriate application.

As the packets travel down the layers of the sending host, headers containing control and formatting information and directions are added. When the packets reach the destination host, that information is read and stripped as the packets move upward through each layer. For example, if you FTP a file from Computer A to Computer B, the data in the file is *packetized* at the application layer and sent through all layers on Computer A. By the time the packets are sent out across the wire, they have gained some "weight" (all that added network information). After the roly-poly packets reach the destination host, they start to slim down; when they arrive at the top layer and deposit your file, they're positively svelte again.

Figure 2-5 shows a Web browser request that uses the Hypertext Transfer Protocol (HTTP) to start at the application layer. The packet travels from the application layer on Computer A (Sarah's computer) onto the network and then up to the application layer on Computer B (Emily's computer). You can see how the packet gains weight at each of Computer A's layers and then goes on a diet (so to speak) as it moves up through computer B's layers. Yo-yo dieting may be unhealthy for humans, but it works well for packets on the network.

The *TCP/IP stack* (or *suite*) is a large collection of protocols, named after the two original pieces: TCP and IP. You may say, "A suite is too big. Can I just have the protocols I need?" Nope. (Sorry.) The protocols in the TCP/IP suite move the data from one layer to another and interact with each other. You can't have a truly functional network by using just one of the TCP/IP protocols.

Figure 2-3, earlier in this chapter, shows the TCP/IP five-layer "cake" with some protocols drawn on the individual layers. You don't need every protocol on the stack to run a network application, but you need at least something from each layer in the stack. So, even though you may not use every protocol on each layer, you definitely need more than one.

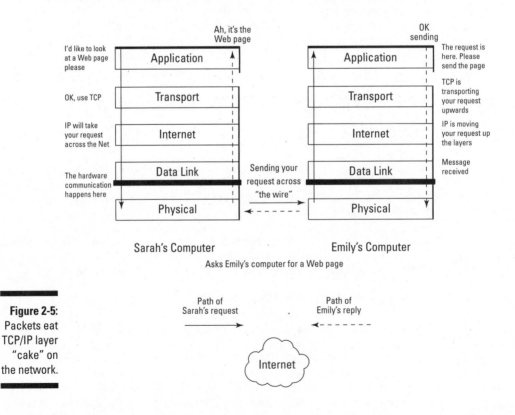

Figure 2-5:
Packets eat
TCP/IP layer
"cake" on
the network.

Now that you've gotten used to the idea that TCP/IP includes numerous protocols in its stack, you're about to find out that TCP/IP is even more than the stack. TCP/IP also includes services and applications. The stack alone would be useless if there were no services and applications to take advantage of them. Most of these services and applications sit at the top layer of the TCP/IP "cake," and Parts III and IV of this book describe them in detail. The following section uses FTP as an example of a TCP/IP component that functions as protocol, service, and application.

Understanding TCP/IP: More than just protocols

Many pieces of the TCP/IP suite have multiple functions: protocols, applications, and services. As we talk about all the useful things you can do with TCP/IP, we let you know whether you're using a TCP/IP protocol, a service, or an application — and highlight the places where the same name applies to one or more of these concepts.

The layered design of TCP/IP works the same way as a new cake recipe does. Suppose that you're a pastry chef and you create a new recipe for the cake components — the layers, the frosting, and the decorations. If you decide that you want to change the frosting to chocolate, you can simply swap out the vanilla recipe — no problem. You don't have to change the layers or the decorations. At the same time, you're thinking about using a new serving plate to show off your fabulous cake. When your cake is done baking, you serve your clients (friends and customers, for example), and they happily consume the result of your tasty baking service.

The layered design of TCP resembles baking a cake: You can easily add new components. If you're a programmer who dreams up a new network service (such as applying the frosting) and then you design the client and server applications, you can simultaneously design a new protocol to add to the TCP/IP suite. The protocol enables the server application to offer the service and lets the client application consume that service. This level of simplicity is a key advantage of TCP/IP.

Determining whether your network has a protocol, an application, or a service

In a network, you find the protocol/application/service relationship so tightly bound together that you might have difficulty determining what's what. We use the File Transfer Protocol, or FTP, as an example. It's not only a protocol — it's also a service and an application. (Don't worry about FTP itself at this point — it's just an example. If you need to find out how to use it, check out Chapter 18.) In the following list, we show you how the FTP service, application, and protocol work together to move files on the network:

- ✔ **FTP is a service for copying files:** You connect to a remote computer running the FTP service, and you can then pull files from, or push files to, that computer.

  Pull is a more technical term for *download*, and you may have already realized that *push* is a technical synonym for *upload*.

- ✔ **FTP is also an application for copying files:** You run a client application on your local computer to contact the FTP server service on the remote computer. The client application is either FTP or your Web browser. The browser uses the FTP protocol behind the scenes for downloads. The server application is known as the *file transfer protocol daemon,* or *FTPD.* (The term *daemon* comes from Unix — think of friendly demons haunting the computer to act on your behalf.) You tell the client what you want to do — pull or push files — and it works with the service to copy the files.

- ✔ **Finally, FTP is a protocol for copying files:** The client and server applications both use this to communicate, to ensure that the new copy of the file is, bit for bit and byte for byte, identical to the original.

FTP is an application, a service, and a protocol. Suppose that you need to copy a file from a remote computer. Without the application, your computer doesn't know that you want to copy. Without the service, your computer doesn't make a connection to the remote computer that has the files you need. Without the protocol, the client and server can't communicate.

Most of the time, you know from the context whether someone is referring to the service, the application, or the protocol. If you can't quite tell, maybe it doesn't matter.

Plowing through the Protocol List (In Case You Thought Only Two Existed)

Hold on tight — here come the pieces in the TCP/IP protocol suite, listed by layer. We start at the bottom with Layer 1, the physical layer, and move to the top application layer, which has the highest number of protocols.

Physical layer protocols

The protocols in this hardware layer aren't strictly TCP/IP protocols. Instead, they define how the hardware should be used to run a network. For example, the IEEE standards for Ethernet LAN (Local-Area Network) speeds and cables are in the physical layer. Don't worry about this concept too much. Save your brainpower for reading about the upper-layer protocols.

Data link layer protocols

The data link layer moves data through the higher layers for transportation across networks and through tunnels to VPNs. The data link layer also includes MAC protocols that understand your network interface card.

Internet layer protocols

The internet layer is the third layer in our imaginary layer cake. IP is the most important protocol in not only the network layer but also the TCP/IP stack. Without IP, TCP wouldn't know where to send anything.

IP: Internet Protocol

The Internet Protocol, IP, is responsible for basic network connectivity. IP resembles a plate in a basic place setting: When you're eating, you need a plate to hold your food. When you're networking, you need a place to put (send and receive) data — and that place is a network address.

The core of IP works with Internet addresses. (You can find the details about these addresses in Chapters 4 and 9.) Every computer on a TCP/IP network must have a numeric address. The IP protocol understands how and where to send messages to these addresses. In fact, all the other protocols — except for ARP and RARP — depend on IP to move information from one computer to another.

Although IP can take care of addressing, it can't do everything to ensure that your information reaches its destination correctly and in one piece. IP doesn't know (or care) when a packet of data gets lost and doesn't arrive, so you need some other protocols to ensure that no packets and data are lost and that the packets are in the right order.

Two versions of IP exist: IP version 4 (IPv4) and IP version 6 (IPv6). When very large networks, such as the Internet, found IPv4 too restrictive, especially in terms of addressing and security, IPv6 (described next) was developed. Both versions of IP are in use across the Internet. Some sites use both. A common practice is to say "IP" to mean either IPv4 or IPv6, or both.

IPv6: Internet Protocol version 6

IPv6 is a bigger and better version of IPv4 that adds features. The IPv4 information (with certain modifications) also holds true for IPv6. (If IP is an Internet plate, IPv6 is an Internet serving platter.)

Chapter 9 describes how IPv6 differs from IPv4 and how to use both versions together.

ARP: Address Resolution Protocol

ARP is the salad plate of the network place setting. With its load of addresses for the devices on the network, ARP works closely with IP, the dinner plate. When all you know about the remote computer is its TCP/IP address, the Address Resolution Protocol (ARP) finds the computer's NIC hardware address. Every NIC comes with a unique MAC address built into it. You cannot change it. ARP is the coordinator between a NIC's hard-coded MAC address and an IP address. By the way, ARP is a protocol, a service, and an application, although you rarely see the application.

RARP: Reverse Address Resolution Protocol

When a computer knows only its own MAC address, the Reverse Address Resolution Protocol (RARP) lets it find out the IP address it has been assigned. In addition to being a protocol, RARP is also a service. These days, the use of the Dynamic Host Configuration Protocol (DHCP) has mostly replaced RARP. In our dinner analogy, RARP is the salad fork that goes with the ARP salad plate. Okay, we realize we're stretching the analogy a bit.

ICMP: Internet Control Message Protocol

ICMP reports problems and relays other network-specific information, such as an error status, from network devices. IP detects the error and sends it to ICMP. (It reminds us of a crystal goblet in our imaginary TCP/IP dinnerware set.) The goblet "pings" when you hit it. In addition to being a protocol, ICMP is a service and an application, although the application is named *ping*. Chapter 22 describes how ping helps you.

Mobile IP

The proposed Mobile IP standard describes how you can connect your mobile device to the Internet from various locations, such as your office, hotel room, and car, while keeping the same IP address.

IPSec: IP Security Protocols

The IPSec protocols provide security services for other TCP/IP protocols and applications. For example, as the security protocol for VPNs, IPSec includes some strong encryption (coding) techniques to protect your data in the public and private world of VPNs. IPSec also ensures that the computer accessing your private network across the public Internet is truly a part of your network and not a pretender trying to sneak into your VPN. We describe VPNs in Chapter 1, and you can read more about IPSec in Chapter 22.

L2TP: Layer 2 Tunneling Protocol

L2TP uses IPSec to encrypt messages moving through VPN tunnels. (Chapter 1 introduces virtual private networks, or VPNs.) L2TP often replaces Point-to-Point Tunneling Protocol (PPTP), an older encryption protocol.

CIDR: Classless Inter-Domain Routing

CIDR is the beverage at the network table that helps addressing flow smoothly. Before IPv6 was developed, people worried that the Internet would run out of addresses. CIDR allows the more efficient allocation of IP addresses for the Internet and also helps in routing packets. (Chapter 8 has more information about using CIDR.)

Transport layer protocols

The protocols in the transport layer include TCP and UDP and some of the routing protocols.

TCP: Transmission Control Protocol

If IP is the network "plate," TCP is the network "spoon." After food is plopped on your plate, you need something to send it into your mouth without spilling it into your lap. Sure, you could use a fork, but try eating soup with a fork. You can probably eat peas from your knife without dropping any, but a spoon is the most reliable implement for most Western foods.

When your packets travel across a network, IP doesn't promise that the packets will arrive in order. In fact, IP doesn't even guarantee that all your packets will arrive. One or more packets may get dropped while on their trip from the source to the destination. IP doesn't care — TCP takes care of it. Figure 2-6 shows how an e-mail message is "packetized," or sent across the Internet and reassembled.

Just like a spoon, TCP ensures that nothing is dropped, no matter what kind of data you're sending. TCP uses IP to deliver packets reliably to those upper-layer applications. Two of the most important TCP functions are

- **Error checking:** Ensures that every packet arrives undamaged
- **Sequence numbering:** Puts the packets back into the right order. Refer to Figure 2-6 to see packet sequencing.

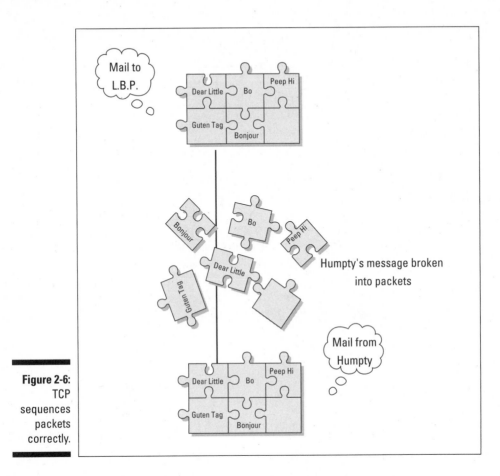

After a packet arrives at the correct IP address, TCP goes to work. It establishes a dialogue between the sending and receiving computers to communicate about the data that's being transmitted. TCP is said to be *connection oriented* because it tells the network to resend lost data.

Theoretically, you can have TCP without IP. A network mechanism other than IP can deliver the data to an address, and TCP can still verify and sequence that data. But in practice, TCP is always used with IP.

UDP: User Datagram Protocol

UDP provides functions similar to TCP. The big difference is reliability. As mentioned, TCP does the best job of moving packets across a network. In our dinnerware analogy, where IP is the network plate and TCP is the network spoon, UDP is your Internet fork: Using it gets most of your food to your mouth, even if you drop some bites. Although it's not as reliable as

TCP, UDP nevertheless moves a lot of data safely across the network. UDP uses IP to deliver packets to upper-layer applications and provides a flow of data among computers. The reason that UDP is less reliable than TCP as a transport protocol is that UDP provides neither error checking nor sequence numbering.

UDP is said to be *connectionless* because it doesn't provide for resending data in case of error. Figure 2-7 illustrates one difference between UDP and TCP.

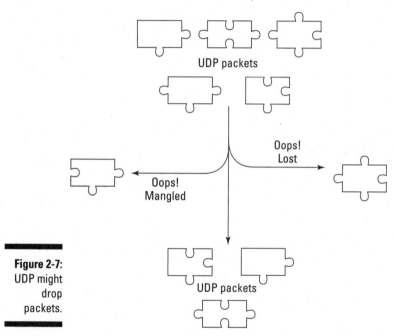

UDP packets

Oops!
Lost

Oops!
Mangled

UDP packets

Figure 2-7:
UDP might
drop
packets.

Another difference between TCP and UDP is that many TCP implementations are polite: They don't intrude on a congested network — they wait before sending their packets. UDP, on the other hand, has no worries about network congestion. It rudely sends packets across even the most congested network. Some of the services and applications that use UDP include:

- ✔ Domain Name System (DNS)
- ✔ Network File System (NFS)
- ✔ SNMP (Simple Network Management Protocol)
- ✔ Various online games
- ✔ Voice over IP (VoIP)

Some protocols use both TCP *and* UDP. DNS runs on top of either TCP or UDP depending on packet delivery needs. For short messages, DNS uses UDP. For longer requests that require absolutely reliable delivery, DNS uses TCP.

TCP versus UDP: Connection oriented versus connectionless?

TCP/IP communicates among the layers in two different ways:

- ✔ **Connection-oriented** communication is reliable and easy to understand. When two computers are communicating with each other, they connect: Each one understands what the other one is doing. The sending computer lets the receiving computer know that data is on the way. The receiver then *ACKs* (acknowledges) or *NACKs* (denies or negatively acknowledges) receipt of the data. A receiver NACKs if the error checking shows a problem. A sender that receives neither an ACK nor a NACK assumes that the data was lost and automatically resends the data.

  This process of ACKing and NACKing is known as *handshaking*.

  Suppose that you send a fax to your friend Ken in Tokyo. If you want to be sure that he receives the fax, you might call and say, "I'm faxing you the baseball results now. Call me when they come through." After Ken receives the fax and ensures that it's readable, he calls you and says, "Thanks. I'm thrilled to hear that the Red Sox finally won the World Series." That's how TCP behaves.

- ✔ **Connectionless** communication occurs when you send a fax without first notifying your friend and, for some reason, it never reaches its destination. Ken doesn't know to expect anything, so he doesn't know that anything is lost. When data are sent via the connectionless method, the computers involved know nothing about each other or the data. If you're on the receiving end, no one tells you that you're about to receive anything. If you're sending data, no one bothers to mention whether they received the document or whether it was garbled. That's how UDP behaves.

With this information in mind, you might wonder why any applications use connectionless mode. But there's a time and place for everything. First, communication is faster without the ACKs and NACKs. Second, not every network message needs to be as accurate as your e-mail messages. Finally, because some applications do their own error checking and reliability processing, they don't need the connection-oriented overhead of TCP.

Figure 2-8 shows the packet beginning its trip at the physical layer. When the packet reaches the internet layer, one of two things happens:

- ✔ The packet takes the TCP path.
- ✔ The packet takes the UDP path.

The double-headed arrow shows that packets move up and down the layers.

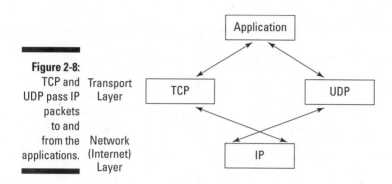

Transport
Layer

Network
(Internet)
Layer

Routing protocols: Interior and exterior

Routing is the process of moving packets between networks.

TCP/IP is a banquet of protocols, services, and applications. IP is the network "plate" that holds your food: That is to say, IP is underneath the data. The other protocols represent various pieces of your network dinnerware. Under your network "place settings" is a network tablecloth of sorts, spread with gateways and routers, which use a mixture of gateway and router protocols. A *router* is a physical device that connects networks to allow data to move between them. A *gateway* translates information from one format to another. Several routing protocols are defined in the TCP/IP suite.

Some of these routing protocols are:

- **Border Gateway Protocol (BGP):** The core routing protocol for the Internet. BGP keeps track of the network numbers that connect to the Internet. BGP runs over TCP.

- **Interior Gateway Protocol (IGP):** A protocol used by routers to exchange network information.

- **Open Shortest Path First (OSPF):** When networks change — perhaps a segment becomes unavailable because a cable breaks — whole pieces of the Internet would become available without OSPF. OSPF calculates an alternate route that a packet should follow when a path fails. This ability to recalculate a route is called *dynamic routing*. OSPF runs directly over IP.

TLS: Transport Layer Security

The TLS protocol provides privacy for client/server communication, such as online shopping, Voice over IP (VoIP), and Web browsing. TLS prevents eavesdropping and tampering with the communication between the client and server. TLS is similar to SSL. Though TLS is the Internet standard, SSL is more frequently used, even though it's vendor proprietary.

RSVP: Resource Reservation Protocol

Packets need to be delivered as quickly as possible and always in the correct order to provide the best experience when you're using multimedia applications, such as videoconferencing, on the network. Otherwise, you see strange pauses or blank spots. The Resource Reservation Protocol (RSVP) was created to provide for high quality of service (QoS). We realize that the RSVP acronym doesn't match the protocol's name. It's *RSVP* (from the French phrase *Respondez s'il vous plait,* or "Respond, if you please") because you *reserve* network resources in advance in the same way you reserve a seat at a party by replying to the invitation.

Application layer protocols

The application layer protocols, applications, and services provide a user interface to the rest of the TCP/IP stack.

DNS: Domain Name Service

The Domain Name Service is critical to the operation of the Internet (and to any other large network). DNS translates the names that we humans love, such as RFC-Editor.org, into the numbers that machines like. Thanks to DNS, you can type `www.sorbonne.fr` rather than `195.220.107.2` in your Web browser. DNS servers are distributed throughout the Internet.

More than just the service that makes the name-to-number translation work, DNS refers to the entire system of DNS servers and databases. In that case, the name changes slightly to Domain Name *System*.

Chapter 4 discusses DNS in more depth, and Chapter 10 adds details about how DNS translates names and addresses.

DNSSEC: Domain Name System Security Extensions

DNS alone is not particularly secure. DNSSEC is a suite of proposed standards to add extensions to the original DNS Protocol. Chapter 10 describes DNS security.

FTP: File Transfer Protocol

The File Transfer Protocol (FTP) helps you copy files between two computers. You use FTP to either pull the files from the remote computer or push them to the remote computer. Keep in mind that FTP is also the name of an application and a service, so we tell you about it again (and again) elsewhere in this book. Check out Chapter 18 for more on FTP and other file sharing protocols.

Telnet

The telnet protocol lets you connect to a remote computer and work as though you were sitting in front of that computer, no matter how far away the computer may be. By using telnet, you can lounge around in Tahiti and work on a remote computer in Antarctica as though you were there and sur-rounded by penguins — without suffering even a shiver. In addition to being a protocol, telnet is a service and an application — three for the price of one. If you've only ever used a graphical operating system, such as a flavor of Microsoft Windows, you might not understand the value of telnet. But your friendly neighborhood Linux, Unix, and Mac OS X often telnet to remote com-puters to run applications that might not exist on their computers.

Making telnet a verb (refer to the previous sentence) is easy and comfortable to do. (Grammarians — and editors — would cringe.) Remember that verbing weirds language.

Chapter 20 explains telnet — the protocol, the application, and the service — and describes telnet security.

TFTP: Trivial File Transfer Protocol

The Trivial File Transfer Protocol (TFTP) is a specialized form of FTP. One common use is to copy and install a computer's operating system from a TFTP server's files. RFC2349 states that "The basic TFTP protocol has no security mechanism." TFTP servers are available (many of them free) from various sources that claim to add security to the basic TFTP protocol. We haven't tried any of these extended TFTP servers, so be careful.

SNMP: Simple Network Management Protocol

SNMP functions as the maitre d' at your network feast, overseeing the entire dining experience. The Simple Network Management Protocol (SNMP) is used to

✔ Monitor and manage networks and the devices connected to them

✔ Analyze network performance

You can get a network monitoring (or management) system from your choice of vendors or use an open source version. These products can show the state of your network by using some attractive graphics.

SMTP: Simple Mail Transfer Protocol

The Simple Mail Transfer Protocol (SMTP) is the protocol for transferring e-mail messages among computers. Messages can move directly from the sender's computer to the recipient's computer, or proceed through interme-diary computers in a process known as *store and forward*. In Chapter 13, you can read more about mail protocols and technologies.

POP3: Post Office Protocol version 3

The Post Office Protocol (POP3, or often just POP) provides basic client/server features that help you download your e-mail from a mail server to your computer. POP3 is designed to allow home users to move their e-mail from their Internet service provider's (ISP's) computers to their own. You need a POP3 mail client to communicate with a POP3 mail server. Again, you can read more about mail protocols and technologies in Chapter 13. POP3 is your network corkscrew because it gets your e-mail wine out of the bottle and into your wine glass.

IMAP4: Internet Message Access Protocol version 4, revision 1

IMAP4 is the fancy decanter that holds the wine better than the bottle does, but still helps you get the e-mail wine into your wine glass. The Internet Message Access Protocol (abbreviated as IMAP4rev1 or IMAP4 or just IMAP) provides more sophisticated client/server capabilities than POP3 does. You need an IMAP4 client to communicate with an IMAP4 mail server, but it gives you more choices for handling your e-mail.

POP3 and IMAP4 don't interoperate. You can't use a POP3 client with an IMAP4 server or use an IMAP4 client with a POP3 server, but these days most clients and servers speak both protocols.

Chapter 13 has more information about mail protocols.

LDAP: Lightweight Directory Access Protocol

The Lightweight Directory Access Protocol (LDAP) is a way to look up and possibly change information such as usernames, passwords, e-mail addresses, and lots more in an X.500-compatible directory service. (Whew! That's a mouthful.) You pronounce it "el-dap," which rhymes with "cap."

Many people refer to the directory service as an LDAP server, but keep in mind the *A* in the name. LDAP is the method that applications use to *access* the directory to reach the data it holds. This communications protocol doesn't mention managing the directory server product or the data. Microsoft and Apple build directory servers into their operating systems (Active Directory for Windows and Open Directory for Mac OS X, respectively), and many stand-alone LDAP server products — both freeware and commercial — are available.

By the way, it's the access protocol that is lightweight — not the directory service or the data in it.

NTP: Network Time Protocol

The time-of-day clocks that computers maintain are synchronized by the Network Time Protocol (NTP). Time-stamping is important in all sorts of applications, providing everything from document creation dates to network routing date-and-time information to banking transactions and stock transfers.

Using NTP, you can configure a computer to set its clock, and keep it accurate, by retrieving current time data from a time server computer, such as `time.microsoft.com` or a member of the NTP pool.

HTTP: HyperText Transfer Protocol

The HyperText Transfer Protocol (HTTP) is the key protocol for transferring data across the World Wide Web. HTTP transfers HyperText Markup Language (HTML) and other components from the Web servers (on the Internet, your intranet, or extranet) to your browser client. (You can find lots more information about the Web in Chapter 11.) With all the different Web languages, HTTP works like a large pitcher filled with Sangria — many different, delicious ingredients that combine to make something wonderful.

HTTPS: HTTP over Secure Sockets Layer

HTTPS is a secure version of HTTP that encrypts sensitive data, such as your credit card information, whenever you buy something over the Internet.

Technically, HTTPS isn't a separate protocol. It's HTTP with security turned on. Although most of the protocols we are talking about can be used with security turned on, few get special names for their secure versions.

Another secure form of HTTP is the Secure HyperText Transfer Protocol (S-HTTP), but it's older and rarely used. HTTPS is much more popular.

BOOTP: Boot Protocol

Not every computer has an operating system preinstalled — sometimes you have to install it yourself. If the computer has no disks for storage (sometimes it happens for good reasons), you can download the operating system into memory from another computer on the network. The diskless computer uses the Boot Protocol (BOOTP) to load its operating system, and other applications, over the network.

BOOTP has no security. Dynamic Host Configuration Protocol (DHCP) has features that have mostly replaced BOOTP.

PPTP: Point-to-Point Tunneling Protocol

The Point-to-Point Tunneling Protocol (PPTP) helps you create a VPN on the public Internet. Using PPTP, you can have a secure link to your organization's network — as though you were inside the building and on the LAN — even though you're connected to the Internet by way of an ISP. (It's like having a secret tunnel into the office.) When you use PPTP, your communication traffic can even be encrypted to ensure that no miscreants can see your data. You get all the benefits of a global private network with none of the hassles of launching your own satellites, laying your own undersea cables, or working with any of the pieces we describe in Chapter 5. Think of PPTP as your network napkin because it augments the tablecloth provided by the router protocols mentioned earlier in this section.

L2tP (see the section "L2TP: Layer 2 Tunneling Protocol," earlier in this chapter) has mostly replaced PPTP for VPN security in most networks because PPTP doesn't provide encryption for security. It relies on the protocol being tunneled to provide privacy.

DHCP: Dynamic Host Configuration Protocol

If IP is your fine dinner plate at the network banquet, DHCP is your recyclable paper plate. DHCP is a client/server solution for sharing numeric IP addresses. A DHCP server maintains a pool of shared addresses — and those addresses are recyclable. When a DHCP client wants to use a TCP/IP application, that client must first request an IP address from the DHCP server. The server checks the shared supply and if all the addresses are in use, the server notifies the client that it must wait until another client finishes its work and releases a TCP/IP address. If an address is available, the DHCP server sends a response to the client that contains the address.

This shared-supply approach makes sense in environments in which computers don't use TCP/IP applications all the time or in which not enough addresses are available for all the computers that want them. Flip to Chapters 4 and 5 for more detailed information about DHCP.

SSL: Secure Sockets Layer

SSL (the Secure Sockets Layer) version 2 is an older protocol developed by Netscape Corporation that allows applications to encrypt data that goes from a client, such as a Web browser, to the matching server. (*Encrypting* your data means converting it to a secret code. We introduce encryption in Chapter 12.) When you buy that Lamborghini over the Web, no one other than the dealer can read your credit card number. SSL version 3 allows the server to authenticate that the client is who it says it is. While SSL is the more frequently used protocol, the TLS protocol is the standard that has replaced SSL in some newer applications.

IPP: Internet Printing Protocol

As the time of this book's publication, no standard for printing exists. You may now need to use different printing methods depending on how your printer is attached and the maker of your printer. The goal of the application layer IPP is to standardize most Internet printing tasks. In other words, regardless of who makes your printer and how it's attached, you need to know only one way to

- Print
- Cancel a print job
- Discover the printer's status
- Find out what a printer can do (print in color or draft quality, for example)

Before IPP, a proposed standard, can become a standard, it needs to include strict authentication and security.

Kerberos Network Authentication Service

Kerberos is the three-headed dog that guards the entrance to hell. Or, is it a TCP/IP service? If your network security is hellish, Kerberos is both. The TCP/IP service Kerberos is designed to allow users, computers, and services to identify themselves to each other without lying. Without this identity-checking process, called *authentication,* a computer or service could potentially say that it is anything or anyone, and TPC/IP would accept the identification without checking. In this age of computer hacking and intrusions, trusting that network services and computers are who they say they are can be dangerous.

Kerberos is a trusted impartial authentication service — or maybe it's just paranoid. It assumes that unauthorized programs try to read and modify packets that are traveling along a network. This paranoia is what makes Kerberos impartial: It doesn't depend on other programs, the host's operating system, the physical security of the network, or IP addresses to do its work. Instead, it works alone with its own, validated tickets. (See Chapter 21 for details on the Kerberos service.) Kerberos is the default authentication mechanism in the Microsoft Windows 2000 operating system.

Kerberos is the bouncer at an exclusive party — it guards the door and kicks out anyone who isn't invited.

IMPP: Instant Messaging and Presence Protocol

Although instant messaging (IM) is a handy application for people to send quick messages back and forth across the Internet, IM vendors have traditionally used different, proprietary protocols that don't work together. The goal of IMPP is for different IM applications to be able to talk to each other easily across the Internet.

SIP: Session Initiation Protocol

SIP is a protocol for connecting multimedia sessions — such as voice, chat, games, and video.

And many, many more

You can find many more existing pieces of TCP/IP, and new ones are being developed right now. The ones we describe in this chapter are some of the most important and most commonly used.

Chapter 3

Serving Up Clients and Servers

- -

In This Chapter

▶ Understanding the definition of client/server architecture

▶ Looking at both sides of the client/server equation

▶ Exploring how TCP/IP takes advantage of client/server computing and vice versa

▶ Finding out how an old technology — peer-to-peer computing — became new again

- -

Client/server solutions comprise the foundation of most TCP/IP services and applications. As you take a look at what client/server means to a network computer user, you see that TCP/IP is an excellent protocol choice for client/server computing because TCP/IP allows so many different computers and network devices to communicate as both clients *and* servers.

The *client/server (C/S)* distributed style of computing spreads computing from central data centers to desktops, laptops, handheld devices, and even cars regardless of where people are located.

Contrary to popular belief, software, not hardware, defines client/server. In the client/server game, a client application on one computer requests services from another computer running server software. The client and server software can run on any kind of hardware. Sometimes they even run on the same computer! You might even use a gigantic supercomputer running client software to request services from a tiny little PC by way of a network protocol, such as TCP/IP.

In this chapter, we discuss client/server (C/S) basic concepts, including both server side and client side software.

Understanding the Server Side

Although we write that the client/server computing style is defined by software, you hear most people refer to computer hardware as clients and servers. In this section, we extend the definition to include more informal definitions of clients and servers. Even though the word *client* comes first in client/server, we need to start with the definition of the server.

Examining the server's job

A *server* is software that provides a resource or a service to share with clients. In this chapter, when we write about the technically correct definition of server, we use the term *server software* to avoid confusion with hardware.

When we write about *servers,* we're using the term to mean computers that run server software. Servers may be specialized or multipurpose. A specialized server provides just one element, whereas a multipurpose server provides more than one. Another way to think about the difference is that multipurpose servers can be reached using several different TCP/IP protocols.

People often call the computer that's running the software *the server*.

Identifying types of servers

Specialized servers include the ones in this list:

- ✔ **Web server:** Software that accepts requests from browser clients to deliver Web objects, such as home pages, documents, graphics, and applets. Also known as a *web application server.* Popular Web servers include Apache HTTP Server, Microsoft proprietary IIS (Internet Information Services, formerly named Internet Information Server), Google Web Server, and lighttpd.

- ✔ **Commerce server:** A type of Web application server that enables you to conduct business over the Web. The server software includes security features, such as TLS (Transport Layer Security), so that you can use your credit card without worrying. You still have to worry about your bills, though. Some people still refer to the security protections by the older name SSL (Secure Sockets Layer) even though TLS has replaced it.

- ✔ **File server:** A computer or group of linked computers (a *cluster*) that shares disk space. One advantage of having a file server is that the shared files still look like they're on your own computer.

  The computers that borrow the file server's disk space are the *clients*. These clients may use an operating system that's different from the server's. When you have various operating systems, you have various file formats. The server's job is to hide those format differences.

- ✔ **Compute server:** A computer that runs a program for you and sends the results back to you. For example, analyzing weather patterns requires enormous amounts of computer power. The meteorologists' client workstations often aren't capable of solving the complex mathematics involved, so they send the problem from their workstations to a super-computer, which completes the calculations and sends back the results. That supercomputer is the compute server.

Using dedicated servers

Often you dedicate a server computer to one task only. For example, you don't usually run a file server together with an e-commerce server. Reasons to use dedicated servers include

- ✓ **Management:** Different servers require different system administration tasks. For example, a file server might require a large disk farm and nightly backups, whereas a compute server, which needs only weekly backups, may require more fine-tuning and a more powerful CPU.

- ✓ **Performance:** Running different server programs on a single computer can slow down all the servers.

- ✓ **Security:** Some of the tasks involved in protecting the servers are quite different. For example, protecting an e-commerce server requires that you set up secure transactions and protect customer information.

On the other hand, you can have good reasons for running multiple servers on the same computer. For example, if your mail server is also running Web server software, you can read your mail with a Web browser in addition to the mail client you would normally use.

Understanding the Client Side

If you read the previous section about servers, you know that a client/server network relies on specialized central points — namely, servers — to provide services. Having all these services available unless something *needs* service, however, doesn't make sense. That needy something is the client. A network contains many, many more clients than servers because a single server can satisfy hundreds (sometimes thousands) of client requests.

Defining a client

It's this simple: A *client* is software that asks for and receives a resource or service from a server. Clients do all sorts of work — anything they want. We could write a whole book on the types of clients that are out there.

People often call a computer that runs client software *the client.*

Clients, clients everywhere

For each server we describe in the previous section, you have a choice of many different clients. Consider these examples:

- ✔ **Browser:** Likely the most often used clients on the Internet, this client software receives services from a Web server.

- ✔ **E-mail:** If you and someone else in your household access the same e-mail server, one of you might use Microsoft Office Outlook for your e-mail client and the other might use Mozilla Thunderbird.

- ✔ **Mobile:** When companies want employees to be able to work anywhere, at any time, they make their mission-critical applications accessible by way of wireless handheld devices. The BlackBerry, smartphone, two-way pager, and personal digital assistant (PDA) are examples of *mobile clients*. Most contain a wireless internet browser, or WIB (also known as a mobile browser, microbrowser, or minibrowser), that knows how to use Wireless Application Protocol (WAP) to find information and display it on the small screen. These clients communicate over cellular networks or wireless LANs. The data is in Extensible Hypertext Markup Language (XHTML), Wireless Markup Language (WML), or even just the standard HyperText Markup Language (HTML), used for normal Web browsers. Many organizations also interconnect their e-mail and voice messaging systems with inbound and outbound fax services to create *unified messaging* solutions.

Answering the Question "Are You Being Served?"

Because of the software that any computer is (or isn't) running, the computer can be

- ✔ Either a client or a server
- ✔ Both a client and a server
- ✔ Neither a client nor a server

The computer can also change as often as necessary to provide and access any number of services.

Figure 3-1 shows an example of multiple roles: One computer provides a shared printer and is thus a print server. The same computer is also a file server and accesses some files from another computer, which means that it's also a client of a file server.

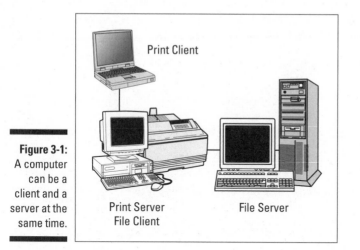

Figure 3-1:
A computer can be a client and a server at the same time.

Print Client

Print Server
File Client

File Server

Supporting TCP/IP with Client/Server and Vice Versa

Not only is TCP/IP a major enabler of client/server computing, it's also one of the biggest users of it. The layered and modular design of TCP/IP makes it easy to design and implement new network services.

TCP/IP is a key element of many, but not all, client/server solutions. Other network protocols can be used on the network at the same time as TCP/IP.

TCP/IP is accepted as *the* protocol that links computers to not just each other but also all the different computers and servers in the world, from the smallest palmtop to the mightiest mainframe. TCP/IP makes all of them candidates for clients or servers.

Recognizing Other Internetworking Styles: Peer-to-Peer Computing

Although TCP/IP itself is built on a client/server architecture and enables most client/server computing, other internetworking architectures also run across TCP/IP networks. Peer-to-peer (P2P) is an older networking style that has become new again as the Internet has become accessible to much of the world's population. Everything that's old becomes new again.

Years ago, peer-to-peer networks were everywhere. They provided an easy way for a few cooperating users to share files and other computer resources. These users were considered a *workgroup*. In a *peer-to-peer* network, no computer is better than any other. A peer-to-peer network requires no dedicated servers.

Determining whether peer-to-peer workgroups are still handy

Although small workgroups are convenient, peer-to-peer networking has its downsides:

- ✓ **Decrease in speed:** It slows down when too many users (more than 15) try to share.

- ✓ **Unreliable resource access:** Imagine that your colleague's computer has a file that many people share. And then suppose that one day your colleague's computer has a disk failure! The result: A critical file resource is lost to many users.

- ✓ **Disintegration into a collection of separate computers:** When resources in a workgroup are limited, the workgroup can disintegrate into a collection of separate computers. Suppose that members of your workgroup use so much of your computer's shared disk space that no space remains for your files. You then have to decide whether to turn off disk sharing or disconnect the network cable.

P2P applications — P2P across the Internet

The earlier P2P section talks about the P2P computing style. P2P sharing applications have sprouted all over the Internet. Although these users don't comprise a neatly formed private workgroup, they usually number in the millions. Figure 3-2 shows the architecture for a large, Internet-wide, P2P application.

Our teenage niece was once a big fan of P2P applications for sharing music. Little did she know that P2P software is subject to its fair share of worms and viruses. Read Chapter 12 for the minimum amount of information you need to know about these security nightmares. P2P programs can also bring lots of adware to your computer along with the videos and music you're downloading. One of our computers became almost useless because of the amount of adware that made its way on there. The computer ground along slower than slow, and we almost cried from seeing all the pop-up ads, pop-under ads, and ads that were all over our screen. You would think we would know better. Unfortunately, when your teenage niece is using your computer, stuff happens.

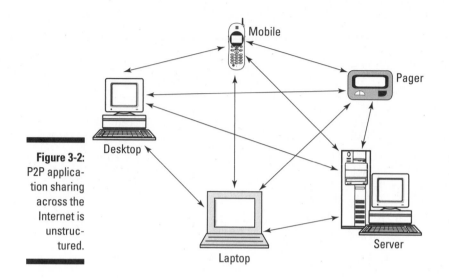

Mobile

Pager

Desktop

Laptop

Server

Figure 3-2:
P2P applica-
tion sharing
across the
Internet is
unstruc-
tured.

Here's a list of possible solutions, in case this situation happens to you:

- ✔ Make your teenager use the computers at the public library. They don't let you download stuff.

- ✔ If you're really nice, get your teen a computer of her own.

- ✔ Threaten all sorts of dire consequences if the computer gets clogged again — if that method works with your teenager.

Network administrators can use applications to manage network traffic, such as PacketHound from Palisade Systems, Inc., at www.palisadesystems. com, to block Gnutella (a popular file-sharing network) traffic from a network. Reasons to do this might include

- ✔ An effective but brute force way for an organization to protect against employees possibly violating copyright laws is to block all unauthorized P2P sharing.

- ✔ Overenthusiastic file sharers can clog an organization's network band-width. Blocking P2P downloading activity relieves network stress.

Depending on the P2P program you use, security may be extremely lax or non-existent.

Chapter 4

Nice Names and Appetizing Addresses

*1*f your computer is already on a network *and* you always call computers by name *and* you're not interested in what TCP/IP is doing to your computer's name behind the scenes, you can breathe easy in this chapter. The only thing you need to know now is another term for a computer — a *host* — and what it means. In other words, you can move on to some other chapter, if you want. This chapter is high-tech.

However, if you need to get your computer on the network or the Internet, or if you want to know the meaning of all those strings of numbers and dots you see when you use an application such as FTP or telnet, stay right here. Most of the information in this chapter is aimed at you — especially if you're a beginning network administrator.

What Did You Say Your Host's Name Is?

If your computer uses TCP/IP, your computer must have a name. You can choose it yourself for your home computer. Most likely, your work organization has a naming policy that helps you select a name or limits your choices. In some cases, a system manager or network administrator gets to have all the fun and assign a name to your computer for you.

The network used for the examples in this book consists of a few hosts. Some of them are named this way:

woodstock   baldEagle   hawk   tweety   pinkflamingo

Your *host* or *computer* — we use the names interchangeably from now on — has a name and a number. The name alone may not be unique, but in Chapter 10, you discover that each host on an internet also has a longer unique name. For now, we'll stick with just simple host names. Your computer's number is an address. Chapter 2 discusses the unique MAC address hardcoded onto your NIC, whether your computer participates in a network or not. This chapter delves into the IP addresses that internets, including the Internet, use to identify hosts.

Playing the numbers game

Your computer has a number, known as your host's *IP address,* and the greater part of this chapter is devoted to its format. Your computer may have more than one IP address, depending on how many networks it's connected to.

Your computer's name and IP address can change. Your computer can take on nicknames, change names, and have multiple identities.

You could have a network where all the computers had numeric addresses and no names, but it would make life difficult, (almost impossible) for most of us. Here are two reasons why names are important:

- **Name recognition:** Humans like to name things (dogs, cats, goldfish) and can remember those names. Computers like dealing with numbers and only numbers

- **Ease of use:** Knowing a particular computer's name makes it easier to connect to a specific computer when you need to use the services it offers. For example, you can connect to `192.168.253.9`, but remembering and typing `pinkflamingo` is much easier.

Table 4-1 lists the host names and IP addresses in our *TCP/IP For Dummies* network.

Table 4-1	Computers in Our Network
Host Name	*IP Address*
woodstock	192.168.253.5
baldEagle	192.168.253.6
hawk	192.168.253.7
tweety	192.168.253.8
pinkflamingo	192.168.253.9

Identifying a computer as uniquely yours

Suppose that your computer name isn't unique on your network or the Internet. Let's compare two companies named Lotus: One makes cars; the other makes software. If you try to connect by way of FTP to a computer named lotus, would you find files related to cars or software?

TCP/IP and the Internet require that every computer on the network (and in the world) be uniquely identified by both name and address. To identify a computer named lotus, for example, you need more names — kind of like first, middle, and last, and maybe more.

A computer's full name is its *fully qualified domain name,* or *FQDN.* (Go ahead — try to say it three times fast.) The FQDN for the computer named lotus might be

```
lotus.wileiden.com
```

Here's a breakdown:

- ✔ **Computer name:** lotus
- ✔ **Organization name:** wileiden
- ✔ **Internet top-level domain:** com (short for *com*mercial organization)

Here's another example:

```
lotus.carcollege.edu
```

And here's what's in it:

- ✔ **Computer name:** lotus
- ✔ **Organization name:** carcollege
- ✔ **Internet top-level domain:** edu (short for *edu*cational institution)

Translating names into numbers

A numeric IP address identifies hosts on a network. Yes, you usually type the host's name, but somewhere along the way a TCP/IP service resolves that name into the numeric IP address.

- **Host just a few translations:** On a small network, your computer may have a *hosts file,* which translates host names into IP addresses. This simple text file lists a computer's name and its IP address. Chapter 10 gives you some advice about how and when to build a hosts file.

- **Translate big-time with DNS:** On a big network (none bigger than the Internet), where the hosts file is enormous, the DNS performs the name/address resolution. Later in this chapter, you can read a brief introduction to DNS. The hosts file and DNS are discussed in detail in Chapter 10.

Taking a Closer Look at IP Addresses

The address where you live is made up of several parts. It can include many elements that identify you — your street name, post office box, city, region (province, state, canton, or county), country, and postal code, for example. The same is true of your computer (host). The difference is that you know your home address — it consists mostly of text with a few numbers — but you may or may not know your computer's IP address, which comprises numbers and dots.

Two versions of IP are now in use: IPv4 and IPv6. Although IPv6 is the next generation of IP addressing, IPv4 is still much more widely used. You can use both IPv4 and IPv6 together. Frequently, people refer to both v4 and v6 as simply *IP.* In this chapter, we explain IPv4 addressing; Chapter 9 talks about IPv6. But don't head to Chapter 9 yet, unless you already understand IPv4 addresses, because

- IPv6 addressing builds on the IPv4 foundation.

- IPv4 and IPv6 will exist together for a long time to come.

- If you're not ready for IPv6, you can use a workaround if you have an IP address shortage.

The *IP address* (to be specific, the *IPv4 address*) is a set of numbers separated by dots. It identifies one host. Every device on the TCP/IP network (that is, every network interface on the network — some devices may have more than one) needs a unique IP address. If your host is on a TCP/IP network, that host has an IP address, even if you always call your computer by name.

You may have noticed this numeric address showing up in messages and wondered what it was. For example, telnet reports the IP address as it tries to connect to the remote host. Here's a brief sample; you connect to flyingpenguin by name, and telnet announces the flyingpenguin IP address:

```
% telnet flyingpenguin
Trying 0.241...
Connected to flyingpenguin.
```

Savoring Classful Addressing

If you've seen a few numeric IP addresses, you've most likely seen classful addresses. *Classful* addresses have four numbers separated by dots, such as the address for flyingpenguin, in the preceding section. This IP addressing format is the conventional addressing method used by IPv4.

Note: This chapter talks about IPv4 classful addressing. Chapter 8 juices up addressing with details on *classless* addressing and Class Inter-Domain Routing (CIDR) protocol, and Chapter 9 serves up IPv6 addressing.

An *IPv4 address* is a 32-bit number that has two sections: the network number and the host number. (You can't see the division. Read the section in Chapter 5 about subnet masks.) Addresses are written as four fields, 8 bits apiece, separated by dots. Each field can be a number ranging from 0 to 255. This style of writing an address is *dotted decimal notation*.

All hosts on the same network must use the same network number. Each host or network interface on the same network must have a unique host number. The following excerpt is from a hosts file, which translates names into numbers and vice versa. The last two digits of each address, the *host numbers,* are unique. The rest of each address comprises the *network number.* Notice that the network number is the same for every host because all the hosts are on the same network:

```
# Cardinal Consulting, Inc. LAN
# IP address          Name            Comment
192.168.40.55         flyingpenguin   #Candace-Linux
192.168.40.56         bluebird        #MarshallVista
192.168.40.61         oldestbird      #VMS server
192.168.40.63         bigbird         #Unix server
192.168.40.64         mazarin         #Windows 2008 server
192.168.40.65         macbird         #Mac OS X
192.168.40.72         uselessbird     #ancient 386
192.168.40.75         pinkflamingo    #Candace-XP
```

An IP address has four parts, and those parts divide into two pieces: the network piece and the host piece.

Figure 4-1 shows how the size of the network and hosts parts differ, based on the class of the network. The hosts in the Cardinal Consulting, Inc. LAN are part of a Class C network. (See the next section for more on network classes.)

A | Network . . . | Host . . . . | . . . . | . . . . . .

B | Network . . . | . . . . | Host . . . . | . . . . . .

C | Network . . . | . . . . | . . . . | Host . . . .

Class A address 1.1.1.1

Class B address 130.103.40.210

Class C address 192.9.200.15

In the figure, the parts of the address that represent the network comprise the *network prefix*.

The basic structure of an IP address consists of two sections: the network ID and the host ID. Where this 32-bit address is divided depends on the network class.

Recognizing the Parts of an IP Address

If you've read this far, you know that a classful IPv4 address has four parts and looks like this:

```
part1.part2.part3.part4
```

The Internet is divided into classes because Internet addresses were handed out in specific groups called classes.

The meaning of these parts depends on your network class. TCP/IP has four classes of networks, as described in the following sections. Although only three classes are now widely used, the fourth has a special purpose. Whether your organization connects to the Internet or is a private intranet, the first three classes work the same way.

Class A is for a few enormous networks

Theoretically, only 127 Class A networks can exist on the Internet, but each one of those can have a huge number of hosts: about 17 million apiece (16,777,216, to be exact). Only a few very large organizations need Class A networks. By the way, no Class A network starts with the number 0, and the entire Class A network numbered 127 is reserved, leaving only 126 Class A networks.

Class B is for lots of big networks

Although Class B networks aren't nearly as enormous as Class A networks, they're still hefty. Each Class B network can have about 65,000 hosts — the size needed by large universities and larger companies. The Internet can support as many as 16,384 Class B networks.

Class C is for millions of small networks

Class C networks are much smaller than Class A and B networks, and the Internet has more than 2 million (2,097,152) of them. Most networks connected to the Internet are Class C. Each one can have only 254 hosts.

Class D is for multicasting

Class D networks are completely different from the other classes — they're used for *multicasting,* which is a special way of transmitting information from a server to a set of clients all at the same time. Multicasting is the technology that supports such cool applications as audio- and video-conferencing and radio and television stations that exist only on the Internet.

Days or weeks before a "broadcast," the sponsoring organization announces (by way of e-mail or Usenet news) the Class D network address that the server will use for the transmission. (Radio and television stations are assigned permanent addresses so that they can transmit constantly if they choose to.) Plenty of channels are available because Class D addresses range from 224.0.0.0 to 239.255.255.255. At the assigned date and time for the broadcast, you tune *(configure)* your client software to the proper Class D address. The broadcast works just like ordinary radio and television except that it's on the Internet.

Real-time applications require special-purpose, multicast-aware *routers* so that the packets always arrive in the proper order and none is missing. These routers on the Internet form the IP *multicast* back*bone,* or MBone.

Biting Down on Bits and Bytes

You might wonder who first determined the number of hosts in Class A, B, and C networks, and you might wonder why only 127 Class A networks exist when (almost) a zillion class C networks exist.

It all has to do with the arrangement of the bits inside the addresses. For example, Class A addresses use the first field as the network section and the next three fields as the host section. The more fields a section has, the larger the number that results. Because Class A has only one field in the network section, it can have only a small number of networks. But the three fields in the hosts part allow each of those 127 networks to have a ton of computers.

Table 4-2 shows how the four fields of the IP address are assigned to the network section and host section.

Table 4-2	The Two Sections of the IP Address	
Network Class	*Network Section*	*Host Section*
A	field1	field2.field3.field4
B	field1.field2	field3.field4
C	field1.field2.field3	field4

Danger — math ahead! If you already understand binary numbers and how to convert from decimal to binary, skip ahead to the next section. If you don't understand binary numbers, this section takes you back to school. Get ready to look at place values in a whole new way.

Figure 4-2 takes the number 127 apart to show how it's constructed in binary. A computer looks at the number 127 as an arrangement of 0s and 1s. Computers ultimately do everything in *binary,* or base 2. So if you look at the place value columns in Figure 4-2, you don't see the familiar 1s, 10s, 100s, and so on, from the decimal system. Rather, you see the 1s, 2s, 4s, 8s, 16s, 32s, 64s, 128s, and so on. (**Remember:** In binary, the only possible values in a column are 0 or 1. Also remember that a byte contains 8 bits.) In the decimal system, it takes three columns — the 1s column, the 10s column, and the 100s column — to represent the number 127. To get to 127, therefore, a binary number has 7 columns: the 1s, 2s, 4s, 8s, 16s, 32s, and 64s.

TECHNICAL STUFF

Classy bits

In a computer, each place-value column in a binary number is represented by a *bit*. In the early days of computers, you could look inside the cabinet and *see* circular magnets, or cores; each magnet was a bit. A core magnetized in one direction (clockwise, for example) meant that the bit was set to 1. A core magnetized in the other direction (counterclockwise) meant that the bit was set to 0. Modern transistors and semiconductors have replaced the magnets so that seeing what's going on inside is more difficult — but the computer still uses bits of 1 and 0. All numbers inside the computer, from 0 to 1,000,000,000,000 and higher, are made from bits. The computer keeps adding the 1s and 0s until it reaches the total, such as 127.

If every bit of the Class A network piece were set to 0 or 1, that would result in a higher number than the 127 allowed by the Internet. Figure it out:

128+64+32+16+8+4+2+1

But TCP/IP requires that the high-order bit for a Class A network is always 0. According to this rule, when you add up the bits, you get 0+64+32+16+8+4+2+1 for the number of Class A networks that a 32-bit address allows. To determine how many networks and hosts were allowable for each Internet class, the maximum value was calculated for the field combinations of each section. The rules for Class B state that the first two high-order bits must be 1 and 0. For Class C, the first two high-order bits must be 1 and 1.

The high-order bits are the bits at the end of the number. Which end they're on depends on whether your computer reads from right to left or from left to right. If a computer reads from right to left, as does a PC, the high-order bits are the ones on the far left end.

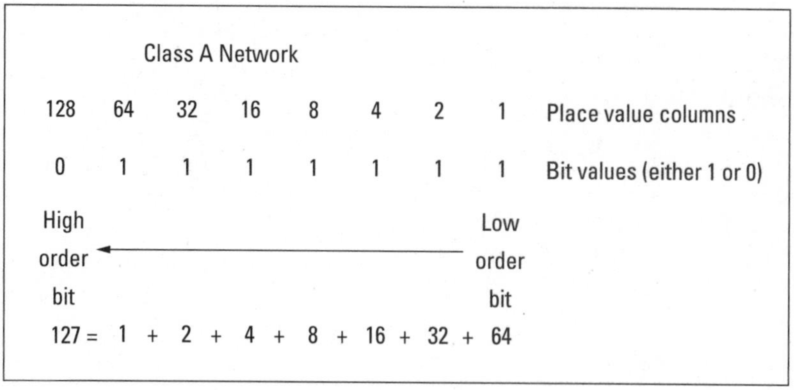

Figure 4-2:
Binary numbers are as easy as 1-2-3. Oops — make that 0-1-0.

Class A Network								
128	64	32	16	8	4	2	1	Place value columns
0	1	1	1	1	1	1	1	Bit values (either 1 or 0)

High order bit ◄———————————— Low order bit

127 = 1 + 2 + 4 + 8 + 16 + 32 + 64

Obtaining an IP Address

Before you obtain an IP address for your network, we first have to ask whether you want a private address or a global Internet address.

The answer depends on whether you need an address for a private network or a global public network, such as the Internet.

Choosing whether to go public or stay private

A *private* network is also known as a *nonroutable* network because it isn't connected to the Internet — at least not directly. The *TCP/IP For Dummies* network is a private network hidden behind a firewall. None of our computers connects to the Internet. We can use any IP addresses on our private network we want because the Internet doesn't know anything about them, and it doesn't care. However, the Internet powers that be have reserved a set of addresses just for private networks. These addresses, which can be within the range of 192.168.0.0 to 192.168.255.255, appear often in the examples in this book.

Figure 4-3 displays a private network. That network's router connects the network to an ISP, and the ISP connects to the Internet. So we have Internet access without having to put ourselves "out there" publicly.

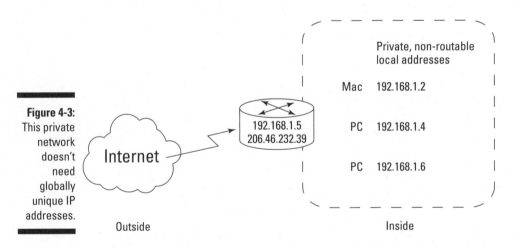

Figure 4-3:
This private network doesn't need globally unique IP addresses.

Private, non-routable local addresses

Mac 192.168.1.2

192.168.1.5
206.46.232.39

PC 192.168.1.4

PC 192.168.1.6

Internet

Outside   Inside

Any device connected directly to the Internet must have a unique IP address. If you aren't directly connected to the Internet, for example, your computers connect to your ISP (Internet service provider), and you can still get a global, unique IP address if you need it.

The IP address powers that be

The Internet Assigned Numbers Authority (IANA) manages the worldwide assignment of IP addresses. IANA delegates its responsibility by passing out massive blocks of addresses to the Regional Internet Registries, or RIRs.

RIRs hand out IP addresses in their respective regions. As of this writing, these five RIRs serve different regions:

AfriNIC: Africa

APNIC: Asia Pacific

ARIN: North America and several Caribbean and North Atlantic islands

LACNIC: Latin America and the rest of the Caribbean

RIPE NCC: Europe, the Middle East, and parts of central Asia

Check out how to request an IP addresses from one of the organizations by reading the document at www.arin.net/registration/guidelines/ipv4_initial_alloc.html.

Obeying the network police

If you work in an organization that uses a private network — granted, it might be much bigger than the private network shown earlier (refer to Figure 4-3), don't think that you can pick any address you like for your computer.

Large organizations employ network administrators (known affectionately as the network police) who tell you what to use for an address so that yours doesn't conflict with anyone else's. Your network police officer is there to ensure that no one "squats" at a network address that's already in use. If the network police force doesn't do its job and you set up your computer to use an existing address, don't come complaining to us that you never receive your e-mail or that you're receiving someone else's junk mail.

If your organization uses the Dynamic Host Configuration Protocol (DHCP), the DHCP server software automatically assigns an IP address to your host. We hand over the DHCP details in Chapter 5.

Obtaining a globally unique IP address

On the Internet, where many thousands of networks are interconnected, the assignment of the network number portion of the IP address keeps the organizations clearly identified and separate.

To connect your network to the Internet, you need an official block of addresses and a registered domain name (to append to your computers' names to create their fully qualified domain names).

Now, if you need a global IP address, you won't go to IANA (described in the nearby sidebar, "The IP address powers that be") unless you're a giant telecom company. Most organizations receive global addresses from an Internet Service Provider (ISP), such as Comcast, Verizon, Deutsche Telekom, NTT Communications, and many more around the world.

Acquiring a static address

When you have a *static* address, your IP address is always the same. When your computer starts up, it immediately knows your address. Your address never changes. But static addresses have some problems, such as

- ✔ **More work for the network administrator.** Even in a small home network, extra work can be annoying because you have to set up each computer's address separately. If something changes in your network, you have to change all the addresses.

- ✔ **Possible waste:** If your computer goes off the network, its IP address isn't needed and is therefore wasted. It might not seem like a problem in a small office/home office (SOHO), but imagine a large corporation with thousands of static addresses. If half its computers don't need to be networked all the time, its addresses go to waste part of the time.

Getting dynamic addresses with DHCP

DHCP gives network administrators a break. If you hate the idea of doing the math, you can let DHCP help. DHCP is the TCP/IP protocol that automatically assigns and tracks IP addresses while the network administrator does something else (like take a stroll on the beach).

Besides giving network administrators a rest, DHCP saves waste. A computer gets an IP address only when it needs one. To find out how DHCP works, see Chapter 5.

Finding out your IP address

Most likely, you know the name of your computer, but if you don't, you can easily find out its name and address by using the ipconfig command (Windows) or the ifconfig command (Mac OS X, Linux, and Unix). The ipconfig and ifconfig commands provide lots of information about your computer's network settings. Using the command works a little differently depending on your operating system, but the results are the same.

Using ipconfig in Windows to digest network information

Whatever flavor of Windows you like to munch, you need to run ipconfig in a command window. (It has no cute little icon.) Follow these steps to run ipconfig:

1. **Click the Start button to open the Start menu.**

2. **Click Run.**

3. **Type** command **or** cmd **in the Run box.**

4. **Type** ipconfig **in the black command window.**

5. **If you want to see much more than your computer's IP address, such as whether it's static or dynamically allocated by a DHCP server, type** ipconfig /all.

Figure 4-4 shows the output from a basic ipconfig command. You can find out a lot about your computer's network configuration by using the ipconfig command.

```
Windows IP Configuration

Ethernet adapter Local Area Connection:

        Media State . . . . . . . . . . : Media disconnected

Ethernet adapter Wireless Network Connection:

        Connection-specific DNS Suffix  . : home

        IP Address. . . . . . . . . . . : 192.168.1.2

        Subnet Mask . . . . . . . . . . : 255.255.255.0

        Default Gateway . . . . . . . . : 192.168.1.1
```

Figure 4-4:
The output from a basic ipconfig command.

Using ifconfig in Mac OS X

Follow these steps to find your computer's IP address in Mac OS X:

1. **Use Finder to open the Applications folder.**

2. **Go to Utilities.**

3. **Open a terminal window.**

4. **Type** ifconfig **at the prompt in the terminal window.**

   When you see en0 (wired) or en1 (wireless), you're looking at information about your NIC.

5. **Find your IP address on the line labeled with** inet.

In Mac OS X, Linux, and Unix, if you want to see all the information, rather than use the /all option, as in Windows, use –a instead:

```
ifconfig -a
```

Using ifconfig on Linux or Unix

To find your IP address on Linux or Unix, you do basically the same thing as on Mac OS X: Open a terminal window and follow the Mac OS X instructions in the preceding section. Linux and Unix typically use eth0 or eth1 as your NIC.

Resolving Names and Addresses with DNS

In this section, you discover another TCP/IP service: the Domain Name System (DNS, pronounced by saying the letters "D N S"). But when you fish for information with the DNS rod and reel, you're fishing around not just on your own intranet but also on the Internet. All servers connected to the Internet use DNS to translate Internet host names into IP addresses.

Understanding the minimum amount of information about DNS

A name service *resolves* (translates) a computer name into a numeric address. The Domain Name System, which is the name service for the Internet, translates computer names into TCP/IP numeric addresses.

Another way to say that DNS translates or resolves names and numeric addresses is to say that DNS *maps* names to addresses.

If your organization's network is connected to the Internet, you *must* use DNS. If your organization has a private intranet, you can either use DNS to provide the name service for your network or create a hosts file with the names and addresses of the devices on your intranet.

DNS was created specifically to handle the requirement that every computer needs to be uniquely named on the network. By adding some pieces to your computer name to make it unique, DNS solves the problem of duplicate computer names.

Using DNS to "Do Nifty Searches"

In techie terms, DNS is the *name-and-address resolution service* used on the Internet. In more straightforward terms, DNS is a kind of directory service. It searches for the numeric Internet address for a computer name and vice versa. (Of course, if we could remember those complicated numeric addresses, we wouldn't need a name-and-address resolution service, but brain cells being what they are, we'd rather think of a computer as bigbird rather than as 192.168.0.1.)

As mentioned earlier in this chapter, hosts on a TCP/IP network have both a name and a numeric IP address. When you use a name, either the hosts file (see Chapter 6) or DNS must translate the names into numbers behind the scenes.

Let's look at the mythical address abc.university.edu. Remember that the first piece of this address, abc, is the computer's name; the last piece of the address, on the right, edu, represents a domain name — a DNS top-level domain name. The intermediate piece (university) is a secondary domain name, which represents such elements as organization names.

Describing Fully Qualified Domain Names (FQDNs)

Various products and applications use the term *domain* to mean different things. The Internet is so huge that it organizes its participating computers into groups of administrative units; these units are *domains*. DNS defines *domain* in the context of a large network, such as the Internet. The domains themselves are organized hierarchically into a tree structure, as shown in Figure 4-5. The next sections explain more about the ICANN (see Chapter 1) domain labeling system.

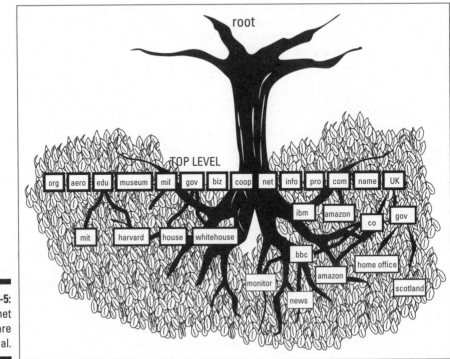

Figure 4-5:
Internet
domains are
hierarchical.

Branching out into domains

The Internet's "tree" (refer to Figure 4-5) is upside down: The root is at the top, and branches extend from the *top-level domains,* or *TLDs.* Your computer sits in the leaves, at the edge of this hierarchy of domains. There are two types of TLDs:

- **Generic top-level domain (gTLD):** These domains have the generic organization types listed in Table 4-3. You might recognize the suffix in the first column as the last part of many Internet and Web addresses.

- **Country code top-level domain (ccTLD):** A country code domain ends with a two-character country code specified by the International Standards Organization (ISO). We last counted almost 300 country code domains, including those reserved for future use. Not all are independent countries. Antarctica, for example, and certain protectorates and territories also have ccTLDs. Table 4-4 lists a few of these country code top-level domains.

Table 4-3	Generic Top-Level Domain Names
Domain Suffix	*What It's Used For*
.com	Commercial enterprise
.net	Network service
.org	Organization
.edu	Educational institution
.gov	United States government
.mil	Military service
.aero	Air transport industry
.biz	Business
.coop	Cooperative organizations
.info	Unrestricted
.museum	Museum
.name	Individual
.pro	Accountant, lawyer, physician, or other professional

Table 4-4	A Few Country Code Top-Level Domain Names
Country Code	*Country It Represents*
ac	Ascension Island
ca	Canada
cz	Czech Republic
uk	United Kingdom (The ISO code is gb, but the popularly used domain is uk.)
uz	Uzbekistan

If you're using the United States' domain structure as a model, be aware that the subdomains may (or may not) have different names. In Australia, they use the same style as in the U.S. (com.au or edu.au, for example). But in the U.K., some administrative domains are named differently, as in co.uk (corporation) and ac.uk (academic community), and some stay the same, as in gov.uk (government).

Stalking new domains

The Internet's current system of generic top-level domains (gTLDs) is about to change. The 21 generic top-level domain names are still available, but organizations can apply to have their own gTLDs. For example, the Octal Octopus Corporation, LLC might apply for its own gTLD. If ICANN approves the application, we must change the top level of the tree shown in Figure 4-5 to add Octal Octopus Corporation. If your friend Olive works at Octal Octopus Corporation and her computer's name is molluska, whenever you send her e-mail, you send it to `olive@molluska.OctalOctopusCorporation`. These new gTLDs are allowed to be as long as 64 characters.

If you decide that you want to have a gTLD of your very own, start saving up. To apply and register costs about US$185,000. (We guarantee that you'll never see a gTLD named Wilensky or Leiden.)

Determining Whether the Internet Will Ever Fill Up

Theoretically, the Internet could fill up in two ways:

- ✔ Run out of addresses.
- ✔ Run out of bandwidth.

Bandwidth is the amount of data you can send through a network connection. It's usually measured in bits per second, or bps.

Choking on bandwidth

You can think of bandwidth as a superhighway. More data flows through the highway as more lanes are added. Data slows down on the information superhighway because there's not enough bandwidth. Just as a chain is no stronger than its weakest link, a data pathway is no faster than its slowest network segment.

The way to ensure that enough bandwidth is available to keep the Internet from slowing to a crawl is to keep adding more and increasingly powerful routers and servers and to upgrade the transmission. Of course, this process is for telecom companies and nations to figure out and pay for. Some doomsayers predict that the Internet will slow to a turtle's pace in a couple of years because of limited bandwidth. An Internet that sluggish isn't likely to happen, however, as long as the big Internet companies and countries keep spending billions to improve its backbone and skeleton.

Panicking about not having enough addresses

The days of panicking that the Internet would run out of addresses have come and gone. IPv6 increases the Internet address space enormously and also seriously decreases the inefficient IPv4 allocation of addresses. Two more technologies, Network Address Translation (NAT) and Classless Inter-Domain Routing (CIDR), are helping to solve potential IP address shortages. Chapter 5 introduces you to NAT, and Chapter 8 includes CIDR information.

Dishing Up More Kinds of Addresses

An IP address is not the only address that identifies your host. Every host with a NIC also has a hardware address (one per NIC), called a Media Access Control (MAC). In addition to IP addresses and MAC hardware addresses, network services and protocols also use an identifier — a *port number* — similar to an address.

MAC: Media Access Control

The NIC manufacturer hard-codes a unique hardware address, a Media Access Control (MAC), on every NIC. The ARP (Address Resolution Protocol) translates IP addresses to MAC addresses. Because your MAC address is a unique hardware ID, ARP is the way a message travels from an IP address through the lower layers of the TCP/IP layer cake and winds up at a specific hardware device. Earlier in this chapter, you can find sections on using the ipconfig and ifconfig commands. In Figure 4-6, the `ipconfig/all` command lists the MAC address as the physical address. This address doesn't look anything like an IP address. The format for your MAC address is six sets of two characters separated by colons.

The computer in Figure 4-6 runs Mac OS X, which uses both IPv4 and IPv6. The dotted decimal notation, such as `inet 127.0.0.1`, represents the IPv4 addresses, explained in this chapter. The double colon (::) notation, such as `inet6 fe80::20a:95ff:fe9d:68`, represents the IPv6 addresses, explained in Chapter 9.

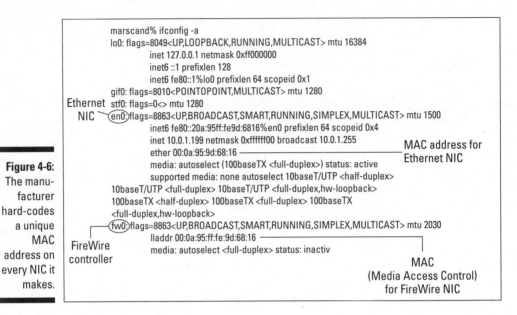

Ethernet NIC

FireWire controller

MAC address for Ethernet NIC

MAC (Media Access Control) for FireWire NIC

Figure 4-6: The manufacturer hard-codes a unique MAC address on every NIC it makes.

Port numbers

Port numbers function as addresses for network services. If you remember the TCP/IP layer cake from Chapter 2, IP (in the internet layer) passes data to the transport layer, and the transport protocol (either TCP or UDP) passes the data to the correct network service. Port numbers identify the network services. Table 4-5 lists a few well-known port numbers and their accompanying service or protocol. Programmers use these port numbers to write new TCP/IP services and applications.

Table 4-5	Sample Port Numbers
Port	**Service or Protocol**
20, 21	FTP (File Transfer Protocol)
22	SSH – Secure Shell (secure remote login)
23	telnet
53	DNS (Domain Name Service)
80	HTTP (HyperText Transfer Protocol)
143	IMAP (Internet Message Access Protocol)
194	IRC (Internet Relay Chat)
546, 547	DHCP (Dynamic Host Configuration Protocol

Figure 4-7 shows the FTP service receiving a request by way of Port 21.

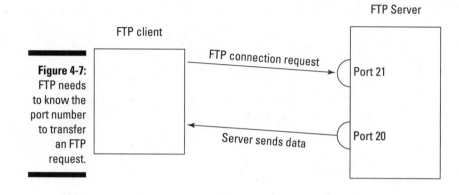

Figure 4-7:
FTP needs
to know the
port number
to transfer
an FTP
request.

FTP Server

FTP client

FTP connection request

Port 21

Server sends data

Port 20

Chapter 5

Need More Addresses? Try Subnetting and NAT

. . . .

In This Chapter

▶ Protocols in this chapter: IP, DHCP, NAT, NAT-PT

▶ Using IP addresses economically

▶ Understanding subnets and why they wear masks

▶ Letting DHCP do the work and save on IP addresses

▶ Understanding how NAT helps ease an IP address shortage

▶ Drinking in NAT security

▶ Using NAT to move between IPv4 and IPv6

. . . .

*T*CP/IP is like a restaurant. When the restaurant runs out of a popular dish, it substitutes another one on the menu. When IP runs out of addresses, it also substitutes other dishes.

The Internet is running out of 32-bit IPv4 addresses! You must have heard that before, maybe many times. But is that shortage still a problem? Maybe not; the TCP/IP restaurant has a delicious addition to the menu: Have a look at IPv6 in Chapter 9 to see how the next generation of IP — and its 128 bits — will hold us for a long time, provide a massive boost in address space, and offer built-in security. Yum. But many organizations and people haven't moved to IPv6 yet. So, we need some other items on the menu to keep surviving with the limited number of IPv4 addresses still available while the great migration goes on. In this chapter, we describe some ways to conserve IPv4 addresses without giving up any Internet connectivity.

So take heart as you peruse some appetizing subnet techniques and a tasty short menu of protocols to help satisfy the Net's short-term appetite for addresses.

Working with Subnets and Subnet Masks

Subnets divide one network into multiple smaller networks, normally inter-connected by network devices called *routers*. (See Chapter 7 for more about routers.)

Not every network environment requires subnets. For example, if your orga-nization's network has 254 or fewer hosts — and the network lives in one building (what a concept), there's no reason to subnet it. But if your organi-zation's network expands into multiple locations, the network administrator needs to look at a couple of options:

- ✔ Ask for another entire network number for every new facility — which is greedy if your existing network still has enough unassigned host num-bers to go around.

- ✔ Split your existing network into pieces (subnetworks — subnets for short), one piece for each location.

Class C networks are the smallest. When you get a Class C network, you get 254 addresses whether you need them or not. Imagine The Crepe Place in Paris (TCPiP), a restaurant with 3 branches. Each branch has a separate Class C network, but there are only 100 network devices in each branch res-taurant. That means in each branch, 154 addresses go unused. That's greedy (or at least wasteful)!

When subnets are necessary and the network administrator (this may mean you!) uses good common sense to subdivide the network, subnets yield some advantages over one large network:

- ✔ Smaller networks are easier to manage and troubleshoot, even though there are more pieces.

- ✔ Network traffic overall is reduced and performance may improve because most traffic is local to its location's subnet.

- ✔ Network security can be applied more easily at the interconnections between the subnets. (For some exhausting details about network secu-rity, read Chapters 20 and 21.)

Figure 5-1 shows a main network with two subnets. Whether wired or wire-less, each network and each host has an address. Look carefully at `field3` in each address; can you find some subtle differences?

Part of the address for a subnet includes the address for the main network:

```
192.168
```

and borrows some bits from the host part to extend the network section. The borrowed bits enable each subnet to have its own unique network address: `192.168.1`, `192.168.2`, and so on.

What are routers? And how big do they get?

A *router* is a computer that runs software that figures how a packet should be forwarded on the route to its destination. A router works at the internet layer of the TCP/IP layer cake, and connects to at least two networks. Most routers are in homes and offices and send Web, e-mail, and other Internet messages from the local area network (LAN) through your broadband connection (such as cable or DSL modem) to your ISP. Your ISP sends your routed messages out to the Internet. A combination cable modem/ router connects the home LAN to the ISP. Some of the fancier routers combine routing functions with a DHCP server and a firewall. Chapters 4 and 5 contain information about DHCP. Chapter 12 gives you an introduction to firewalls.

The routers at the biggest ISPs that connect the Internet backbones (major Internet segments) have huge capacity. Cisco Systems Inc., for example, makes most of the Internet routers, including one that's so powerful, it's listed in the Guinness World Records. This enormously powerful router can move up to 92 Tbps (*tera-bits*, that is, trillion bits) of data per second. Just one of these routers on the Internet will allow 1 billion people to play an online game, and use real-time voice-and-chat — all at the same time. (For that matter, it would let everyone who's ever read any edition of this book watch a video simultaneously.) Whew! Luckily, most of us don't really need a router that costs half a billion U.S. dollars.

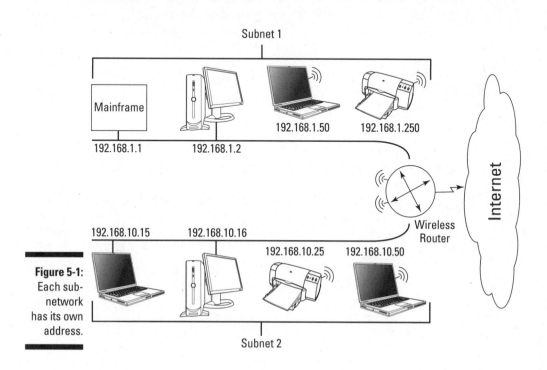

Subnet 1

Mainframe

192.168.1.1   192.168.1.2   192.168.1.50   192.168.1.250

Internet

Wireless Router

192.168.10.15   192.168.10.16   192.168.10.25   192.168.10.50

Figure 5-1: Each sub-network has its own address.

Subnet 2

Because the subnet addresses come from the main network's address, you don't have to ask a registrar to assign them. These addresses already belong to your organization; you've just decided to use them differently.

Defining subnet masks

When the network administrator borrows bits from the main network address's host section, TCP/IP needs to know which bits of the host section are borrowed to be used as the network address. The administrator uses a *subnet mask* to borrow those host bits. A subnet mask is 32 bits that overlay an IP address.

An IPv6 subnet mask is 128 bits, but IPv6 subnet masks are only rarely needed.

The mask sets all the bits for the network address to 1, and all the bits for the host address to 0. The mask tells the router, "Look only at the bits that lie under the 1s. Forget about any bits that lie under the 0s." Because the router can skip the masked-out bits (that is, the zeroed-out bits), it can send packets on their way faster than if it had to look at the entire address.

Before defining a subnet mask, the network administrator needs to figure out how many subnets to create and how many hosts will be in each subnet. This determines how many bits should be set to 1.

The more bits used for the subnet mask, the fewer hosts can be on each subnet created.

Why a network has a mask when it has no subnets

Your network always has a subnet mask even if it doesn't use subnets. Most TCP/IP implementations supply a default subnet mask, which says, "Hi. I'm a network that's not subnetted." Figure 5-2 shows the default subnet mask for each class of network. Most TCP/IP vendors automatically set the default subnet mask for you.

Regardless of your operating system, you can see the mask when you look at your network properties.

The subnet mask must be the same for each computer on that part of the network; otherwise the computers don't understand that they're on the same subnet.

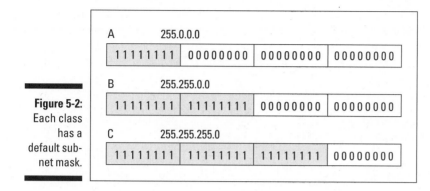

Figure 5-2:
Each class
has a
default sub-
net mask.

The subnet mask is applied to the IP address in every message in order to separate the network number and the host number. For example, when your computer examines the address 192.9.200.15 and applies the default subnet mask of 255.255.255.0, it sees the network number 192.9.200 and the host number 15.

Okay, how do you *know* this works? Hold on to your techie hats. It's done by converting nice decimal numbers, such as 255, to not-so-nice binary numbers, such as 11111111. Then, after all the numbers are converted to binary, they get ANDed. AND is a binary mathematical operation. If you aren't fed up AND bored by now, read the upcoming sidebar "Boolean arithmetic: AND." Just remember: Although this stuff may seem incomprehensible to you, your computer lives, breathes, and eats binary — and thinks this is Really Fun!

(The authors of this book cannot be held responsible for any medical or mental complications that result from reading the Boolean arithmetic sidebar.)

Subnetting 101

Say, for example, that you're going to split one Class C network with 256 addresses into two equal subnets of 128 addresses each. First order of business: Change the Class C default subnet mask of 255.255.255.0 — along some very specific lines . . .

For this example, you use network number 192.9.202, which means the 256 addresses are numbered 192.9.202.0 through 192.9.202.255. To split the network into two parts — giving one part addresses 0 to 127 and giving the other addresses 128 to 255 — you need the custom subnet mask 255.255.255.128. The 0 becomes 128 because you borrow the high-order bit from field4. (In binary, 128 is 10000000. Refer to the "Classy bits" sidebar in Chapter 4 if you need help with the math.)

Boolean arithmetic: AND

In the AND operation, regardless of the value in the data bit, a mask bit of 0 yields a result of 0. And a mask bit of 1 preserves the value in the data bit, also regardless of the value in the data bit. Another way to say this is that the result bit is a 1 if and only if both the data bit and the mask bit contain 1. Otherwise the result bit is 0. This table demonstrates:

	0	1	0	1	Data
AND	0	0	1	1	Mask
	0	0	0	1	Result

Here's an overview of how a subnet mask is used to obtain the network number part of an IP address. In your computer, the fields of the dotted decimal IP address 192.9.200.15 are already in binary as

11000000 00001001 11001000 00001111

The fields of the dotted decimal subnet mask 255.255.255.0 are also already in binary:

11111111 11111111 11111111 00000000

The AND operation yields the network number 192.9.200, as shown here:

11000000 00001001 11001000 00001111 IP address: 192.9.200.15

11111111 11111111 11111111 00000000 Subnet mask: 255.255.255.0

11000000 00001001 11001000 00000000 Result: 192.9.200.0

To get the host number, your computer inverts the bits of the subnet mask — each 1 becomes a 0 and each 0 becomes a 1 — and does another AND. Easy as pi, right?

11000000 00001001 11001000 00001111 IP address: 192.9.200.15

00000000 00000000 00000000 11111111 Subnet mask: 0.0.0.255

00000000 00000000 00000000 00001111 Result: 0.0.0.15

In the 192.9.202 network, there are 128 addresses that happen to have the high-order bit of field4 set to 0 and another 128 addresses that happen to have the high-order bit set to 1. If you thought the custom subnet mask would be 255.255.255.1, you were close, but that mask borrows the low-order bit of field4. It puts all the even-numbered addresses (0, 2, 4, 6, and so on up to 254) in one subnet and all the odd-numbered addresses (1, 3, 5, 7, and so on up to 255) in the other.

Before subnetting this example network, it was easy to say that all the hosts were in the 192.9.202 network. The good news: After subnetting, they still are.

Probably the most common example of subnetting is splitting a Class B network into 256 Class C networks. To accomplish this, every host sets its subnet mask to 255.255.255.0.

TIP If you're a network administrator and you hate this math, Google "free subnet calculators" for some handy tools to ease the pain. Also read about IPv6 in Chapter 9, and rejoice: The expanded address size removes the need for subnetting.

TIP If you don't know your subnet mask and you want to know it, the `ipconfig` or `ifconfig` command is an easy way to find out. (Use `ipconfig` if you're running some form of Windows. Use `ifconfig` if you're running some form of Linux or Unix.) Chapter 4 illustrates using the basic command to see your IP address. If you add the following command option, as shown in Figure 5-3, you can see your subnet mask:

```
/all
```

Figure 5-3: Use the /all option on the ipconfig command to see the sub-net mask.

```
C:\WINDOWS\system32\command.com
Microsoft(R) Windows DOS
(C)Copyright Microsoft Corp 1990-2001.

C:\DOCUME~1\CANDACE>ipconfig/all

Windows IP Configuration

        Host Name . . . . . . . . . . . . : woodstock
        Primary Dns Suffix  . . . . . . . :
        Node Type . . . . . . . . . . . . : Broadcast
        IP Routing Enabled. . . . . . . . : No
        WINS Proxy Enabled. . . . . . . . : No

Ethernet adapter Local Area Connection:

        Media State . . . . . . . . . . . : Media disconnected
        Description . . . . . . . . . . . : Broadcom 440x 10/100 Integrated Cont
roller
        Physical Address. . . . . . . . . : 00-15-C5-22-D7-9A

Ethernet adapter Wireless Network Connection:

        Connection-specific DNS Suffix  . :
        Description . . . . . . . . . . . : Intel(R) PRO/Wireless 3945ABG Networ
k Connection
        Physical Address. . . . . . . . . : 00-13-02-B8-58-51
        Dhcp Enabled. . . . . . . . . . . : Yes
        Autoconfiguration Enabled . . . . : Yes
        IP Address. . . . . . . . . . . . : 192.168.1.103
        Subnet Mask . . . . . . . . . . . : 255.255.255.0
        Default Gateway . . . . . . . . . : 192.168.1.1
        DHCP Server . . . . . . . . . . . : 192.168.1.1
        DNS Servers . . . . . . . . . . . : 167.206.254.1
                                            167.206.254.2
        Lease Obtained. . . . . . . . . . : Saturday, December 27, 2008 2:23:16
PM
        Lease Expires . . . . . . . . . . : Sunday, December 28, 2008 2:23:16 PM

C:\DOCUME~1\CANDACE>_
```

Letting the DHCP Protocol Do the Work for You

If you could use some help with the complexities of subnetting, DHCP (Dynamic Host Configuration Protocol) provides some. It's the TCP/IP protocol that automatically assigns and keeps track of IP addresses and subnet masks while the network administrator takes a stroll on the beach. DHCP has three major benefits:

  ✔ DHCP gives out IP addresses only when they're needed

  ✔ DHCP automatically recycles IP addresses

  ✔ DHCP reduces network administrators' workloads

So here's a look at how **gnarly** subnetting can be, and how DHCP can help you through the maze.

One administrator's nightmare is another's fantasy

Imagine you're the person in charge of the White Pages of the telephone book. What a hard job it must be! You have to be sure that every customer's name and number are in the book correctly and in alphabetical order. When people move into your area and get phone service, you have to assign every one of them a number and list it in the directory. If people discontinue service, you have to remove their names and numbers. If you live where people move frequently, you spend all your time keeping that directory up to date.

Now fantasize that the telephone company gets a new system that's magical — and whenever someone needs to be assigned a telephone number, you don't have to do anything. The telephone system magically assigns a number automatically. If someone no longer needs a number, the telephone system automatically removes it and later recycles the number to someone else. And forget about keeping the telephone book up to date. The telephone system magically does that, too. In fact, there's no permanent telephone book. If someone wants to call Emily, she picks up the telephone and says, "Please connect me to Emily's telephone, wherever that is." This system would make your life as a telephone administrator so easy that you could work at the beach with a novel in one hand and a cold drink in the other.

Fantasy? Yes, for telephone administrators — but not necessarily for network administrators. People communicate on a network — big or small, Internet or intranet — via computer names and IP addresses. The network administrator keeps these names and addresses up to date in a hosts file or a DNS database. Maintaining this information is tedious and time-consuming in a volatile network environment, just as it is in a real-life telephone company.

In IPv6, DHCP changes its name to DHCPv6. Chapter 9 gives you the lowdown on IPv6.

Understanding how the DHCP protocol works — it's client/server again

DHCP does its magic by using a well-established approach to networked computers: client/server networking. The DHCP server holds pools of IP addresses to *lease* to clients. When you turn on your computer (a DHCP client), it contacts your network's DHCP server and asks to lease an address. The client and server negotiate the lease and — voilà! You have an IP address to use for the duration of the lease.

Here's how it works:

1. You turn on your computer.

   TCP/IP starts, but remember, you're leasing. You have no permanent IP address.

2. Your DHCP client software asks to lease an IP address.

   This request is called a *DHCP discover message*. The DHCP discover message contains the name of your computer and its MAC hardware address. Your hardware address comes on your NIC (network interface card), so the DHCP software already knows where to look for it.

3. Your DHCP client keeps broadcasting its lease request until a DHCP server responds.

   The response is usually so quick, you don't notice any wait time. A DHCP server is software that usually runs on a large host. The server software provides DHCP services, such as storing a large pool of IP addresses in a central database and leasing you an IP address. If there's no DHCP server — maybe an earthquake destroyed it — your computer keeps trying, but never gets its address. In that case, you can't use any TCP/IP applications or services.

4. All the available DHCP servers answer your message by offering your proposed IP address, the servers' IP address, a subnet mask, and the duration of the lease in hours.

   The server's response is called a *DHCP offer message*. Your computer grabs an IP address so no one else can take it while you're negotiating.

   The client and server negotiate in Figure 5-4.

5. Your DHCP client takes the first offer and broadcasts its acceptance.

   The client responds to the server's offer message with a *DHCP request message*. The request message asks the DHCP server to verify the address it offered. Then the other servers can cancel their offers.

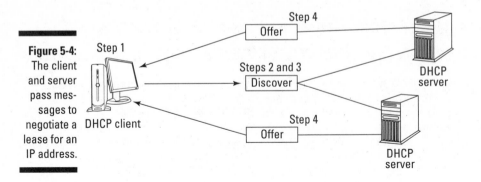

Figure 5-4:
The client
and server
pass mes-
sages to
negotiate a
lease for an
IP address.

6. Your selected DHCP server makes your IP address permanent and sends you an "acknowledged" message (DHCP*ACK*).

7. Congratulations! You have an IP address.

Figure 5-5 congratulates the DHCP client on obtaining an IP address.

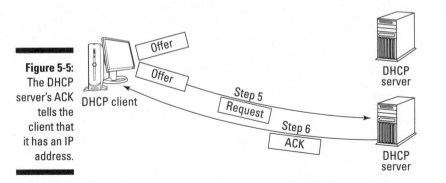

Figure 5-5:
The DHCP
server's ACK
tells the
client that
it has an IP
address.

You can use TCP/IP applications and services as long as you want — or until your lease expires.

Being evicted after your lease expires

Usually a DHCP server renews your lease with no problem. In fact, you don't have to do anything. The entire process is automatic and doesn't interfere with what you're doing.

If the DHCP server dies during your lease, you keep your IP address until its lease expires. You won't be able to renew the lease. When your lease expires, so does your ability to use TCP/IP services and applications.

Because any DHCP server on the network can renew your lease, your network administrator should configure more than one DHCP server. That way, a lone DHCP server is not the single point of failure on a network.

Sharing Addresses with Network Address Translation (NAT)

NAT (also called IP NAT) consists of two parts:

- ✔ A pass-through between your private intranet and the outside world (public Internet)
- ✔ A translator to and from private IP addresses to global IP addresses

NAT allows multiple computers on one intranet to share one officially registered IP address. Only one computer on the intranet must have a registered IP address to get to the Internet; the device that has the official IP address is called a *NAT router*. Requests from the hosts on your intranet go through the NAT router on their way to and from the Internet.

Using IPv6 removes the need for NAT because IPv6 provides so many addresses that there's no need to share. If you're running IPv6, pat yourself on the back, have a piece of layer cake, and skip the sections about NAT. If you stay with this chapter, you get a glimpse of how NAT works behind the scenes, how to ensure your NAT configuration is secure, and how NAT and DHCP work together.

Understanding how NAT works

When packets move from inside your intranet through the NAT router, those packets seem to come directly from the router; they have the router's external address. Here's how it works. When a request comes from one of the hosts on your intranet, the NAT router replaces that host's local IP address with its own global address. The NAT software then sends the message out to the world on behalf of the local requester. When a response comes back, the NAT router reverses the procedure and removes its own IP address from the message and restores the originating computer's address. Figure 5-6 shows NAT running on a router.

NAT comes in two flavors:

- ✔ **Static NAT** requires you to assign a permanent public address to each host on your private intranet.
- ✔ **Dynamic NAT** automatically assigns public addresses on an as-needed basis.

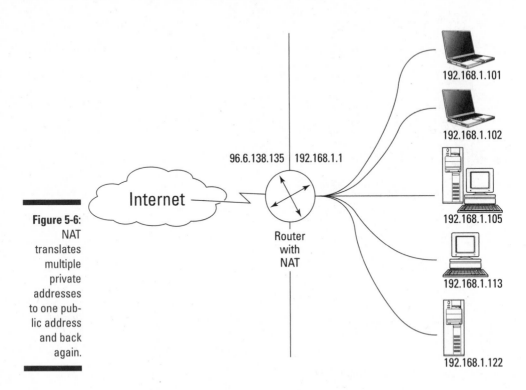

96.6.138.135 | 192.168.1.1

Router
with
NAT

192.168.1.101

192.168.1.102

192.168.1.105

192.168.1.113

192.168.1.122

Figure 5-6:
NAT
translates
multiple
private
addresses
to one pub-
lic address
and back
again.

Securing NAT

Using Dynamic NAT has the added benefit of adding security to your network because your internal addresses are not available to the outside world. It's impossible for a hacker/cracker to see the address of your computer when it's hidden in a private network behind a NAT router.

Your private hosts can only see the NAT router. They can't see the Internet. For example, when you browse the Web, all your requests go through the NAT router with the NAT router's address. When there is any kind of incoming request to your private host, Internet routers cannot see your host. As far as the Internet is concerned, your IP address doesn't exist. Any incoming requests for your host see only the NAT router's address. You are invisible.

Although NAT offers a side benefit in the security it provides, it's *not* a substitute for the bare-bones minimum security features listed in Chapter 12.

Using NAT and DHCP to work together

The computer acting as a NAT router can also be the DHCP server that leases IP addresses to the other computers on the intranet. The computer that serves as the NAT router might also be a DHCP client, getting its official

IP address from the ISP. Microsoft's Internet Connection Sharing (a feature of older Windows operating systems, such as Windows 98 Second Edition, Windows 2000, and Windows XP Professional) functions as a DHCP server and NAT router. The network we use for most of this book's examples uses NAT and DHCP. Instead of requesting a Class C network for our small intranet, we have one computer with an IP address assigned by our ISP. Figure 5-7 shows a piece of our intranet and how a Web-browser request goes through our NAT router and out to the Internet.

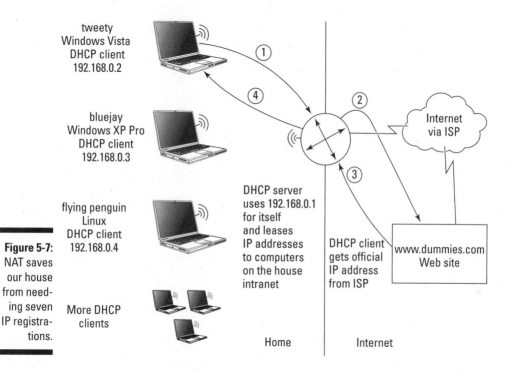

tweety
Windows Vista
DHCP client
192.168.0.2

bluejay
Windows XP Pro
DHCP client
192.168.0.3

flying penguin
Linux
DHCP client
192.168.0.4

More DHCP
clients

DHCP server
uses 192.168.0.1
for itself
and leases
IP addresses
to computers
on the house
intranet

DHCP client
gets official
IP address
from ISP

Internet
via ISP

www.dummies.com
Web site

Home   Internet

Figure 5-7:
NAT saves
our house
from need-
ing seven
IP registra-
tions.

Here the router, with multiple NICs inside, serves three roles:

- ✔ **NAT router:** Again, this is the computer that has the official IP address.
- ✔ **DHCP Client:** It gets our official IP address from our ISP. One NIC connects us to our ISP through a cable modem.
- ✔ **DHCP server:** It leases IP addresses to the other computers on our in-house intranet. The other NIC goes to a hub that connects all the in-house computers.

The browser request follows these steps:

1. Marshall, on tweety, types a URL, such as www.dummies.com, in his browser. The packet includes tweety's address, and it goes to the combination router/DHCP server. The router removes tweety's IP address from the packet and inserts its own address.

2. The router sends tweety's browser request to the www.dummies.com Web site.

3. The www.dummies.com server packages up a response to send to the router. The router's IP address is part of the packet. The router receives the response packet. The router also removes its own IP address and replaces the address with tweety's IP address.

4. The router forwards the response to tweety.

Swallowing NAT incompatibilities

Thank goodness the TCP/IP Restaurant at the End of the Universe allows address substitutions. A NAT router works by rewriting IP addresses in the packet header. NAT assumes that IP addresses only occur in the Internet layer of the TCP/IP model. NAT's assumption is usually true, but not always. Figure 5-8 shows the fields in an IP packet header.

← 32 bits →			
Version	IHL	Type of service	Total length
Identification		Flags	Fragment offset
Time to live	Protocol		Header checksum
Source address 206.46.232.39			
Destination address			
Options (+ padding)			
Data (variable)			

Figure 5-8: NAT rewrites the IP addresses in the IP packet header.

Some applications also include IP addresses in applications. NAT doesn't look beyond the IP packet header. The problem arises when some applications repeat the IP address in its data. FTP, the File Transfer Application, is an application that embeds the IP address in its data. NAT never sees the IP addresses that FTP includes. When you download a file, the FTP message specifies one destination address, and NAT rewrites and specifies a different address. Result (oops): You don't get your file.

This incompatibility between the IP address embedded in application-layer data and the rewritten address provided by the NAT router affects other applications besides FTP. Applications that have compatibility difficulties with NAT include IPSec (the most effective security protocol for VPNs), video games (such as Halo), and the Internet Relay Chat (IRC) protocol.

There are various workarounds to solve these NAT/application address compatibilities, but remember that IPv6 is coming. IPv6 makes NAT processing unnecessary in most situations. If you're already using IPv6, the workarounds are yesterday's news; if you're not there yet, read on.

Digesting NAT-PT (Network Address Translation-Protocol Translation)

NAT-PT does what NAT does — it hides a private network behind a NAT router, and the router substitutes a global IP address for the addresses of the computers in the private network — but it doesn't stop there. NAT-PT lets IPv6 hosts communicate with IPv4 hosts and vice versa. Of course, you have to put a *dual-stack router* (a router that understands both IPv4 and IPv6) on the boundary between the IPv4 network and the IPv6 network to get NAT-PT to work. (Chapter 2 includes a brief definition of routers and routing protocols.)

When IPv6 packets go to IPv4 hosts, NAT-PT overwrites the IPv6 address with an IPv4 address. When IPv4 packets go to IPv6 hosts, NAT-PT overwrites the IPv4 address with an IPv6 address. You can see how NAT-PT works in Figure 5-9. Don't worry about the weird-looking address that has a colon (:).That is an IPv6 address. You can read about the IPv6 addressing format in Chapter 9.

NAT-PT is especially useful for an organization that has started to move to IPv6 and has a mix of IPv4 and IPv6 computers on its networks.

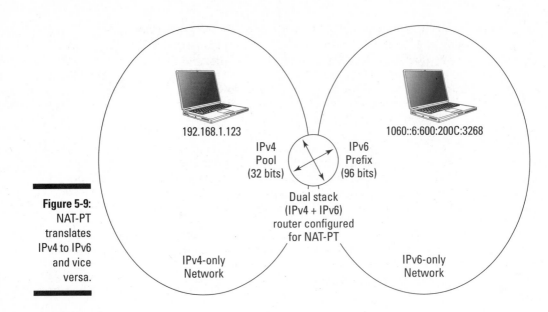

Figure 5-9:
NAT-PT
translates
IPv4 to IPv6
and vice
versa.

Part II
Getting Connected

The 5th Wave   By Rich Tennant

"You the guy having trouble staying connected to the network?"

In this part . . .

*P*art II ranges from getting started with easy TCP/IP installations to such serious technical topics as IPv6 and routing protocols. Feel free to skip the technical parts — you probably need them only if you're managing a very large organizational network.

Part II shows you hands-on, in six easy steps, how to configure TCP/IP on lots of different operating systems, including Linux, Mac OS X, Windows 7, Windows Vista, Windows Server 2008, and Unix. Then you become familiar with the files created by installing and configuring TCP/IP. You find out what those files are for, what they look like inside, and when you may need to change them.

Then it's on to setting up a wireless network for a small office or home office (SOHO). The minimum hardware details are painless, and we give you four easy steps to setting up your wireless network. Security is everywhere in this part and in this book. After you have a wireless network, we show you how to secure your hardware so that no one can break in.

Then it's back to IP addressing. You find out that you don't always need to assign an address the hard way — that is, manually. You can let a handy protocol and service, the Dynamic Host Control Protocol (DHCP), lease you an address just for the asking. If you want to be on the cutting edge, Part II takes you into the world of IPv6, the next generation.

Keep in mind that people like names and computers like numbers. Venture into DNS (the Domain Name Service) to see why people can be happy with names and our computers can still use numbers. We show you how DNS and special hosts files make the conversion from names to numbers for us.

Finally, we get seriously technical with routing protocols, router jargon, and ways to secure routers.

Chapter 6

Configuring a TCP/IP Network — the Software Side

. . . .

In This Chapter

▶ Protocols in this chapter: IPv4, IPv6, DNS, DHCP

▶ Installing no more

▶ Checking on IPv4 and IPv6

▶ Configuring TCP/IP in six steps

▶ Setting up clients and servers

▶ Investigating the network files that hold TCP/IP information

▶ Seeing that once again, "people like names, computers like numbers"

▶ Resetting a corrupted TCP/IP stack on Microsoft Windows systems

. . . .

TCP/IP is software, and just like any software, it has to be installed. This chapter describes the steps needed to get TCP/IP up and running. If you're lucky, you might have *no* steps. Yet. After TCP/IP is installed — *that's* the time you have to get to work and configure your system. Read on to see what to do, and to examine the contents of some network files that work for you behind the scenes.

If you're using an operating system or TCP/IP product that's different from the ones that our examples show, your files may vary slightly from what you see in the figures in this book. Don't worry. The steps you follow to set up your system are the same, regardless of how a window or command line may look. The files may be in a slightly different location, but the general content and the purpose of those files are the same, regardless of what folder or directory they're stored in. The principle of *RTFM — Read the Fishy Manual* that came with your TCP/IP product — always applies.

Installing TCP/IP? Probably Not

First of all, do you need to install TCP/IP? Most computers come from the factory with basic TCP/IP already installed. So your first step is

to check whether TCP/IP is installed; if it is, be sure you find out what version
of IP (IPv4 or IPv6) is on your computer (more about that in a minute).

Detecting whether TCP/IP is installed

There are lots of ways to find out whether TCP/IP is installed on your computer, but here is the easiest way (in your authors' opinion anyway). Do
you remember the ifconfig and ipconfig commands from Chapter 4? If not,
take a look, because the existence of those commands tells you whether TCP/
IP is already installed. If you can't find those commands, we're so sorry —
because that means you don't have TCP/IP, and you need to check out the
section "Installing TCP/IP from Scratch," later in this chapter. If you do have
those commands, Whoopee!; TCP/IP is already installed . . . "piece of cake"—
TCP/IP layer cake that is.

Use the ipconfig command on any flavor of Windows. Use the ifconfig command on Linux, Unix, and Mac OS X. Figure 6-1 shows the output of the Mac OS
X command ifconfig -a (equivalent to ipconfig/ all in Windows).

Figure 6-1:
This Mac
runs a dual
protocol
stack with
both
versions
of IP.

```
% ifconfig -a
lo0: flags=8049<UP,LOOPBACK,RUNNING,MULTICAST> mtu 16384
        inet 127.0.0.1 netmask 0xff000000
        inet6 ::1 prefixlen 128
        inet6 fe80::1%lo0 prefixlen 64 scopeid 0x1
gif0: flags=8010<POINTOPOINT,MULTICAST> mtu 1280
stf0: flags=0<> mtu 1280
en0: flags=8863<UP,BROADCAST,SMART,RUNNING,SIMPLEX,MULTICAST> mtu 1500
        inet6 fe80::20a:95ff:fe9d:6816%en0 prefixlen 64 scopeid 0x4
        inet 10.0.1.199 netmask 0xffffff00 broadcast 10.0.1.255
        ether 00:0a:95:9d:68:16
        media: autoselect (100baseTX <full-duplex>) status: active
        supported media: none autoselect 10baseT/UTP <half-duplex>
10baseT/UTP <full-duplex> 10baseT/UTP <full-duplex,hw-loopback>
100baseTX <half-duplex> 100baseTX <full-duplex> 100baseTX
<full-duplex,hw-loopback>
fw0: flags=8863<UP,BROADCAST,SMART,RUNNING,SIMPLEX,MULTICAST> mtu 2030
        lladdr 00:0a:95:ff:fe:9d:68:16
        media: autoselect <full-duplex> status: inactive
```

IPv6 address

IPv4 address

MAC (NIC hardware)
address

Determining whether it's IPv4, IPv6, or both

If TCP/IP is already installed (and it usually is), you need to discover which
version of IP is running: IPv4 or the newer IPv6. Chapter 9 has more detail
about IPv6 than you want to know. In a nutshell, IPv6 is the next generation of
IP. It allows for billions more IP addresses to service all the computers, smart
phones, video games, MP3 players, and all sorts of devices that have made
computing so pervasive. To figure out which version of IP you have, look at
the IP address in the ipconfig or ifconfig output. If the address is extra long

(128 bits if you do the math), you have IPv6. If the address looks "normal" — that is, 4 sets of numbers in dotted decimal notation (for example, 192.168.5.1) — then you're running IPv4.

Savoring TCP/IP right out of the box

Although almost all computers come with TCP/IP software, differences between operating systems exist. For example, your new computer might be supplied with IPv4 or IPv6 or both. This section lists several factoids about Mac, Windows, Linux, and Unix:

- *Mac OS X:*

  - All Mac OS X systems have TCP/IP preinstalled.

  - All Mac OS X systems have both versions of IP installed (IPv4 and IPv6) and active.

- *Windows Vista, Windows 7, and Microsoft Windows Server 2008:*

  - All Windows Vista, Windows 7, and Windows Server 2008 systems have TCP/IP preinstalled.

  - All Windows Vista, Windows 7, and Windows Server 2008 systems have a dual stack of both IPv4 and IPv6 preinstalled (both versions of IP, just like Mac OS X).

  - You can't uninstall IPv6 in Windows Vista, Windows 7, and Windows Server 2008, but you can disable it if you want to use IPv4 only.

    Figure 6-2 shows an example from Windows Server 2008. In the Network and Sharing Center, open the Network Connections folder, select the properties of an adapter, select the Configuration tab, and look for the IPv6 information.

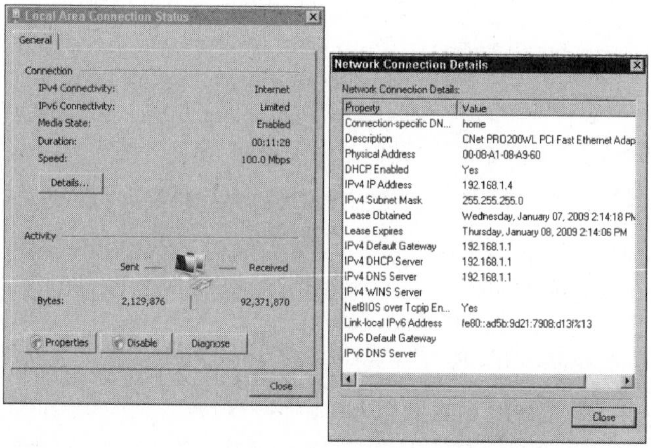

Figure 6-2: You can examine the IPv6 protocol from the Windows Server 2008 Network Connections folder.

✔ *Linux and Unix:*

- Most Linux and Unix distributions are IPv6 ready — all the IPv6 software is there, but you may or may not have to set up IPv6, depending on the distribution you're using.

- Recent Linux and Unix distributions allow you to run IPv4 and IPv6 at the same time.

- The IPv6 module may or may not be automatically loaded at startup.

- If the IPv6 module is not automatically loaded, you can load it manually.

Six Steps to a Complete TCP/IP Configuration

If your computer comes with TCP/IP already installed, it doesn't necessarily mean that the installation has all the settings you need. For example, if you're the administrator for a large server, you probably need to assign a static address for your server and configure various services. If you're setting up a small business network, you'll probably want a DHCP server to lease addresses automatically to your clients. Even in a small home network, you need to decide on a couple of options. Plan ahead.

Follow the same steps in this software chapter whether you're working on a wired or wireless network. The software-side steps are the same. When you get to hardware and security, there are variations for wired versus wireless.

Follow these steps to configure TCP/IP:

1. **Decide whether your computer is a client or a server.**

   Setting up a client is much simpler than setting up a server because you don't need to configure server services — you'll be getting those from the server.

2. **Gather client information.**

   The installation procedure for your operating system usually asks you for the hostname. After you provide that vital bit of information, the installation program sets the domain name and IP address automatically. The bottom line is that if you're configuring a TCP/IP client, it's all been done for you automatically. Cheers.

3. **Set up your NIC(s).**

   Installing the operating system usually takes care of this step too.

4. **Decide on a static IP address or a DHCP leased address.**

5. **Choose how your host will translate names into addresses — either with a hosts file or with DNS (Domain Name Service).**

6. **Gather server (or multifunction router) information.**

   If your computer is a server or a router, you need to continue with optional configurations.

We discuss these steps in detail in the following sections.

Step 1: Determining whether your computer is a client or server or both

First of all, we don't recommend setting up a host to be both a client and server. Just because something is possible doesn't mean you should do it. A computer that tries to do everything has more congestion than Marshall's sinuses.

If you're going to be a client, you'll use services but not provide them. All you have to do is set up your NIC and your IP address. If you're a DHCP client, you don't even need to set up your IP address; the DHCP server leases you an address automatically.

If you're setting up TCP/IP as a server, you need to know what service(s) to provide. Is your server going to be an HTTP server, FTP server, DHCP server, or what (the list goes on)?

Step 2: Gathering client information

Client information includes how the client will get its IP address and how a client will get other hosts' addresses, either from a private list of hosts or from a DNS server.

Step 3: Setting up your NIC (s)

This step should already be done for you. But just in case it's not, read on.

Your computer connects to a network through a NIC. (You already know this, right?) If you connect to more than one LAN, you need a NIC for each connection. In most cases, your computer recognizes your NIC when you install the operating system. If you add a NIC after installing the operating system, your computer (Windows, Mac, and most Linuxes and Unixes) recognizes the new NIC automatically.

"NIC" names

The figures in this book show Ethernet network adapters because all the NIC cards on our network, regardless of the operating system, are Ethernet adapters. While Ethernet is by far the most popular network architecture, don't be surprised if you run into others (such as FDDI and token-ring). The handy-dandy command — okay, two versions of a command — to use when you want to see your NIC (and find out whether it's Ethernet or another connection) is ipconfig or ifconfig. There are examples of the ifconfig and ipconfig commands in Chapter 4. The ifconfig or ipconfig output varies depending on your operating system:

✔ On **Microsoft Windows** operating systems, the ipconfig output shows your NIC as "Ethernet adapter Local Connection" for a wired network or "Ethernet adapter Wireless Network Connection".

✔ **Mac OS X** shows your Ethernet adapter(s) as "en0, en1" and so on for each NIC in your computer.

✔ **Linux and Unix** show your Ethernet adapter(s) as "eth0, eth1" continuing on for each NIC in your computer.

If you're on a large network that uses FDDI, look for "fddi0, fddi1", and so on.

If you're a token-ring user, some of the names you see in the ifconfig output are "tr0" for IBM AIX, "tra0" for other Unix distributions.

Each Linux and Unix distribution seems to work a little differently when you add a NIC. Red Hat Linux, for example, has a program called Kudzu, which detects NICs. Then you configure the network settings for that new NIC. The procedure is similar with Ubuntu Linux. Usually Ubuntu recognizes the NIC and you configure the NIC settings by running System➪Admin➪Networking. Our advice is RTFM (Read the Funky Manual) to see how to add a NIC to your specific Linux or Unix distribution.

If you use more than one NIC, you need to set up protocols, services, and applications for each LAN.

To avoid confusion, it's a good idea to rename each local area connection. Choosing descriptive names for each connection makes sense, such as ROOM1LAN and ROOM2LAN. Sometimes organizations have naming standards, and you *have* to name your local area connections something that is not meaningful like LAN0. Sorry.

Step 4: Deciding on a static IP address or a DHCP leased address

Usually small servers in small networks, such as a SOHO (small office home office), and all clients use DHCP addresses, which is the default in a TCP/IP setup. You don't have to do anything to assign the IP addresses. The whole process is automatic. Hooray! If you're configuring a larger server, of course, you have to fill in a static IP address for whatever interface you're using. Also, sometimes you might have a special reason to assign a static IP address manually for a client or small server.

You can get your official IP address from your ISP. If you're an ISP, you can get IP addresses from these Internet Registries:

- ✔ In America, from ARIN (American Registry for Internet Numbers) at `www.arin.net/registration/index.html`
- ✔ In Europe, from RIPE NCC (Réseaux IP Européen) at `www.ripe.net/rs/`
- ✔ In Asia and Australia, from APNIC (Asia Pacific Registry) at `www.apnic.net`

Step 5: Choosing how your host will translate names into IP addresses

If you're on a small private intranet, you might be fine with a simple hosts file (which you can read about in the section "The local hosts file," later in this chapter). If you're joining a large network, you need DNS to resolve names and addresses; without it, you'll be constantly busy updating your hosts file. Be sure to get the IP address of the DNS server from your network administrator. If you need a reminder about DNS, Chapter 4 introduces you to DNS. Chapter 10 contains technical details about DNS and how to set it up. If you decide to use DNS, you can still keep a local hosts file with name/address translations for the sites you visit most often.

Step 6: Gathering server information

Configure the server software (such as e-mail, DHCP, NAT, FTP, Web, or DNS) that you provide. Chapters 9 through 20 help you set up servers.

Setting TCP/IP Client Properties

The operating system may vary, but the client configuration process is pretty much the same. Remember, you may not need to do anything. The sections and examples that follow show a few of the different steps and looks that you might encounter when you configure your client system.

"There's more than one way to do it"— unknown Unix sage

There are as many ways to get to your Linux and Unix networking configuration windows as there are distributions of these operating systems. (Has anyone actually counted these?) Besides graphical interfaces, you can also use command-line interfaces to get started with your networking set up work. Here are just a few ways to get to a graphical Networks window:

✔ With Ubuntu Linux, the distribution we use for the Linux examples in this book, choose System⊳Administration⊳Networking.

✔ RedHat Linux comes with the redhat-config-network utility, which provides both a graphical and a command-line interface.

✔ On Suse Linux, you can use the YAST or YAST2 utilities configure network.

✔ The Gnome graphical interface runs on most Linux systems and uses gnome-network-preferences.

✔ The KDE graphical interface also runs on most Linux and Unix systems. Select the Network Settings option in the KDE Control Center. Select the Network Interfaces tab to manage TCP/IP configuration.

Whenever you configure TCP/IP settings, be sure to log in to an account with Administrator privileges.

Keep in mind that if you want to change client properties after you configure TCP/IP, you do so in the same window where you set them. For example, if you want to change a DHCP address to a static IP address, open the window where you originally accepted DHCP, uncheck the DHCP option, and fill in the IP address you want the client to use.

Configuring TCP/IP on a Mac OS X client

Follow these steps to set up and configure TCP/IP on your Mac OS X client:

1. **Choose System Preferences from the Apple Menu at the upper-left of the screen.**

2. **Click the Network icon⊳Location pop-up menu and choose Automatic.**

3. **Access the Configure pop-up menu and choose your connection media, such as Built-in Ethernet.**

4. **If the lock icon (bottom left) is locked, make sure that you click the icon and enter your password to unlock it.**

   This allows you to save the changes you make in the following steps.

5. **Click the TCP/IP tab, and from the Configure pop-up menu, choose Manually or Using DHCP, depending on how you plan to get the IP address.**

   Figure 6-3 shows the configuration window.

6. **If you're adding the address manually, type the subnet mask (if your network uses one).**

7. **If you're not using DHCP to get an address, type your IP address in the IP Address box.**

8. **Click the Apply Now button.**

To test your configuration, try using a beloved command of network administrators: the ping command. Ping checks for a host's availability on the network. To test your own connection, use the command

```
ping localhost
```

Figure 6-4 shows that localhost (Woodstock) is alive and well on the network. If the ping command doesn't give you a reply, your network configuration has a problem. Check out the troubleshooting tips in Chapter 22.

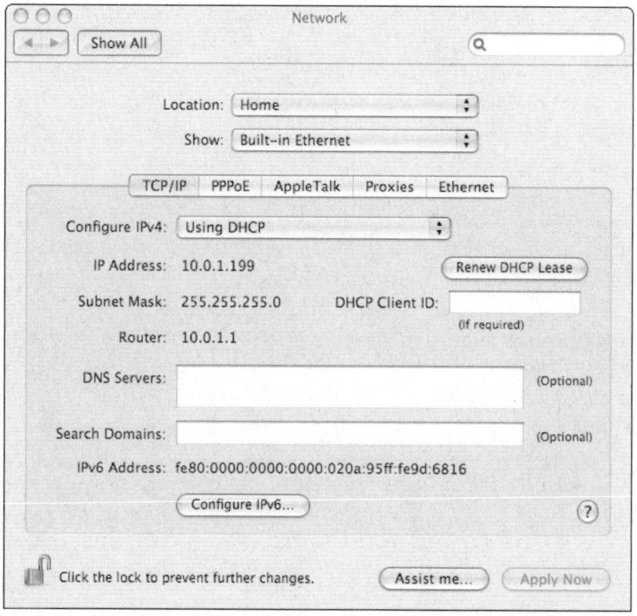

Figure 6-3:
Set your IP address for Mac OS X.

Figure 6-4:
The ping
command
tests your
network
configura-
tion.

The ping command is available on all the operating systems used in this book.
It runs from a terminal or command window.

Configuring TCP/IP on a Linux or Unix client

When you install Linux or Unix, the operating system installation procedure
assumes that you're also setting up networking — and asks you to provide
the following information:

- ✔ The network interface that you want to use
- ✔ Whether you want a DHCP server to assign your IP address
- ✔ Your IP address and subnet mask (if you didn't choose DHCP in the preceding step above)
- ✔ The host name
- ✔ Whether you want to use DNS to translate names into IP addresses: If you don't choose DNS, you have to put entries in the hosts file (which is coming up later in this chapter).

The operating-system installation procedure also sets up networking files. If
you choose not to set up networking during the installation procedure, you
can use the upcoming steps to set up and configure TCP/IP at any time on
your Linux client.

Don't panic if your installation screens look different from ours. Our computer
is running Ubuntu Linux software with the popular Gnome interface. Although
every Linux vendor designs its screens differently, the steps to follow for
setting up TCP/IP and your network are essentially the same.

Follow these steps to configure TCP/IP on a Linux or Unix client:

1. **Log on with the root password and select System from the main menu.**

2. **Choosing Administration then Networking opens the Networking Settings Window.**

3. **Choose either Wireless or Wired Network Connection and select the Properties tab to see the settings for your Ethernet connection.**

   The NIC information shows the DHCP client.

   Figure 6-5 shows the automatic DHCP setting. If you want to set a static IP address, click on the drop-down Automatic Configuration box to input your IP address.

4. **If you want to set a static IP address, fill in the IP address, subnet mask, and gateway address (if you have one) in the Settings for Interface window.**

   Figure 6-6 shows you how manual IP settings look.

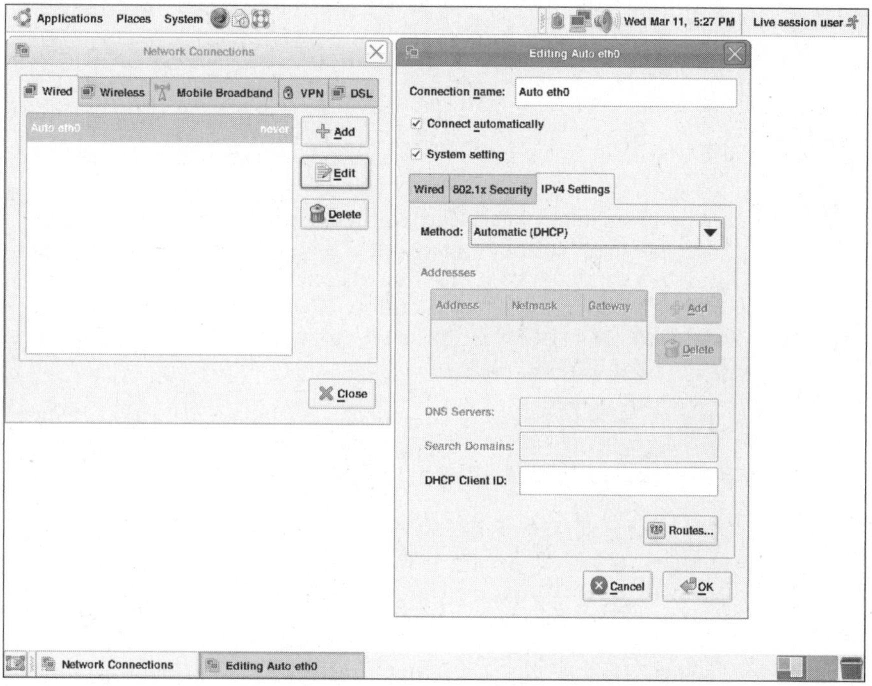

Figure 6-5:
A TCP/IP client automatically receives an IP address from a DHCP server.

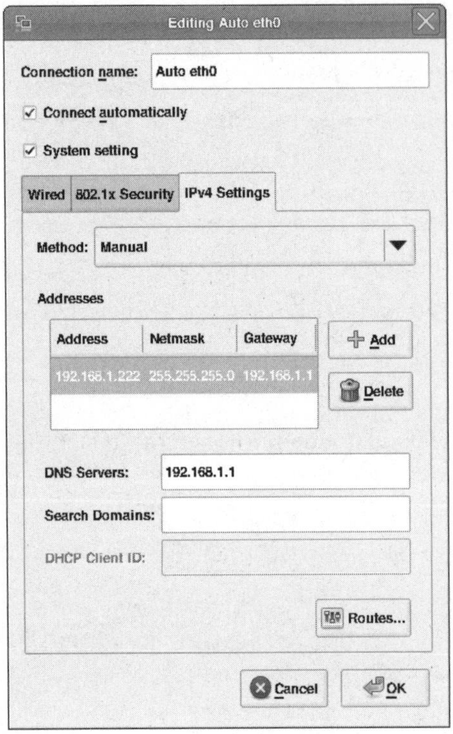

Figure 6-6:
If you want
to assign
a static IP
address to
your client,
you have
more work
to do.

As you can see from the Mac example (from the previous section) and this Linux example, setting up a client is a simple procedure — even though the setup windows look different. Client setup works the same way in Microsoft Windows XP and Windows Vista, although getting to the actual setup window is different for each variation of Windows; see the next two sections for details.

Configuring a TCP/IP client on Windows Vista

Follow these steps to get started setting up your network client on Microsoft Windows Vista (see Figure 6-7):

1. **Click Start⇨Control Panel.**

2. **Choose Network and Internet⇨Network and Sharing Center.**

3. **Click Manage Network Connections.**

4. **You probably want to add a DHCP address, which is already there. If not, enter your IP address.**

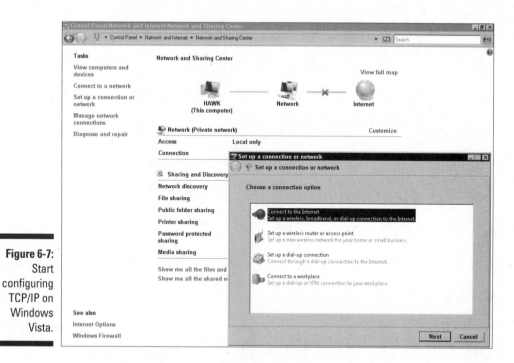

Figure 6-7:
Start
configuring
TCP/IP on
Windows
Vista.

Configuring a TCP/IP client on Windows XP

1. **Click My Network Places from the Start Menu.**

   The My Network Places window opens, as shown at the top of Figure 6-8.

2. **Click on the Network Setup Wizard.**

   The Wizard searches for network hardware, and then opens the dialog box shown at the bottom of Figure 6-8.

3. **Choose the network connection you want to set up (or change).**

4. **Follow the Network Setup Wizard's directions.**

   Fill in the computer's name and description. The Network Setup Wizard continues to guide you through various screens until your network's set up. Mostly you just have to click "Next" until you're done with the Wizard.

It's always a good idea to answer "Yes" to any query that asks whether you want to create a backup disc.

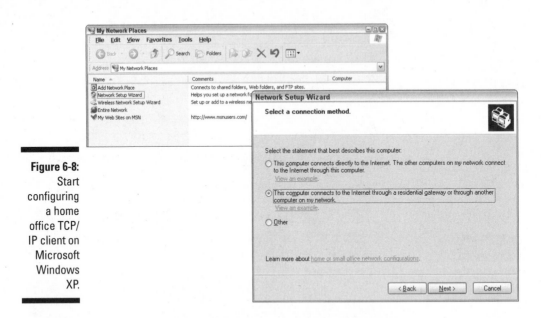

Figure 6-8:
Start
configuring
a home
office TCP/
IP client on
Microsoft
Windows
XP.

Setting TCP/IP Server Properties

Setting up a server starts out with the same steps as setting up a client, but you'll need to go beyond the default client setup steps described in the preceding section. Server software has lots more work to do than client software. A server reacts to requests from multiple clients. For example, a Web server receives requests from Web browsers and sends the requested information back to the browser. The Web server provides services to browser clients using the HyperText Transport Protocol (HTTP) or the Secure HyperText Transport Protocol (S-HTTP).

The most popular Web-server software is *Apache* (Chapter 11 has details). After you set up the basics, such as IP address, your next steps depend on what kind of server you're configuring. Figure 6-9 demonstrates how to get started on Windows Server 2008.

The simplest way to get started setting up TCP/IP on Windows Server 2008 is to follow these steps:

1. **Click the Network icon at the far right of the taskbar. This takes you to the Network and Sharing Center.**

   The Network and Sharing Center shows a map of your network and lists various server setup tasks (refer to Figure 6-9).

Another way to start working with TCP/IP on Windows Server 2008, is to click Start⇨Control Panel. What you do next depends on which view you're using:

- If you're in the Control Panel Home view, click Network and Sharing Center⇨View Network Status and Tasks.

- If you're in the Classic View, click Network and Sharing Center.

2. Choose Set Up a Connection or Network from the Task Center.

The Set Up a Connection or Network Wizard appears (refer to Figure 6-9).

Now you're ready to get down to business and configure the specific services you want to offer. Chapters 10, 11, 13, 15, 18, 19, and 20 describe different kinds of servers, how those servers work behind the scenes, and how to set them up.

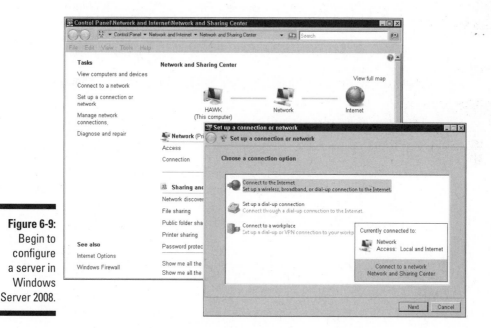

Figure 6-9: Begin to configure a server in Windows Server 2008.

Installing TCP/IP from Scratch

Installing TCP/IP software separately from your operating system is a rare task. In fact, some operating systems try to protect you from having to reinstall them. Microsoft Windows XP, for example, considers TCP/IP a core component of the operating system and won't let you *un*install it. When you're looking at the NIC properties, look carefully at the Uninstall button next to TCP/IP. The button is not enabled.

Before you have a big layer cake to celebrate the fact that you will never have to install TCP/IP from scratch on Microsoft Windows (yeah, right), think again: It's always possible that some software component may become corrupted and impossible to repair. If the corrupted software is TCP/IP, then yes, in unusual cases, you *do* have to install TCP/IP from the beginning.

If you run the netsh utility in a command window, you can delete and reinstall TCP/IP on Microsoft Windows XP and Vista. The only reason to do this is if your TCP/IP stack is corrupted and you have to reinstall the protocols.

```
netsh interface ip reset [log]
```

The [log] option is not required. This option is a file specification that tells netsh where to create a log file of the command's activities. If you don't fill in this option, netsh doesn't log its activities.

Don't omit the log file. It might come in handy later for debugging.

Behind the scenes, the netsh utility is changing the following Windows Registry keys:

```
HKEY_LOCAL_MACHINE\SYSTEM\CurrentControlSet\Services\Tcpip\Parameters
HKEY_LOCAL_MACHINE\SYSTEM\CurrentControlSet\Services\DHCP\Parameters
```

On Windows Server 2008, you can use netsh for these ticklish procedures:

- ✔ Uninstall IPv4:

```
netsh interface ipv4 uninstall
```

- ✔ Install IPv4:

```
netsh interface ipv4 install
```

- ✔ Reset your IPv6 configuration:

```
netsh interface ipv6 reset
```

If you decide to disable IPv6 in Windows Server 2008 and/or Vista, you do that by opening a command prompt and using the reg add (add to Registry) command to set IPv6 to disabled:

```
reg add hklm\system\currentcontrolset\services\tcpip6\parameters/v
            DisabledComponents /t REG_DWORD /d 255
```

If you are running any applications that depend on IPv6, those applications will break if you disable IPv6, even though you still have IPv4 running.

Feasting on Network Files

Your operating system automatically creates most of the network files that TCP/IP needs. Nevertheless, you may need to edit these files based on your network setup. For example, you might want to make your account available to someone who's working on another computer.

Linux, Unix, and Mac OS X usually store these files in a directory called /etc or sometimes in a subdirectory of /etc. Microsoft Windows operating systems store some of the files as files and others as Registry entries. Regardless of where and how the information is stored, the purpose of these files is the same — to tell TCP/IP to function the way you want it to.

The local hosts file

We start with the most fundamental file that you need for communicating with other computers on your network — the local hosts file. (In Chapter 4, we added the word *host* to your networking vocabulary — the host computer on the network.) If you think it's host as in "Be our guest," take a look at the security chapters: Chapters 12, 20, and 21.

A hosts file can improve network performance because you don't have to go out to the network, ask for a translation, and have the translation sent back to you. You know the address of where you're going lickety-split, in a trice, *tout de suite*.

When you access another host by name on the Internet or any intranet/internet, your computer needs to know the remote host's IP address. You can get remote host addresses from DNS (see Chapters 4 and 10) or from your computer's local hosts file. This file is extremely convenient. It lists the names and addresses of other hosts known by your computer. If you list your frequently accessed computers in the hosts file, your own host won't have to access a host on the network to ask for a name/address translation.

On the other hand, when you need to know about thousands of hosts on the Internet, maintaining the local file is really too cumbersome a mechanism. Imagine having to spend all that time updating it as computers come and go — or relocate — on the Internet! In that case, you need DNS to locate remote hosts. (See the handy sidebar for more about that.)

Let DNS share the job with a hosts file

TCP/IP allows you to use a combination of DNS and a hosts file to find remote hosts by putting the most frequently accessed hosts into your hosts file. That way, you won't have the performance overhead of accessing a DNS name server on the network to get an address for the hosts that you connect to on a regular basis. Let DNS help you find addresses for hosts that you access only occasionally. This is really the best of both worlds: performance and reliability. When a host name needs to be translated to an IP address, the application looks first at the local hosts file. If the application can't find the translation it needs, it then goes across the network to a DNS server for the translation.

The location and name of the hosts file depend on the operating system and version of TCP/IP you use. Table 6-1 lists the hosts file locations for a few implementations of TCP/IP.

Table 6-1	Popular Locations for Hosts Files	
Location	*Operating Systems*	*Vendor*
`/etc/hosts`	Linux, UNIX	Various
`c:\windows\system32\drivers\etc\hosts`	Windows XP, Vista, Server 2008	Microsoft
`/etc/hosts`	Mac OS X	Apple

Discovering another appetizing use for your local hosts file

Your hosts file lets you redirect IP addresses to another location. Looking at Candace's local hosts file in Figure 6-10, you see that the file is full of redirections to the IP address, 127.0.0.1. This address is the localhost — your own computer. It functions like a trash can. You throw out any messages from annoying sites if you redirect them to yourself (localhost). Candace's hosts file has loads of redirections created by a wonderful, free program, *Spybot – Search & Destroy* (`www.safer-networking.org`). Spybot finds and destroys spyware. (Spyware is one of the malware threats we describe in Chapter 12.)

Any line in the local hosts file that starts with # is a comment.

Figure 6-10:
Candace
lists her
e-mail
program in
her local
hosts file.
Spybot has
made lots of
redirections
too.

Improving the digestion of your local hosts file

Listing the computers in most frequently used order is a good idea. TCP/IP searches the hosts file sequentially from top to bottom until it finds the computer it's looking for, so if you have a large hosts file, ordering the computers appropriately gives you a performance advantage. That's why Candace lists google and her e-mail provider at the top.

The trusted hosts file, hosts.equiv

On Mac OS X, Linux, and Unix operating systems, the file /etc/hosts.equiv lists the other hosts on the network that your computer trusts; this is your *trusted hosts file.* This file is easy to create with any text editor. It has only one column — the host name of each computer you trust.

Be very careful with the hosts.equiv file. *Any* remote computer listed in this file is a trusted host — and all of its users can log on to your computer without having to know a password.

Don't look for hosts.equiv on a Microsoft Windows operating system. Instead of using a trusted hosts file, you set up trust relationships when you set up security policies for your computer or Active Directory for your domain. Trust relationships are between domains as opposed to individual hosts.

Freddie's nightmare: Your personal trust file

You should be aware of a special (and dangerous) file that exists on a per user basis on Mac OS X, Linux, and Unix. You and all the other users on a computer can create a personal trust file in your home directories. This file is named .rhosts, pronounced "dot are hosts." And yes, the dot is part of the filename.

The .rhosts file holds two pieces of information: the host name and the account name. Here are the contents of our niece Sarah's .rhosts file in her home directory on computer elmst:

```
#  host   user    comment
mainst    emily  # Let in Emily from mainst
```

The file allows her sister, Emily (from computer mainst), to have the run of computer elmst without a password. If you live on Elm Street or elsewhere in cyberspace, don't let personal trust become a nightmare. Please be careful about letting evil players into your computer.

 Most network administrators, like Freddie, consider .rhosts files to be potential security problems. These files list *trusted remote users* — those who are permitted to log on to your account without entering a password. Logging on without a password allows users to copy any files from your directories and to remotely execute any command on your computer.

This is scary. Why would I ever want .rhosts?

If you do a lot of work on various hosts, it's quite convenient to rlogin as yourself on all the computers on which you have accounts. Your account may be Marshall on one computer, Wilensky on another, and Mwil on a third — with three different passwords. If all of these computers have a .rhosts file that lets you in from anywhere, you can skip remembering all those passwords.

Surprise! The curse of the network administrator lives

If Emily has been wandering all over computer elmst because Sarah lets her, Emily may get a big surprise one day when she tries to log on remotely and permission is denied. Network administrators frequently hunt down and kill these .rhosts files. After Sarah's .rhosts file is gone, Emily needs to know a valid password in order to log on, unless she gets Sarah to re-create the file.

The services file

The services file lists the network services being used on your computer. TCP/IP automatically maintains this file as you enable or disable new services. Most of these services are daemons (described in the next section) — although, in a Microsoft file, daemon names don't end in "d". Each line in the file has the following columns:

- ✔ Service name
- ✔ Port number
- ✔ Protocol (separated from the port number by a /)
- ✔ Aliases (other, optional names for the service)

The following example shows an excerpt from a Windows Server 2008 services file. If the Status column is blank, the service is not started. The entire services file lists about 300 services. An enterprise-class server must do a lot of work because a Windows XP Pro system has only about 115 services.

```
# Copyright (c) 1993-2004 Microsoft Corp.
#
# This file contains port numbers for well-known services defined by IANA
#
# Format:
#
# <service name>  <port number>/<protocol>  [aliases...]   [#<comment>]
#

echo            7/tcp
echo            7/udp
discard         9/tcp     sink null
discard         9/udp     sink null
systat          11/tcp    users               #Active users
systat          11/udp    users               #Active users
daytime         13/tcp
daytime         13/udp
qotd            17/tcp    quote               #Quote of the day
qotd            17/udp    quote               #Quote of the day
chargen         19/tcp    ttytst source       #Character generator
chargen         19/udp    ttytst source       #Character generator
ftp-data        20/tcp                        #FTP, data
ftp             21/tcp                        #FTP. control
ssh             22/tcp                        #SSH Remote Login Protocol
telnet          23/tcp
smtp            25/tcp    mail                #Simple Mail
ldap            389/tcp                       #Lightweight Directory Access
                                               Protocol
https           443/tcp   MCom                #HTTP over TLS/SSL
https           443/udp   MCom                #HTTP over TLS/SSL
```

People like names, and computers like numbers

You've heard it before, and you'll hear it again. Many applications, services, and protocols are named the same. Take FTP, for example, which is the name of an application, a service, *and* a protocol.

Applications communicate with services via a *port id number.* ID numbers 1 through 255 are reserved for the most commonly used services, such as telnet and FTP. You can create port numbers as needed. If you write your own TCP/

IP application and service, you simply use a port number greater than 255.

When an application, such as FTP, says to TCP/IP, "Here I am, ready to work," TCP/IP doesn't really care about the application's name. Instead, TCP/IP sees only these numbers:

✔ The IP address of the host that provides the service

✔ The port number through which the application intends to communicate

You can find the services file in /etc/services in Mac OS X, Linux, and Unix. The file location for Microsoft Windows operating systems is C:\WINDOWS\system32\drivers\etc\services.

It's a little more work to see the services on Microsoft Vista. Choose Start⇨Control Panel⇨System and Maintenance⇨Administrative Tools⇨ Services.

With so many services, how does an application know which one it should use? See the nearby sidebar for details.

Daemons Aren't Devils

There's nothing devilish about daemons. A *daemon* is a program that automatically runs in the background, where users can't get their hands on it. Daemons manage most of the services shown in the services file (described previously).

Relishing your daemons

The inetd program (pronounced "eye net dee") is the father of all daemons. It manages the other daemons (and there are lots). Many programs spawn other programs called *children.* The inetd program works so hard managing its children that it's often called the "superserver." The following list describes a few other TCP/IP daemons that you should know about:

✔ **routed:** The routed daemon manages routing tables (which we explain in Chapter 8). No, don't say "row-ted" or even "roo-ted." It's either "rowt dee" or "root dee." The routed daemon uses RIP, the Routing Information Protocol (which we also explain in Chapter 8).

✔ **named:** The named daemon is pronounced "name dee." (Are you getting the hang of it yet?) This handy daemon runs on your name server to manage DNS and to do the host name/IP address resolution that we cover in Chapters 4 and 10.

✔ **Other handy-dandy daemons:** All other daemons have names that end with *d* and are pronounced by saying the name of the service followed by "dee." We list some of the more famous daemons in Table 6-2, along with the services they provide.

Finding the daemons on your computer

In Figure 6-11, the ps command (process status) shows some popular daemons running on a UNIX system. You can also use the ps command on Mac OS X and Linux. Look for the daemons in the last column of each line. The rest of the information for each daemon is performance information.

If you have a problem using one of the services in Table 6-2, a quick trouble-shooting technique is to check and see whether the daemon is started. On Windows NT and 2000, use the Services applet to see whether it's running. On Linux and Unix, you can do this with the ps command, one of the tools that we cover in Chapter 20. Look for the name of the daemon in the ps output (refer to Figure 6-11). If you don't see the daemon required for the service, that's the problem. To use the service, you need to get the daemon started in whatever way your operating system allows.

Figure 6-11: This computer is running some of our favorite daemons.

```
$ ps auwx
USER        PID %CPU %MEM   VSZ  RSS TT  STAT STARTED  TIME COMMAND

root         65  0.0  0.0  1160  992 ??  Ss   Thu12PM  1:31.58 named
root         68  0.0  0.0    52  108 ??  Ss   Thu12PM  0:08.83 rwhod
root         70  0.0  0.0    60  108 ??  Is   Thu12PM  5:13.29 nfsiod 4
root         77  0.0  0.0    56   16 ??  I    Thu12PM  1:47.96 nfsiod 4
root         78  0.0  0.0    56   16 ??  I    Thu12PM  0:48.53 nfsiod 4
root         79  0.0  0.0    56   16 ??  I    Thu12PM  0:20.84 nfsiod 4
root         80  0.0  0.0   444  132 ??  Ss   Thu12PM  0:17.39 inetd
root      22947  0.0  0.0    96   72 ??  I    10:28PM  0:00.48 rlogind
root      15491  0.0  0.0   120  172 ??  I    1:00PM   0:00.35 telnetd
root      20008  0.0  0.0   224  556 ??  S    3:03PM   0:00.40 ftpd
root      20033  0.0  0.0    28  232 ??  S    3:03PM   0:00.07 ntalkd
```

Table 6-2	Popular Services and Their Daemons
Service	*Daemon*
chat (internet relay chat)	`ircd`
ftp	`ftpd`
telnet	`telnetd`
rlogin	`rlogind`
rsh	`rshd`
rexec	`rexecd`
talk	`talkd`
NFS client	`nfsiod`
NFS server	`nfsd`

Chapter 7

Networking SOHO with Wireless

- -

In This Chapter

▶ Protocols in this chapter: IP, DHCP, IEEE security protocols (WEP, TKIP, WPA, WPA2)

▶ Plunging into the joys of Wi-Fi

▶ Setting up SOHO (Small Office/Home Office) hardware

▶ Chewing up wireless security tips

▶ Spreading broadband out with WiMAX (Worldwide Interoperability for Microwave Access)

- -

*W*ireless networking is networking without using wires, satellite, regular cable, or fiber optic cable. Okay. Of course you know that, but we felt we had to say it so everyone who's reading this chapter uses the same definition as a starting point. So, the transmission medium is air in this chapter. According to our definition, wireless networking could be semaphore signals or carrier pigeons, but let's not get too silly.

Aside from computer networking, wireless applications include cell phones, satellite phones, wireless radio, remote controls for TV and other appliances, pagers, point of sale devices, and more. Even if you've never knowingly used a computer in your life, you've probably got some wireless applications in your house: a baby monitor, security camera, remote controls for TV, video games, cordless phones, printers, and toasters, just to name a few. One of our favorites is the remote control for our ceiling fans.

You've probably noticed that we often say "cables or air" when we refer to transmission media. In earlier editions, we simply said "cables" because Wi-Fi (pronounced "why-fye" — the "-" is silent) was not widespread. Wi-Fi is a networking technology that provides high-speed network connections without the use of physical cables.

In this chapter, we discuss how to set up the hardware and software components of a small office/home office (SOHO) and how to keep your wireless connections secure.

The Wi-Fi Alliance owns the Wi-Fi registered trademark. The Wi-Fi Alliance specifies that the IEEE's 802.11 standard should be the basis of any Wi-Fi technology that uses the registered trademarked name.

Gulping the Minimum Hardware Details

The bare minimum wireless networking hardware includes computers with NICs, a broadband connection, cables and air (for wireless connections), and a wireless router with NICs.

Believe it or not, you need a wired component to set up your wireless network. We know, it's weird. Stay tuned till later in this chapter.

It's possible for SOHO networks to have more hardware components, but let's keep it simple. In the following sections, we describe NICs and routers in more detail.

NICs

You've read about computers with NICs in Chapters 4 and 6. You can't do a lot to set up a NIC. Remember that a NIC comes from the factory with a MAC address already hard-coded.

Most computers have the NIC built in. If you have an older computer, you may need to purchase a NIC for it. In Figure 7-1, you can't see the NICs. Trust us — they're inside the computers. Figure 7-1 shows a wireless NIC in a laptop communicating with a router and a wired NIC communicating with a router.

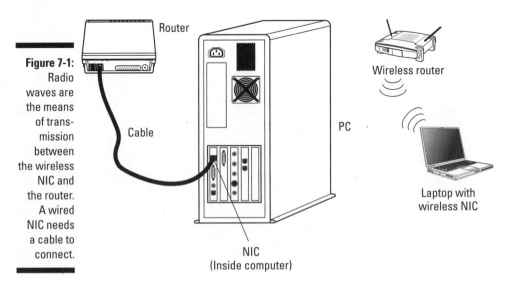

Figure 7-1: Radio waves are the means of transmission between the wireless NIC and the router. A wired NIC needs a cable to connect.

Rowter or rooter? Doesn't matter

According to *Webster's*, a *router* (pronounced "rowter") is a woodworking tool. A *router* (pronounced "rooter") is a sports fan with a bet on the big game; it's also a horse that's trained for distance races. In networking, however, you can pronounce it any way you want, so pick a side and join the battle. People pronounce it both ways, and some are willing to fight for their choice. We prefer to remain nootral.

Routers

Routers connect networks. If you want your SOHO network to connect to the Internet, you need inside routers that connect your intranets, and at least one router that faces the outside world. Your outside router gets all network messages from your inside routers and forwards those messages out to the Internet. Your outside router also receives all network messages for your intranets and sends them to your inside routers for delivery.

Your inside and outside router can be one and the same router in a small network like the one shown in Figure 7-2. Three NICs are inside the little router, one to face the outside world (the Internet) and two more for each of the inside intranets (subnets).

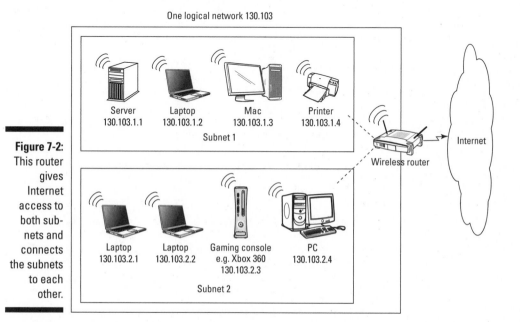

One logical network 130.103

Server 130.103.1.1 Laptop 130.103.1.2 Mac 130.103.1.3 Printer 130.103.1.4

Subnet 1

Wireless router

Internet

Laptop 130.103.2.1 Laptop 130.103.2.2 Gaming console e.g. Xbox 360 130.103.2.3 PC 130.103.2.4

Subnet 2

Figure 7-2: This router gives Internet access to both subnets and connects the subnets to each other.

Software routers

While most routers are dedicated hardware devices (also known as specialized computers) running specialized software, you can use a general-purpose computer to perform like a router. Using a regular computer as a router works best if only a few networked computers share a connection to the Internet via cable modem or DSL. You can use the one computer attached to the network device as your router. You need to add some kind of Internet sharing software to this computer. Microsoft's ICS (Internet Connection Sharing) is one example of Internet sharing software. Software packages are available for other operating systems as well. The routing software checks to see whether packets should stay on the local net or go out to the Internet.

Remember: The routing computer must have two or more NICs and must be connected to two or more network segments.

Each router has two or more NICs, one for each network it's connecting. The router also has two or more IP addresses for the same reason.

Setting Up a Home Wireless Network in Four Steps

Setting up a SOHO network is as easy as 1, 2, 3, oh yes, and 4. Or, if you want to do nothing, your ISP is more than willing to do all the work for you. For you do-it-yourselfers, we show you the four steps:

1. **Choose your wireless hardware.**

2. **Connect your wireless router.**

3. **Set up your wireless router for your network.**

4. **Connect your computers to your router.**

We describe each of these steps in detail in the following sections.

Step 1: Choose your wireless hardware

First, you need a broadband network connection, such as cable modem or DSL (Digital Subscriber Line). If you don't already have a broadband connection, contact your ISP. After you have your broadband connection, you only need two (plus) pieces of hardware to get started with a wireless network:

✔ The wireless NIC inside your computer

✔ The wireless router

✔ Believe it or not, a wired connection between your wireless router and one computer (just to get started, you don't need to maintain the wired connection after you're set up).

If you want wired Internet connections as well as wireless, most desktop computers come with a wired NIC. You might have to buy a wireless NIC to put inside as well. Most laptops come with two NICs — one for wireless and one for wired connections.

When you subscribe to an ISP, they usually provide all the wireless gear you need. Of course, you usually have to pay, but when our ISP was running a special deal, they gave us the router for free. We already had the NICs we needed inside the computers.

The IEEE (see Chapter 1) defines four wireless networking technologies. Whatever gear you buy, NICs and routers should conform to the same standard:

✔ **802.11b:** The original Wi-Fi runs at 11 megabits (millions of bits) per second, just about the same as the original Ethernet.

✔ **802.11a:** Created along with 802.11b, but finished after .11b. The 802.11a standard is incompatible with both .11b and .11g. You don't want this in a SOHO network.

✔ **802.11g:** A 54 megabit version. 802.11g offers the fastest performance for SOHO and is compatible with 802.11b.

✔ **802.11n:** As of this writing, .11n is the newest standard for Wi-Fi gear. It's fast — over 100 megabits (1 gigabit) per second and has a longer-distance range than 11.g. Because 802.11n is new, products that comply with it are still expensive.

Most routers implement all the preceding IEEE standards.

A wireless router can do more than just hang around being a router. For example, our home wireless router is also a base station (a wireless access point), a cable modem, a DHCP server, and a firewall. That's a lot for a device no bigger than a hard-cover novel. (The router shown in Figure 7-3 looks much like the router we use for our home office connection.) A wireless router works by converting the signals from your Internet connection into radio waves.

Wireless broadband router

Step 2: Connect your wireless router

Step 2 is really several baby steps. Here's what you need to do to connect your wireless router:

1. **Plug the router's power cable into an electrical outlet.**

   Isn't it odd that we call them wireless, but still need cables? If the router has a separate power switch, use it to turn the router on.

   Your ISP will be happy to connect and set up your wireless router and connect your computers (as described in this and the following two sections), usually for free, when you subscribe.

2. **Plug one end of an RJ-45 Ethernet cable into one of the router's LAN ports. Plug the other end of the cable into a nearby computer's Ethernet NIC.**

   RJ-45 cable is the most common form of Ethernet cable. Figure 7-4 shows you what an RJ-45 cable looks like.

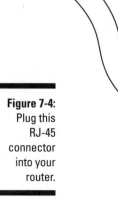

Figure 7-4:
Plug this
RJ-45
connector
into your
router.

3. **Connect the appropriate cable to the router's WAN port and the wall jack that connects to your ISP.**

   Here's how to decide what cable you need:

   - If you have DSL service and your router has a built-in DSL modem, you use a telephone cable to connect the router to the wall jack.

   - If you have cable Internet service and your router has a built-in cable modem, you use a coaxial ("co-ax") cable to connect the router to the wall jack.

   - If your router does not have a built-in modem, you use an RJ-45 Ethernet cable to connect the router to the modem. Some other kind of cable connects the modem to the wall jack.

   - You also use an RJ-45 Ethernet cable to connect your router to another router. (One router's WAN port connects to a LAN port on the other router.)

   - In some cases, you use a USB cable.

Step 3: Set up your wireless router

This step may seem complicated. That's because it is. It's also required. The good news is that you should only have to do it once, or (at most) once in a blue moon.

Start with the wired side

Gather this information from the router's documentation and your ISP:

- ✔ The router's default intranet IP address. In many cases, it is 192.168.0.1 or 192.168.1.1.

- ✔ The router's default administration username and password. In many cases, the username is admin or nothing. The password might be password.

- ✔ The username, password, and connection method that your router must use to authenticate with your ISP. It might be something like PPPoE (Point-to-Point Protocol over Ethernet).

Don't try to guess these answers. You'd just waste a lot of time and maybe get needlessly annoyed before gathering the right information anyway.

Now you're ready to configure the router's connection to your ISP and the Internet. Here goes:

1. **Open a Web browser on the computer and surf to the router's intranet IP address.**

   The router's built-in Web server gives you a login page.

2. **Enter the default administration name and password to log in to the router's administration interface.**

   After you've surfed to your router, you can check the status. Figure 7-5 shows the status display of an ActionTec router in our *For Dummies* test network. Depending on your router's supplier, your display will differ slightly. However, the basic information remains the same.

3. **Set the date, time, and time zone if your router gives you the option.**

   Don't worry if your router doesn't let you control these settings. They may come automatically from your ISP after the router is connected to the Internet.

4. **Enter the username, password, and the connection method that your router needs to authenticate itself with your ISP.**

   Without these, the router cannot obtain an IP address and connect to the Internet.

Typically, your router gets an IP address from your ISP via DHCP. That's right; your router is a DHCP client. Figure 7-5 shows that this router gets its IP address from DHCP. Later on we show you that it's also a DHCP server. Many ISPs use a basic security control. Their DHCP server only responds to requests from registered MAC addresses, so they have to know your router's MAC address.

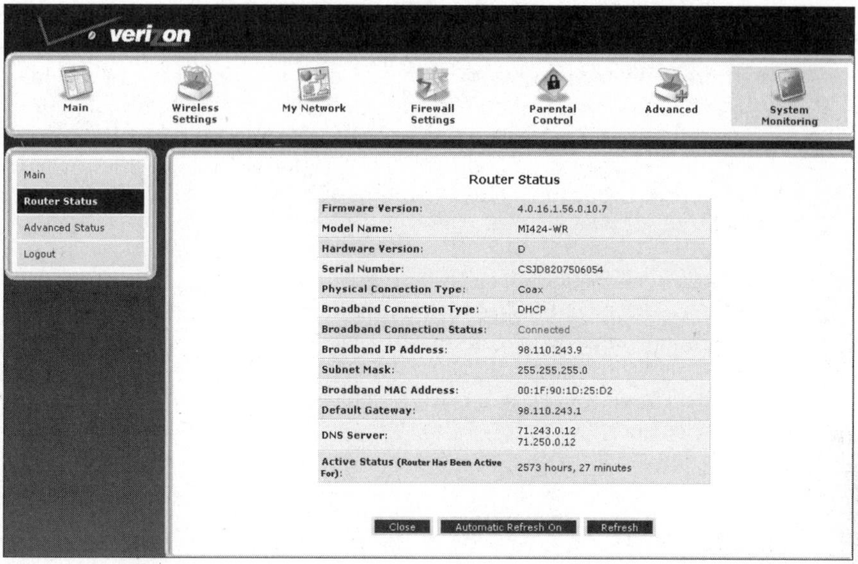
verizon
Main
Wireless Settings
My Network
Firewall Settings
Parental Control
Advanced
System Monitoring
Main
Router Status
Advanced Status
Logout
Router Status
Firmware Version: 4.0.16.1.56.0.10.7
Model Name: MI424-WR
Hardware Version: D
Serial Number: CSJD8207506054
Physical Connection Type: Coax
Broadband Connection Type: DHCP
Broadband Connection Status: Connected
Broadband IP Address: 98.110.243.9
Subnet Mask: 255.255.255.0
Broadband MAC Address: 00:1F:90:1D:25:D2
Default Gateway: 98.110.243.1
DNS Server: 71.243.0.12 71.250.0.12
Active Status (Router Has Been Active For): 2573 hours, 27 minutes
Close
Automatic Refresh On
Refresh

Figure 7-5: The router's broadband connection status is connected.

If you have arranged with your ISP for a static IP address, enter the information they gave you:

- The IP address itself
- The routing prefix (also known as a subnet mask)
- The default gateway
- The addresses of DNS servers

As soon as you have this information in place correctly, your computer — the one wired directly to the router — can access the Internet! If it can't, then either your settings are wrong for username, password, and connection method or your ISP may be experiencing trouble.

Now for the wireless side

Gather these default values from the router's documentation, or if you use an ISP to install your router, get these values from the ISP:

- The SSID (*service set identifier*), also called the *wireless network name*. It's usually the manufacturer's name.
- Is the SSID being broadcast or not? It often is.
- Is the wireless network enabled or disabled? Most of the time, it's enabled.

These days, most wireless routers come pre-configured to provide an open, public wireless network. That helps you get up and running quickly, but there is no security. Anyone can get on your wireless network! People called *wardrivers* drive around with their laptops booted up looking for available networks. If you broadcast your SSID and have no security on your network, these wardrivers park and connect to your network. Often these people are harmless. They just want to borrow a little of your bandwidth to access the Internet. However . . .

Beware the malicious wardriver! If one of these troublemakers uses your network to hack into a site and do damage, the origin of the hacking will trace back to *your* network. Uh-oh.

A little later, we tell you how to tighten security and limit who can use your wireless network.

Step 4: Connect your computers

Here's how to connect your computers, based on whether their NICs are wired or wireless:

- ✔ **If a computer has a wired NIC,** plug one end of an RJ-45 Ethernet cable into one of the router's LAN ports and the other end into the computer's Ethernet NIC. Make sure the computer is set to be a DHCP client.

- ✔ **If a computer has a wireless NIC,** whether inside or attached to the computer, there is no cable to connect. Use the software that's built into the operating system (or that came with the NIC) to specify the SSID you want to connect to; then set the computer as a DHCP client.

In either case, the computer is ready to go as soon as it gets an IP address from the DHCP server inside the router.

The wired side of your network provides a little security because strangers can't easily plug network cables into your router without your knowledge. The wireless side, however, is a totally different story — Insecure City. So, in the following section, we look at how you can tighten things down.

Securing Your Network

After you've set up your wireless network, it's time to enable security. You need to protect both the wired side and the wireless side.

Securing the wired side

From a computer with a wired connection to the router, open a Web browser and return to the router's administration interface. (Use the router's default intranet IP address, and then enter the default username and password.) Consult the router's documentation to find the specific ways to accomplish these tasks.

Change the administrator's name (if possible) and the password. Don't forget either of those!

By default, you can only access the router's administration interface from a wired connection. However, you may find it more convenient to use a wireless connection. If you choose to lift the restriction, however, remember: Doing so means that anyone on the Internet can manage your router if they know — or guess — the password!

Securing the wireless side

Always remember that if you change the router's wireless settings, you must make matching changes on the computers! If you don't, they can't reconnect to the network.

Your router's documentation will help you find the specific ways for your hardware to accomplish the following tasks:

- ✔ **Change the SSID from the default value.** Pick something that doesn't identify you or your location.

- ✔ **Disable broadcasting the SSID.** This is not a real security protection — it's "security by obscurity" — but it does make it a bit harder for people to connect to your wireless network.

- ✔ **Restrict use of the wireless network to those NICs whose MAC addresses are recorded on the router.** This technique is called *MAC filtering*.

- ✔ **Enable wireless security.** You have several 802.11i security protocols to choose from. Use the strongest combination possible, keeping in mind the phrase "lowest common denominator." That is, use the strongest combination that *all* the computers and wireless devices have in common. These protocols depend on some form of encryption. (You can read about encryption in Chapters 12 and 21.) Basically, encryption translates your data into a secret code so snoopers can't read it. On the receiving end, the secret code is decrypted back into readable form. So here's the list of protocols, from strongest to weakest:

- WPA2: *Wi-Fi Protected Access version 2*. The latest and strongest wireless security protocol. You may need to buy the newest hardware to enable this WPA2.

- WPA: *Wi-Fi Protected Access* is much more intelligent than previous wireless security protocols.

- TKIP (pronounced "tee-kip") *Temporal Key Integrity Protocol* was a solution to replace WEP. TKIP eventually became the first version of WPA.

- WEP: Wired Equivalency Privacy, the original wireless security protocol, comes in different strengths: 64-bit, 128-bit, and 256-bit, the higher the better.

Hackers find WEP extremely easy to break, and there are programs for cracking WEP posted on the Web. Bottom line: WPA2 is best, WPA/TKIP is okay, and WEP is better than nothing.

The router in the *For Dummies* SOHO network uses WEP, as you can see in the router's administration interface in Figure 7-6. Unfortunately, you may want to use a strict level of security, such as WPA2, but if even one device on your network doesn't support your preferred security choice, you must use the lowest common denominator. In the case of the network in Figure 7-6, we unwillingly use WEP. All of the devices on our wireless network are state of the art except for one ancient wireless printer. Because that printer only supports WEP, we're stuck with lax security until we replace the old printer.

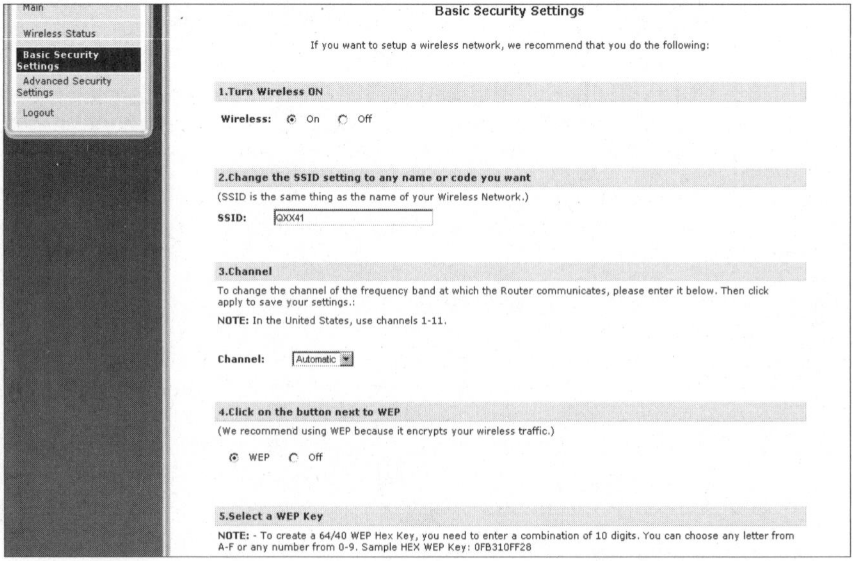

Figure 7-6:
It's time to replace the old printer in order to upgrade wireless network security.

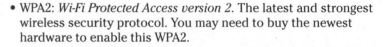

Figure 7-7 shows three wireless networks, two with security enabled, one that is wide open. The MAHGUEST network is a public network at a wireless hotspot. It has no security or encryption enabled. *Public networks open to all are by their very nature not very secure.* Candace uses this particular hotspot often, but you can be sure she does not shop or bank online from the MAHGUEST network.

Figure 7-8 shows another network at the same location as MAHGUEST. We don't know the name of the network because its SSID is not broadcast. This network also uses the TKIP security protocol. Interestingly, whether secure or not secure, you can see the MAC addresses of both networks.

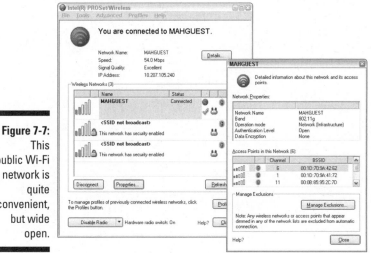

Figure 7-7:
This public Wi-Fi network is quite convenient, but wide open.

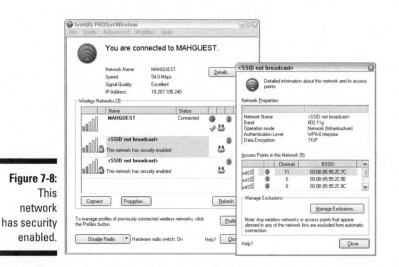

Figure 7-8:
This network has security enabled.

Each wireless vendor provides an interface for checking and troubleshooting network connections. Figures 7-7 and 7-8 were snapped from an Intel interface. Different NICs will have different interfaces, and your screen may look different from Figure 7-7, but the data collected will be the same.

Broadband for Everyone? We Hope

WiMAX (Worldwide Interoperability for Microwave Access), pronounced "why max," is wireless over very long distances up to a couple of thousand miles. It's based on the IEEE 802.16 standard, also called Broadband Wireless Access. Although WiMAX is still in the early stages and is not widely used, WiMAX could become important for home networkers who live in rural areas. Cable and DSL providers have ignored rural areas for a long time, and rural users have been stuck with dial-up or satellite networking. WiMAX means people out in the countryside (Hi, Dad!) will be able to have wireless broadband connections.

Depending on your needs, you can have different types of mobility:

- Using wireless hotspots
- Paying for broadband wireless service within a cellular area
- Going anywhere you want to connect to the Internet

We describe these different levels in the following sections.

Level 1: Using wireless hotspots

You must go to them. Wireless hotspots let you go out of range of your home base station to use the hotspot's Internet connection. Sometimes you must pay to connect to the hotspot. Sometimes these are free. Sometimes you have to pay. If Candace goes to the Lexington library to connect via their wireless hotspot, there's no charge. She doesn't even need to bring a computer. The library supplies one if you want. (It's a fantastic library. Shameless plug for the Cary Memorial Library in Lexington, MA.)

There are a couple of cafés that Candace spends too much time in that also are free wireless hotspots. Although you do need to buy a cup of coffee or tea or whatever is your beverage, so is it technically free? We think so, but not everyone agrees. You can also get free Wi-Fi with your fast food. McDonald's has Wi-Fi hotspots on every continent except Antarctica. Well, DUH! There are no golden arches in Antarctica. However, Antarctica has other Wi-Fi hotspots so you can stay in touch with the rest of the world while dining with the penguins. (Hey — we said dining *with* the penguins, not *on* the penguins!)

Level 2: Paying for broadband wireless service

Some cellular providers let you subscribe on a daily/weekly/monthly basis for wireless access anywhere they provide cell phone service. Your NIC needs to be a broadband cellular modem. Most newer NICs support wired, wireless, and cellular connections in one NIC. This kind of service is similar to smart phones, such as the iPhone and the G1 by Google that let you access the Internet. Marshall has one of these phones so he can perform very important activities: play online games and access e-mail.

Level 3: Going anywhere you want to connect to the Internet with WiMAX

The dream of WiMAX technology is to let you connect to the Internet no matter where you are on the planet (and beyond — maybe even the Restaurant at the End of the Universe).

The reality is that WiMAX access is scattered around here and there, depending on who's providing it. You don't need any fancy hardware, just a standard wireless NIC. There are no distance limits. Theoretically WiMAX lets you roam as far as you want or just stay home to access the Internet. WiMAX is just getting started as an Internet connection for real life. There are plenty of test sites and demonstrations, but a good site is hard to find.

Here are some examples of WiMAX in action:

- ✔ In the United States, entire towns, such as Sandersville, a town in rural Georgia, are already using WiMAX. The coverage extends for about 300 square miles. Besides household and business subscribers, the police and fire departments use the network. If you live in Sandersville, you don't need an ISP; you subscribe to the town's WiMAX provider.

- ✔ Internationally, cities such as Tripoli and Benghazi in Libya and Okinawa in Japan have deployed WiMAX networks. Also, the military is using WiMAX to connect remote sites. In Japan, UQ communication offered free, introductory WiMAX to residents of Tokyo, Yokohama, and Kawasaki, followed by an inexpensive monthly fee.

- ✔ Do you want to be connected on your entire trip wherever you roam? Last month, Stockholm, Sweden started a pilot program to provide WiMAX service on the Stockholm-to-Norrtalje route 676 commuter bus. Everyone on board gets free Internet access. Airplanes have started pilot programs (so to speak) as well.

Think of Wi-Fi as your LAN connectivity, as it's pictured in most of this chapter. Think of a WiMAX network as an ISP's entire WAN (Wide Area Network), but no wires — just WiMAX towers (similar to cell towers) every couple of thousand miles. Actually, a WiMAX tower that connects directly to the Internet will use a high-speed wired line. Don't worry that the landscape will become blighted by WiMAX towers. There are already many cell towers out there that you don't see. (There's one hidden in the steeple of our church, in fact.) WiMAX towers don't always have to be in front of your eyes.

WiMAX roaming is similar to cellphone roaming. When you're traveling outside your home network's service, you can still access its wireless services (including Internet, e-mail, voice, and video) by automatically using a network outside that of your home network provider. Of course, your home network service must have a prior agreement in place with those other services before you can use their networks.

The WiMAX Forum is a non-profit, industry-sponsored organization to watch over and certify WiMAX devices as compatible with each others. This group supports the compatibility and interoperability of broadband wireless devices, using the IEEE 802.16, Broadband Wireless Access Standards. The WiMAX Forum coined the term "WiMAX" and serves as a watchdog for how it's used. For example, the WiMAX Forum sponsors the global roaming program to help manufacturers learn how to build compatible roaming products.

Chapter 8

Advancing into Routing Protocols

● ●

In This Chapter

▶ Protocols in this chapter: IP, RIP, OSPF, OLSR, BGP, CIDR

▶ Looking at how packets travel through the TCP/IP layers

▶ Understanding how routers work

▶ Discovering routing protocols

▶ Gorging on routing tables

▶ Putting routing tables on a diet with CIDR

▶ Recognizing attacks on routers

● ●

*A*ll *routers* connect networks — small networks, gigantic networks. Every router's job is to connect networks.

In Chapter 7, you find out how to set up a wireless SOHO (Small Office/Home Office) network. The small multifunction routers shown in that chapter's SOHO figures connect a home or small office's subnets to each other — and to the Internet. These small routers can forward packets at a rate ranging from 10 to 20 megabits (millions of bits) per second. That seems plenty fast, but get this: Routers for large private networks (major corporations and organizations) have to be able to forward tens of millions of packets per second. Routers for the Internet forward hundreds of millions of packets per second. Oh, by the way, these big-to-huge routers also cost big-to-huge amounts of money.

No matter how many networks are attached, the router's job never changes: It connects networks. We can't say it enough. The job may get more complicated, though, when a router has to figure out where and how to send millions of packets. Special routing protocols help the large routers do their complex jobs.

This chapter introduces some of the added functions, protocols, and terminology associated with the big routers.

Understanding Routing Lingo

Routing and routing protocols have a jargon all their own. Before devouring the meat of this chapter, here are some bite-size definitions that make the reading easier:

- ✔ **Packet switching:** The TCP transport layer divides messages into *packets* before they move out onto a network. Routers use *packet switching* to move messages from one place to another on a network. During transmission, each packet is independent of the others. In fact, each packet in a message could take a different route to the destination. That's packet switching. The point is that all the packets in a message get to the destination, not *how* they get there. In Figure 8-1, the packets from the original message travel by different paths to the same destination. TCP reassembles the packets.

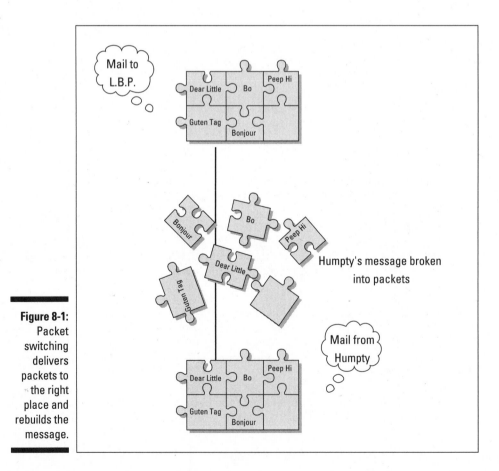

Figure 8-1: Packet switching delivers packets to the right place and rebuilds the message.

✔ **Routing:** *Routing* is the process of forwarding a packet to a destination IP address. The router decides how to forward the packet. The *route* is the path to the destination IP address. One way of measuring the efficiency of the route is in hops.

✔ **Hop:** A *hop* is each leg of the journey that a packet takes on its route. No, it's not because the packet has to jump on one leg. In the network shown in Figure 8-2, the lines between the routers represent hops. Not every router connects directly to another, so the hop count is one or sometimes more than one. For example, the direct path from router A to G is one hop. Router A could also hop to router H and hop again to router G. A packet could also hop around the outside the network — A to B, B to C, and so on.

✔ **Routing table:** Routers try to determine the most direct route that is also the most trustworthy route. The router checks a lookup table, called a *routing table,* which stores routes for data to travel. The router gets most of its intelligence from *routing tables*. Routing tables contain information about the following:

  • Paths (routes) to particular networks

  • How to handle special kinds of traffic

  • Priorities for certain connections

On big fancy routers, the routing tables also store statistics on which routes are fastest and shortest. You can use the command `netstat -rn` in Mac OS X, Linux/Unix, or Windows to display the routing table for your computer. The netstat command option `-r` means to show the routing table. The option `-n` means to display the addresses in numeric form. The routing table shown in Figure 8-3 is a small IPv4 table from Windows 7. Because Windows 7 runs a dual stack, there is a separate routing table for IPv6 destinations.

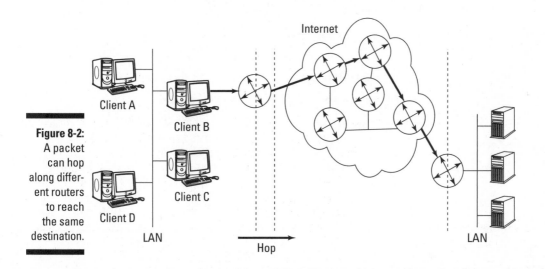

Figure 8-2: A packet can hop along different routers to reach the same destination.

Client A

Client B

Client C

Client D

LAN

Internet

Hop

LAN

How the cold war gave us dynamic routing

TCP/IP has its origins in the United States agency, DARPA (Defense Advanced Research Projects Agency) in the 1960s. In those days of the Cold War, the U.S. was worried about the threat of nuclear attack. DARPA's job was to design a way to connect computers and maintain the connection even if the network was disrupted. For example, if a network segment was taken out by enemy attack, the traffic on that segment would automatically move to another network segment. This reliable scheme is call *dynamic routing*. Eventually, this network became the ARPANET, where TCP/IP was born. Complex routing protocols weren't needed back then because the ARPANET could only support 256 networked computers. Of course, the ARPANET gradually morphed into the Internet, with its mammoth traffic, and now routing protocols are a big deal. Your system doesn't have to be a victim of an enemy attack for dynamic routing to be valuable. Thanks to dynamic routing, if a forklift cuts a cable in a warehouse inventory and blocks one route, data can take a different route across the network.

Figure 8-3: netstat −r shows an IPv4 routing table on a Windows 7 host.

```
C:\WINDOWS\system32\command.com                                    _ 8 X
Route Table
─────────────────────────────────────────────────────────────────────
          edited

═════════════════════════════════════════════════════════════════════
Active Routes:
Network Destination        Netmask          Gateway       Interface  Metric
          0.0.0.0          0.0.0.0      192.168.1.1    192.168.1.3      25
        127.0.0.0        255.0.0.0        127.0.0.1      127.0.0.1       1
      192.168.1.0    255.255.255.0      192.168.1.3    192.168.1.3      25
      192.168.1.3  255.255.255.255        127.0.0.1      127.0.0.1      25
    192.168.1.255  255.255.255.255      192.168.1.3    192.168.1.3      25
        224.0.0.0        240.0.0.0      192.168.1.3    192.168.1.3      25
  255.255.255.255  255.255.255.255      192.168.1.3    192.168.1.3       1
  255.255.255.255  255.255.255.255      192.168.1.3    192.168.1.3       1
Default Gateway:       192.168.1.1
Persistent Routes:
  None
C:\DOCUME~1\CANDACE>_
```

To display the IPv6 routing table, you need to use the netsh command:

1. Open a command window.

2. Type **netsh** at the command prompt. Press Enter.

3. Type **interface ipv6** at the prompt. Press Enter.

4. Type **show routes**. Press Enter.

The netstat command can show you a lot more than the routing table on your machine. It can also display all your computer's network connections, ports, protocols, and Ethernet statistics. Netstat can be a helpful diagnostic tool when you need to know what processes and programs are active on your network. You can also use netstat to monitor network communications, looking for malware running. You can specify that the netstat display updates itself at a regular interval so you can watch your network statistics change.

Starting TCP/IP automatically creates a routing table. You can add more entries either manually or automatically.

✔ **Routing protocols:** *Routing protocols* are the rules routers follow to send packets on their way. The protocols specify how a router should figure out a path to send packets. The protocols also spell out whether the router can change its mind about a route (*dynamic routing*) or whether it should stick with pre-set routes (*static routing*).

✔ **Metrics:** Routers use statistics called *metrics* to choose the fastest and most reliable route for a packet to travel. Some metrics include

- *Bandwidth:* The data-transfer rate between two points on a network.

- *Delay:* The time it takes for a packet to get from its source network to its destination network.

- *Reliability:* The error statistics for a router or network segment to travel.

Routing Through the Layers — the Journey of a Packet

Packets go up and down the TCP/IP layers as they travel from one location to the next. Let's say you want to initiate a Google search. The browser running on your PC — the source computer — needs to send a message to the Web server running on www.google.com — the destination computer — in order to get Google's home page. There's going to be a lot of layer travel involved. Figures 8-4 through 8-8 display a packet's travel through the network layers, to and from routers, until it reaches its final destination. We also provided a list of the steps that the packet travels until it reaches its final destination, shown later, in Figure 8-8.

A new message heads out across the Net

These first steps occur on the source computer, your PC. Figure 8-4 illustrates how the request starts on your computer at the application layer. The following text describes Steps 1 through 6 in detail:

1. **(Application Layer - outbound) Begin to construct the message.**

   The data in the message is a simple HTTP Get request. The source address is your computer's FQDN (fully qualified domain name). The destination address is the FQDN www.google.com.

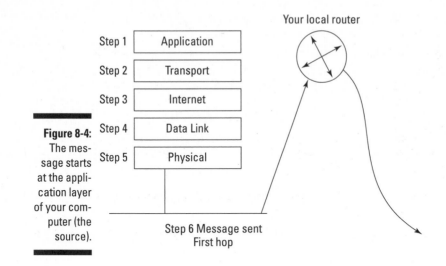

Figure 8-4:
The mes-
sage starts
at the appli-
cation layer
of your com-
puter (the
source).

2. **(Transport Layer - outbound) Choose TCP or UPD; add the source and destination port numbers.**

   TCP is connection-oriented, provides error detection, and ensures that the message arrives at its destination. UDP is connectionless, generally doesn't check for errors, and doesn't ensure that the message arrives. Your message uses TCP.

   Because many applications can be running on the same server (that is, mail server, Web server, file sharing, and so on), they listen on different TCP/IP *ports*. Every server application has a *default port number*, in fact it often has 2 — one for non-secure and one for secure communication. For example, a Web server normally listens on the default ports 80 and 443. This outbound HTTP request needs to specify port 80.

   When the response finally arrives, it needs to be delivered to your Web browser (not your e-mail client or any other application you're running), so the message sets a source port number. (The actual port number isn't important the way it is for a service.)

3. **(Internet Layer - outbound) Replace the names with their IP addresses.**

   Because computers talk to each other using numbers rather than names, the message needs the IP addresses rather than the FQDNs. In this example, the IP address of your computer is 192.168.0.2, and the IP address of www.google.com is 64.233.169.147. (Actually, there are multiple addresses for www.google.com because there are multiple servers handling the workload of Google searches.)

4. **(Data Link Layer - outbound) Set the MAC (Media Access Control) addresses.**

   If the destination computer was on your local intranet, your PC could send the message directly there. Because the destination computer in this example is not local, your PC doesn't know how to get the message there. The best it can do is to send the message in the right direction — to a local router. As part of its TCP/IP configuration, every computer has a *default route*. (It's also known as a *default gateway*.)

In either case, local destination or not, the IP addresses aren't enough information. The message needs the MAC addresses:

- The *source* MAC address is set to the hardware address of the NIC that forwards the message.

- The *destination* MAC address is the hardware address of the NIC that receives the message.

In this example, even though you're going to Google, you'll have several destinations along the way. At this stage, the destination MAC address is your local router's intranet NIC.

5. **(Physical Layer - outbound) Pick a NIC.**

"Which of my NICs should I use?" your PC asks itself. If it has multiple NICs, it selects the correct one — the one that communicates with the local router. (Because it has only one, the choice is simple.)

6. **Send the message.**

This is the first hop along the route.

The message visits the router

The message travels across the transmission medium and arrives at your local router. These next steps take place there. The next steps occur at the router's bottom three layers. Figure 8-5 illustrates Steps 7 through 14: how the router receives and processes the request, and then consults routing tables and the MAC address to determine how to forward the message on the next part of its journey.

Here are the router Steps 7 through 14:

7. **(Physical Layer - inbound) Receive the message.**

"Oh, look! A message," your local router says.

8. **(Data Link Layer - inbound) The MAC address in the message matches the NIC's.**

"Hey. This message is addressed to me!" your local router continues.

9. **(Internet Layer - inbound) Which computer is this message for?**

Your local router examines as few bits as possible in the destination IP address until it can decide what to do with the message. For example: "Wait a minute! This IP address starts with 64. That's not one of my intranets. I need to send this message on its way."

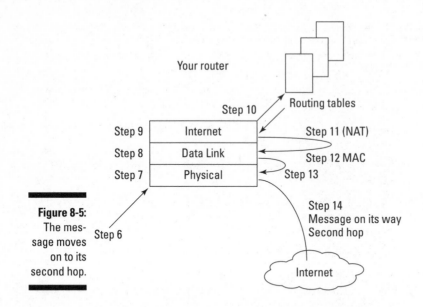

Your router

Step 10

Routing tables

Step 9	Internet
Step 8	Data Link
Step 7	Physical

Step 11 (NAT)

Step 12 MAC

Step 13

Figure 8-5:
The mes-
sage moves
on to its
second hop.

Step 6

Step 14
Message on its way
Second hop

Internet

10. Your local router consults its routing tables.

Your local router picks the appropriate routing-table entry, or its default route if necessary. The entry tells your local router the best path for the next hop.

11. (Internet Layer - outbound) Adjust the IP addresses?

Because this router is also performing NAT (Network Address Translation), it replaces the source IP address — your PC's non-routable IP address — with the router's own external IP address. The destination IP address remains the same. You can review NAT (Network Address Translation) in Chapter 5.

When the response finally arrives, your local router reverses this action. It replaces its own external IP address with your computer's IP address.

12. (Data link Layer - outbound) Set the MAC (Media Access Control) addresses.

Because the destination computer in this example is still not local, the router sends the message in the right direction. It sets the source MAC address to the MAC address of the NIC that will forward the message. The destination MAC address is an Internet router's NIC.

13. (Physical Layer - outbound) Pick a NIC.

"Which of my NICs should I use?" your local router asks itself. It selects the correct one — the one that communicates with the selected Internet router.

14. Send the message.

This is the second hop along the route (refer to Figure 8-5).

Into an Internet router and out again

The message travels across the transmission medium and arrives at an Internet router. These next steps repeat for each hop that takes the message from one Internet router to another. For this example, there is just one hop because the next router is the one that can reach Google's router: Steps 15 through 22 describe the message's movements at the Internet's router. The message only travels through the bottom three layers of the Internet router (just as it did at the local source's router). Figure 8-6 summarizes the steps the message passes through on an Internet router:

15. **(Physical Layer - inbound) Receive the message.**

    "Oh, look! A message," the Internet router says.

16. **(Data Link Layer - inbound) The MAC address in the message matches the NIC's MAC address.**

    "Hey. This message is addressed to me!" the router continues.

17. **(Internet Layer - inbound) Which computer is this message for?**

    The Internet router examines as few bits as possible in the destination IP address until it can decide what to do with the message. "This address starts with 64. That's not one of my intranets. I need to send this message on its way."

18. **The Internet router consults its routing tables.**

    The Internet router picks the appropriate routing-table entry. The entry tells the Internet router the best path for the next hop.

19. **(Internet Layer - outbound) Adjust the IP addresses?**

    The Internet router leaves the IP addresses alone. "This message didn't come from any of the computers on my intranets, and it's not going to any of the computers on my intranets so the IP addresses are none of my business."

20. **(Data Link Layer - outbound) Set the MAC (Media Access Control) addresses.**

    Because the destination computer in this example is still not local, the Internet router sends the message in the right direction. It sets the source MAC address to the MAC address of the NIC that will send the message onward. The destination MAC address is the NIC of the next router. In this example, the next router is Google's.

21. (Physical Layer - outbound) Pick a NIC.

"I better use the NIC that talks to Google's router," the Internet router decides.

22. Send the message.

This is the next hop along the route.

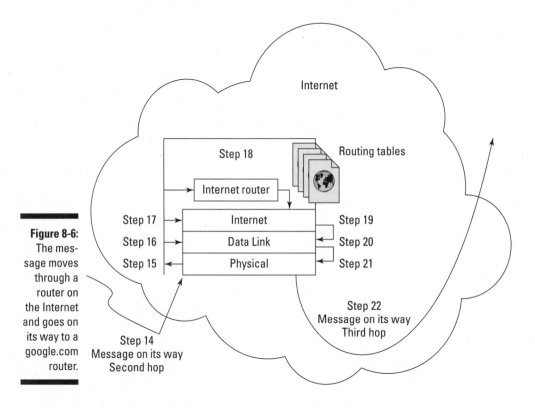

Figure 8-6: The message moves through a router on the Internet and goes on its way to a google.com router.

Reaching the destination

The message travels from the Internet's router across the transmission medium and arrives at Google's router, as shown in Figure 8-7.

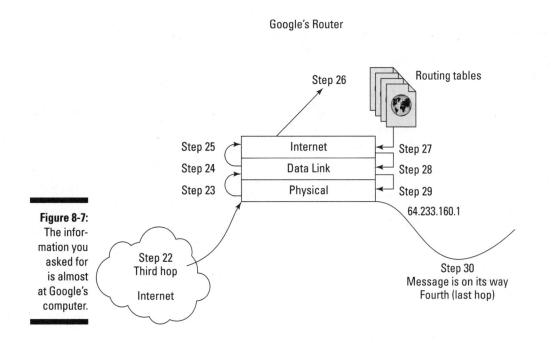

Google's Router

Step 26

Routing tables

Step 25 — Internet — Step 27

Step 24 — Data Link — Step 28

Step 23 — Physical — Step 29

64.233.160.1

Figure 8-7:
The information you asked for is almost at Google's computer.

Step 22
Third hop

Internet

Step 30
Message is on its way
Fourth (last hop)

These next steps take place there:

23. (Physical Layer - inbound) Google's router receives the message.

"Oh, look! A message," Google's router says.

24. (Data Link Layer - inbound) The MAC address in the message matches the NIC's.

"Hey. This message is addressed to me!" the router continues.

25. (Internet Layer - inbound) Which computer is this message for?

Google's router examines as few bits as possible in the destination IP address until it can decide what to do with the message. "Hey! This IP address is for one of the computers on my intranets."

26. The router consults its routing tables.

Google's router picks the appropriate routing-table entry that says where (that is, on which intranet) the computer sits.

27. (Internet Layer - outbound) Adjust the IP addresses?

If Google's router is performing NAT (Network Address Translation), it changes the destination IP address — its own external IP address — to the destination computer's internal IP address. The source IP address remains the same. (It is still the external IP address of your local router.)

28. (Data Link Layer - outbound) Set the MAC (Media Access Control) addresses.

Since the destination computer — www.google.com — is now local, the router sets the destination MAC address to the MAC address of that NIC. The source MAC address is the hardware address of the NIC in the Google router that is sending the message.

29. (Physical Layer - outbound) Pick a NIC.

30. Send the message.

This is the last hop along the route (refer to Figure 8-7).

The message travels across the transmission medium and arrives at www.google.com. These last steps take place there, as shown in Figure 8-8.

31. (Physical Layer - inbound) Receive the message.

"Oh, look! A message," www.google.com says.

32. (Data Link Layer - inbound) The MAC address in the message matches the NIC's.

"Hey. This message is addressed to me!" www.google.com continues.

33. (Internet Layer - inbound) Which computer is this message for?

"Wow! That's my IP address. This message really is addressed to me!"

34. (Transport Layer – inbound) Which service is this message for?

"The port number, 80, means the message is for the Web server I'm running." (Step 2 is where the destination port number was set.)

35. (Application Layer - inbound) Deliver the data to the service.

The Web server receives the HTTP request. Yay!

When www.google.com sends its HTTP response, the message makes a journey just like the one in this example. The source computer is www.google.com and the destination computer is your PC. The destination port number is the source port number your PC put in the original request. The route might be longer or shorter — and it may go through completely different Internet routers — but the routing process is the same.

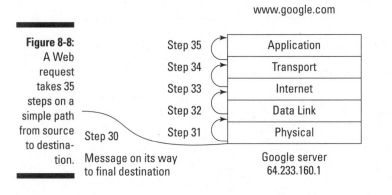

www.google.com

Figure 8-8:
A Web
request
takes 35
steps on a
simple path
from source
to destina-
tion.

Step 35	Application
Step 34	Transport
Step 33	Internet
Step 32	Data Link
Step 31	Physical

Step 30

Message on its way
to final destination

Google server
64.233.160.1

Getting a Handle on How Routers Work

Routers work at the internet, data link, and physical layers of the TCP/IP structure. A router resembles an octopus, and the tentacles are all your different transmission media. Routers understand the multiple paths that your data packets can take across the network to their final destination. Your router also knows about other routers on the network, and chooses the most efficient path (route) for your data to travel. This efficient route may change as network devices change, and as traffic comes and goes.

For example, on Monday, the most efficient path may be from network A to network C to network B. On Tuesday, however, the most efficient path may be from network A to network D to network B because network C is broken. Because the router knows about any problems on the network path, it can detour your data when necessary. Not only are routers intelligent, they can route traffic dynamically according to network conditions. Routers that use dynamic protocols talk to each other and share knowledge, especially traffic reports: "Route A is jammed right now. Take route B instead. Route C has disappeared." Figure 8-9 shows an example of dynamic routing. Each packet travels a different route, and they all arrive at the same, intended destination.

Routers use routing protocols to find out information about the entire network and to determine the optimal path for sending a packet on to its destination. What's optimal? Is it the shortest path (fewest hops from one host to another)? The fastest path (more hops on speedier links)? Or the least congested path?

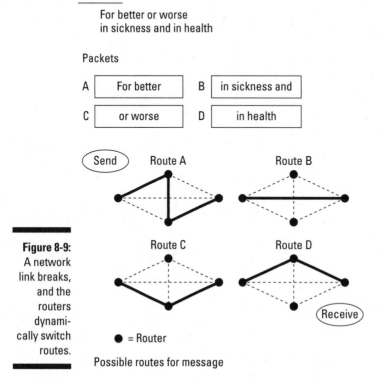

Message
_____

> For better or worse
> in sickness and in health

Packets

| A | For better | B | in sickness and |
| C | or worse | D | in health |

Figure 8-9:
A network
link breaks,
and the
routers
dynami-
cally switch
routes.

● = Router

Possible routes for message

Suppose you want to go from Sydney, Australia to visit Government House in Canberra. Your top three choices are probably these:

  ✔ Drive from Sydney to Canberra and use a tourist map to find the Government House.

  ✔ Drive to Sydney Airport. Fly to Canberra Airport. Take the Airliner Bus to the city. Take a shuttle bus to Government House.

  ✔ Take a bus to Sydney Central Station. Take the train to Canberra Railway Station. Take a taxi to Government House.

Which way do you think gets you there faster?

  ✔ Driving seems like it takes the most time.

  ✔ If you've never driven to Sydney Airport during rush hour, you might guess that flying is the fastest route. However, depending on city traffic in Sydney and Canberra, flying may actually be the slowest way when you add in the time getting to and from each airport.

✔ The high-speed train sounds like a really fast option, but depending on how many people get on and off at the many stops, the train may ultimately be less-than-high-speed.

The shortest way isn't always the fastest way. Nor is the most direct route always the fastest way. If you never go to Canberra even once in your life, these facts are still rules to live by on the network. For example, in Figure 8-2 (earlier in this chapter), the direct path from Router A to Router B may not be the fastest path. Perhaps the link between the two routers is handling an unusual traffic load.

The router permits each connected network to maintain its independent identity and address. Figure 8-10 shows a small intranet consisting of two subnets. The router connects the subnets and connects the entire intranet to the Internet.

When someone at address 130.103.2.1 sends e-mail to 130.103.2.4, the router is smart enough to see that the message is staying on the same subnet. There is no need to investigate any routes to the other subnet or to the Internet. When 130.103.2.1 sends e-mail to 130.103.1.4, however, the router forwards the message to the other subnet. When someone from anywhere within the intranet sends a message outside the 130.103 intranet, the router forwards the message out to the Internet.

What makes routers special is that they're intelligent enough to understand IP addresses. In fact, the router makes decisions about directing the packets of your message based on the network portion of the IP address. A router contains a network interface card for each segment of the network that it connects. Each network interface card has a different IP address because the router itself is a member of each network.

Gateways are devices that sit between networks and translate different protocols and data formats. Routers used to be called gateways. That's why you might see the term "default gateway" meaning router. This is the router that faces the outside world, usually your ISP or the Internet. "Facing the outside world" means that the router sends and receives all network traffic to and from the Internet before sending the packets on to the appropriate subnet LANs and hosts.

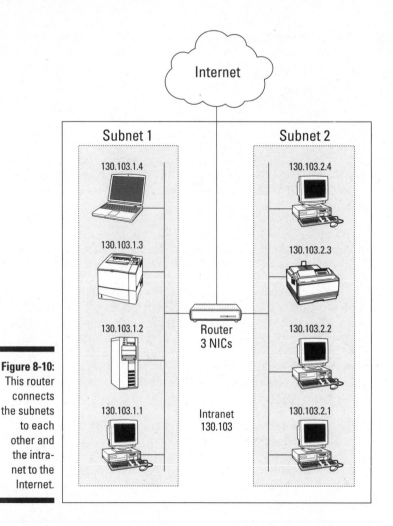

Figure 8-10:
This router
connects
the subnets
to each
other and
the intra-
net to the
Internet.

Getting Started with Routers

A router looks at the IP address of the packets that make up your message
and figures out where to send those packets. A *route* is the path along which
the router chooses to send your packets.

Figure 8-11 displays two LANs that connect to the Internet. If you follow the
paths, C-LAN can connect to M-LAN only by going from their respective routers and through the Internet. If people on these LANs communicate

frequently, it would make sense to reduce Internet traffic and speed up communications between the two LANs. Adding direct connection between C-LAN and M-LAN would improve the network design. As you can see in Figure 8-10, you have to add a NIC to a router in each LAN to make the direct connection.

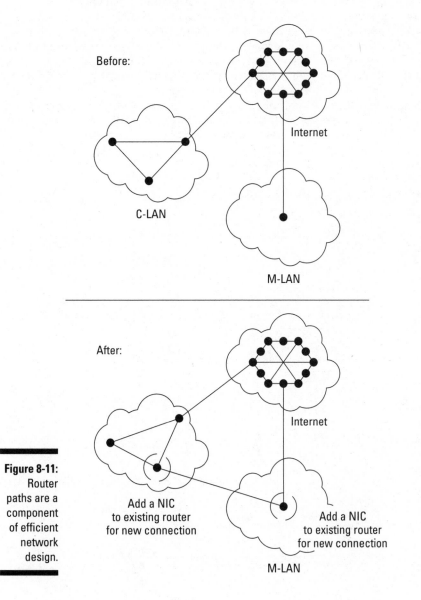

Before:

Internet

C-LAN

M-LAN

After:

Internet

Add a NIC
to existing router
for new connection

Add a NIC
to existing router
for new connection

M-LAN

Figure 8-11:
Router
paths are a
component
of efficient
network
design.

Swallowing Routing Protocols

Routers know how to do their jobs thanks to a set of TCP/IP routing protocols. Routing protocols tell routers how to communicate with each other and how to select efficient routes between other routers. Regardless of the protocol, every router starts knowing only about the network(s) attached to it. Routing protocols share information about their immediate neighbors among their close neighbors. Each router tells another router and that router tells another router and so on. Eventually, routers learn to map out parts of the network into their routing tables. When a router first appears on a network, it has to find its neighbor routers and advertise its own presence. If the new router sends a message to the broadcast address, 255.255.255.255, the neighbors who use the same routing protocol will greet the new router.

There are two types of routing protocols:

- ✔ Interior Gateway Protocol (IGP)
- ✔ Exterior Gateway Protocol (EGP)

Figure 8-12 shows the relationship between IGP routers and EGP routers.

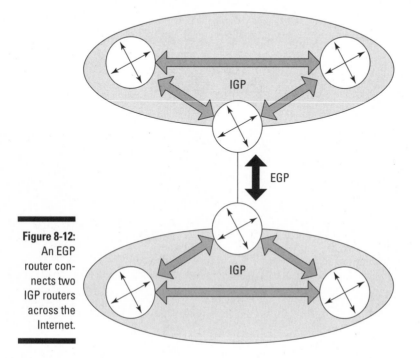

Figure 8-12:
An EGP router connects two IGP routers across the Internet.

Nibbling on IGP protocols

IGP protocols are the rules for routers on the same intranet. The intranet may be as small as a home office or as large as the location of a major organization. These protocols tell intranet routers how to share data about routes. Three of the best-known IGP protocols are RIP, OSPF, and OLSR.

Routers that talk to each other using an Interior Gateway Protocol (IGP) are doing (as you might expect) internal routing. Basically, there are two styles of IGPs, and each style has different protocols. Each implementation compensates for some issue that cropped up earlier, as when other protocols

✔ Couldn't handle large networks

✔ Took too long for the routers to learn what they needed to know

✔ Caused routers to send too many messages too often

And so on. Fortunately, many smart people have been working on these issues for a long time.

The four styles of IGP routing protocols are described in this list:

✔ **RIP:** The oldest and simplest IGP is the Routing Information Protocol (RIP, also sometimes called RIP-1) though there are also RIP version 2 (also sometimes called RIP-2) and RIPng. (RIP-1 and RIP-2 are for IPv4 while RIPng is for IPv6.) Cisco developed its own Interior Gateway Routing Protocol (IGRP) that it later replaced with the Enhanced Interior Gateway Routing Protocol (EIGRP).

✔ **OSPF:** The Open Shortest Path First (OSPF) protocol is the most common IGP, especially on large intranets.

✔ **OLSR:** Optimized Link State Routing Protocol, an experimental protocol for routing requests in mobile networks.

✔ **IS-IS:** The Intermediate-System-to-Intermediate-System (IS-IS) routing protocol is not strictly a TCP/IP protocol. It is an OSI (Open Systems Interconnect) standard that has been adapted for the Internet. Although it does not follow IETF standards, Internet Service Providers (ISPs) commonly use it.

Regardless of the style or protocol(s) in use, each router sends out periodic IGP messages that say what it can do for the network — such as which other routers it talks to directly. Every router uses the information to maintain the internal data it needs to route packets along the most efficient paths.

RIPping through all the RIPs

The Routing Information Protocol (RIP) is one of the Interior Gateway Protocols, which means that RIP is used within an organization and not on the wider Internet.

RIP is one of the first routing protocols, and is still commonly used. RIP does not have dynamic routing features. RIP has been part of Unix TCP/IP since the beginning, and is a part of every TCP/IP product on the market today. RIP counts hops to determine the best route.

Are you thinking that RIP is old? Some people think it's old as in Old Reliable. Some people think it's old as in Rest In Peace. Although RIP is intelligent and routes your packets to their destinations just fine, it's a slow learner when it comes to network changes, such as the appearance of new routers and faster paths.

RIP has its advantages and disadvantages, depending on network size. RIP has an advantage in a small network. RIP is as easy to set up as setting an IP address for the router and turning the router on. Here are some of the disadvantages:

- ✔ The main problem with RIP is that it uses static hop counts to compare alternate routes. As a result, RIP cannot adapt to real-time network problems, such as delays, loss of a router(s), and network load. Using RIP on a very large intranet could slow down network performance.

- ✔ All versions of RIP limit paths to a maximum of 15 hops: that is routing tables can only list 15 routers. If two intranets within a RIP routing domain (a collection of intranets and routers using RIP) have 15 or more routers between them, they cannot communicate. This is a problem for organizations with large intranets that need to work together.

- ✔ RIP wastes IP addresses even though IPv4 addresses are in short supply.

- ✔ Each RIP router broadcasts the full list of all the routes it knows — every 30 seconds — if the routing tables don't change. (Routing tables change, for example, when a new network link appears; the routing tables receive their updates immediately.) Given the large size of routing tables, RIP can use excessively large amounts of network bandwidth by constantly broadcasting everything on the list of routes.

RIP is an example of a *distance vector protocol,* which uses various metrics to figure out the best route for forwarding packets. RIP, however, uses hop count as the only metric to determine routes. One of the jobs of the protocol is to send copies of its routing table regularly to nearby routers. Sending routing-table data keeps the routers up to date, but doesn't help if a network segment gets cut or a router becomes so congested that it runs slower than molasses.

RIP was developed by Xerox, which was way ahead of its time as a computer company — so ahead of its time, in fact, that it didn't catch on as a computer company. Nevertheless, the legacy of Xerox lives on in networking, including Ethernet.

RIP version 2 (RIPv2)

RIPv2 has the same 15-hop limitation as the original RIP, but RIPv2 includes important features that extend the life of its ancient ancestor, RIP.

✔ RIPv2 doesn't waste IP addresses, as the original RIP does; that's because RIPv2 uses CIDR.

CIDR (Classless Inter-Domain Routing) gets a thorough once-over later in this chapter, in the "Juicing Up Routing with CIDR" section.

✔ RIPv2 provides security with authentication — and this is its most important improvement.

Briefly, *authentication* is the process that proves you are who you say you are. For example, credit-card companies require you to sign the cards so salespeople can authenticate that the card is really yours. RIPv2 makes sure that messages routed across your intranet are really from the router that claims to be forwarding those messages. Without authentication in place, hackers can get into certain software and substitute a fake IP address. The consequences of this hack could be that you receive a virus from a source you think you trust because of its IP address, which turns out to be bogus.

Chapter 12 gives you the lowdown on the minimal security facts you need to know. Chapters 20 and 21 drone on and on about security technologies; if you need to know more, they could save your bacon.

RIPng

RIPng is a "new generation" of RIP to support IPv6 (formerly known as IPng, where *ng* is short for *the next generation*). IPv6 uses a much different addressing format than IPv4, which is what people mean when they say "IP." You may remember from Chapter 4 that an IP (IPv4) address is 32 bits long. Chapter 9 spills the details of IPv6, such as a 128-bit IP address.

RIPng does not perform authentication.

OSPF (Open Shortest Path First)

"Open" in OSPF isn't a verb. In this case, it's an adjective, as in *open systems*. OSPF is built on the concept of *designated routers* — that is, all routers start out equal, but some get elected to positions of importance. OSPF has more features than RIP, but is more complicated to set up and manage. Usually, large networks use OSPF, and small networks use RIP as their Interior Gateway Protocols.

The Internet today uses mostly the OSPF protocol inside intranets (interior) and the BGP-4 protocol in the outside world (exterior). Both of these protocols can reroute packets if necessary. When networks change, — perhaps a segment becomes unavailable because a cable fails — OSPF quickly recalculates the route a packet should follow. *Dynamic routing* is this handy ability to recalculate a route in just about no time (ideally, anyway).

OSPF enables routers to calculate on the fly the shortest path between two networks, regardless of the changes that constantly happen.

OSPF routers keep an up-to-date map of the network. Any time there's a change to the network, OSPF has the routers update the map to reflect the changes. OSPF routers work together to keep their maps synchronized.

OSPF is an example of a *link state* protocol. The map of the network used by the routers is also called the *link state database*.

OSPFv3

OSPFv3 is a new version that supports those long, long, long IPv6 addresses.

Optimized Link State Routing Protocol (OLSR)

The OLSR protocol is designed for routing on mobile ad hoc networks. The RFC-Editor lists OLSR's status as Experimental (as of this writing). However, the protocol is in use. The RFC standards process drags on for a long time; by the time most protocols become standards, they've been in use for a while. Although the OLSR protocol is experimental, it is in production mostly in research institutions and universities.

Exterior Gateway Protocols (EGP)

External routing has become more and more vital as the Internet has grown (and grown) — and as the amount of traffic it carries has grown (AND GROWN). Now, you are probably thinking that external routing is done by routers that talk to each other using an exterior gateway protocol (EGP). Oooh, so close! There used to be an EGP, and it even got as far as version 3, but not anymore.

The Internet's most important routers, and many ISPs, use the Border Gateway Protocol (BGP) version 4 (BGP-4), which is the first version to support CIDR (pronounced like the drink, cider, and detailed later in this chapter). Exterior Gateway Protocols, such as BGP-4, share routing information with the routers that connect networks. That is, routers in the outside world, connected in the Internet.

Interior protocols, such as RIP and OSPF, only allow routers on the same intranet to communicate, so the Internet needs a protocol that allows routers to send information outside and between intranets.

Please be careful not to confuse the obsolete EGP protocol with the EGP *general description* of protocols that connect networks.

The big, big, enormously expensive routers at the top of the Internet food chain talk to each other differently. They have to use different protocols in order to forward the whopping and relentless amount of Internet traffic as quickly as possible. Most organizations don't need or use routers like the six figure (in U.S. dollars) giants that run BGP.

BGP-4

BGP-4 is the heart of the Internet. BGP-4 keeps a table of IP networks. It is one of the most important protocols of the Internet. Most of the routers in the ISP core networks (very large central high-speed networks that connect millions of smaller networks to the Internet) have to trade information about several hundred thousand networks. BGP-4 continues to carry out that task.

Other routing protocols have an easy job compared to BGP-4. The other protocols simply have to find the ideal path to the routers it knows about. BGP-4 cannot take this simplistic approach because the agreements between ISPs almost always result in complex routing policies. In the earlier section "Routing through the Layers — the Journey of a Packet," a packet hopped from its intranet to `google.com` on the Internet. The following steps explain how the protocols work when a packet is routed from an intranet to the Internet:

1. When a request for an IP address comes through on an intranet, each OSPF router advertises its links (interfaces). The routers who know where the IP address is on the network calculate the best path.

2. When a router receives a request to forward a packet to an IP address, the router must find the best route to the requested destination (the IP address).

To find the best route, the router scans its BGP table, where information on routes is stored. The "best" route is the one that corresponds as closely as possible to the address the router is actually looking for.

For example, say that a router is looking for IP address 123.255.189.25. It might find a dozen routers advertising that they connect to 123.xxx. xxx.xxx, but that's a very broad location. Presented with its options, the router chooses to send its data to the ISP or other network that's advertising itself as connecting to 123.255.xxx.xxx over sending it to an ISP that just advertises itself as 123. Once the data reaches 123.255, the new router checks *its* BGP table, and forwards the packets along to the closest address it can find.

Understanding How BGP Routers Work

When a BGP router first comes up on the Internet — whether as a new router or one that was off but has been turned back on — it connects with other BGP routers. It immediately copies the routing tables of each neighbor router. Then, after initially getting the routing tables, the BGP router only sends and receives update messages to and from the other BGP routers.

The list of update messages changes depending on the preferred route for a host's IP address. The router also updates its own routing tables when this new path is more efficient. Updating the routing tables can be very intensive and may slow the routers down, and, therefore, slow down part of the Internet. There is an addressing technique called CIDR (Classless Inter-Domain Routing), described in the next section, that reduces the size of the routing tables to help the routers perform faster.

Juicing Up Routing with CIDR

When you use *classful* IP addressing (as described in Chapter 4), you need a separate entry in a router's routing table for each network. You wind up with a bloated routing table with heaps of entries because of the large number of networks that exist. Depending on the size of the router, large routing tables lead to degraded performance and the eventual crash of the router. If you use

CIDR (instead of the traditional Class A, B, and C addressing scheme), you can use one routing-table entry to represent a whole group of networks. This keeps your router nice and lean and fit. This technique is called *route aggregation*. Don't worry. You haven't lost the routes to individual networks. Those routes simply exist in another router down the path.

This scheme works because each entry in the router has a network prefix associated with it. The network prefix identifies the correct network for a given IP address. Figures 8-13 and 8-14 show a network before and after "CIDRizing."

Another benefit of CIDR is that it reduces the demand for classful Class C networks. Okay, we know — how can something that's class*less* work on something that's class*ful*? Please have patience and read on.

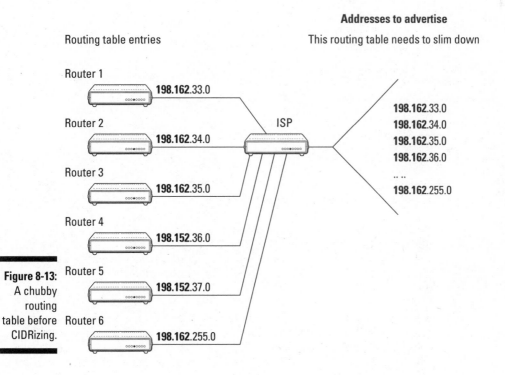

Figure 8-13: A chubby routing table before CIDRizing.

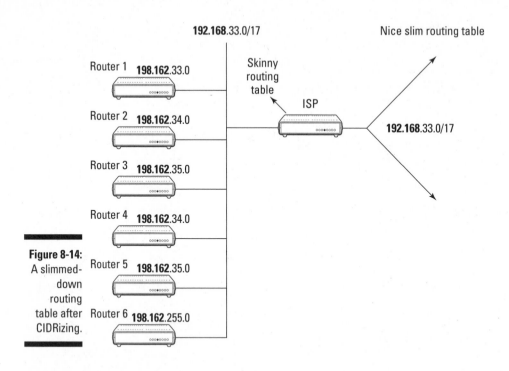

192.168.33.0/17   Nice slim routing table

Router 1   **198.162**.33.0

Skinny routing table

ISP

Router 2   **198.162**.34.0

192.168.33.0/17

Router 3   **198.162**.35.0

Router 4   **198.162**.34.0

Figure 8-14:
A slimmed-
down
routing
table after
CIDRizing.

Router 5   **198.162**.35.0

Router 6   **198.162**.255.0

C Is for Classless

If you use classful addresses, described in Chapter 4, the key letter in CIDR is *C* — for classless addressing.

With the enormous growth of the Internet, everyone needs to accept that IP addresses are an endangered resource that must be managed for the good of the many. CIDR replaces the system of A, B, and C classes with a way to allocate IP addresses that allows the Internet to grow without getting ungainly and sluggish.

Scott Bradner, the Secretary to the Board of Trustees of the Internet Society (ISOC) AND University Technology Security Officer at Harvard University, told us that "no one has been assigned a Class B address since 1992." With CIDR, the remaining — enormous — Class A networks are split into various sizes, including the traditional Class B *size*. The Internet backbone's routers understand CIDR and distribute packets to the right destinations. The following sections describe how CIDR works to conserve IP addresses and, most importantly, how it makes routing tables more efficient.

CIDR pressing the routing tables

CIDR is an addressing and routing scheme that enables routing decisions to be made more efficiently by reducing the size of routing tables. Reducing the size of anything in the Internet is a good thing. (Too bad TCP/IP doesn't have a protocol for reducing the size of our waists — excuse the digression).

If you're an Internet user who doesn't need to configure IP addresses on your computer, then you now know all you need to know about CIDR to discuss it intelligently. Stop here if you don't want to read too many stressful techie details. But if you're a network administrator, read on.

The problem

In late 1990, there were 2,190 routes to be managed by routing tables. In early 1999, that number exceeded 40,000 routes. It takes almost 64 MB of computer memory and a powerful CPU to store 60,000 routes. If you use CIDR, you can save lots of router memory and CPU power, too.

The solution

CIDR offers a solution to the growing demand for IP addresses without making the Internet address space too hefty to manage. One way CIDR does this is to replace a Class B address with a group of contiguous Class C addresses that can be allocated differently. This technique is called *address space aggregation*. Aggregation has two benefits:

- ✔ Fewer Class B addresses are wasted.
- ✔ The routing table size is nice and slim and manageable.

CIDR specifies that every IP address include a network prefix that identifies either one gateway or an aggregation of network gateways. The length of the prefix is also part of the IP address.

A CIDR network address looks like this:

```
130.103.40.03/18
```

130.103.40.03 is the IP address, and /18 declares that the first 18 bits are the network part of the address. The last 14 bits (because 32 bits minus 18 bits equals 14 bits) represent the host address. A /18 address-space aggregation holds 16,384 hosts — that's equivalent to 64 Class C networks and is one-fourth of a Class B network. Table 8-1 lists more details.

Taking CIDR apart

C is for *classless*— which means "Let's revolt against the 4-class structure of IP addresses, especially Class B networks (65,533 hosts), which often waste lots of IP addresses."

I is for *inter.* Inter-domain means that CIDR is used between domains. The routers on the Internet's backbone network that use BGP also use CIDR for routing between each other. The Internet's regulating authorities now expect every ISP to use CIDR.

D is for *domain.* RFC 1518, "An Architecture for IP Address Allocation with CIDR," defines a domain as the group of "resources under control of a single administration." Internet service providers (ISPs) are domains *of* domains; that is, an ISP lets other domains hook into its network. Subscribers are the domains that connect to ISPs. A domain can be both an ISP and a subscriber simultaneously.

R is for *routing.* This paragraph is a brief review. A router is a computer that runs software that connects two or more networks. Routers determine the path a packet should follow on the network as it moves toward its final destination. A router stores a table of the available routes for packet travel and figures out the most efficient route that a packet should follow.

Table 8-1	CIDR Address Space Aggregations	
Bits in Network Part	*Number of Hosts*	*Number of Class C Networks*
/12	1,048,576	4,096
/13	524,288	2,048
/14	262,144	1,024
/15	131,072	512
/16	65,536	256 = 1 Class B network
/17	32,768	128
/18	16,384	64
/19	8,192	32
/20	4,096	16
/21	2,048	8
/22	1,024	4
/23	512	2
/24	256	1
/25	128	1/2
/26	64	1/4
/27	32	1/8
/28	16	1/16

CIDR also works with the OSPF routing protocol.

You say "subnet," aggregating.net says "aggregate"

Okay, just trust us — it's *aggregating* not *aggravating*. Consider the example of a fictional Internet service provider (ISP) named "agregating.net." Agregating. net is allowed to give out addresses 162.9.*.* (where * represents 0 to 255). When you sign up with aggregating.net, you get a piece — some subnet — of its address space (numeric IP address range). From aggregating.net's perspective, it is aggregating your address space into 162.9.*.*. For example, a mythical company called "example.com" gets 162.9.200.0/24, and your company gets 162.9.201.0/24. Remember: Table 8-1 says that the "/24" part of the address means you can have 256 hosts. With CIDR, it's easier for agregating. net to give all of its customers the number of IP addresses they need without wasting too much.

Assume that aggregating.net has 100 customers. Before using CIDR, aggregating.net's routing table had 100 entries — one for each customer's address. But now it has just one entry on the Internet that benefits all 100 clients. That routing table entry says, "Send me all packets addressed to 162.9.*.*." That makes for a much smaller and, therefore, more efficient routing table. This is what CIDR does. Now, apply this sample routing efficiency across the entire Internet address space. The efficiency savings are impressive! We wanted to say staggering, but maybe we're getting carried away — or maybe we drank too much hard CIDR.

The many free IP calculators that you can find on the Web also do CIDR calculations.

Securing Your Router

There's not much you can do about Internet router security unless you're a network administrator at an ISP, but threats and attacks do exist at the highest levels. Most routers are multi-purpose and include a firewall as a first line of defense.

The United States government is sponsoring the BGPSEC program to secure BGP operations that are currently vulnerable to assault. BGPSEC is a multi-million-dollar, multi-year project. Why spend so much time and effort on one protocol? Remember, BGP is the core routing protocol *of the whole Internet.*

If you want to bring the Internet to its knees, bring down BGP. Unfortunately, the firewall doesn't prevent attacks on Internet routers and BGP — in particular, these:

- Denial of Service (DoS)
- Router (IP) hijacking
- BGP eavesdropping

We describe each of these types of attacks in the sections that follow and end with a couple of proposals from private industry to shore up BGP router security.

Coring the apple with Denial of Service (DoS) Attacks

Along with the Domain Name System (DNS), BGP routers form the core of the Internet. In the year 2000, there was a rash of DoS assaults on popular Web sites. The goal of DoS is to prevent Web users from getting any information from their favorite sites. The attackers flooded the routers with far too many requests to be managed.

Routing protocols have rules that won't allow millions of requests from the same address in a short time space. If a router receives too many requests, it throws away the extra requests. However, if you really want to outsmart the routers, you can do what the bad guys did: They inserted programs on various computers that sent thousands of requests per minute to a Web site. These programs *spoofed* the sender's IP by putting a false IP address on each packet. IP spoofing (see Chapter 12) let the bad guys get around the routers' security rules. As the routers received this flood of legitimate-looking packets, they couldn't handle the deluge. The routers discarded millions of packets and sent messages to other routers that the connection was full. Soon enough, honest traffic couldn't get through the routes to the Web servers they wanted.

Hijacking routers

A *router hijacking* (also called an IP hijacking) can make it seem that a Web site has been wiped off the face of the earth. For example, in 2008, Pakistan Telecom hijacked YouTube traffic from around the world. Although YouTube was up and running, all the content it sent out was basically going into a black hole. No matter where in the world you were, you could not get to YouTube because it was clogged with false "advertisements" about the YouTube network sent to the Internet routers. Oddly enough, this hijack was not maliciously intended. It was a mistake — but a serious mistake.

When a router decides on the best path to reach an IP address, it checks a BGP table for the best route. That BGP table consists of "advertisements" issued by large networks, such as ISPs. The advertisements declare a list of IP prefixes (a mass of IP addresses) to which they'll deliver Internet traffic.

The routing table searches for the destination IP address among those prefixes. To intercept data, someone with a BGP router advertises a smaller range of IP addresses than the mass other networks advertise. Because the BGP protocol likes smaller masses, it will go with the hijacker. The hijacker's advertisement would take only minutes before data headed to legitimate addresses would be hijacked to the wrongdoer's network.

Eavesdropping on BGP

BGP Eavesdropping tricks BGP routers into re-directing Internet traffic from a legitimate address to the eavesdropper's network. Anyone with a BGP router (ISPs, large corporations) can intercept data headed to a group of IP addresses or to one address. Eavesdropping attacks only steal data headed to network destinations. They can't affect outbound data.

It's so sad

You might wonder, "How can someone shut down an entire Web site or spy on others' data? It's the Internet's history of trust again. BGP's architecture assumes routers are trustworthy. When a router says a route is the best path, BGP assumes the router is telling the truth. Attacks like those detailed here sadly prove that BGP's assumption of trust is naïve and gullible when compared with Net realities.

S-BGP (Secure BGP): Proposals to make BGP routing secure

In addition to the U.S. government's BGPSEC research program described earlier, private corporations are looking for solutions to the BGP security problems. BBN Technologies, the company that launched the ARPANET (later to become the Internet) in 1969, has proposed S-BGP as an architectural solution to improve BGP security by adding additional data and checks to the existing BGP protocols. BGP relies on the IPSec group of protocols (see Chapter 21 for information about IPSec) to add needed security features to BGP routing. BBN has implemented a test system for S-BGP.

Cisco Systems (the largest router vendor) has proposed Secure Origin BGP (SoBGP). So far, no BGP security research has been put into production because the proposed security features require too many changes to routers.

Chapter 9

IPv6: IP on Steroids

*I*f you're interested in the new IPv6 protocols and addresses, this chapter is for you. At first glance, IPv6 protocols and addresses seem more complicated than in IPv4. Take a deep breath, count to ten, and rest assured that IPv6 can make your life a lot easier. Several IPv4 limitations led to the development of IPv6.

Say Hello to IPv6

IPv6 is the Internet protocol designed to replace IPv4. The IPv4's address space offers 4,294,967,296 possible unique addresses. That's not nearly enough, though, to meet the demand for globally unique IP addresses. Remember that it isn't just the obvious computers and routers that need IP addresses — other devices include smartphones, the computer under your car's hood, your GPS device, robots, and medical devices, such as select pacemakers and their monitoring systems. As you can see, one person might need several IP addresses, and the IPv4 address space just isn't large enough to cover the demand that's expected in the next couple of years.

IPv6 offers 340,282,366,920,938,463,463,374,607,431,770,000,000 unique global addresses, so it might be easier to say "340 billion billion billion billion." In any case, IPv6 provides more than enough global unique addresses for every device on the planet. Chapter 2 equates IPv4 to an Internet plate that holds many other protocols and services. Now you have a mammoth IPv6 *platter* so that billions more devices that are hungry for addresses can enjoy the TCP/IP banquet.

In the following sections, we discuss in more depth the limitations of IPv4 and the advantages of IPv6.

Digesting IPv4 limitations

Keep in mind some of the limitations of IPv4:

- ✔ In the late 20th century, Internet architects realized that the Internet was in danger of running out of network numbers. They created temporary solutions involving Network Address Translations (NATs) and classless inter-domain routing (CIDR), but using those workarounds isn't a final solution. The Internet is still running out of addresses.

- ✔ You know that the IPv4 32-bit numbering provides for 4 billion addresses. How many networks is that? We don't know. The Internet probably won't run out of IPv4 addresses for another year (around 2010). That's just a guess. If we could predict the future, do you think we would be authors?

- ✔ The IPv4 classful addressing strategy wastes a lot of Class C addresses. You can review classful addressing in Chapter 4.

- ✔ Large, cumbersome routing tables of addresses slow down the Internet.

- ✔ The NAT workaround causes other problems.

If you're a network manager and you haven't begun to plan for IPv6, start now to plan your migration path to IPv6. Start now! In the meantime, while you plan, IPv4 and IPv6 can coexist. In fact, you should be considering a coexistence plan now if you want to be ahead of the conversion tidal wave.

Absorbing IPv6 advantages

IPv6 has a variety of benefits in addition to the huge address space. We write about these benefits in the section "Exploring Other Delicious IPv6 Morsels," later in this chapter. For now, here's a brief list:

- ✔ Improved security

- ✔ Mobile IPv6 — better support for mobile devices

- ✔ Improved VoIP transmissions (We describe Voice over IP in Chapter 17.)

In Chapter 4, we urge you to call your computer a "host," but in this chapter, we use a new name. We're not trying to drive you crazy, we promise! In the IPv6 world, a computer is now known as a *node*. And, it isn't just computers — any device, such as a router, on an IPv6 network is a node.

If It Ain't Broke, Don't Fix It — Unless It Can Be Improved

IPv6 retains most IPv4 characteristics — especially the stuff that works. For example, fully qualified domain names (FQDNs) stay the same. Thank goodness!

Some things change, though. Every piece of TCP/IP is affected by a new, longer address format. Although the name resolution services (local hosts file, NIS, and DNS) still exist, the availability of autodiscovery, autoconfiguration, and autoregistration should make them less necessary. (See the section "IPv6 — and the Using Is Easy," later in this chapter.)

Other things can become unnecessary, such as supernet masks (described in the sidebar "What About Subnet and Supernet Masks?" later in this chapter) and ARP (see Chapters 2 and 4), while still other things could simply stand some improvements (such as switching to a different network number). In this chapter, we highlight IPv6 addressing and other key topics that become important when using IPv6.

If you need a refresher course on IPv4 addressing, see Chapter 4.

Wow! Eight Sections in an IPv6 Address?

A 32-bit IPv4 address provides 4 billion addresses. To be able to offer more addresses on the Internet, IPv6 changes the address format. It works like adding a country code to telephone numbers. If you think that you have to discover a new way to access the Internet because of IPv6, relax. The IPv6 task force mandates that IPv4 and IPv6 addresses must coexist.

IPv6 has its own Web site at `www.ipv6.org`.

Every IPv6 address is 128 bits long, or four times longer than an IPv4 address. More than four times as many IPv6 addresses are available, however (an enormously *huge* number of IPv6 addresses are available) because we're talking about exponential growth! The number is so big that we broke three calculators trying to work it out. It's more than 340,000,000,000,000,000,000,00 0,000,000,000,000 addresses.

An IPv6 128-bit address consists of 8 groups of 16-bit numbers, separated by colons. Each number is written as 4 hexadecimal (hex) digits. So, IPv6 addresses range from

```
0000:0000:0000:0000:0000:0000:0000:0000
```

to

```
FFFF:FFFF:FFFF:FFFF:FFFF:FFFF:FFFF:FFFF
```

Here's a sample IPv6 address:

```
EFDC:BA62:7654:3201:EFDC:BA72:7654:3210
```

(Hey, these are even more agonizing than IPv4 addresses.) Aren't you glad that fully qualified domain names are still valid?

The next few sections get extremely mathematical, and you can use an IP calculator, freely available on the Internet, to perform the calculations. We show your inquiring minds "the hard way" to perform IPv6 calculations.

Don't these long addresses clog network traffic? The format of the packets is so improved that even though the IPv6 long addresses use more of the network's capabilities, the new packet format offsets any performance penalty of the longer address fields. The streamlined packet headers make the e-mail store-and-forward process faster (see Chapter 13).

Why use hexadecimal?

Hexadecimal is quite compact inside a computer, which saves memory and disk space. Writing large numbers in hex is also easier than in decimal.

Most operating systems have a calculator tool that can convert between decimal and hexadecimal.

There's good news and there's bad news

The good news is that if you're what the computer industry calls an end user, you don't need to worry about hexadecimal, decimal, or any other numbers. You still send e-mail to Candace by typing her address, `cleiden@ bigfoot.com`.

The bad news is that if you're a system manager or network administrator, you may have to type these awkward IPv6 addresses into files to set up the network for the lucky end users.

Take advantage of IPv6 address shortcuts

We know that it seems like a lot of work to read and write these long IPv6 addresses. Thank goodness IPv6 has some shortcuts to make them easier to handle.

The leading zero (0000) shortcut

When you write an IPv6 address, you can omit any leading zeros (and there may be lots of them) in each group of four hex digits. If all four digits are zero, you need to write just one. For example, you can write the line

```
1060:0000:0000:0000:0006:0600:200C:326B
```

as

```
1060:0:0:0:6:600:200C:326B
```

The double-colon (::) shortcut

In an address, you can replace one sequence of single zeros and colons with a double colon, which is quite a shortcut. You can use it only once in an address, though. For example, you can write

```
1060:0:0:0:6:600:200C:326B
```

as

```
1060::6:600:200C:326B
```

To expand a double-colon address again, you have to figure out how many colons, and which ones, are missing. You may want to draw an address template with asterisks (*) rather than hex digits and with all seven colons in place, like this:

```
****:****:****:****:****:****:****:****
```

Then look at the address you need to expand and find the double colon, : : — everything to the left of it must start at the beginning of the address. Line up any colons you can. Everything to the right of the : : must end at the end of the address. Again, line up any colons you can. Insert spaces or leading zeros to help. Now you can tell which colons are missing and how many.

For example, to expand `1060::6:600:200C:326B` again, the `1060` (in front of the `::`) must start at the beginning of the address, and the `6:600:200C:326B` (behind the `::`) must be placed at the end, like this:

```
****:****:****:****:****:****:****:****
1060:    :    :    :   6: 600:200C:326B
```

Now you can tell that `0:0:0` is missing. Don't worry about the leading zeros before the `6` and `600`. They're optional.

Be careful. Sometimes, the double-colon appears at the start or end of the address — as in `::8267:2805` or `FEC0:1:A0::`.

The IPv4 coexistence shortcut

IPv4 addresses are a subset of the IPv6 address space. You can convert an IPv4 address into an IPv6 address by inserting zeros at the beginning and converting the decimal digits to hexadecimal. All of IPv4 fits in

```
0000:0000:0000:0000:0000:0000:****:****
```

which can also be written as

```
::****:****
```

For example, the IPv4 address `130.103.40.5` is also the IPv6 address

```
0000:0000:0000:0000:0000:0000:8267:2805
```

or

```
::8267:2805
```

In the hybrid notation *IPv4 mapped addresses,* you can still use dotted decimal notation. It looks like this:

```
0000:0000:0000:0000:0000:0000:0000:130.103.40.5
```

or this:

```
::130.103.40.5
```

Thanks to mapped addresses, you can reduce the risk of typos caused by broken calculators.

Special IPv6 Addresses

IPv6 reserves certain addresses for special purposes. These special addresses include

- **Unspecified address:** The *unspecified address* is $0:0:0:0:0:0:0:0$ (or just $::$). It can be used by a system that needs to send a packet for broadcasting or DHCP client requests but hasn't yet received an address. An unspecified cannot be used as a destination address.

- **Loopback address:** The *loopback address* is $0:0:0:0:0:0:0:1$ (or just $::1$). It lets a system send a message to itself for testing.

- **Site-local addresses:** *Site-local addresses* begin with $FEC0:$ — they're designed for use within an organization's intranet and cannot be routed on the Internet.

- **Link-local addresses:** *Link-local addresses* begin with $FE80:$ — they're designed for use on a single network segment and aren't forwarded by any router. Link-local addresses permit communication with only those neighboring systems directly connected to the same part of the network (link). They allow a system to learn about its neighbors and their services without involving a router. (If you're feeling brave, read all about routers in Chapters 7 and 8.)

  This address type saves time and has a side security benefit: A system can automatically generate an IPv6 address for itself from the link-local address prefix ($FE80$), the double-colon shortcut ($::$), and the 48-bit hardware address from its network interface card (NIC). Every NIC comes with a unique, hard-coded hardware address — the Media Access Control (MAC) address — built in to it. For example, your link-local address may be $FE80::0800:2BBE:1124$. You can find out more about NICs in Chapter 2.

IPv6 — and the Using Is Easy

Suppose you receive a new computer that you need to connect to your office intranet. How does your computer get an IP address? In the IPv4 environment, with a static IP address, you have to contact your network administrator. He configures your laptop with an IP address and updates the appropriate network management files (see Chapter 6). In two or three days (assuming the network administrator isn't on holiday or swamped with requests), your IP address is ready, and you can sign on to the network and start working. If your site uses DHCP (see Chapters 4, 5, and 6), you may be able to connect your laptop to the branch office intranet and request an address from the DHCP server.

IPv6, which can automatically connect your host to a network, automatically builds your IP address. You don't even need DHCP — it's magic! (Those first two sentences are the most important ones in this chapter. If you aren't in the mood for technical, behind-the-scenes, head-breaking information, stop reading here.)

Your computer automatically gets an IPv6 address by using autodiscovery, autoconfiguration, and autoregistration. Together, they provide easier management of a dynamic network with no manual intervention. The following sections are technical in nature and more than a little boring, but we spent a lot of time on them, so humor us — give them a try.

Checking out the network with autodiscovery

Autodiscovery, or *neighbor discovery*, uses the link-local addresses and the new Neighbor Discovery Protocol (NDP) to find out about the network and its nearby systems. Available only in IPv6, NDP uses ICMPv6 (Internet Control Message Protocol version 6 — see Chapter 2) informational messages. The routers on the network segments use Router Advertisement (RA) multicast packets to

- ✔ **Advertise the routers' existence:** It says, "I'm here. Send data through me."

- ✔ **Announce the *on-link prefix* (the "network part" of an IPv6 address):** It says "Here's my network."

- ✔ **Signal whether systems should perform stateless or stateful configuration:** "Here's how to create my address."

Other nodes hear these advertisements and can generate their own addresses *(stateless)* or request an address from a DHCPv6 server *(stateful)*. (See the autoconfiguration discussion in the later section "Automatically assigning addresses.")

So how does your computer exchange address information with other computers on the network? We're so glad you asked — although you may regret it. The following process isn't just for computers but also for routers and every other network-attached device.

Whenever your node creates an IPv6 address for itself, it transmits a Neighbor Solicitation (NS) query to that address and waits for a response. If your node doesn't receive a response, the address is available. If another system responds with a Neighbor Advertisement (NA), the address is already in use. Try again. Your system caches the address for that neighbor in case it needs to use it later.

Your node listens to all the NA confirmations and all the data communication traffic on the network to discover which neighbors are still alive and which addresses they're using.

In the absence of NA confirmations and data traffic, your node periodically sends out an NS query. An NA response is a "Yes, I'm here" confirmation that includes the hardware address. If there's no response, your neighbor is unreachable. Address information can be deleted when it expires this way. You can call this process *autoforgetfulness* — it's an important piece because it supports system renumbering.

The process involving NS, NA, and Duplicate Address Detection (DAD) replaces the Address Resolution Protocol (ARP). Take a look at Chapters 2, 4, and 8 to find out about ARP.

Ensuring that your address is unique

IPv6 supports two different autoconfiguration techniques:

- **Stateless autoconfiguration** allows systems to generate their own IPv6 addresses and also checks for address duplication. In stateless configuration, your node automatically builds an IPv6 address; you don't have to do anything.

  Stateless configuration builds your IP address by appending the hardware address to the on-link prefix. Of course, the configuration must now use DAD to ensure that the address is okay to use. Figure 9-1 shows how a node (also known as your computer) uses DAD.

- **Stateful autoconfiguration** uses DHCPv6, an upgrade to the current DHCP protocol. In stateful configuration, your computer *requests* an IPv6 address from a neighboring DHCPv6 server.

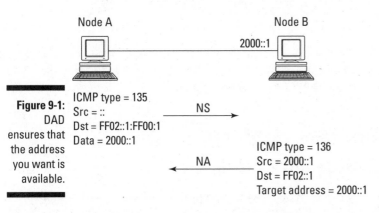

Figure 9-1:
DAD ensures that the address you want is available.

Node A

Node B

2000::1

ICMP type = 135
Src = ::
Dst = FF02::1:FF00:1
Data = 2000::1

NS

ICMP type = 136
Src = 2000::1
Dst = FF02::1
Target address = 2000::1

NA

TECHNICAL STUFF

What about subnet and supernet masks?

IPv6 addresses still consist of a network part and a host part, but it's much harder to say where the division between the two parts comes. Subnet masks, which we discuss thoroughly in Chapter 5, have mostly disappeared in IPv6. You don't need subnet masks because the IPv6 address space is so large. The systems know what to do, and that's what matters. Don't worry about it. Supernet masks are obsolete under IPv6. We're absolutely positive that it will be years before anyone will need to link multiple chunks of IPv6 address space. (At least we hope so.)

In both stateless and stateful configurations, your address has a lifetime.

The steps involved in DAD illustrate one way that NS and NA messages are used. After node A receives an IPv6 address, it performs DAD to find out whether another node is already using that address. NS and NA messages put DAD into action. Figure 9-1 lays out these steps:

1. Node A sends an NS message whose source address is the unassigned address :: d. The destination address is the IP address that node A wants to have. The NS message contains the requested IPv6 address.

2. If node B is using the requested address, node B returns an NA message. The NA message contains node B's IPv6 address.

3. The NA message tells node A that node B is already using the requested IPv6. If node B isn't using the IPv6 address, node A is welcome to it.

Automatically assigning addresses

Autoconfiguration is an IP address "plug-and-play" technique. It automatically assigns an IPv6 address to your NIC. As we describe in the earlier section "Checking out the network with autodiscovery," the Router Advertisement (RA) packets contain the on-link prefix and indicate whether systems should perform stateless or stateful configuration.

Realizing that autoregistration says "Let us serve you"

If your computer is just acting as a client of the services on your organization's network, it should be completely satisfied by autodiscovery and autoconfiguration. But now you need to know how the servers — the computers responsible for the services on the network — ensure that the clients can find them.

The answer is *autoregistration*. It automatically adds or updates a computer's hostname and address information in DNS. A server receives an address from autoconfiguration, just as a client does. Autoregistration makes the new IPv6 address available to the clients whenever they need it (so maybe you won't have typos and broken calculators, after all). Even now, we can hear the contented sighs of network managers everywhere. Too bad they have to wait for more IPv6 deployment.

IPv6 Installation

On new computers, IPv6 usually is installed by default. For example, because Windows Vista, Windows 7, and Windows Server 2008 have a dual IP architecture, they support both IPv4 and IPv6. Computers running these operating systems come from the factory with IPv6 already installed and enabled. You cannot uninstall IPv6, but you can disable it if you want only IPv4.

Mac OS X users are in luck, too: IPv6 comes preinstalled. All those new Macs connected to the Internet contribute to the growing number of IPv6 installations. Newer releases of Unix and Linux, such as Ubuntu Linux, come with a dual stack.

If you're running Windows XP Service Pack 2 (SP2), Windows Server 2003, or a Unix, or Linux, read on to find out more about installing IPv6.

Configuring IPv6 on Windows XP and Windows Server 2003

If you want to run IPv6 on Windows XP SP2 (Service Pack 2) or Windows Server 2003, you need to install the protocol. Follow these steps to install the IPv6 protocol:

1. **Make sure you're running from a privileged account.**

2. **Choose Start⇨Control Panel. Then double-click Network Connections.**

3. **Right-click any local-area connection and click Properties.**

4. **Click Install.**

5. **In the Select Network Component Type dialog box, select Protocol. Then click Add.**

6. **In the Select Network Protocol dialog box, select Microsoft TCP/IP version 6 and then click OK.**

7. **Click Close to save the change you just made.**

If you aren't sure whether IPv6 is already installed, type **ipv6 if** at the command prompt, as shown in Figure 9-2.

When you're using Microsoft's IPv6, the familiar network commands add the number 6 at the end of the command name. For example, the ping command, which checks to see whether a computer is reachable, becomes ping6 in IPv6. Figure 9-3 shows sample output from using the ping6 command. Notice the long IPv6 address.

You can ping either an IP address or a host name.

```
C:\>ipv6 if
Interface 6: Ethernet: Wireless Network Connection ────── You have IPv6
  Guid {685A0B57-6DD7-4514-92A6-1D6DD7FE19CF}
  uses Neighbor Discovery ┐
  uses Router Discovery   ┘────────── Autodiscovery here
  link-layer address: 00-1f-3c-1b-7f-05
       preferred link-local fe80::21f:3cff:fe1b:7f05, life infinite
       multicast interface-local ff01::1, 1 refs, not reportable
       multicast link-local ff02::1, 1 refs, not reportable
       multicast link-local ff02::1 ff1b:7f05, 1 refs, last reporter
  link MTU 1500 (true link MTU 1500)
  current hop limit 128                     ── Lots of IPv6 addresses
  reachable time 36000ms (base 30000ms)
  retransmission interval 1000ms
  DAD transmits 1 ──────────────── DAD's here
  default site prefix length 48
  routing preference 2
  link-layer address: 0.0.0.0:0
       preferred link-local fe80::ffff:ffff:fffd, life infinite
       multicast interface-local ff01::1, 1 refs, not reportable
       multicast link-local ff02::1, 1 refs, not reportable
  link MTU 1280 (true link MTU 1280)
  current hop limit 128
  reachable time 31500ms (base 30000ms)
  retransmission interval 1000ms
  DAD transmits 0
  default site prefix length 48
```

Figure 9-2:
Checking
the IPv6
installation
and its
parameters.

```
C:\>ping6  fe80::21f:3cff:fe1b:7f05

Pinging fe80::21f:3cff:fe1b:7f05
from fe80::21f:3cff:fe1b:7f05%6 with 32 bytes of data:

Reply from fe80::21f:3cff:fe1b:7f05%6: bytes=32 time<1ms
Reply from fe80::21f:3cff:fe1b:7f05%6: bytes=32 time<1ms
Reply from fe80::21f:3cff:fe1b:7f05%6: bytes=32 time<1ms
Reply from fe80::21f:3cff:fe1b:7f05%6: bytes=32 time<1ms

Ping statistics for fe80::21f:3cff:fe1b:7f05:
       Packets: Sent = 4, Received = 4, Lost = 0 (0% loss),
Approximate round trip times in milli-seconds:
       Minimum = 0ms, Maximum = 0ms, Average = 0ms

C:\>
```

Figure 9-3:
Remember to add the numeral 6 to IPv6 commands in Windows XP.

Non-Windows operating systems don't usually add a 6 to the command name.

Welcoming IPv6 to Mac OS X

Hurray! IPv6 comes pre-installed on Mac OS X. All those new Macs connected to the Internet contribute to the growing number of IPv6 installations.

Getting started with IPv6 in Unix and Linux

In most Linux distributions, IPv6 is active by default, as in Ubuntu, the Linux distribution we use on the *TCP/IP For Dummies* network. Fedora, OpenSUSE, Red Hat Linux 7.1 and later, and most other Linux distributions also support IPv6.

On the Unix side of the street, some distributions that include native IPv6 are AIX 4.3.3, Solaris 8, and all recent BSD distributions (FreeBSD, NetBSD, and OpenBSD).

Just because a Linux or Unix operating system's kernel supports native IPv6 doesn't mean that all applications also support IPv6. If you aren't sure whether an application supports it, read the white paper "Current Status of IPv6 for Networking Applications," by Peter Bieringer, Federico Baraldi, Simone Piunno, Mauro Tortonesi, Emanuele Toselli, and Dario Tumiati. You can find it on the Web at

```
www.deepspace6.net/docs/ipv6_status_page_apps.html
```

If you need to run IPv6 on a Unix or Linux computer, you must be sure that the operating system kernel supports IPv6. For Linux, at the time this book was written, the latest stable kernel is version 2.6.27, and it has IPv6 support. Linux and Unix kernels have had IPv6 support for several years.

To find out the version of your kernel, type the `uname -r` command:

```
# uname -r
```

which yields this version of the ancient kernel:

```
2.4.13
```

In Unix systems, you can find out whether your kernel has IPv6 support by using the `sysconfig -q ipv6` command this way:

```
# sysconfig -q ipv6
```

The command's output lists the IPv6 subsystems that are in the Unix kernel.

If your kernel is set up with IPv6, you see sysconfig messages that start with inet6, such as the following one, which displays an IPv6-format address:

```
inet6 efdc:ba62:7654:3201:efdc:ba72:7654:3210
```

Other Delicious IPv6 Morsels

IPv6 delivers other features, too. Some are continuations of features that work under IPv4, and others are new concepts. We don't go into detail here, but we thought you should hear a little about them.

Security for all

Security services, such as packet authentication, integrity, and confidentiality, are part of the design of IPv6. These capabilities guarantee these packet characteristics:

- ✔ They are from the indicated sender.
- ✔ They haven't been altered in transit.
- ✔ They can't be seen by hackers.

Because security services are built into IPv6, they're available to all the TCP/IP protocols, not just specific ones, such as PPTP, S-HTTP, and SSL. Your organization's network, therefore, can be easily made more secure without add-ons.

Here are a couple of IPv4 security problems that IPv6 solves:

- ✔ **IP spoofing:** Tricks a computer into believing that a message comes from an authorized IP address. IP spoofing can fool a computer into revealing passwords and data to hackers and crackers. Spoofing is also a common form of denial-of-service attacks, in which crackers flood a site with so many requests that genuine users can't access the site.

  The problem: IPv4 doesn't know how to determine whether the packets it receives are from the end node they claim to be from. Malicious users can impersonate genuine nodes. You need to install good firewall software to use on state-of-the-art routers, to guard against IP spoofing. (See Chapters 12, 14, and 20 for an explanation of how firewalls work.)

  The IPv6 solution: The IPv6 packet includes an authentication header that lets you determine that a packet you receive actually comes from the address it claims to come from. The authentication header also ensures that the packets you receive haven't been altered. You don't need any add-on software or hardware to prevent the bad guys from masquerading as good guys.

- ✔ **Sniffers:** Monitor and analyze network traffic. Network managers use sniffer programs to find bottlenecks and problems on networks. Sniffers also cause security holes on networks — and we mean all, not just TCP/IP, networks. Because a sniffer can read the data inside the packet, a cracker can use a sniffer to read data as it moves along the network wires.

  The problem: By itself, IPv4 transmits data, including account names and passwords, mostly in regular text. When crackers "sniff" out accounts and passwords, they can truly do some damage to your computer and network. Most Unix and Linux operating systems have tools so that you can search for sniffers on your network, but these tools can be difficult to use and time consuming. For other operating systems, you need to buy sniffer-detection tools. And it still takes time to use and analyze the data they return. You can also buy certain specialized hardware and software that prevent sniffer attacks.

  The IPv6 solution: End-to-end encryption at the network layer. An IPv6 packet includes a special extension header saying that the *payload* (the data that follows this special header) is encrypted.

IPSec protocols, a component of IPv6, add a level of security and create a secure, TCP/IP-level, point-to-point connection. In fact, IPv6 offers security to applications that now lack built-in security, and adds security to applications that already have minimal security features. You can find IPSec information in Chapter 21.

Faster, better multimedia

IPv6 provides new capabilities for high-quality, streaming, multimedia communications, such as real-time audio and video. Huge opportunities for research and experimentation exist in this area of communication, especially as the Internet continues to grow and evolve.

Support for real-time applications

IPv6 improves the performance of real-time applications, such as live radio and television broadcasts and video conferencing.

The IPv6 term *flow* is a noun that means a set of packets that needs special handling along the way between source and destination. Real-time services, for example, need special handling. A flow of packets has a label that's stored in the packet header. By checking this header, a computer on the network can decide how to forward these special packets without taking the time to look at the rest of the headers for each packet in the flow. The result is that IPv6 strips some of the fat from real-time transmissions. In a videoconference, the picture doesn't seem so jerky, and you don't miss what people are saying.

Improved support for mobile computing

IPv4 has trouble with mobile computers. A mobile computer not only moves around geographically but also attaches to the Internet at different addresses. When Candace teaches a database class in Tokyo and connects to her client's intranet, she needs a different address for her laptop. When Marshall delivers a network presentation in Buenos Aires and connects his notebook to the convention center's intranet, he needs a different address. At the same time, both Candace and Marshall need to be connected to their companies' networks. IPv4 has a hard time keeping up with these changes in location.

IPv6 has many benefits for mobile users. We don't go into detail here, but check out the RFC 3002, titled "Overview of 2000 IAB Wireless Internetworking Workshop," at `www.ietf.org/rfc/rfc3002.txt`. It discusses the advantages of IPv6 support for wireless users and road warriors. The improvements involve some of the topics we discuss in this chapter, such as autoconfiguration, special headers, encapsulation, security, and cast addresses. As you read this chapter, some satellite work in Europe has already become IPv6 based.

Share the Planet — IPv6 and IPv4 Can Coexist

Now that IPv6 is here, do you have to use it? No. Most organizations still use IPv4. Also, IPv6 is built to manage both v4 and v6 addresses. If your server has the latest and greatest IPv6, your client computer with IPv4 doesn't have to change. IPv6 server software is *backward compatible* — it understands both IPv4 and IPv6 dialects. Your server knows what to do.

Don't bother upgrading your client computer to IPv6 until your network administrator upgrades your servers and routers.

A key reason to upgrade your routers is to enable the "autos" (autodiscovery, autoconfiguration, and autoregistration), thereby giving network administrators a well-deserved week at the beach.

Stacking IPv4 and 1v6

The dual stack concept is quite handy. You can configure both IPv4 and IPv6 on the same node. When you dual-stack a node, IPv4 and IPv6 share the same TCP and UDP. Figure 9-4 shows you how the two stacks share the upper layers of the TCP/IP layer cake.

Here are a couple of benefits of dual-stacking both protocols:

- ✔ IPv4 hosts and routers can connect to both IPv4 and IPv6 nodes on the Internet.

- ✔ On a network that is moving from IPv4 to IPv6, but hasn't gotten all the way there, the old IPv4 applications and protocols run along with the new IPv6 applications and protocols.

Figure 9-4: Both IP protocols share protocols at the transport layer.

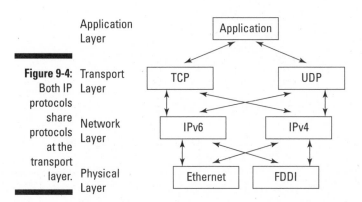

Tunneling IPv6 through IPv4

Tunneling involves carrying IPv6 packets encapsulated (inside) IPv4 so that your IPv6 data can go across the networks that are still using IPv4. So your starting and destination nodes can both be IPv6 even if they have to cross an IPv4 network. When the IPv6 data reaches its destination, the IPv4 encapsulation layer is stripped off.

Whew — You Made It!

If you made it all the way through this chapter without skipping anything, wow, are we ever impressed. If you're interested in more details regarding IPv6 and its advanced features and capabilities, you can find many RFCs, articles, and books, or you can get on the Internet and see what's happening. Oh, by the way, we're not done with IPv6 in this book. As you look in other chapters, you can read how specific protocols and services work in IPv6.

Chapter 10

Serving Up DNS (The Domain Name System)

DNS (the Domain Name System) is a *distributed* system — it's stored in pieces across the network; no single computer holds all the information. The core of DNS is the database that stores information about domain names and addresses. Think of the DNS database as a kind of Internet telephone directory. Instead of looking up a name and finding a telephone number, you look up a computer's name in the DNS database and find its IP address (or look up an IP address and find its name).

The heart of the Internet consists of DNS cooperating with the BGP-4 protocol (see Chapter 8) so that messages travel from source computers to their destinations. DNS lives a triple life, in the form of these three elements:

▸ Protocol

▸ Service

▸ Database

On the Internet, if DNS knows an IP address, the BGP-4 protocol figures out how to get the message there. Without collaboration between DNS and BGP-4, the Internet wouldn't work.

Lots of pieces collaborate for DNS: hardware, software (programs and TCP/IP protocols), data files, and people. Working together, these components provide the ability to take a computer's FQDN (fully qualified domain name) and look up its IP address or take a computer's IP address and look up its FQDN. Remember, people prefer to use names, and computers prefer to use numbers. Luckily for us, TCP/IP has quite a few services, including DNS, that let people use names while computers use numbers.

Chapter 4 simplifies some basic DNS concepts. This chapter gets you into the core workings of DNS. If you're simply interested in what DNS does, but not how it does it, all the information you need is in Chapter 4. Feel free to move on to another chapter.

Taking a Look at the DNS Components

Here's a brief introduction to the DNS components discussed in this chapter:

- ✔ **Distributed database:** Holds information about computers' names and their addresses in domains on the Internet or on your intranet
- ✔ **Domain:** A logical collection of computers whose requests for name/address lookups are handled by the same server or servers
- ✔ **Name server:** A program that implements DNS by accessing information from the database and responding to client queries
- ✔ **Client:** A program that requests name/address lookups from the name servers
- ✔ **Resolver:** Client software that asks name servers to convert Internet host names to their IP addresses and to convert IP addresses to their Internet host names
- ✔ **Cache:** Stores DNS data in memory for quick access
- ✔ **Zone:** A group of computers created by network administrators to make managing them easier
- ✔ **System and network administrator:** Set up everything and maintain the databases

DNS domains are different from — and unrelated to — Microsoft Windows Server domains. Please forget (or at least ignore) everything you know about the Microsoft definition of a *domain* while you read this chapter.

Going Back to DNS Basics

All servers connected to the Internet use DNS to translate FQDNs into IP addresses and vice versa. If you have a small intranet that never accesses the Internet, you could do without DNS and rely on your local hosts file. (See Chapter 4 for a description and an example of a local hosts file.) For each fully qualified domain name, such as `www.example.com`, the DNS database stores the domain name/IP address pair.

The database structure is a hierarchy (an upside-down tree) of FQDNs. Figure 10-1 illustrates the tree starting with the root, which is a dot (.). DNS is organized into an upside down tree with the DNS root domains at the top.

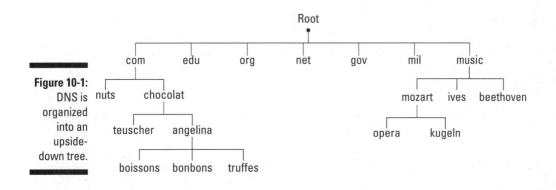

Figure 10-1: DNS is organized into an upside-down tree.

The DNS database is distributed (decentralized) so that hundreds of different organizations share database management. With more than 80,000,000 branches in the `.com` domain alone (and growing every day), a central database would be so large as to be unmanageable.

By default, DNS doesn't think about DHCP and IP addresses leased on request. DNS assumes all IP addresses are stable and do not change. Remember, when DNS was designed, DHCP servers were just a gleam in some pre-teen whiz kid's eye.

Whenever you register a domain, your registrar adds a record to the DNS database.

In techie terms, DNS is the Internet's *name/address resolver*. It translates FQDNs into IP numbers and IP numbers into FQDNs.

Revisiting Client/Server with DNS

A *service* is functionality, such as resolving a name into an address. The *server* is the software that implements the functionality.

DNS runs in a client/server style. Clients such as an e-mail client or a browser pass their FQDN requests to your *resolver* software. The resolver is a client of the server software called a *name server*. The following sections describe how DNS clients and its various servers operate behind the scenes.

Dishing up DNS client/server definitions

Client and server software work together so that DNS can translate an FQDN, such as the fictional `www.angelinachocolat.com`, to its IP address. DNS client and server terminology includes these elements:

- ✔ The *DNS client* software is part of TCP/IP, so it runs on your client machine automatically.

- ✔ The *resolver* is a library of programs that make up the client software. The resolver software asks the *name server* software for IP addresses.

- ✔ The *cache* is memory. When DNS responds to a name/address query, the information gets put into the cache, so that the next time you ask for the name/address resolution, the answer already sits in memory. That makes for much faster access than traipsing all over the Internet to solve the query again.

- ✔ The *name server* program responds to queries from the resolver to translate a name to an address and vice versa. The most common DNS server software is *bind* (Berkeley Internet Name Daemon). *Bind9* is the latest version, with added performance features. BIND is usually included in TCP/IP. In many Unixes and Linuxes, BIND is there, but you might have to build it before it's available for use. The name server program is part of TCP/IP.

Usually name servers are managed by ISPs. No worries for you. If you take a look back at the ipconfig example shown in Figure 5-3, you can see the IP address for the DNS server.

Snacking on resolvers and name servers

You don't need to worry about installing any special resolver software because the resolver is part of TCP/IP. You need it. You have it. No problem. Unless you're a TCP/IP programmer, your resolver is invisible.

If you're a programmer writing an application that needs to know a computer's address, you need to call the resolver routines.

When you run an application, such as e-mail or a Web browser, your DNS resolver looks for the domain name/address translation in your computer's cache. If the IP information is not in cache, your resolver queries its primary *name server* (which is probably at your ISP) for a computer name-to-IP address translation:

✔ If the name server can answer the query, it responds with the requested information and all is well.

✔ If the first name server can't answer the query, it starts a process of forwarding to other name servers until one has the name/address resolution. Figure 10-2 shows how a query may need to go to more than one name server to get the information it requests. The references to SRV1 and SRV2 are not to the computer; the references are to the BIND9 name server programs that the computers are running.

If, for some reason, you don't like BIND9, you can use other name server software, such as NSD (Name Server Daemon) from `www.nlnetlabs.nl/projects/nsd` and PowerDNS from `powerdns.com`.

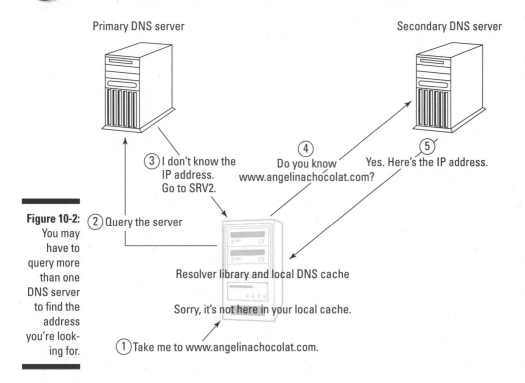

Figure 10-2: You may have to query more than one DNS server to find the address you're looking for.

Primary DNS server

Secondary DNS server

③ I don't know the IP address. Go to SRV2.

④ Do you know www.angelinachocolat.com?

⑤ Yes. Here's the IP address.

② Query the server

Resolver library and local DNS cache

Sorry, it's not here in your local cache.

① Take me to www.angelinachocolat.com.

All DNS queries, except those in its cache, get forwarded to DNS servers (in this case, the primary DNS server and/or secondary DNS server). Even those responses from the cache are not authoritative. (See the later section "Who's Responsible for Name and Address Information?" for more on authority.) Therefore, a heavy dependence still exists on the primary and secondary DNS servers in the network. If a long DNS disruption occurs, the data in the cache eventually expires.

When your client asks the name server for a name/IP address, you're usually asking a name server program at your ISP. Most DNS name serving happens at an ISP. Sometimes very large organizations will choose to run private DNS name servers on their intranets before going out to the ISP.

Who's in charge here?

In DNS, a name server can be in one of three different states when queried by a client:

- ✔ **State 1:** The name server knows the IP address *authoritatively,* meaning it's *responsible* for the data and has the answer in the database on its hard drive. The network administrator maintains a set of the data files that comprise a DNS database.

- ✔ **State 2:** Because the name server knows the address, but not authoritatively, it has stored (cached) the data in memory from a previous query.

- ✔ **State 3:** The name server doesn't know the address and has to ask another DNS server. Refer to Step 2 in Figure 10-2 for an example: The address isn't in the name server's cache (memory), and the name server doesn't know the answer.

Serving a DNS client's needs

If the client's main name server can't supply the information requested, two things may occur, depending on whether the name server is or is not *responsible for* the information (more on this in the next section):

- ✔ If the name server is responsible, it responds with a message that says the information doesn't exist.

- ✔ If the name server isn't responsible for the information, it forwards the query to, or at least toward, the name server that's responsible. (The name server knows to do this based on how the network administrator sets things up.) When the answer comes back, it travels all the way back down the chain to the client.

When the client receives the IP address for `angelinachocolat.com`, it caches the address. If the client needs the address later, the address will be right there in the client's memory. The client won't have to find a name server.

Oops! Can't help you

The chain of DNS servers can't always satisfy the client's request. There are two reasons this can happen:

✔ Your client *times out* — grows tired of waiting for a response — which is the same as receiving a "No Information" answer from the queried name server.

✔ Your client asks for a nonexistent Web site and IP address. If you try to browse `www.angelinachocolat.com`, you see this response on your screen:

```
Sorry, 'www.angelinachocolat.com' does not exist or is not
        available.
```

If, at this point, *you* have timed out, too, hang in there. We clarify this "responsibility" thing next.

Who's Responsible for Name and Address Information?

What does it mean for a server to be "responsible for" name and address information? The DNS term for responsibility is *authority.* Several different types of name servers may be deployed in your environment. In the DNS world, there is no single master server. Instead, various servers know, via the DNS database, the names and addresses of the computers in your organization. These name servers are responsible for this information, and the answers they give to client queries are said to be *authoritative.*

Because the DNS database is *distributed* (that is, stored in pieces across the network), no single computer has all the information you need about all the addresses. Can you imagine the number and size of the disks you'd need to hold the addresses of *all* the computers on the Internet? Not practical, even if it were possible. Therefore multiple name servers work together to translate names to addresses.

When you look at the DNS domain tree, at the very top is a dot (.). That dot is the root of the tree. There are 13 root name servers across the world that hold the master list of DNS records.

The root name servers send a file (the *root zone file*) to other DNS servers and clients on the Internet. The root zone file lists the IP addresses of the authoritative servers for the DNS top-level domains (TLDs), in other words: which servers store authoritative (totally trustworthy) data about the TLDs, such as .com, .org, .net, .nl or .au.

Each organization that operates the root name service is labeled with an ID consisting of a single letter. Table 10-1 lists the operators (administrators).

Table 10-1	Root Name Service Operators
Alphabetical Designation	*Organization*
A	VeriSign Global Registry Services
B	University of Southern California Information Sciences Institute
C	Cogent Communications
D	University of Maryland
E	NASA Ames Research Center
F	Internet Systems Consortium, Inc.
G	U.S. Dept. of Defense Network Information Center
H	U.S. Army Research Lab
I	Autonomica/NORDUnet
J	VeriSign Global Registry Services
K	RIPE NCC
L	ICANN
M	WIDE Project

No there's no mistake in the table: VeriSign operates *two* root name services, A and J. The Root-Servers Technical Operations Association, www.root-servers. org, displays a map of the locations of all the Root Name Service Operators and their IP addresses.

If you're curious, but don't want to browse the Web, you can get a very brief look at the root servers if you have access to a Windows Server 2008. Use the DNS Manager in the Microsoft Management Console to list the servers' IP addresses. Figure 10-3 shows an excerpt of a list of root servers. The display is nowhere near as interesting as the map at www.root-servers.org, but it's a quick-and-dirty look at root servers.

Understanding Servers and Authority

You can have three types of servers in your DNS domain:

- ✔ The primary name server
- ✔ The secondary name server(s)
- ✔ The caching name server(s)

Before we examine their roles in the scheme of things, be sure you know your authority figures. Read on.

Primary name server: Master of your domain

Primary name servers are the master authorities for their domains. Its database contains a list of registered domain names and a translation between each name and one or more IP addresses. No single name server holds the entire DNS database. Each primary name server maintains just one subset (zone) of the domain tree. A zone is often the same as a domain, but not always. (More on that in the section "Zoning Out: Understanding Domains and Zones," later in this chapter.) The primary name server stores the database for its zone. Also, a primary name server can delegate authority to a secondary name server, to lessen the primary's workload and to give it a backup. (Is this starting to sound like life at the office? To relieve stress, delegate!)

The primary server is the ultimate repository of truth — at least as far as the names and addresses in the domain are concerned. When the primary name server delegates authority, it ships the truth — in the form of the database (or at least part of it) — to the secondary name server. That action is called a *zone transfer*. So a zone can be the entire domain, or just a subsection. The more the primary can delegate, the more stress relief it gets.

For reliability and performance, every domain should have a primary and at least one secondary name server.

Secondary name servers

In school, the little kids in primary school look up to the big kids in secondary school. But on the Internet, it's just the opposite: The big kids are the primary name servers. Secondary name servers download copies of name/address information from a primary or another secondary name server. Secondary name servers relieve primary stress.

The more secondary name servers a large organization has, the less risk it runs of clogging up the primary name server — and the better protected it is from a failure of the primary.

Secondary name servers are the backups for the primaries, and if the primary delegates authority, the secondary can answer address queries from any other name server in its zone.

The big difference between a primary name server and a secondary name server is where each gets its information. The primary gets it from the database files; the secondary gets it from a primary or another secondary name server. In Figure 10-4, a primary server receives database changes and passes them along to a secondary server (SRV2). SRV2 also acts as a primary to SRV3, and passes the database changes down the chain.

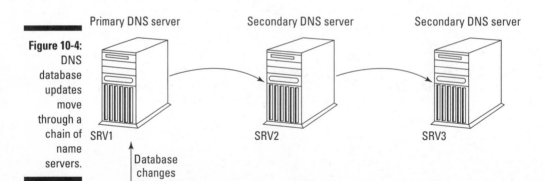

Figure 10-4: DNS database updates move through a chain of name servers.

Suppose you have a chocolate craving and you browse the fictional site, angelinachocolat.com. Your HTTP request needs to ask more than one server for an authoritative response. Figure 10-5 shows the question-and-response sequence that processes your request.

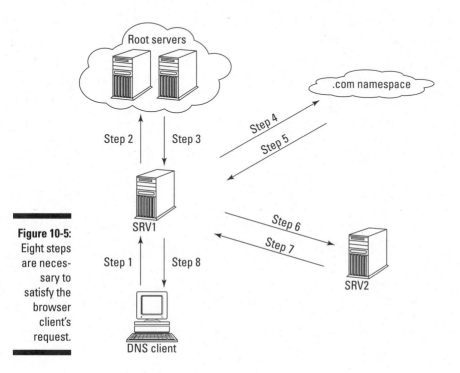

Figure 10-5: Eight steps are necessary to satisfy the browser client's request.

Here's what's happening in Figure 10-5:

1. You want to browse www.angelinachocolat.com, so you go to your main DNS server SRV1. You ask, *What is the IP address?*

2. Your DNS server has no authority (responsibility) for www.angelina chocolat.com, so it asks a root server how to find the IP address.

3. The root server doesn't know the IP address. It tells SRV1 to look in the .com *namespace* (a term for the structure of the DNS database).

4. SRV1 checks the namespace for the name server that knows the IP address for www.angelinachocolat.com.

5. The namespace tells SRV1 where to find the name server that knows the www.angelinachocolat.com IP address authoritatively. Let's call that name server SRV2.

6. SRV1, your main name server, goes back across the network to ask SRV2 for the www.angelinachocolat.com IP address.

7. SRV2 responds to SRV1, "Here's the `www.angelinachocolat.com` IP address." Finally, one last step remains.

8. SRV1 goes back to the client and says, "Here's the IP address you're looking for. Now you can browse for chocolates."

Caching servers

All name servers, including those that are authoritative, are also caching servers. A name server *caches* (keeps in memory) all the name/IP address translations. The reason is simple: Retrieving DNS information from memory is a lot faster than getting the data from disk. Of course, the server updates the cache regularly with new information it receives. Otherwise the memory cache would get out of date and send people to the wrong Web or e-mail sites.

Caching-only name servers are never authoritative. Their purpose is strictly to relieve network performance stress. From a security standpoint, they're not entirely trustworthy because they don't have the "real truth" in the form of database files on disk. They have what they "believe" to be the truth in memory. Caching servers have no authority in a DNS system; they depend on the kindness of other name servers for information. The caching servers query other servers for name-address information and cache (that is, store) it in memory for users who are geographically close.

All servers do caching, especially of data for which they're not responsible. Specialized caching servers do *only* caching; they have no data files and aren't responsible for any information.

If Katherine wants to browse `angelinachocolat.com`, for example, her local caching server looks up `angelinachocolat.com` in DNS and keeps (caches) the information in memory. When Katherine sends another mail message to Angelina, the `angelinachocolat.com` IP address is now quickly available from the caching server, and her request for the name-to-address translation is spared a long trip across the network.

 If `angelinachocolat.com` changes its IP address, Katherine's caching server may still hold the old address information. To avoid this problem, the cached data in a name server expires after a specified period, called the Time To Live, or TTL.

If you get DNS errors trying to access a network site, but you can get to the same site on another computer, your DNS cache is probably out of date, and you should flush and renew your DNS cache.

Each of the Big Three computer operating systems (Microsoft Windows, Linux/Unix, Mac OS X) has a different mechanism for clearing the DNS cache:

✔ **Microsoft Windows** (various editions):

    1. Start a command window. (Choose Start⇨Run⇨command.)

    2. Type the following command:

```
ipconfig /flushdns
```

✔ **Linux**: Restart the ncsd program (name service cache daemon)

    1. Log in as root.

    2. Type the following commands to restart the ncsd:

```
# cd /etc/rc.d/init.d
# ./nscd restart
```

The dot (.) is part of the file name. Don't forget to type it. The # is the command prompt.

✔ **Mac OS X:**

    1. Start a terminal.

    2. Type the following command (the "$" is the command prompt; don't retype the command prompt):

```
$ dscacheutil -flushcache
```

If you're running an older version of Mac OS X (older than Leopard, that is), type this command:

```
$ lookupd -flushcache
```

Understanding Domains and Zones

The concept of domains and zones can get a bit confusing. Domains may be part of zones. Zones may be part of domains. A domain may be its own zone. Here's what these two concepts mean in general terms:

✔ A *domain* is a branch, and everything below that branch of the upside down tree represents the DNS domain namespace. Refer to Figure 10-1. It shows the top-level domains in the DNS namespace tree. For example, chocolat is part of the .com domain — chocolat.com. The imaginary angelina would be part of the chocolat domain — angelina. chocolat.

✔ A *zone* describes how the namespace is divided for management purposes. A zone can include pieces of a domain, or a zone can be an entire domain.

The top-level domains, such as .com and .net, have millions of domains under them. No single organization could possibly manage all that. The namespace gets sliced and diced so that different organizations can manage portions of it. A zone is one of the administrative slices. The `.com` domain just happens to be its own zone. So `.com` is two entities:

- ✔ **A domain with lots of subdomains beneath it:** Remember, the `.com` namespace has more than 80 million domains under it. (What a management nightmare!)

- ✔ **A zone with nothing below it:** And you can bet that those 80 million lower domains are broken into manageable zones!

In Figure 10-6, the `chocolat` *domain* isn't the same as the `chocolat` *zone*. The `teuscher.chocolat.com` domain is managed by some other zone.

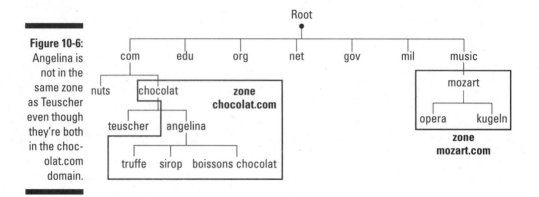

Figure 10-6: Angelina is not in the same zone as Teuscher even though they're both in the chocolat.com domain.

Let DNS and a hosts file share the job

TCP/IP allows you to use a combination of DNS and a hosts file to find remote hosts by putting the most frequently accessed hosts into your hosts file. That way you won't have the performance overhead of accessing a DNS name server on the network to get an address for the hosts you regularly connect to. Let DNS help you find addresses for hosts that you access only occasionally. This is really the best of both worlds: performance and reliability. When a host name must be translated to an IP address, the application looks first at the local hosts file. If the application can't find the translation it needs, then it goes across the network to a DNS server for the translation.

The hosts file is only good for storing stable IP addresses, not the ever-changing addresses given out by DHCP. Even so, "permanent" IP addresses can change. It's your (or your network administrator's) responsibility to keep your hosts file up to date.

If you're not a high-level network administrator, you can forget about zones. You'll never be aware of them. You'll never use them.

The owner of a domain decides whether to break up the domain into zones. If the owner is going to use administrative zones, she decides how to slice up the domain into zones.

Problem Solving with Dynamic DNS (DYNDNS)

As explained in Chapter 4, DHCP allows computers to lease an IP address only when needed and that addresses expire and may be extended or expired. DHCP and DNS have difficulty working together. The DHCP-DNS combination creates the following problem, and DYNDNS solves it:

- ✔ **The DHCP-DNS problem:** Because DNS was developed long before DHCP, DNS is clueless about how to handle DHCP addresses coming and going. The problem is almost obvious: How do you keep DNS servers up to date when you can't count on stable IP addresses?

- ✔ **The DYNDNS solution:** Dynamic DNS lets hosts update their own DNS data in real time. For DYNDNS to work, computers have to let their DNS server know that they (the individual hosts) have updated knowledge of IP addresses.

Most home networking routers have DYNDNS already built in. The major operating systems (Microsoft Windows, Linux/Unix, and Mac OS X) support DYNDNS clients. In Microsoft Windows Servers, Dynamic DNS is part of Active Directory.

Diving into DNSSEC (DNS Security Extensions)

By now, you probably realize that the Domain Name System (DNS) is a core piece of the Internet's functionality. Without DNS' translating FQDNs into IP addresses, most people would give up on the Internet. Remember, people like names. Computers like numbers. How many of us would really *like* to type http://74.125.19.99 rather than google.com? With IPv6 addresses, such as 2001:4860:0:2001::68, finding your favorite Internet sites would be even more daunting.

Because DNS is the key to the Internet's ease of use, DNS security, or a lack thereof, is an issue that RFC 3833 (www.ietf.org/rfc/rfc3833.txt) addresses thoroughly. The RFC describes potential threats to DNS and ways in which DNSSEC addresses these threats.

Why does DNS need DNSSEC?

The DNSSEC Deployment Initiative (www.dnssec-deployment.org) news-letter published in June 2006 brings up a potentially disturbing point about the near future:

> "Some 10 percent of servers in the network today are vulnerable to domain name system (DNS) attacks, and many experts expect a serious attack on the underlying infrastructure within the next decade."

DNS was developed in the early days of the Internet, when Internet users were a friendly, trusting community. As the Internet has grown, not all users are so nice and friendly, and security has become necessary. Because of its importance to the working of the Internet, DNS has become a major target of abuses and attacks. Even if when you type a legitimate Web address, a bad guy can forge a fake address to steal information, including usernames and passwords. The technical term for this fakery is *packet spoofing.* Another hacker gambit is to send you to a phony Web site where files contain viruses, worms, and Trojan horses for you to download innocently.

The reason DNS is so vulnerable is that it uses UDP as its connection medium. Because UDP doesn't verify packet information, such as the source of the packet, DNS is open to packet spoofing and falsifying source addresses. (You can review connection-based and connectionless protocols in Chapter 4.)

DNSSEC is a work in progress, but some of its specifications include these:

✔ **Digital signatures:** that provide:

- *Data integrity:* They certify that the data has not been changed since it left the source.

- *Authentication of the sources of DNS data:* In effect, this is a way to make sure that the data really is coming from where it says it's coming from (no spoofing allowed).

✔ **Authenticated denial of existence:** DNSSEC responds with a special record format if DNS data (for example, an IP address) is not found.

Even so, DNSSEC doesn't solve all security problems. For example, it doesn't help detect these hazards:

✔ Lack of confidentiality: When DNS servers respond to requests, the requests are authenticated *but not encrypted,* so although the responses can't be messed with, they *can* be watched. Oops.

✔ DoS (Denial of Service) attacks.

✔ Snoopers who can see the host names being looked up.

Glimpsing behind the scenes of DNSSEC

DNSSEC means that DNS zones can be digitally signed. DNS then uses the digital signatures to verify that the network data received is *authentic* — that is, the data has not been altered. Server software and resolver software need to be configured with a Trust Anchor. The Trust Anchor sets up "chain of trust" to the signed zone. Data from this signed zone can then be validated.

In Figure 10-7, the part of the DNS tree inside the box is protected by DNSSEC. The child zones have been signed by the parent zones. Parent and children together make up an "island of trust". As is often the case with Internet diagrams, parents and children live in an upside-down tree. The entire island of trust can be validated with only one key. This key and its associated information is a *trust anchor* because it provides a firm footing for the security of all zones within the island.

Windows 7 — DNSSEC client?

Yes and no. It's close, and it may be a matter of semantics, but the Microsoft Windows 7 DNS client does not perform its own DNSSEC validation. Instead, the client relies on its DNS server to perform validation on its behalf. Because of this method, the client doesn't need a trust anchor, which saves some setup time on the client. The server handles the trust anchor for the client. So, at the time this book was written, the Windows 7 client were considered *security aware* (along with many other products that don't complete their own DNSSEC validation). Such products expect the DNS server to do all the DNSSEC work, such as returning the validation status of a client's query. By the way, Windows starts the DNS client software automatically.

The Thunderbird mail client is an example of a DNSSEC validation client. Windows Server 2008 R2 supports DNSSEC, as do Linux and Unix, depending on the distribution, Mac OS X, and BIND 9.6 and higher.

As of this writing, DNSSEC is not widely used, so there are small separate islands of trust floating around the Internet. In the future, some of these islands will converge, extending the protection of DNSSEC. Maybe someday, in the far, far future, the entire DNS might become one island of trust. Realistically, we wouldn't bet the farm on it. There are always slowpokes and holdouts on new technology. If there weren't, we'd all be using IPv6 already.

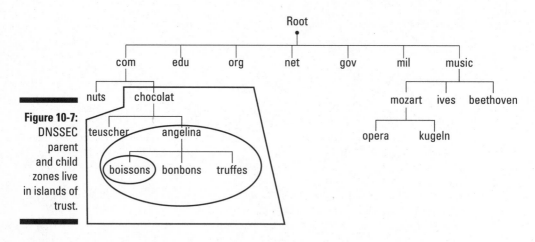

Figure 10-7:
DNSSEC parent and child zones live in islands of trust.

When a non-security-aware resolver generates a query and sends it to a security-aware server for information contained in a secured zone, the security-aware server can respond with either Authenticated or Insecure data.

Part III

Configuring Clients and Servers: Web, E-Mail, and Chat

The 5th Wave   By Rich Tennant

"Hello?! Hello, Phillip?! You're breaking up! Listen, put a penny on the tone arm and turn the speed up to 45 RPM!"

In this part . . .

Part III goes from client to server: Web clients and servers, e-mail clients and servers, chat clients and servers, and, finally, Usenet news clients and servers. In most of these cases, both the clients and servers are part of the TCP/IP stack, but a couple of exceptions exist — e-mail clients and chat clients and servers. E-mail clients are vendor proprietary or open source clients. They aren't TCP/IP applications. However, as you see in detail in Chapter 13, e-mail clients use TCP/IP to communicate with e-mail servers. Many chat clients use TCP/IP protocols and, therefore, qualify as TCP/IP applications, but an extensive selection of proprietary clients exists as well.

In addition to describing the protocols that underlie Web browsing, e-mail, and chat, we show you how to set up the most popular Web server software, the Apache HTTP server, and how to make Web browsing safe from cyberdelinquents.

Much of Part III is about security. We walk you through an online shopping transaction so that you can see how the secure protocols SSL and TLS work behind the scenes of a Web server to keep your credit card and other private information protected.

We devote an entire chapter, Chapter 14, to e-mail security on both the client side and the server side. Chapter 12 talks about minimum security — not prison related, but rather the necessary amount of security concepts and terminology to get you through the rest of the book until you read Chapters 20 and 21, where you can delve into advanced security topics if you want to go further.

Chapter 11

Digesting Web Clients and Servers

- -

In This Chapter

▶ Protocols and Web standards in this chapter: HTTP, HTTPS, HTTP over TLS, TLS, SSL

▶ Understanding the languages of the Web

▶ Going behind the scenes to see how a Web browser works

▶ Subscribing to RSS feeds

▶ Amping up your browser's performance

▶ Configuring proxy servers and clients

▶ Keeping Web browsing secure

▶ Setting up a Web server with Apache

▶ Using digital certificates

- -

A common misconception among newcomers is that the Web and the Internet are two different things. The *World Wide Web* (or *Web* or *WWW* or *W3*) is the worldwide hypermedia information service on the Internet. Its definition may sound complex, but it's simply saying that the Web is the graphical interface to the Internet, compliments of the protocols HTTP and HTTPS. This chapter is about both Web standards for Web languages and services as well as TCP/IP standards for protocols and services that underlie the Web.

On the client side, this chapter focuses on how Web browsing works. On the server side, this chapter describes how a Web server works with the client and tells you which steps to follow to set up a Web server.

Like most of the applications and services we talk about in this book, Internet information services are client/server environments. You use a client application, usually a browser, to connect to a Web server.

Standardizing Web Services

Although the Web is part of the Internet and follows TCP/IP standards, the World Wide Web Consortium (W3C) sets standards related to Web services. Some of the practical services the W3C provides include

✔ Sample applications that demonstrate upcoming Web technology

✔ A library of information about the Web and its specifications, which is useful for both application developers and users

Many members of the W3C also belong to Internet Engineering Task Force (IETF) working groups. W3C research and proposals can be put on the IETF track to become standards. For example, the W3C and the IETF work together on the HTTP protocol and the IETF HTML (Web language) working group originally supervised the development of HTML. The working group closed in September 1996 and passed to the W3C the task of defining a standard.

The W3C Technical Reports and Publications Web site, at `www.w3.org/TR`, is much like the RFC-Editor, described in Chapter 1.

Deciphering the Languages of the Web

Web authoring languages, or *Web languages*, tell Web browsers how to display Web pages. Web languages are markup languages. A markup language includes the text to display and text formatting instructions. HTML calls the formatting instructions *tags*. For example, this line of HTML consists of text and tags:

```
<b>This text should be bold.</b>
```

The tags say where the text should start to show bold and where the bolding should end. In case you haven't guessed, the tags are <b> to start bold text and </b> to end bold text.

In the sections that follow, we discuss different types of Web languages.

HTML

HyperText Markup Language (HTML) is the first Web language, the parent of all the others. HTML has portability challenges. Some HTML tags apply to only one or two browsers and not to others. Using these tags means that your pages look different in different browsers. A Web developer has several options:

✔ Don't use those tags.

✔ Use the tags but display a message that the page is meant for a particular browser.

✔ Write different browser versions of the same page.

✔ Try to use XHTML.

In case you're curious about the code that makes up Web pages, most Web browsers give you a way to view the HTML source code for a Web page. To see the code from the Apple Safari browser or Microsoft Internet Explorer, choose View➪View Source from any Web page. If you're using Mozilla Firefox or Google Chrome, simply press Ctrl+U.

The following fragment of HTML code is the beginning of the code that defines the simple Web page shown in Figure 11-1, `http://mysite.verizon.net/vze10yilm/`:

```
<html>
<head>
<meta http-equiv="Content-Type" content="text/html; charset=iso-8859-1">

<title>Welcome to ComputerCatz</title>

<!.......... edited to save space ........


<!--base href="http://mysite.verizon.net/vze10yilm/"-->

<!.......... edited to save space ........


<body leftmargin=»0» topmargin=»0» marginwidth=»0» marginheight=»0»
              bgcolor=»White»
background="/imagelib/sitebuilder/layout/t_gry_back.gif" link="black"
              alink="red" vlink="purple">
```

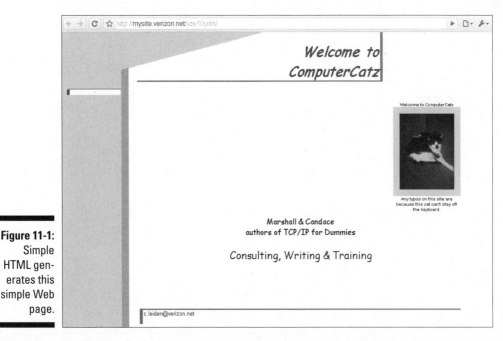

Figure 11-1:
Simple
HTML gen-
erates this
simple Web
page.

XML, HTML — what's the difference?

First, there was HTML. Most elements on a Web page are *hard coded,* which means that most of them are preset in HTML. Although your browser displays pages as best it can, if the Web page creator's intent isn't clear, the browser tries to "guess" at it. If it guesses wrong, it displays an error message.

And then came XML, and browsers began to work harder at processing Web pages. Here are some advantages (and trade-offs) of using XML to create Web pages:

✔ The browser can render elements on the page on the fly (ad lib), which adds flexibility.

✔ The browser does its on-the-fly work at the client. Moving the workload to the client reduces demands on the server. The trade-off for easing up on the server is that some clients have difficulty processing fancier pages.

✔ The same content can look completely different, based on use. For example, an entertaining but complex display can have a simpler format for printing.

HTML is a simpler, less flexible way to publish data quickly on the Web. It's especially useful for simple data, such as meeting agendas and advertising brochures. If the data needs more structure and flash and will remain on the Web for a long time (more than a month), XML is a better choice for Web page creation.

Unless you know HTML, you can't decipher all the tags, but if you glance briefly at the code, you can see that the title of the home page is Welcome to ComputerCatz. If you look toward the end of the code, you can see how the background is constructed. The background color is white. We used a site builder tool (an automatic HTML generator) to automate the creation of our Web page, so the layout of the page x comes from the site builder's image library background named `t_gty_back.gif`. The *image library background* sets the color scheme and style for the Web pages in the site.

You can write your own HTML to build a custom scheme for your Web site, but the tool we used let us build a home page in fewer than 5 minutes, and we didn't have to write any HTML ourselves.

HTML 4

HTML 4, also called *dynamic HTML,* lets you build flashy Web pages with animations and lots more interactive moves. For example, moving the mouse over a graphic makes the graphic speak or play music or change color or any combination.

XML

Extensible Markup Language (XML) builds on HTML so that you have to mark up data only once, no matter how many browsers or other applications — such as print, electronic books (e-books), and mobile documents — might read the data.

XHTML

The Extensible HyperText Markup Language, or XHTML, is supposed to be the best of all possible authoring worlds: HTML and XML. XHTML is still considered a work in progress, so a standard for XHTML is still a long way off. As of June 2009, the W3C categorizes XHTML as a Proposed Edited Recommendation, which means that the W3C doesn't endorse the language as a standard. Although XHTML is envisioned to combine the best of HTML and XML, the W3C can declare its recommendation obsolete or replace it at any time.

HTML + MIME = MHTML

Multipurpose Internet Mail Extensions HTML (MHTML) *has* to be the biggest mouthful in this book. The name refers to how you save and e-mail a Web page in the .MHT file type. If you have ever saved a Web page — and tried to e-mail it — you know that it can be way too much work if the Web page has lots of style. When you choose File⇨Save As in your browser, the HTML code is stored in a file and each graphic and link are stored in a separate file. Then you have to collect all these files and mail them. If you forget even one file, your mail recipient cannot display the complete Web page. MHTML allows you to consolidate into one file the HTML code, graphics, and links on a Web page.

Java and other Web dialects

Besides the *ML languages, different corporations have created programming and scripting languages of their own. Although these languages, described in the following list, aren't considered standard (except for one), they're commonly used on the Web pages you browse:

- ✔ **ActiveX:** Developed by Microsoft specifically for Internet Explorer running on Windows, ActiveX is the Microsoft response to the popularity of Java. *ActiveX controls* (similar to programming plug-ins) run in a Windows ActiveX and Internet Explorer environment. Microsoft has also developed a native Macintosh ActiveX for Macs. Because ActiveX is intended specifically for Internet Explorer, Web pages that use ActiveX controls might not load properly in other browsers.

  Historically, ActiveX has had problems with security, so be careful if you download ActiveX controls.

- ✔ **Java:** Created by Sun Microsystems as a portable Internet programming language, Java has been adopted by most of the major corporations as a major Web programming language. Java is popular because *Java applets* (small computer programs) can run on any operating system in almost any browser. Microsoft hasn't been a fan of Java because it has its own version of a Web programming language (see the preceding bullet). Oracle Corporation recently bought Sun Microsoft, so the future of Java as free and portable is now unknown.

- ✔ **JavaScript:** Developed by Netscape, JavaScript is a scripting (miniature programming) language for HTML pages. Web browsers know how to interpret JavaScript scripts.

Hypertext and hypermedia

Hypertext is text that contains in-line pointers to other text in a file. A common example of hypertext is a Web page, where you click a highlighted object to see more information related to the topic you clicked. The linked, multipage information you click in is the hypertext.

Hypermedia extends the hypertext concept beyond just text and into multimedia. In hypermedia applications, a pointer can take you to a sound bite, graphical image, video clip, or other nontext object. You can see links to both hypertext and hypermedia in Figure 11-2.

There's much more to life on the Internet than just text! You can check out what's happening in space, take courses, listen to foreign language radio stations, and even climb Mount Kilimanjaro — all thanks to hypermedia.

Links to hypertext and hypermedia

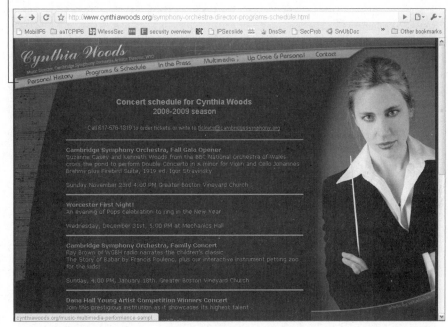

Figure 11-2:
This con-
ductor's
Web page
contains
links to
hypertext
and hyper-
media.

Understanding How Web Browsing Works

Web browsers are the graphical interface to the Web. They communicate with Web server software by way of these protocols:

- ✔ HyperText Transfer Protocol (HTTP)
- ✔ HTTP over SSL/TLS (HTTPS)
- ✔ Secure HTTP (S-HTTP)

Serving up a Web page

A *Web browser* is an HTTP client that sends requests to Web server software. When you type a *Uniform Resource Locator,* or *URL,* or click a hypertext link, your browser creates an HTTP request and sends it to the IP address repre-sented by the URL. Figure 11-2 shows the URL `http://www.cynthia woods.org/music-multimedia-performance-samples.html`.

Browsers aren't just for WWW

Your browser can take you to a non-HTTP resource, such as an FTP or LDAP application. The following two URL examples point to an anonymous File Transfer Protocol (FTP) site and a Lightweight Directory Access Protocol (LDAP) server:

```
ftp://ftp.microsoft.com
ldap://ldap.bigfoot.com
```

The browser follows these steps to send you the Web page you request:

1. Your browser separates the URL into these elements:

   - http — the protocol

   - www.cynthiawoods.org — the name of the Web server storing the page you asked for

   - /music-multimedia-performance-samples.html — the file-name of the Web page (Good thing long filenames are allowed, eh?)

2. Your browser asks a DNS server to translate the name www.cynthia woods.org into an IP address.

   If you're on a small intranet and your Web server is local, the browser may find the name-address translation in your local hosts file. We explain DNS and host files in Chapters 4 and 10.

3. Using HTTP, your browser connects to the Web server's IP address through port 80 and sends a GET request for the file that holds the Web page.

4. Your browser checks your hard drive for cookie files containing information about you. If the browser finds any cookies for this site, it sends them to the server. Maybe you've browsed the site already. If your browser finds a cookie, it can welcome you back by name. (See the next section for more on cookies.)

5. The server sends to the browser the Web page's source code, written in a special language (HTML) and again using the HTTP protocol.

6. Your browser reads the HTML instructions *(tags)* and text and then displays the page.

Although we begin URLs in this book with the letters www (as in www.home page.mac.com), it isn't always necessary — you can simply enter the domain (homepage.mac.com) in your browser's address window and it works. It isn't magic: It happens because a network or system administrator set up the browser to assume that the URL begins with www.

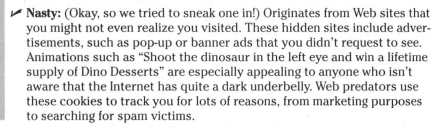

> ## The colors of HTML — names or numbers?
>
> The HTML for Figure 11-1, listed earlier in this chapter, spells out color names, including gray. You can also choose to use numeric symbols for colors, as shown in this excerpt from the HTML in Figure 11-2:
>
> ```
> <p align="center">
> <font color="#666666" style="font-size: 6.5pt" face="Verdana"><br>
>  Content
> Copyright © 2008 CynthiaWoods.org.
>  <font color="#666666">Design and layout Copyright © 2008 <a target="_
>     blank" href="http://www.vstudios.us/">
> ```
>
> The symbol for dark gray is #666666. The HTML that creates the page shown in Figure 11-1 spells out the word *gray.* Use either names or numbers. It's the coder's choice, although numeric color symbols give you a wider range of colors to choose from.

Storing user information as cookies

Cookies are small files that Web sites use to keep track of visitors. A Web server may store one or more cookies on your local hard disk. For example, a Web page might ask for your postal code. The server stores the postal code and a unique ID number within a cookie file on your own computer. The next time you visit the Web site, the server knows where you live and the browser displays your local weather automatically. This list describes the two types of browser cookies:

- ✔ **Temporary or session:** Deleted whenever you exit your browser. Web servers also use temporary cookies to keep track of short-term information, such as items in your shopping cart.

- ✔ **Persistent:** Remains on your computer after you exit your browser. Web servers store information, such as your username and password, so that you don't have to sign in every time you browse a particular site.

- ✔ **Nasty:** (Okay, so we tried to sneak one in!) Originates from Web sites that you might not even realize you visited. These hidden sites include advertisements, such as pop-up or banner ads that you didn't request to see. Animations such as "Shoot the dinosaur in the left eye and win a lifetime supply of Dino Desserts" are especially appealing to anyone who isn't aware that the Internet has quite a dark underbelly. Web predators use these cookies to track you for lots of reasons, from marketing purposes to searching for spam victims.

Managing cookies with your browser

All major browsers let you manage cookies, at least to block them or accept them. Some browsers have gone beyond simple cookie management and given you extra flexibility in how you handle cookies.

If you use more than one browser, you need to learn how to deal with cookies on each one. The good news is that the principles of managing cookies are the same, no matter which browser you use. The bad news is that each browser has a different way for you to point and click your way to the cookies. When you reach the cookie management page in a browser, remember that different browsers have different degrees of cookie control.

The Microsoft browser, Internet Explorer in its many versions, lets you manage cookies. Internet Explorer 8 gives you even more options for managing cookies. IE8 lets you specify which cookies to allow a Web server to store on your computer.

To change your privacy settings for cookies, follow these steps:

1. **Choose Tools⇨Internet Options⇨Privacy.**

2. **Move the slider to your preferred level of cookie privacy.**

   Your choices range from blocking all cookies to accepting all cookies with four levels between these extremes.

Some Web sites don't work if you're too restrictive about blocking cookies.

Microsoft Internet Explorer (IE) privacy settings let you set cookie privacy in general and also for particular Web sites. For example, if you want to block all cookies except from one Web site, you block all cookies using the preceding general steps. Then you customize those general cookie settings for the specific Web sites where you accept cookies.

Using Microsoft IE8, you customize cookie settings for an individual Web site by following these steps:

1. **Choose Tools⇨Internet Options and then, on the Privacy tab of the Internet Options dialog box, click the Sites button.**

   Figure 11-3 displays a list of blocked sites on our computer.

2. **Type the complete URL of the Web site where you want to customize settings.**

3. **If you want IE8 to allow a server to store cookies from the specified Web site on your computer, click Allow. If you want IE8 to block a server from storing cookies on your computer, click Block.**

4. **Click OK.**

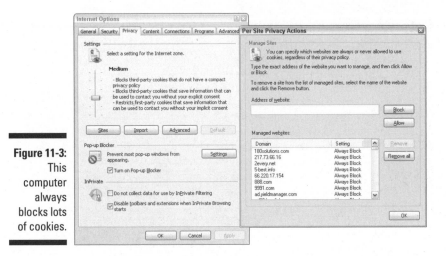

Figure 11-3:
This
computer
always
blocks lots
of cookies.

You manage cookies on most browsers by following the same principles as you use in IE. The menu choices and tabs you click vary from browser to browser.

For example, on the Safari browser (from Apple Computer), follow these steps:

1. **Choose Edit➪Preferences➪Security.**

2. **In the Accept Cookies section, choose how you want Safari to handle cookies. Click Help to see the available options.**

When you select the Show Cookies option, Safari shows you complete cookie information (see Figure 11-4):

- ✔ The name of the Web site that stored the cookie

- ✔ The name of the cookie

- ✔ The location on your computer where the Web server stored the cookie

- ✔ The cookie's security status (cookies marked Secure are sent over an encrypted connection)

- ✔ The expiration date (when the cookie will be deleted)

- ✔ The content (normally a string of code)

Some cookies never expire.

As in most browsers, if you set Safari to block cookies, you might need to accept cookies temporarily to view a Web site. Repeat the cookie management steps (refer to Figure 11-4), but in Step 2 select Always instead. When you're done with the page, turn off cookies again and manually delete the page's cookies.

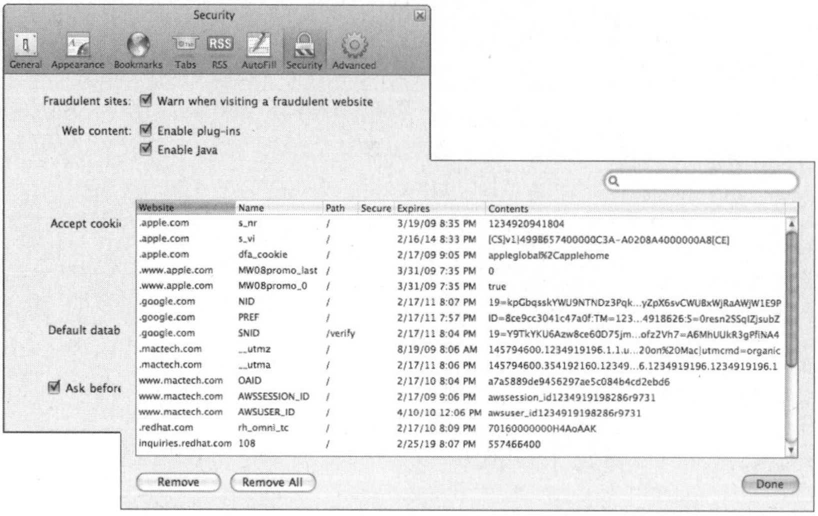

Figure 11-4:
Too many
cookies can
give you
an upset
stomach.

To delete cookies manually, follow these steps:

1. **Choose Edit⇨Preferences⇨Security⇨Show Cookies.**

2. **Select one or more cookies and click Remove, or click Remove All.**

3. **Click Done.**

Dishing up multimedia over the Internet

Most people, even Internet newbies, have probably heard about multimedia on the Web — listening to audio, watching animations and videos, playing 3-D games, and even attending conventions and training seminars. Life online is more enjoyable when you can access more than words and pictures.

The Internet, compliments of TCP/IP protocols, lets you listen to CD-quality music with a click of your mouse. The *MP3* file format shrinks digital audio files (which are usually quite large) while preserving audio quality. You can download MP3 music fairly quickly. One minute of music is about 1 megabyte, so an average song is about 4 megabytes. Using our cable modem, it takes only seconds to download MP3 files. To play a song, you need an MP3 player, usually bundled with your operating system. If you don't have or don't like your built-in player, try a free one, such as the free WinAmp high-fidelity player (www.winamp.com).

Sound and videos use lots of hard drive and memory space on your computer. You *need* hardware power. Some of the recommendations we see on the Web are ridiculously low. You need a broadband connection and lots of memory (no less than 1 gigabyte) to watch videos.

Multimedia also uses *plug-ins.* Your browser uses this type of software to turn your computer into a radio receiver, television set, or meeting place.

If you browse a Web page that uses a plug-in you don't have, you usually see a message asking whether you want to download it immediately. If you use lots of plug-ins, create a folder to store them in the same place.

The Microsoft Internet Explorer browser uses ActiveX controls rather than plug-ins. The controls perform much the same tasks as plug-ins do.

Table 11-1 lists some popular, free multimedia plug-ins.

Table 11-1	Plugging In with Free Plug-Ins	
Plug-In Name	*What It's Used For*	*Web Site for Download*
Adobe Reader	View and print Adobe Portable Document format (PDF) files.	`www.adobe.com`
Flash Player	Watch vector graphics and animation, including cartoons, interactive seminars, and comedy routines.	`www.adobe.com`
Multimedia apps for Linux	Watch QuickTime movies, listen to music, and lots more.	`www.linux.org/ apps/all/ Multimedia/ Video.html`
RealPlayer	Listen to radio or watch TV from around the world.	`www.real.com`
Shockwave	Enjoy interactive Web content, such as games, presentations, and entertainment.	`www.adobe.com`

Packets stream over the Internet using either the TCP protocol over port 1755 or the HTTP protocol over port 80. TCP provides the highest performance. HTTP works fine but is slightly less efficient than TCP because of the HTTP overhead. Multimedia *streams* because your browser receives the data in a continuous stream from the server so that you don't have to wait to download large multimedia files.

Feeding Web Pages with Atom and RSS

Syndicated Web feeds are an optional way of seeing a Web page. Web sites, such as news sites, often use *syndication pages,* which list recent articles by displaying a line or two of each article's content. The page also includes a link to the complete article. Web sites can have more than one syndicated feed. For example, a newspaper's Web site may have separate feeds for news, sports, finance, and entertainment.

Two syndication protocols are described in this list:

- ✔ **Atom Publishing Protocol, or AtomPub:** Finding a Web page with the Atom icon is difficult because of the wide acceptance of RSS. If you're looking for an Atom feed, look for an icon that's similar to the symbol for an atom. As with RSS, you click the icon to open the syndication page.

- ✔ **Really Simple Syndication, or RSS:** Sites that offer RSS feeds show the RSS *icon*, a small button that looks like an orange box with either white stripes or the letters *XML* (see Figure 11-5.) When you press the orange button, the Web site displays a page where you can sign up for feeds. The *New York Times* page lists almost 30 main categories of feeds, from Home and Garden to Obituaries. Most categories list several subcategories. It's like browsing the magazine section in the solar system's biggest bookstore.

Figure 11-5:
Click an RSS icon to sign up for a feed.

Syndication skirmishes

Atom Publishing Protocol, or AtomPub, is the Internet standard for syndicating Web feeds — you can find five RFCs detailing it. In terms of standards, RSS is built on standards, but there's no RFC for RSS. It's a dialect of XML, which is defined by both an RFC and an official W3C Recommendation. To add to the confusion, RSS dates must conform to the RFC Date and Time Specification. And, another standards group is rearing its head — the RSS Advisory Board (www.rssboard.org). As of this writing, RSS is more widely used than AtomPub.

RSS feeds can be addictive, so don't be greedy. The thing is, who has time to read all of them? Marshall loves the news. As you can see in Figure 11-6, he subscribes to several RSS services. He also has almost 500 unread articles, with more automatically arriving every day.

Figure 11-6:
You can receive these news feeds by way of RSS or AtomPub. Be selective!

Reducing the Web's Wide Waistline to Increase Speed

Even though HTTP is an efficient Internet protocol, some people think that WWW stands for World Wide Wait instead. Web speed ranges from tortoise speed to warp speed. All those fancy graphics you see on Web pages are high fat and take a long time to open.

To speed things up, follow a few tips:

✔ **Be frugal in reading RSS feeds.** Subscribe only to the feeds you know you'll read. Select a High setting for your browser's RSS update frequency. For example, Apple Safari 4 has a default value of 30 minutes. That means every 30 minutes, the program searches for new and updated RSS articles. If the millions of people who subscribe to RSS feeds have their feeds updated every half hour, much of the Internet's bandwidth is sucked up by RSS data that's floating around. (And you wonder why sometimes browsing seems slow.)

✔ **Use faster hardware.** Use a broadband connection, either cable modem or DSL at home, especially for multimedia. Add more and faster memory. Use faster disk drives.

✔ **Clean your browser cache.** Your browser *cache* is an area of temporary storage on your hard disk. Caching is good. When you browse a Web page, your browser caches the data into memory (if you have enough of it) and onto your hard disk. If you return to that same page, your browser retrieves it from the cache, and the page loads quickly. Using your cache rather than requesting the file again from the Web server speeds up Web browsing. On the other hand, if you're low on disk space and you browse lots of different sites during your session, your browser cache might fill up. Full disks slow down overall computer performance, so if your disk is almost full, cleaning your cache manually is particularly helpful to speed up performance.

A side effect of clearing your cache is that you protect your privacy by erasing evidence of sites you visited from your computer. Depending on your browser, you click your way through the Internet menus until you find a Clear Cache or Empty Cache option. For example, in Apple Safari, choose Edit➪Empty Cache➪Empty.

If you use the Google Chrome browser to clear the cache, be very careful when you click the wrench icon and choose the Clear Browsing Data option. Be warned, not only does this choice clear your cache, it also clears your browsing history.

✔ **Turn off multimedia.** By default, IE displays all multimedia (such as pictures, videos, and sounds) on Web pages. Turning off all or some of the multimedia objects speeds the loading of Web pages. Follow these steps:

 1. *Choose Tools➪Internet Options➪Advanced.*

 2. *In the Settings section, select Multimedia and clear all these check boxes to turn off all, or just certain types of, multimedia:*

 Play Animations in Webpages

 Play Sounds in Webpages

 Show Pictures

If you turn off pictures, you can display a picture when you're browsing the page — just right-click the picture's icon and choose Show Picture.

✔ **Use a browser that performs DNS prefetching.** As soon as a Web page loads, Google Chrome, for example, *prefetches* its Web links — it automatically looks up the IP addresses of links on the Web page. Prefetching speeds up browsing because, as you follow the links on a page, Chrome already knows where to find their pages.

✔ **Use a proxy server.** It stores Web pages as you browse them. If you return to that page, it's already in the computer's memory or disk drive, saving you a trip across the Internet to find the page all over again. Some organizations require you to use a proxy server to get past their firewalls. (You can read about proxy servers later in this chapter, in the section "Proxy Serving for Speed and Security.")

✔ **Automate downloading.** You don't have to sit in front of your computer at prime time to download Web pages, files, and fun toys such as iTunes. You can "sexercise" and work off the junk food that this book makes you crave by using *download scheduling* software. You can then use it to download Web pages and files automatically on schedule. These scheduler programs disconnect from the Internet when your download is complete. You can find free download schedulers by searching for *download scheduler* at www.google.com. Mac OS X, Linux, and Unix include a native, flexible scheduling text-based application, cron (short for "cron"ological). If you're a Mac OS X user who prefers a graphical interface, you can download cronnix, a graphical front end to cron. Figure 11-7 demonstrates using cronnix to automate the downloading of iTunes. You can download cronnix from www.h775982.serverkompetenz. net:9080/abstracture_public/projects-en/cronnix.

✔ **Use Lynx.** Little-known Lynx saves lots of time. When surfing for text, use the Lynx browser for speed. It outperforms most browsers when reading pages of text and FAQ files. You can get a free copy of Lynx for Windows at www.fdisk.com/doslynx/lynxport.htm. You can also download Lynx for Unix, Linux, and Mac OS X from

```
www.apple.com/downloads/macosx/unix_open_source/
        lynxtextwebbrowser.html
```

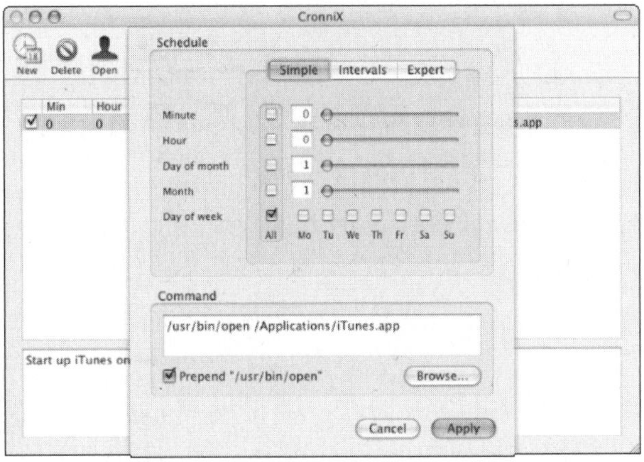

Figure 11-7:
Mac OS X users have an easy way to set up the cron scheduler.

Do you want secure transactions over Lynx? Lynxw32.lzh is an SSL-enabled version of Lynx. The site, at `http://dir.filewatcher.com/d/FreeBSD/4.2-release/i386/lynx-ssl-2.8.3.1.tgz.785278.html`, lists more a dozen FTP download sites for Lynx SSL.

✔ **Create a shortcut on your desktop that links directly to an Internet site.** A shortcut can save you the time and effort of opening your browser and typing a URL. That doesn't sound like much of a savings, does it? If you need to return to the same few places, though, you might be pleasantly surprised at the convenience. To create a shortcut in Internet Explorer, choose File➪Send➪Shortcut to Desktop. From now on, double-click the shortcut to launch Internet Explorer and open the site.

✔ **Multitask.** Let your Internet connection do two things at the same time. Contrary to popular belief, you can surf while you download or perform a couple of downloads at the same time and still get good performance.

✔ **Avoid Web rush-hour congestion.** Check the MAE West traffic report before you start browsing (`www.internettrafficreport.com`). MAE helps you pick the best times to surf and download files. Although the site never mentions it, Metropolitan Area Ethernet (MAE) is a public network exchange point. In the 1990s, the MAE was the center of the Internet universe, where all route information from ISPs was exchanged. At that time, the Internet was of a size where the MAE worked efficiently. But as Internet use expanded, MAE West was born in Silicon Valley, a high-tech area in the western United States. Interestingly, MAE often suffers from Internet congestion.

✔ **Block pop-ups.** If your browser doesn't block pop-up ads, try the free Google pop-up blocker on the Google toolbar for Internet Explorer and Firefox: `http://.toolbar.google.com`.

Proxy Serving for Speed and Security

A *proxy server* (or just *proxy*) helps speed Web page retrieval and adds security to your browsing. The proxy server, acting as a middleman, sits between the HTTP client and server. It looks like the real HTTP server to your client (your Web browser, for example). The HTTP server sees the proxy server as a client. In Figure 3-1, over in Chapter 3, we tell you that a server can be a client of another server. The proxy server acts as an HTTP client and passes your browsing requests to the real HTTP server. Your HTTP client (the browser) sees the proxy server as a server.

After the HTTP server retrieves the Web page, it passes the response (the Web page) back to the proxy, which forwards the response to the client. You can see a proxy server fooling an HTTP client in Figure 11-8.

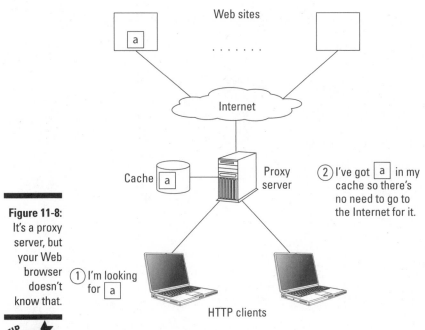

Proxy features are part of the HTTP/1.1 standard.

If you're worried that adding another piece of the pie to the HTTP client/ response sequence will slow down your Web performance, you can relax. Proxies usually increase Web access performance as well as the security of your request.

Caching pages

When your Web browser asks for a page, the proxy server delivers it to you and caches it at the same time. The proxy server maintains a cache of delivered pages, so that if anyone else using the same proxy server wants to see a page that you recently browsed, the proxy server just pops it out of its cache. Voilà! — you see the Web page without spending time and bandwidth on going out on the Internet again.

The cache is a combination of memory cache and disk cache. The network designer or administrator decides how much memory to devote to caching. If the memory cache fills up and new pages are coming in, less frequently used pages in the memory cache are written to the disk cache. Retrieving a page is slower if you have to access the disk, but it's still much faster than searching for the page on the Internet again.

Because all users share the pages in the cache, private pages protected with HTTP authentication aren't cached unless they carry special directives.

Improving security with filtering

You can set up proxy servers to check both outgoing requests and incoming responses to help keep your computers safe. Filtering, which is a useful property to set on a proxy server, can

- ✓ Prevent users from requesting specified content
- ✓ Screen out harmful replies, such as files containing malware

Proxy client setup is a browser option. You might be a client of a proxy server and not even know it.

Setting up a proxy client

If you want to use a proxy, configuring a proxy client in the Apple Safari browser takes only four steps, and more in Microsoft Internet Explorer. The interface for each browser differs, but Step 1 is always the same. You can examine the steps for three different browsers in the following three sections.

First, however, you need to get three pieces of information from your network administrator:

- ✓ The type of proxy server: FTP, HTTP, or HTTPS (if your network requires different proxy addresses for different services)
- ✓ The IP address of the server or its fully qualified domain name (FQDN)
- ✓ The port number for the proxy server

Port 2138 is the default for proxy servers, but your network administrator might have decided to use another port, so be sure to ask.

After you configure your browser settings, the browser sends requests for Web pages to the proxy server rather than directly to the Web server. The proxy server forwards the request to the Web server.

Microsoft Internet Explorer 8

After you gather the necessary information about your proxy server, follow these steps to set up a proxy client in Internet Explorer 8:

1. Choose Tools⇨Internet Options.

2. In the Internet Options dialog box, click the Connections tab and then click the LAN Settings button.

3. Select the Use a Proxy Server for Your LAN check box.

4. In the Address text box, type the address of the proxy server — either the IP address or the FQDN.

5. In the Port text box, type the port number.

6. If you're using multiple proxy servers for FTP, HTTP, or HTTPS, click Advanced.

7. Type the individual proxy server addresses and port numbers and click OK.

8. Click OK to close the dialog box.

Changing these proxy settings affects other Windows applications, such as media players and e-mail clients.

Apple Safari

Follow these steps to set up a proxy client in Safari:

1. Choose Edit⇨Preferences⇨Advanced.

2. Click Change Settings to open the Internet Properties dialog box.

3. Click Settings and enter the settings from your network administrator.

4. Click OK.

Google Chrome

Follow these steps to set up a proxy client in Chrome:

1. Click the wrench icon in the upper-right corner, select Options, and click the Under the Hood tab.

2. In the Network section, click the Change Proxy Settings button to open the Internet Properties window.

3. Open the Connections tab. Click the Local Area Networks (LAN) button to open the Local Area Networks (LAN) dialog box.

4. In the Proxy Server section, select the Use a Proxy Server for Your LAN check box.

Chrome sets 80 as the default port for a proxy server rather than the usual Port 2138. Figure 11-9 shows you the first three steps in setting up the proxy client.

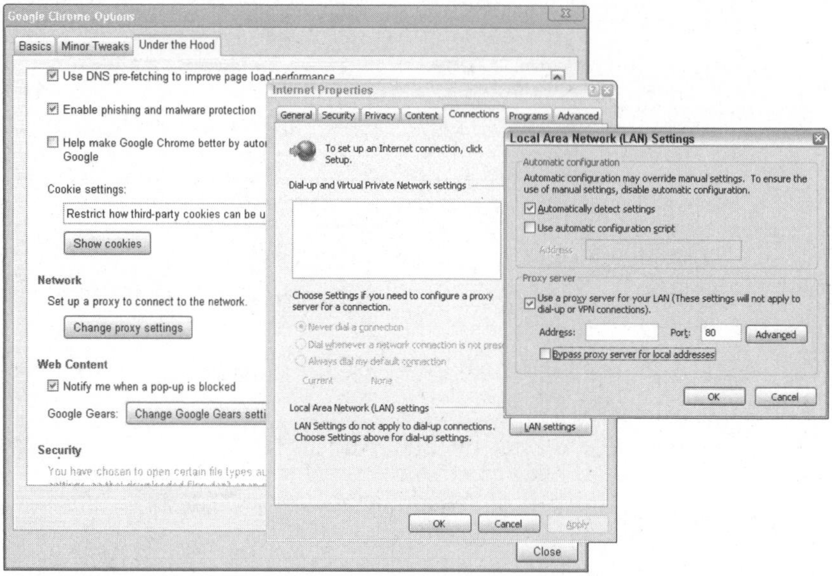

Figure 11-9:
Setting
proxy client
informa-
tion in a
browser.

5. **Click Advanced to set ports for the proxy servers you plan to use.**

Figure 11-10 shows how to set the port numbers for TCP/IP services.

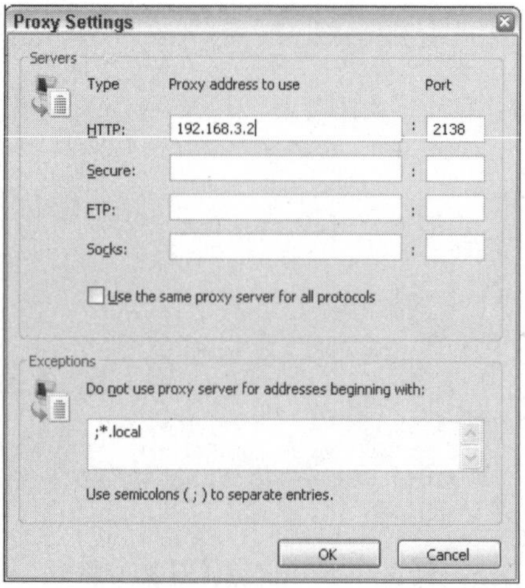

Figure 11-10:
Setting the
HTTP proxy
client.

Google Chrome uses the same connection and proxy settings as Microsoft Windows. Changing the Chrome proxy settings affects Internet Explorer as well.

Finishing touches

To use a proxy, client software must receive explicitly

✔ An instruction to use the proxy

✔ The proxy's IP address or domain name

Then your browser client sends its requests to the proxy rather than to the actual Web server.

Setting Up a Caching Proxy Server

This section talks about caching proxy servers, which are included in most firewall programs. The difference is that plain vanilla proxies provide security protection by letting you filter traffic that's entering your network. The act of caching proxies, in addition to filtering, keeps fetched pages in their caches for reuse. Although hundreds of options are available for choosing a caching proxy, we use squid, for these reasons:

✔ It's free, open source software, with frequent updates.

✔ It's multiplatform, available for all supported versions of Microsoft Windows, Linux and Unix distributions, and Mac OS X.

✔ It uses a similar setup procedure on all operating systems.

✔ It delivers frequently used Web content while putting much less than a normal load on the Web servers.

In the following sections, we explain how to configure squid.

Outlining the general steps for installing and configuring squid

One advantage of using squid is that many popular operating systems include it in their systems. When setting it up, you follow these similar steps on all operating systems (see the next section for the specifics of setting it up on Windows Server 2008):

1. **Find squid and download it.**

   The main squid site, `www.squid-cache.org`, lists both stable and beta (still in development) versions. Choose a version depending on how adventurous you are. Remember that beta versions may not yet incorporate all known features and may have bugs (because these versions aren't fixed as often as stable versions).

2. **Unzip and compile squid.**

3. **Create directories for the configuration files and cache.**

4. **Edit the `squid.conf` file if you want to customize its configuration. (We recommend that you do so.)**

5. **Make squid a service and start it.**

Be sure to check the syntax and file locations for your particular operating system.

Configuring squid for Microsoft Windows Server 2008

The following example shows the steps to follow for getting squid up and running on Windows Server 2008:

1. **If squid isn't part of your operating system, download a free copy from the official squid Web site, `www.squid-cache.org/Download/binaries.dyn`.**

2. **For Windows Server 2008, squid comes in a .zip archive. Extract all files to C:\.**

   Extracting the files creates a folder named `C:\squid`.

3. **Create the folder for the squid cache — `c:\squid\var\cache`.**

   Squid provides default configuration files in the folder `C:\squid\etc`, ending with `.default`. Figure 11-11 shows the `.default` files.

4. **Copy the `.default` files and remove the `.default` extension, as shown in Figure 11-12.**

   Be sure to keep the `.default` versions of the files. They let you restore a basic configuration if your customized configuration doesn't work the way you want.

5. **Configure your squid proxy cache by editing the `squid.conf` file.**

6. **Create the cache by opening a command window and typing** C:>squid\sbin\squid.exe –z, **as shown in Figure 11-13.**

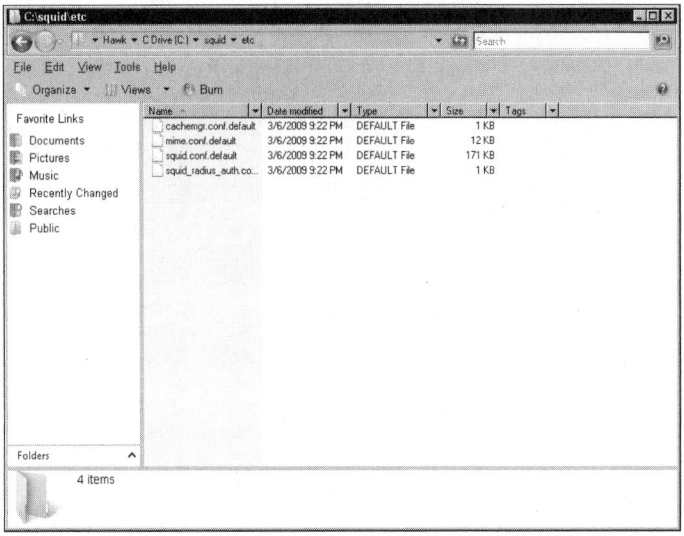

Figure 11-11:
Squid provides a set of default configuration files.

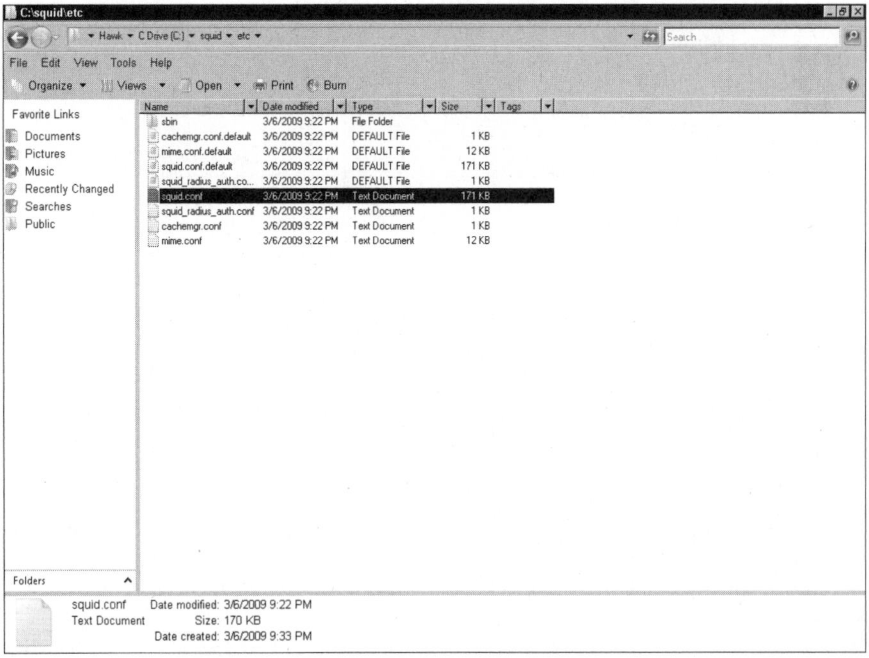

Figure 11-12:
After following Step 4 of the configuration, you have two sets of files.

Set up squid as a service.   Used a stable release.

Start the service.

Figure 11-13:
Build the
caching
space for
Web pages
and create
the squid
service.

This system is short on memory.

7. **Make squid a Windows Server 2008 service. Type the following line in your command window (refer to Figure 11-11):**

```
C:>squid\etc\sbin\squid.exe -d 1 -D
```

The figure shows the information returned from creating the squid service. Most of the information refers to the options that squid enabled.

8. **Type the following command to start the squid service and enable it to start automatically whenever the system shuts down:**

```
C:>squid\etc\sbin\squid.exe -i
```

Now you're caching — see Figure 11-14. You can also use the Windows 2008 Services Manager to create, start, and stop the squid service.

As you can see in Figure 11-15, installing squid creates a tree of folders, subfolders, and files. Looking through the files in the docs subfolders is a good place to find more information about your squid configuration.

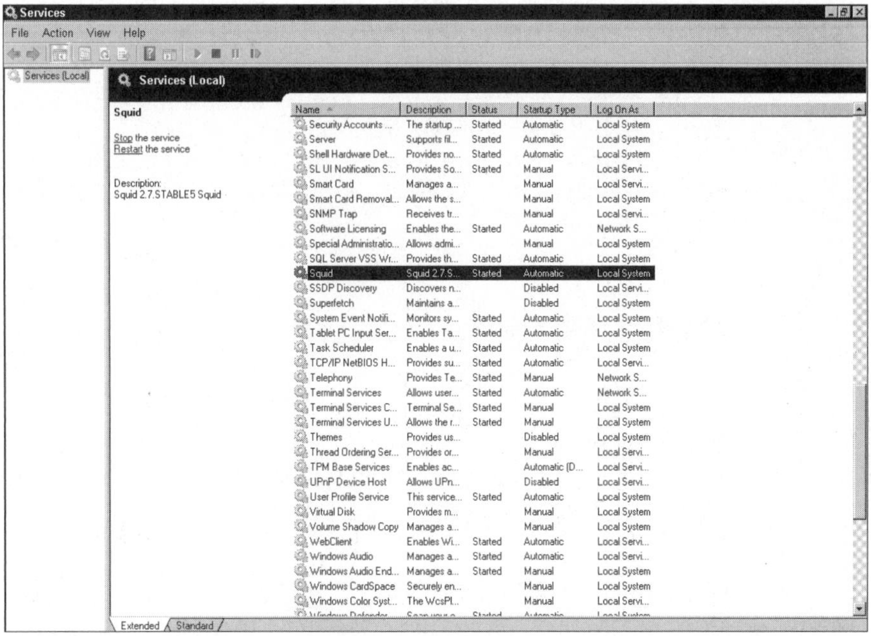

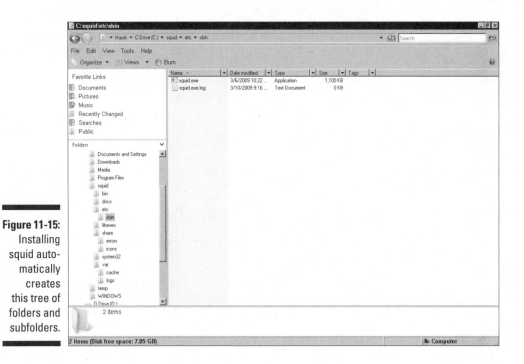

Figure 11-14:
Microsoft
Windows
Server 2008
Services
Manager
shows squid
after you
start it.

Figure 11-15:
Installing
squid auto-
matically
creates
this tree of
folders and
subfolders.

Browsing Securely

The Internet is a wonderful place to make friends, travel the world, shop, and research, but it can also be quite scary. Lots of predators scour the Internet, looking for private information. If you follow a few basic tips for secure browsing, you can protect yourself from cybercriminals and from unwanted cybermarketing.

Ensuring that a site is secure

When you visit a Web site that handles private or financial information, make sure that the Web site is in Secure mode by looking for a *lock icon* in the browser window. All major browsers display the icon — it indicates that the site has a certificate proving that it's a legitimate Web site and that your session on that page is encrypted (see Figure 11-16). To see information about the certificate, click the lock icon in your browser window.

Figure 11-16:
Click the lock icon to show certificate information.

Internet Explorer, Apple Safari, and Google Chrome show the lock icon on the upper right side of the browser window. Just to be different, Firefox displays its lock icon in the lower right corner of the window.

Another way to be sure that you're browsing securely is to check the Web site address. It should begin with https (rather than http), and the protocol should change to https when you're about to make a secure transaction, such as checking out of a shopping site. Some browsers go beyond showing the protocol change. When you connect to a site using https, Firefox, for example, turns the address bar yellow and shows two lock icons: one on the address bar and another on the status bar.

Using your browser's security features

Using a browser that has a wide variety of built-in security protections can help you manage some of your Web client connections with peace of mind. Also, built-in features in your browser can reduce the number of security products you install on your computer. Most browsers provide several options for secure browsing. For example, Microsoft Internet Explorer 8 builds in a suite of defensive tools, including these:

- ✔ SmartScreen Filter
- ✔ A pop-up blocker
- ✔ Alerts
- ✔ Digital signatures
- ✔ A 128-bit secure (SSL) connection, for using secure Web sites

Chapter 12 defines basic security terms, such as phishing, spoofing, and malware.

SmartScreen Filter

In Internet Explorer 8, the SmartScreen Filter protects your computer in three ways:

- ✔ **It analyzes pages and checks to see whether they have any suspicious features.** If you're looking at a suspicious Web page, SmartScreen advises you to proceed with caution. (It runs in the background while you browse the Web.)

- ✔ **It keeps a list, updated hourly, of phishing and malware Web sites.** If you browse a site on the list, a red SmartScreen Filter warning message notifies you that it has blocked the site for your safety.

- ✔ **It compares your downloads against the same list of unsafe sites.** If SmartScreen Filter finds a match, the red warning message notifies you that it has blocked the download for your safety.

Pop-up Blocker

A *pop-up* is a small window that appears uninvited over the site you're browsing. Pop-up Blocker helps you block or limit most pop-up windows. This feature is turned on by default, but you can always turn it off. Pop-up windows often open as soon as you reach a Web site, and they're usually advertisements. You can choose the level of blocking you prefer, ranging from blocking all pop-ups to allowing specific ones that you want to see. When Pop-up Blocker is on, you see a message on the Information bar: "Pop-up blocked. To see this pop-up or additional options, click here." If you want to see the blocked window, you have a couple of options:

   ✔ Click Temporarily Allow Pop-Ups.

   ✔ Click Always Allow Pop-Ups from This Site and then Yes.

Other browsers and toolbar add-ins have pop-up blockers, too.

Alerts

Alerts notify you when a Web site is trying, uninvited, to download files to your computer.

Digital signatures

Digital signatures show who published a file and whether anyone has tampered with it since it was digitally signed. For more information, see the section "Using Digital Certificates for Secure Browsing," later in this chapter.

128-bit secure connection

The 128-bit secure (SSL) connection creates an encrypted connection with secure (look for the S-HTTP protocol in the address) such as banks and online shopping, that handle private information.

Setting Up a Web Server

A *Web server* is software that accepts HTTP requests from browser clients and serves up, to the client, either Web page responses or, sometimes, sadly, error messages. A Web server can also support secure Web connections with HTTPS (with SSL or TLS protocols).

If you plan to set up a Web server, you have several software choices:

   ✔ **Apache HTTP Server:** The number-one Web server software used on the Internet. The Apache server is open source and follows Internet standards. It runs on Unix, Linux, Mac OS X, and Microsoft Windows. Open source software is available for free under the GNU Public License (GPL). In addition to downloading packaged applications and utilities, you can download source code and modify it if you have special needs.

   ✔ **Microsoft proprietary Internet Information Services (IIS):** The runner up. It's bundled with Windows Server, though. It runs only on Windows and doesn't adhere strictly to Internet standards.

   ✔ **The CERN httpd (also known as the W3C httpd):** The first and, for a time, only Web server software. The CERN source code is free, and it runs on most flavors of Unix. You can download the CERN httpd from `www.w3.org/Daemon/Status.html`.

You can also purchase a Web server, such as IBM WebSphere Application Server, Oracle WebLogic Application Server, or Zeus Web Server.

In the following sections, we show you how to set up and configure Apache HTTP Server.

Setting up the Apache HTTP Server

Figures 11-17 through 11-21 illustrate the steps to follow when setting up an Apache Web Server on Windows Server 2008. You follow these same general steps on any operating system. Depending on your operating system, you might have a graphical setup wizard, like the one shown in the example, or you might need to edit the configuration file by hand.

If your operating system has no built-in graphical interface for configuring Apache, don't despair. Use your favorite search engine to search for **Apache GUI**. The list of graphical programs is extensive. Take your pick.

Follow these steps to install Apache HTTP Server:

1. **Download the software.**

   The Web page at `www.apache.org/download.cgi` has links for downloading various versions of the Apache HTTP Server software. The Web page at `www.apachelounge.com/download` has links specifically for Apache in Windows. The page at `www.blackdot.be/?inc=apache/ binaries` has files and instructions for loading Apache on 64-bit versions of Windows. Whether you run Win32 (32-bit Windows versions) or Win64 (64-bit versions) depends on your hardware.

   The Windows 64 version of Apache is an unofficial version of Apache, and its Web page is managed by a kind and hard-working volunteer.

2. **Run the installer program.**

   This step starts the Apache Installation Wizard. Figure 11-17 shows the Welcome screen.

3. **Read the License Agreement and click yes to accept the terms.**

4. **Click Next to fill in the required information. Figure 11-18 shows the four required pieces of information that you enter:**

   a. *Network domain:* The DNS domain where you will register your Web server. Figure 11-18 uses the fictional domain name example. com. You can read about DNS in Chapters 4 and 10.

   b. *Server name:* Your server's fully qualified domain name (FQDN).

   c. *Server administrator's e-mail address:* Whoever is brave enough to volunteer for the task. If you're setting up the server, it's probably your e-mail address.

> d. *Port number for the services to access:* Port 80, the default, is the standard port for a Web server.

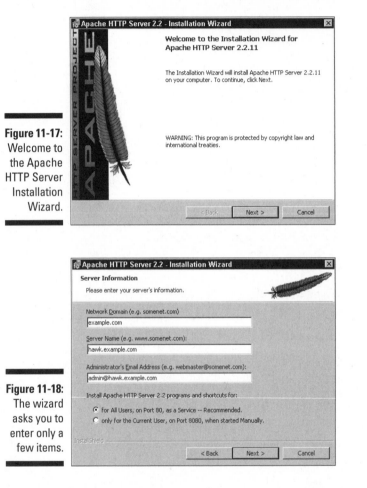

Figure 11-17:
Welcome to the Apache HTTP Server Installation Wizard.

Figure 11-18:
The wizard asks you to enter only a few items.

5. **Close the wizard.**

6. **Make sure that the Web server is running. Start the Windows Task Manager and click to select the Processes tab.**

   You should see the ApacheMonitor (see Figure 11-19) and httpd processes running.

7. Test the Apache configuration. Start any browser and use the server name you entered (refer to Step 4b) as the URL.

You can also use 127.0.0.1 (your localhost address) for testing. Figure 11-20 shows the test result.

Figure 11-19:
The Apache
Web Server
processes
are running.

Image ... ▲	User Name	CPU	Memory (...	Description
ApacheMonito...	Administ...	00	548 K	Apache H...
audiodg.exe	LOCAL ...	00	9,844 K	Windows ...
chrome.exe	Administ...	00	13,960 K	Google Ch...
chrome.exe	Administ...	00	4,444 K	Google Ch...
csrss.exe	SYSTEM	00	1,020 K	Client Ser...
csrss.exe	SYSTEM	00	1,120 K	Client Ser...
CtHelper.exe	Administ...	00	3,144 K	CtHelper ...
daemon.exe	Administ...	00	2,012 K	DAEMON ...
dwm.exe	Administ...	00	832 K	Desktop ...
explorer.exe	Administ...	00	14,148 K	Windows ...
explorer.exe	Administ...	02	10,780 K	Windows ...
GoogleUpdate...	Administ...	00	768 K	Google In...
httpd.exe	SYSTEM	00	1,980 K	Apache H...
httpd.exe	SYSTEM	00	2,404 K	Apache H...
iexplore.exe	Administ...	00	12,032 K	Internet E...
lsass.exe	SYSTEM	00	2,772 K	Local Secu...

Windows Task Manager — File Options View Help

Applications | Processes | Services | Performance | Networking | Users

☑ Show processes from all users   End Process

Processes: 52   CPU Usage: 24%   Physical Memory: 81%

Figure 11-20:
The URL is
your new
Web serv-
er's FQDN.

Oops! This link appear...   http://hawk.example.com/
Customize Links   Apache HTTP Ser...   Other bookmarks

It works!

Installing Apache creates dozens of configuration files with the file type `.conf`. The file `httpd.conf` is the main configuration file. The data you type in the wizard become entries in the `httpd.conf` file. Figure 11-21 lists some of the many configuration files and displays a brief excerpt from the `httpd.conf` file. You can see that the data you entered in the wizard is stored in the file as *directives*.

Installing the Apache Web Server software on Unix, Linux, or Mac OS X creates the same files you see in Figure 11-21.

Data created by the wizard

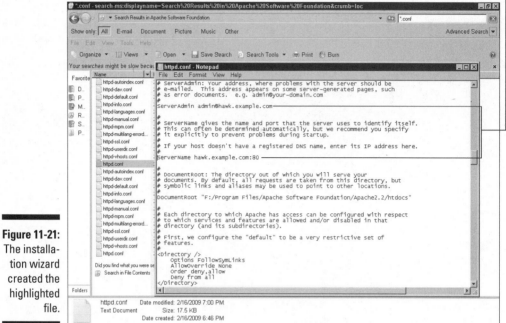

Figure 11-21:
The installation wizard created the highlighted file.

Speeding up Apache

Fortunately, Apache Server consists of efficient code and can perform satisfactorily even on a PC powered by an older Pentium processor with 1GB of memory. If you feel the need to speed up Apache, follow these guidelines:

✔ **Keep the Apache logging function to a minimum.** Then the server can spend more time servicing Web requests and less time logging events. The trade-off is that a significant event, such as a security event, might not appear in the log.

✔ **Run a proxy server to cache Web pages for future requests.** You can either use Apache as a proxy server to filter incoming traffic or install a separate proxy server. (See the earlier sections "Proxy Serving for Speed and Security" and "Setting up a Proxy Server.")

Making Apache more secure

The following tips apply to any Web server software, not just Apache:

✔ **Keep up with security updates.** The Apache HTTP Server announce-
ments list (www.apache.org/lists) keeps you informed of new
releases of the server and its security updates.

✔ **Log critical security warnings and the status of emerg, alert, and crit.**
Table 11-2 lists the Apache log levels. Don't eliminate logging altogether
to improve performance.

✔ **Hide the Apache version number.** As soon as hackers know which version of the software and operating system your server is running, they
have information about your Web server. To hide the version number,
follow these steps:

1. **Edit the** httpd.conf **file.**

2. **Edit (or add) the ServerSignature directive to the Off setting:**
ServerSignature Off.

Table 11-2	Apache Security Log Levels
Level	*Description*
emerg	Emergencies — system is unusable.
alert	Take action immediately.
crit	Critical conditions exist.
error	Error conditions exist.
warn	Warning conditions exist.
notice	Normal but significant conditions exist.
info	Informational level.
debug	Debug-level messages.

Adding Security to HTTP

HTTP is the RFC draft standard protocol, the closest thing to a standard for
communication between Web client requests and Web server responses.
HTTP, having been designed in the 1990s, doesn't offer much in the way of
security. HTTP sends private data such as passwords and credit card numbers
across the Internet in plain text format. Both the older Secure HTTP (S-HTTP)
and HTTP over SSL/TLS (HTTPS) add needed security features to the basic
HTTP protocol.

In addition to HTTP, loads of applications and services rely on SSL and TLS
to provide encryption and authentication. (See Chapter 12 for definitions of
both terms. You can find brief descriptions of both SSL and TLS in Chapter 2.)

Taking a look at HTTPS

HTTP Secure (HTTPS) is HTTP with security enhancements; it addresses the issue of moving data securely across a public environment, such as the Web.

HTTPS provides transaction security services and confidentiality as well as authentication. It builds encryption into the application level before you even reach the Web server. HTTP, on the other hand, makes the client try to access the Web server before issuing a username and password challenge, if needed. Secure HTTP doesn't require any changes to HTML, the language that makes the Web's pages look good. (Although HTML is also getting new features, those additions are driven by other requirements.)

By the way, HTTPS also supports Kerberos security. (For more on Kerberos, flip to the section in Chapter 21 that talks about whether Kerberos is a guardian or a fiend.)

Getting up to speed on SSL

When Netscape introduced SSL in 1995, it made online information, including credit card information, as secure as handing a credit card to a salesperson in a store — and maybe even more secure. Don't shop at a site that doesn't use SSL. Check your browser's status bar for the lock icon (refer to Figure 11-16).

URLs that begin with `https://` use SSL to protect information. (Think of the *s* as *secure*.)

The SSL protocol ensures privacy between a client and server by using certificates to authenticate the server (and, optionally, the client) and ensures confidentiality by encrypting the data they exchange. No one can put a computer on the network and fool SSL into believing that the spoofing server should receive the client's confidential credit card information. If you're shopping on the Web, you want the commerce server to prove that it is who it claims to be. SSL also has an option to authenticate the client so that a server can be sure you're who you claim to be. SSL requires a reliable protocol for the transport — TCP, not UDP.

TLS and SSL aren't tied to a particular application. Protocol independence is typical of the protocols in the TCP/IP stack and is a great advantage. You can layer any application or protocol, such as HTTP or FTP, over SSL or TLS. They sit on top of TCP, taking care of encryption, security keys, authenticating the server, and, possibly, authenticating the client before the application layer sends or receives any data.

Chapter 21 features the IPSec set of protocols, which provide security one layer down, closer to hardware and farther from applications at the network layer, where the IP protocol is. Check out Chapter 2 for a reminder about the TCP/IP network layer cake.

Protocol parenthood: SSL begets TLS

Netscape invented SSL and still owns it. If you're wondering how this proprietary network protocol made its way into this book, the reason is that SSL filled a hole that international standards had left open. The Transport Layer Security (TLS) protocol is on the IETF (refer to Chapter 1) standards track in its first version.

The goal of this protocol is similar to the goal of SSL — to enable client/server applications to operate without the danger of anyone eavesdropping or tampering with their networks or forging either personal or computer identities. In fact, TLS is patterned after SSL, and Netscape is helping the IETF create a standard protocol.

Don't forget that both the client and server computers and applications must also be secure if you want to keep cybercriminals away.

Stepping through an SSL Transaction

Here are the technical details of an SSL transaction, such as sending your credit card number over the Internet:

1. The client program, such as a Web browser, indicates that it wants to send a document using the `https://` protocol.

2. The server program sends its certificate to the client program.

3. The client program checks to see whether the certificate has been issued by a trusted authority — a Certification Authority (CA). See Chapter 21 for details about Certification Authorities.

   If the certificate hasn't been issued, the server sends a message to the user: "Do you want to continue without a certificate or end the transaction?" Sometimes you see a Certificate Expired message at this point.

4. The client program compares the information in the certificate with the authentication key.

   If they match, the client program knows that the site is secure — that is, that the site is who it says it is.

5. The client program tells the server which encryption algorithms it can understand.

6. The server program chooses the strongest encryption algorithms that it has in common with the client program. The server program tells the client which encryption algorithm they will use to communicate.

7. The client program generates a key using the agreed-on encryption.

8. The client program encrypts the key and sends it to the server program.

9. The server program receives the encrypted key from the client and decodes it.

10. The client and server programs continue to use the key throughout the transaction's back-and-forth communication.

Security software can't protect you from disreputable people. In TCP/IP, as in life, security makes you less vulnerable to the bad guys, but in networking, as in real life, you have to trust someone. (Even special agent Bond trusts his boss, M.) When you order a product or a service over the telephone, you trust the person who takes your order with your credit card information. When you buy something over the Internet, you trust the server administrator at the site with your credit card information. If the administrator has set up tight security, your encrypted credit card information should be impossible for her to see.

The server administrator maintains the security software, the physical security of the computers, and the security of passwords and private keys.

Using Digital Certificates for Secure Web Browsing

A *certificate* is a digital document that helps verify the identity of either a person or a server. You can use certificates with a browser to protect your personal information on the Web and to help protect your computer from unsafe software. Browsers use two types of certificates:

✔ **Personal:** Helps prove that you are who you say you are. Even James Bond has to show special identification to prove who he is — his name alone isn't enough. Some Web sites require proof of an ID in the form of a digital certificate. You can also use a digital ID to help verify your identity by storing a private key on your computer. Digital certificates with private keys are also known as *digital signatures*.

✔ **Server:** Proves that a Web site is genuine — not a hacker spoofing the name or address (or both) of the site to steal your personal data. Whenever you send personal information over the Internet, check the certificate of the Web site to make sure that it's truly the site you think it is. When you receive information, such as downloaded programs from a Web site, view the site's certificates: You need to know that the origin of your download is as claimed and that no one has tampered with the file during transport.

Chapter 21 gives you the scoop on how to get a digital certificate and signature and how to examine Web site certificates.

Chapter 12

Minimum Security Facilities

●●●

In This Chapter

▶ Identifying the most serious threats to your computer and intranet

▶ Sampling some basic security terminology

▶ Protecting your network with firewalls, anti-malware, and encryption

●●●

*B*eing connected to a network, especially to the Internet, comes with some security risks. Is it worth it? For most people and organizations, the answer is yes, but a few important precautions are usually necessary.

This chapter lists the nastiest muggings that can happen to your computer and a few basic security practices you can use to protect your computer and your intranet. The information in this chapter introduces the basic security vocabulary and techniques to prepare you for the application chapters that follow. Chapters 20 and 21 delve into network security in much more depth.

What's the Worst That Could Happen?

The frequency of break-ins and hacks on the Internet grows nearly as fast as the Internet itself. If that leaves you hungry for some data safety, this chapter is the first course of your security dinner. Some of the security attacks to worry about on your own computer and intranet include

✔ **Theft:** Scoundrels break onto networks or into hosts to steal computing resources and/or information.

✔ **Spoofing:** E-thieves without network permissions pretend to be other people who have the necessary credentials, often by sending fake e-mail, using someone else's access rights, or getting a host to assume the identity of another host so users access the wrong machine.

✔ **Password cracking:** Another popular technique for attacking your computer is to use a *packet sniffer* to capture plain-text (that is, unencrypted) passwords as they float across the Internet. A sniffer is a program that a network administrator uses to record and analyze network traffic, but the bad guys use them, too. Packet sniffers capture data from packets as they travel over a network. That data is often in plain text: usernames, passwords, and confidential information, such as medical records and industrial secrets. Scoundrels try to break into users' accounts by using data gained from sniffers.

✔ **Phishing:** Sending a Web mail message that looks like it comes from an official site in order to collect your information, usually usernames and passwords. Many popular sites, such as eBay and AOL, list how their official messages look so you won't be taken in.

The Internal Revenue Service never sends an e-mail message to make contact with a taxpayer. If a message (a) claims to be from the IRS, a major bank, or a similar institution, and (b) asks for (or demands) your username, password, account number, or other information you'd never offer a total stranger, somebody's trying to phish you.

✔ **Spear phishing:** Cyber-phishermen usually try to draw hundreds or even thousands of victims into their nets. Spear-phishermen attack one or two famous people, such as Steve Jobs. Urban legend says that Steve Jobs' Amazon account was spear-phished in May 2009.

✔ **Loading malware onto your computer**: Viruses, worms, Trojan horses, and zombies — all these malevolent applications exist to destroy data, create chaos, open secret passages into hosts, and more. Read Chapter 20 for descriptions of malware. And be sure you read about Denial of Service (DoS) attacks in Chapter 8.

Are you worried yet? We hope so — it's realistic — but don't abandon hope. You have a wide assortment of tools and techniques to help protect yourself, your family and friends, your colleagues, and your users. You can and should use the following protections in various combinations.

Jump-Starting Security with the Big Three

There are certainly more than three security practices to implement on your computer and network. Because this chapter is an introduction to the basics that the following chapters refer to, we're keeping it simple. For more in depth security information, please read Chapters 20 and 21. In our humble opinions, the Big Three security protections (described in the following sections) are

✔ Firewalls

✔ Anti-malware, including anti-virus and anti-spyware software

✔ Encryption

Installing a personal firewall

A *personal firewall* is software that you run on a single computer to protect it from attacks. *Webster's Ninth New Collegiate Dictionary* defines a firewall as "a wall constructed to prevent the spread of fire." Notice it doesn't say anything about putting out the fire. A real-world firewall actually only slows the fire's movement through a building. Network and personal firewalls usually catch the arson attempt before it becomes a fire.

Protecting yourself with a personal firewall

A firewall filters out evil traffic and break-in attempts. Personal firewalls are part of most recent operating systems. You can also find many free or low cost personal firewalls available for download from the Internet. Pcmag.com is a reputable site that includes firewall reviews and downloads of free and inexpensive firewalls, such as Comodo, a highly rated free personal firewall. Figure 12-1 shows how to enable a personal firewall in Windows 7.

If an unknown source tries to connect to your computer, a pop-up window, such as the one in Figure 12-2, alerts you to the intrusion and prompts you to choose whether to grant access. The firewall software also writes the details of the access into a log file so you can review it later.

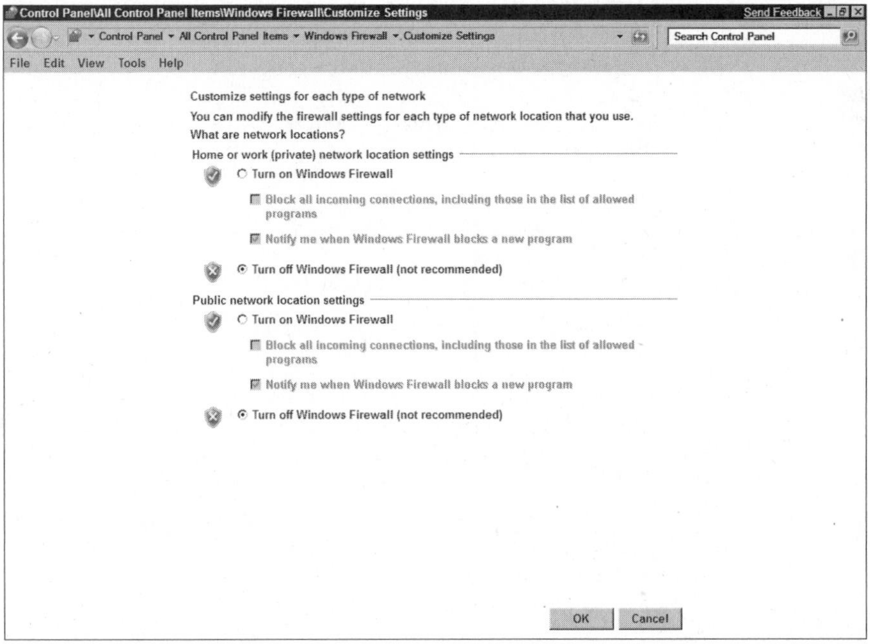

Figure 12-1:
A personal firewall defends your computer.

Personal firewalls protect you not only from outside attacks but also from inside attacks. The attack shown in Figure 12-2 did not come from the Internet. It came from another computer *on the same intranet* trying to break into someone else's files. Figure 12-2 is an excerpt of a thwarted break-in attempt into Candace's laptop, Woodstock. In terms of network traffic, you're more concerned with *inbound* traffic (from your intranet and the Internet to your computers) than with *outbound* traffic.

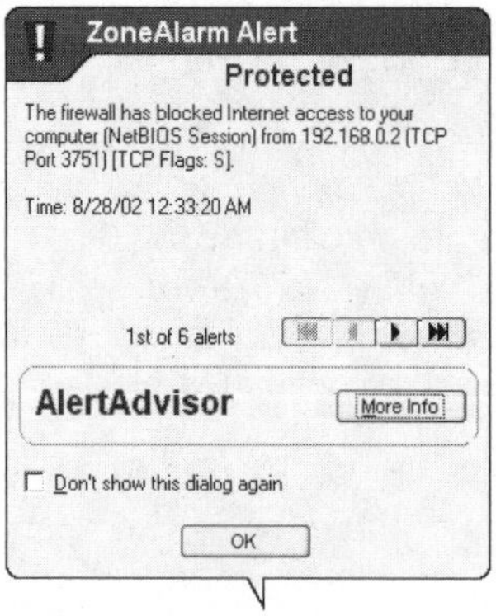

! ZoneAlarm Alert

Protected

The firewall has blocked Internet access to your computer (NetBIOS Session) from 192.168.0.2 (TCP Port 3751) [TCP Flags: S].

Time: 8/28/02 12:33:20 AM

1st of 6 alerts |◄◄ || ► ►►|

AlertAdvisor   [More Info]

☐ Don't show this dialog again

[OK]

Figure 12-2: Woodstock's personal firewall fights back.

Layering firewalls

Besides your personal firewall protecting your own computer, you should have other levels of firewalls for extra protection:

✓ You can set up a separate firewall to protect all the devices on your intranet. Conveniently, this firewall capability is usually built into your router.

✓ Out on the Internet, your ISP's firewall also protects you.

Vaccinating your system with the anti-s

The "anti-" software includes anti-virus and anti-spyware. Run these tools on all the computers in your intranet(s). Many ISPs include a security *suite* (a set of programs to protect against various attacks) with their services; check with your ISP to find out what is available to you. For example, our former ISP included McAfee Security Suite, and Candace's sister's ISP includes Norton Internet Security. With our current ISP, we have to buy a security suite or download free or shareware programs, such as Avast! or the basic version of ZoneAlarm. In any case, be absolutely certain to run some anti-virus program.

Immunizing your system with anti-malware software

Malware is any malevolent application that destroys data, causes your computer to crash, and spreads to other computers. Many malware applications, such as zombies and bots, spread from Web sites. Most security suites protect against various types of malware.

Malware (such as viruses) not only infects your computer, but can also be passed to your entire intranet. Additionally, any infected machine can pass on viruses outside your intranet — because a favorite place for a virus to hide is in an e-mail message forwarded to friends and colleagues.

Whatever anti-virus software/anti-malware you run, be sure you keep your anti-virus software updated. The software reminds you that updates are available. Don't delay. New viruses come out all the time, and anti-virus programs put out updates to inoculate your system against the latest threats.

Detecting spyware

Spyware is a particular kind of malware that works under cover on your computer. It reports on your activities and gathers personal information about you.

Spybot Search and Destroy freeware scans your system for malware, and it actively protects you from being infected, running programs such as TeaTimer. TeaTimer notifies you of changes in the Windows Registry before they happen and asks if you want to allow the change. You can download Spybot Search and Destroy for free from the Spybot site, `www.spysearchdestroy.com`.

Encrypting data so snoopers can't read it

Encryption scrambles human-readable data, also called plain text, into a secret code. To read an encrypted file or e-mail message, you must have access to a secret key that lets you decrypt the message.

Another function of encryption is to scramble the transmission of data. In other words, you can transmit a non-encrypted file, and it's still encrypted. This protection is a big part of why you can shop safely online: No one can just barge in and read your credit-card information because it's encrypted. You can read more about encryption in Chapters 14 and 21.

Adding a Few More Basic Protections

Besides the Big Three listed earlier in this chapter, the following chapters refer to a couple of other basic security concepts: authentication and digital certificates.

Authentication goes beyond identifying yourself. That's just saying you are somebody. You also have to prove that you are who you say you are.

"Knock, knock."

"Who's there?"

"Bond . . . James Bond."

Do you believe the voice on the other side of the door and open up? Or do you authenticate him by looking at his ID? Can you really *believe* his ID? Do you even know what a real British secret service ID looks like? Do you call the MI6 headquarters and try to verify Bond's identity? What if he's really actor Sean Connery in disguise?

Do you believe the Web pages are from the legitimate site and not some imposter? It might *look* like the legitimate site. Authentication makes sure someone or something (in this case, the Web page) is who or what it claims to be. The RFC-Editor lists over 100 RFCs dealing with various aspects of authentication. Chapter 21 describes ways to authenticate users.

A *digital certificate* is a unique electronic ID that provides authentication and encryption and more.

Chapter 13

Eating Up E-Mail

· ·

In This Chapter

▶ Examining the similarities between e-mail and postal mail

▶ Benefitting from the client-server aspect of e-mail

▶ Transferring e-mail by SMTP

▶ Using a Web browser for e-mail

· ·

*A*t the restaurant at the end of the network, the Big Three favorites on the TCP/IP menu are electronic mail (e-mail), Web browsing, and file downloading. Add remote and mobile access for dessert and you have a satisfying meal. E-mail, which is the first network application that most people use, has been around for so long (since 1971, when the Advanced Research Projects Agency Network, or ARPANET, hadn't yet morphed into the Internet) that many of us forget that some folks still don't have it and don't even want it.

We often hear the question: "Is e-mail TCP/IP?" The answer is: No, it isn't. Yes, absolutely it is. Okay, it depends. An e-mail client — such as Mozilla Thunderbird, Microsoft Outlook Express, Apple Mail, or one of countless others — is either a proprietary or open source application with no Request for Comments (RFC) standards for its development. However, the communication among e-mail clients and servers relies on TCP/IP services and protocols.

Getting the Big Picture about How E-Mail Works

Almost every author who writes about e-mail compares e-mail to postal mail. The analogy works well because e-mail is mail — with senders, recipients, mailboxes, and local and regional post offices. Postal mail is stored in local post offices and possibly forwarded to larger post offices for delivery out of the sender's area. E-mail is also stored and forwarded for local and wide area delivery. E-mail in the 21st century is more secure than postal mail unless you write your postal mail in code and seal the envelope with wax. Oh, and if you move around often, your address changes take place immediately.

Table 13-1 shows that postal mail (or *snail mail*) and electronic mail follow the same six steps.

Table 13-1		Mail Step by Step
Step	*Postal Mail (Snail Mail)*	*Electronic Mail (E-Mail)*
1	Write a letter.	Compose a message in a mail user agent (MUA) client.
2	Address envelope.	Address message — user@domain (for example, `emily@eastmail.example.com`).
3	Take to post office (P.O.).	Transfer message to mail transfer agent (MTA) server.
4	Local P.O. delivers to "recipient's post office.	Simple Mail Transfer Protocol (SMTP) connects your MTA to the recipient's MTA.
5	Recipient's post office puts mail in P.O. box.	Recipient's MTA delivers the message to the mailbox.
6	Recipient reads mail.	Recipient reads message with MUA.

Feasting on E-Mail's Client-Server Delights

An Internet *e-mail system* is a client-server environment in which TCP/IP protocols handle the connection between servers. In the sections that follow, we describe different e-mail clients and servers and how e-mail clients and servers communicate to provide a complete e-mail system.

E-mail clients

An *e-mail client,* or, more formally, a *mail user agent (MUA),* is a program that provides your personal entry to an e-mail system. It's the only part you can see. You use MUAs to compose, read, forward, reply, and delete — the actions you take to create, send, and manage e-mail. You can set options for your own MUA, but you may not have to set any of them.

When choosing an e-mail client, you have more choices than you probably realize, and more than we could possibly write about in one book, let alone one chapter. Our personal preferences lean toward free, open source, portable cross-platform clients such as Thunderbird and Mulberry. Of course, lots of vendor proprietary clients are available too, including Microsoft Office Outlook and IBM Lotus Notes.

After you compose your e-mail and click Send, your MUA hands the message to an e-mail server.

E-mail clients versus Web mail clients

E-mail and Web mail serve the same function — to allow you to compose, read, and send electronic mail. When someone sends you e-mail, it's stored on a computer running e-mail server software. This computer is usually called an e-mail server, although only the software is the server. Both Web mail and e-mail clients read and send e-mail across the Internet. The difference between e-mail and Web mail, however, is in how the user interface works. An *e-mail client* is a specialized application for sending and receiving e-mail. The client for Web *mail* is simply a browser.

When you read about an e-mail client in this book, you're reading about a specialized application for e-mail. We carefully distinguish between reading e-mail with an e-mail client versus reading it with a browser client.

E-mail servers

E-mail servers are more formally called *mail transfer agents* (MTAs). All e-mail users who share a computer use the same MTA, even though they can't see it. These programs — such as IBM Lotus Domino, Meldware Mail Server, Microsoft Exchange Server, FirstClass (from OpenText), Postfix, qmail, sendmail, and many others — deliver your e-mail to the right place. For example, after you compose a message and click Send, an MTA takes over and starts your message on its journey. When your message reaches its destination, another MTA delivers it to the addressee. Your system or network administrator configures the MTA on your system. Some MTAs are infamous for the level of tedium involved in configuring their numerous options. Newer MTAs, which are easier to configure, are growing in popularity.

An MTA is your e-mail server software, and it runs at the TCP/IP application layer. The MTA is your postal carrier. SMTP moves your message from MTA to MTA until it reaches the addressee's MTA, which deposits it in the *message store* — that is, the correct mailbox. The addressee then uses an MUA to read the message.

E-mail server data structures

An e-mail server has two structures to store e-mail:

- ✔ A *mailbox* (one per e-mail address) contains delivered messages.
- ✔ A *message queue* contains outgoing messages that are waiting to go.

The implementation of these structures depends on the mail server product. For example, some products use plain-text files. Others use proprietary file formats that offer more security and use less disk space but usually require more sophisticated backup schemes.

E-mail server product choices

Sendmail, with implementations for various operating systems, is the oldest and most widely used MTA. Because sendmail was developed back in the Internet's friendly, trust-everyone days, it's difficult to secure. Newer e-mail servers, such as qmail and Postfix, are rapidly growing in popularity. These three MTAs are free, open source software. They follow Internet (TCP/IP) standards. You can find versions of sendmail for all major operating systems. Postfix, the server software that's rapidly gaining in use over sendmail, runs on almost everything except Microsoft Windows.

Most operating systems are supplied with e-mail server programs. For example, Mac OS X ships with sendmail, the most frequently used e-mail server. Ubuntu Linux includes Postfix as its e-mail server, and Red Hat Enterprise Linux ships sendmail as its default e-mail server.

Network and system administrators: If you don't like the e-mail server software that's bundled with your operating system, that's no problem — just install a different e-mail server. For example, Microsoft offers Exchange Server, but you don't have to use it, especially if you manage a SOHO (small office/home office), where you may not have the budget or time to administer Exchange. So many different e-mail servers exist in the world of free software that you can easily swap in server software (an MTA) that fits your needs better than the one supplied with your operating system. (Be safe, though, and talk to management first!)

Most people don't have to choose an e-mail server program. If you're in a small office or home network, for example, you may leave the management of an e-mail server program to your ISP. If you work for a large organization, your network or system administrator manages your e-mail server program. If you're the network administrator, you may get to choose your e-mail server, and you definitely get to manage it and keep it running (even over your own protests and requests to change products).

Postfix: Configuring the fastest-growing MTA

In the following example, you see how to install and configure Postfix on the fastest-growing (in popularity) Linux distribution, Ubuntu. We use Postfix in the following "HowTo" because it's rapidly replacing sendmail as the most commonly used MTA. In the example, the computer's name is ubuntu, and it "lives" in the special, reserved domain name example.com (which can never be used on the Internet). That makes the computer's fully qualified domain name (FQDN) ubuntu.example.com.

Linux and Unix distributions are supplied with a package manager that helps you install other software. Ubuntu Linux uses the Synaptic Package Manager, which already knows about Postfix, as shown in Figure 13-1.

To install and configure Postfix in Ubuntu Linux, follow these steps:

1. **The message bar at the bottom of the screen (refer to Figure 13-1) shows that the package manager is running. The package manager displays a list of packages and specifies whether they're already installed. When you highlight a package, such as Postfix, a pop-up window asks what you want to do. As the figure shows, we chose to install Postfix.**

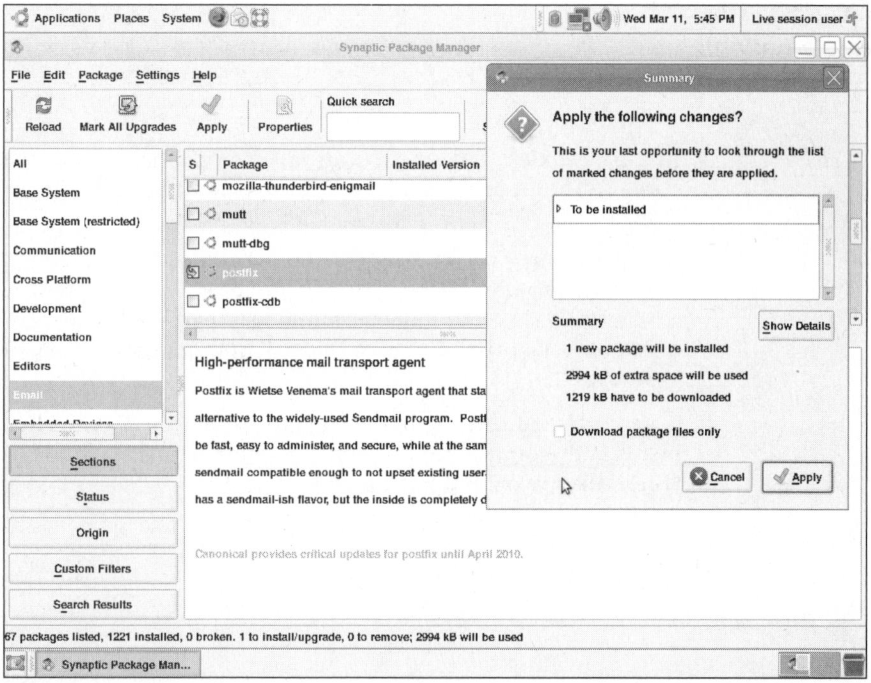

Figure 13-1:
Ubuntu Linux provides a package manager that knows how to install Postfix.

When the package manager finishes installing the files, it automatically launches the Postfix configuration wizard. The wizard asks you a series of questions.

2. **In the next step, shown in Figure 13-2, select the type of configuration you want. When you finish, click Forward.**

The default option is Internet Site, but Internet with Smarthost is probably the most common. When that option is used, the mail server can deliver e-mail locally. It tries to deliver Internet e-mail by itself, but passes to the smart host any messages it can't deliver. We tell you more about that topic in Step 4.

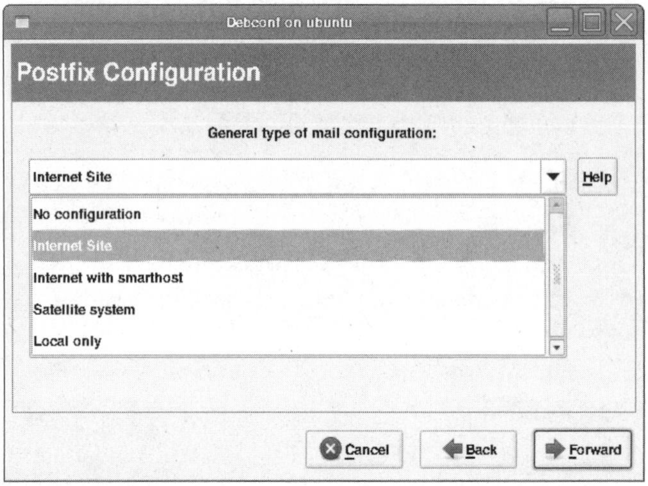

Figure 13-2:
The wizard knows five configuration options for the Postfix mail server.

3. **In the next step, the Configuration Wizard looks up the computer's name (ubuntu) and then you enter the domain name to append (see Figure 13-3). When you finish, click Forward.**

You may have multiple mail servers in your domain that share the workload of managing users' mailboxes and cooperate to handle inbound and outbound e-mail. Using multiple mail servers prevents a mail server from being a single point of failure. All of them should be working in the same domain.

4. **If you selected Internet with Smarthost in Step 2, enter the smart host's name on the next screen that appears, as shown in Figure 13-4. Otherwise, leave the field blank.**

A *smart host*, or *relay host,* is a safety net. When a mail server that's configured with a smart host doesn't know exactly how to handle a message, it sends it to the smart host. In this example, the smart host is our ISP's e-mail server. The explanation of "store and forward" is coming up shortly.

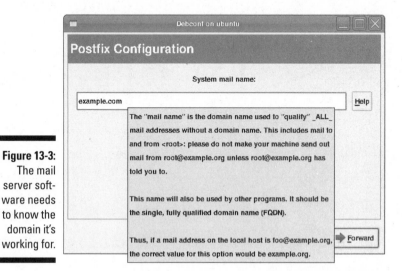

Figure 13-3: The mail server software needs to know the domain it's working for.

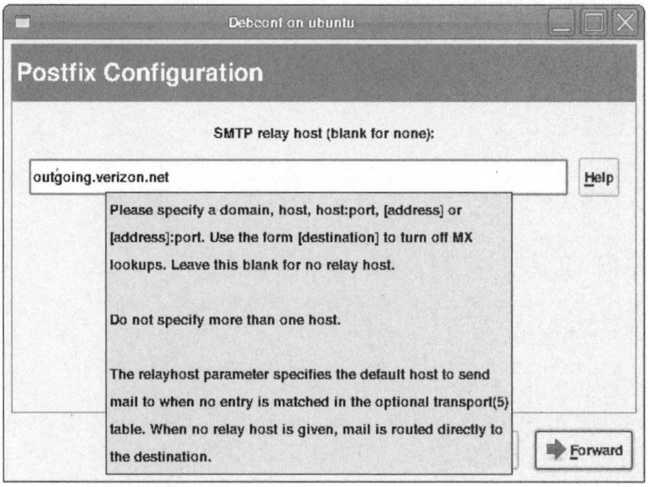

Figure 13-4: You have to tell the mail server the name of the smart host.

5. When you finish, click Forward.

The wizard has no more questions to ask, so it updates the appropriate files. Then it launches Postfix and reports that everything is done!

The main configuration file for the Postfix e-mail server is `main.cf`. It's easy to remember, isn't it? Figure 13-5 shows an excerpt from the file. (Lines that begin with the pound sign, #, are comments.)

Figure 13-5:
The wizard automatically edited the configuration file to get you started.

```
Applications  Places  System                    Wed Mar 11, 8:56 PM   Live session user

                          main.cf (/etc/postfix) - gedit

File  Edit  View  Search  Tools  Documents  Help

New  Open    Save  Print...  Undo  Redo   Cut  Copy  Paste   Find  Replace

main.cf

biff = no

# appending .domain is the MUA's job.
append_dot_mydomain = no

# Uncomment the next line to generate "delayed mail" warnings
#delay_warning_time = 4h

readme_directory = no

# TLS parameters
smtpd_tls_cert_file=/etc/ssl/certs/ssl-cert-snakeoil.pem
smtpd_tls_key_file=/etc/ssl/private/ssl-cert-snakeoil.key
smtpd_use_tls=yes
smtpd_tls_session_cache_database = btree:${data_directory}/smtpd_scache
smtp_tls_session_cache_database = btree:${data_directory}/smtp_scache

# See /usr/share/doc/postfix/TLS_README.gz in the postfix-doc package for
# information on enabling SSL in the smtp client.

myhostname = ubuntu
alias_maps = hash:/etc/aliases
alias_database = hash:/etc/aliases
myorigin = /etc/mailname
mydestination = example.com, ubuntu, localhost.localdomain, localhost
relayhost = outgoing.verizon.net
mynetworks = 127.0.0.0/8 [::ffff:127.0.0.0]/104 [::1]/128
mailbox_size_limit = 0
recipient_delimiter = +
inet_interfaces = all

                                              Ln 30, Col 1        INS
```

Sharpening the Finer Points of Mail Servers

Table 13-1, a little earlier in this chapter, simplifies the task of describing the mail process. For example, how does your snail mail post office know where the delivery office is? For most of us, the address of a letter contains a postal code that maps to a post office in a town or city. With e-mail, SMTP figures out how to communicate between the sender's MTA and the recipient's MTA.

SMTP has two options for sending e-mail from the source MTA to the destination MTA:

- ✔ The store-and-forward method
- ✔ MX (Mail Exchange) records from the Domain Name Service (DNS)

You can review DNS in Chapter 10. One way or another, SMTP sends the e-mail from sender to recipient.

Transferring e-mail by way of store-and-forward

To understand the store-and-forward method, take a look at an example. Suppose that Sarah wants to send an e-mail message to her sister Emily. Here's how the e-mail message is transferred from Sarah to Emily (as shown in Figure 13-6):

1. Sarah composes the message using her favorite mail user agent, or MUA.

2. When Sarah clicks Send, her MUA hands the message to an MTA on her network.

3. Sarah's local MTA passes the message to an MTA on Emily's network. SMTP defines how messages move from one MTA to the next.

4. Emily's MTA receives the message and puts it in Emily's mailbox. The simplest kind of mailbox in an e-mail system is a text file that stores all of a user's messages.

5. After Sarah's e-mail to Emily arrives, it sits in Emily's mailbox until she checks her e-mail. (Knowing Emily, that's about once a month.)

6. When Emily checks her e-mail, either POP3 or IMAP4 takes over and retrieves Sarah's message from Emily's mailbox.

   MUAs that work with both POP3 and IMAP4 include Alpine, Apple Mail, Eudora, IBM Lotus Notes, Microsoft Outlook, Mozilla Thunderbird, Pegasus Mail, and many more. Whether POP3 or IMAP4 takes over depends on how Emily configures her e-mail client. Figure 13-6 shows you the big picture.

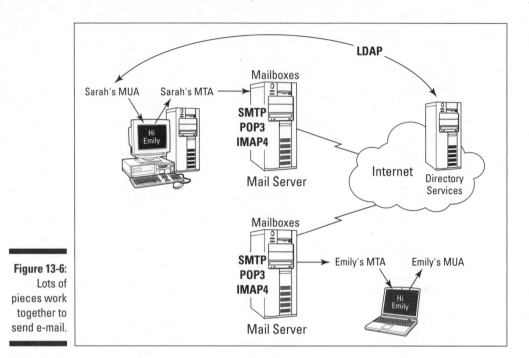

Figure 13-6:
Lots of
pieces work
together to
send e-mail.

Transferring e-mail by way of DNS MX records

Sending e-mail by using store-and-forward works well in smaller intranets. When a message is bound for the other side of the Internet, the message might have to do a lot of hopping from one MTA to another before it finally reaches its destination.

A more efficient way for MTAs to find out where to send e-mail works with special records in the DNS database. MX (Mail Exchange) records list the e-mail servers for a particular domain, such as `example.com`. The outbound (sending) MTA first checks to see whether the e-mail is being sent to a local address. If so, that's great — the MTA only has to hand off the e-mail to the recipient's MUA. However, if the message isn't local, the outbound MTA starts to figure out the recipient's address by using MX records from the DNS database. In an e-mail address, such as `emilyd@example.com`, the second part of the address, `example.com`, represents the DNS domain.

The MX records in DNS define the e-mail servers for a particular domain.

Understanding How SMTP Works with MTAs

Simple Mail Transfer Protocol, or *SMTP,* is the part of the TCP/IP protocol suite that MTAs use to communicate with each other. Without SMTP, MTAs wouldn't know how to send e-mail. SMTP defines how messages move from one computer's MTA to another's MTA, but not which path each message takes. A message can move directly from the sender's computer to the recipient's, or it can proceed through intermediary computers by using the store-and-forward process.

In the store-and-forward style, as each message travels through the network on its way to its destination, it can pass through any number of intermediate computers' MTAs, where it's briefly stored before being sent on to the next computer in the path. The process is sort of like a weary traveler stopping to rest occasionally before continuing the trip across the network galaxy.

SMTP is strictly about moving messages from one computer to another. Although SMTP doesn't care about the *content* of an e-mail message, it limits the formatting attributes of the message. SMTP can transfer only text! It can't handle fonts, colors, graphics, attachments, or any other of those fancy e-mail features that you know and love. The Multipurpose Internet Mail Extensions (MIME) standard was created to overcome this limitation. MIME encodes the deluxe features into plain old text, which SMTP transfers. So go ahead and send e-mail with sounds and pictures of your dog, for example.

MTAs also act as waystations for messages, by accepting messages not meant for them and forwarding the messages to their destinations or to another intermediary MTA. An MTA, which determines how to send messages to the appropriate recipient, sends messages to

✔ Other MTAs

✔ Mailboxes

✔ Other programs, such as spam filters, for advanced processing

Defining E-Mail Protocols

Figure 13-6 shows the protocols that are part of a complete e-mail system. Some protocols, such as POP3 and IMAP4, are optional. The following section, "Adding More Protocols to the Mix," describes protocols that are used when a mail message reaches its destination. The transfer protocols that deliver mail to its destination are described in this list:

✔ **Domain Name System (DNS):** A protocol, a service, an application, and a distributed database. The protocol and service translate server names into numeric IP addresses so that the e-mail can be shipped from computer to computer.

✔ **Lightweight Directory Access Protocol (LDAP):** Another part of the TCP/IP suite. It's optional but can help you address your e-mail by letting your MUA look up e-mail addresses for people and groups.

✔ **Simple Mail Transfer Protocol (SMTP):** The TCP/IP protocol that MTAs all over the Internet use to communicate to send and deliver e-mail. SMTP might be "invisible," but it's a hard worker. Without SMTP, there would be no way for an MTA to deliver e-mail to another MTA on another computer.

Adding More Protocols to the Mix

After SMTP hands off an e-mail message to the final destination MTA (which deposits it in the correct mailbox), the recipient controls what happens next. The e-mail environment often provides options for how and when recipients' MUAs present messages for their reading pleasure (or not) and for where the messages are stored.

Because we're talking about clients (MUAs) and servers (MTAs), there must be protocols — where there are protocols and servers, there are services!

Your mail server must give you a way to access the mail in your mailbox. These days, most mail server software gives you several choices, including these:

✔ Post Office Protocol, version 3 (POP3)

✔ Internet Message Access Protocol, version 4 (IMAP4)

✔ Hypertext Transfer Protocol (HTTP)

✔ Lightweight Directory Access Protocol (LDAP)

In most cases, these services are so tightly integrated with the mail server software that you can't tell them apart.

POP3

By default, POP3 e-mail processing is *offline*. Your MUA connects to the POP3 server by using a valid username and password and then downloads all messages in your mailbox and deletes them from the e-mail server. This means you have to read e-mail on your local computer, but after POP3 downloads your e-mail to your computer, you can disconnect from the network, if you want.

If you read your e-mail from many different computers, you can also wind up with "puddles" of e-mail all over the place! Messages you read at work aren't available at your home computer and vice versa. Fortunately, you can override the default behavior by configuring an option in your MUA to leave messages on the server until you explicitly delete them.

IMAP4

In contrast to POP3, the default for IMAP4 e-mail processing is *online*. Your MUA accesses the IMAP4 server and your mailbox as though it were on your local computer. With IMAP4, you keep e-mail on either the server or your local computer or both. You set the message storage options when you set up your MUA. You can read e-mail from your computer at home, your workstation at the office, and a PDA while on a business trip, all without moving messages off the server or transferring them between your various computers. You can scroll through the headers and download only the messages you want to be local.

Table 13-2 lists the differences between POP3 and IMAP4.

Table 13-2	POP3 versus IMAP4	
Feature	*POP3*	*IMAP4*
Default storage location	User's computer	Server
Default reading style	Offline	Online
TCP port number	110	143
Server overhead	Small	Large
Network connect time	Small	Depends; usually longer
Disk storage restrictions	Size of local drive	Possibility of disk quotas and limits
Ease of configuration	Simple	Complicated
Value for mobile	No	Yes

You must match your MUA's protocol to that of the e-mail server with the MTA you're connecting to. For example, a POP3 MUA cannot communicate with an IMAP4 server.

HTTP

If you read your e-mail with a Web browser, you're using HTTP. It isn't an e-mail protocol, but then your browser isn't an e-mail client either. It works and we like it, so who cares?

LDAP

Lightweight Directory Address Protocol (LDAP) is another optional piece of an e-mail system that makes your MUA more user friendly. If your MUA works with LDAP, you may never need to type another e-mail address. Popular e-mail clients can all use LDAP. When you send a message, LDAP makes it possible for you to enter a name rather than an address for the recipient.

LDAP helps your MUA work with a directory *service,* which is simply a type of database that stores information — in the case of e-mail, information about people, including their e-mail addresses. Here's how it works:

1. Rather than address e-mail to `emilyd@e-mailland.com` (a fictitious address), Sarah presses Ctrl+E (or chooses the Edit➪Find➪People command).

2. Sarah selects a directory service from the Look In menu.

3. She fills in Emily's name and clicks the Find Now box.

4. The MUA contacts the directory service by following LDAP rules and looks up Emily.

5. If the directory service finds multiple instances of people named Emily, it tells the MUA, and the MUA gives Sarah a list of people named Emily to choose from. Sarah selects one and sends the message.

DNS and its MX records

Every MX record contains the name of the domain that the e-mail is being sent to, the priority for the record, and the hostname that receives e-mail for that domain. The MX record with the lowest preference is the first server to try. The following two records list the hosts that can deliver e-mail for `example.com`:

example.com	MX	5	mailsrv1.example.com
example.com	MX	10	mailsrv2.example.com

Both mailsrv1 and mailsrv2 can accept e-mail for `example.com`, but mailsrv1 is the "preferred" server because it has the higher priority.

In the preceding section, Sarah wanted to send an e-mail message to her sister Emily. In Figure 13-7, Sarah's message benefits from an MX record that specifies the e-mail server for Emily's domain.

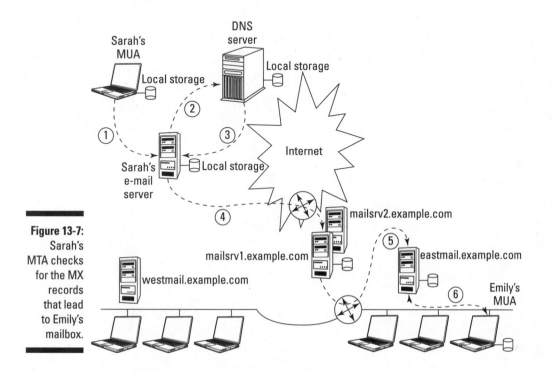

Figure 13-7:
Sarah's
MTA checks
for the MX
records
that lead
to Emily's
mailbox.

Here are the steps for getting Sarah's e-mail to Emily:

1. On her computer, Sarah writes the message in her MUA, specifies Emily's e-mail address (the fictitious `emily@eastmail.example.com`), and clicks Send. The MUA puts the message in local storage for outbound e-mail and sends the stored message to Sarah's e-mail server by using SMTP.

2. The MTA on Sarah's e-mail server receives the message and puts it in local storage for outbound e-mail because the message isn't intended for any user of that e-mail server. The server asks the DNS for information about `eastmail.example.com`.

3. The DNS server's response includes the MX records for the entire `example.com` domain. They declare that this message to Emily can't go directly to her e-mail server. It must go through the "front door," `mail.example.com`.

4. The MTA on Sarah's e-mail server sends the stored message to `mail.example.com` by using SMTP. The MTA on `mail.example.com` receives the message and puts it in local storage for outbound e-mail

(messages it needs to send) because the message isn't intended for any user of that e-mail server. This step represents store-and-forward in action!

5. The MTA on `mail.example.com` sends the stored message to Emily's e-mail server by using SMTP. The MTA receives the message and puts it in Emily's mailbox.

6. When Emily chooses to read her e-mail, her MUA retrieves the message from her e-mail server by using POP3 (or perhaps IMAP4) and puts it in local storage on Emily's computer. The message may or may not be deleted from the server, depending on how Emily configures her MUA.

To discover the MX records that are registered for a domain, you need software that handles name server queries. The most common are dig, host, and nslookup. Here's an example of using nslookup to find Apple Computer's MX records:

```
C:\> nslookup
Default Server:  Wireless_Broadband_Router.home
Address:  192.168.1.1

> set type=mx
> apple.com
Server:  Wireless_Broadband_Router.home
Address:  192.168.1.1

Non-authoritative answer:
apple.com       MX preference = 20, mail exchanger = mail-in2.apple.com
apple.com       MX preference = 20, mail exchanger = mail-in6.apple.com
apple.com       MX preference = 100, mail exchanger = mail-in3.apple.com
apple.com       MX preference = 25, mail exchanger = eg-mail-in2.apple.com
apple.com       MX preference = 10, mail exchanger = mail-in11.apple.com
apple.com       MX preference = 10, mail exchanger = mail-in12.apple.com
apple.com       MX preference = 10, mail exchanger = mail-in13.apple.com
apple.com       MX preference = 15, mail exchanger = eg-mail-in11.apple.com
apple.com       MX preference = 20, mail exchanger = mail-in1.apple.com

mail-in6.apple.com          internet address = 17.254.13.9
mail-in3.apple.com          internet address = 17.254.13.8
eg-mail-in2.apple.com       internet address = 17.112.144.124
mail-in11.apple.com         internet address = 17.254.13.7
mail-in12.apple.com         internet address = 17.254.13.10
mail-in13.apple.com         internet address = 17.254.13.11
eg-mail-in11.apple.com      internet address = 17.112.144.127
mail-in1.apple.com          internet address = 17.254.13.4
mail-in2.apple.com          internet address = 17.254.13.5
>
> exit

C:\
```

Chapter 14

Securing E-Mail

· ·

· ·

E-mail is one of the biggest threats to your client, server, host, intranet, and Internet security. If you think you have nothing to hide, remember that e-mail security is always a personal privacy issue even if you aren't mailing credit card numbers or the secret formula for eternal youth. E-mail security involves three concepts:

✔ **Confidentiality:** An e-mail message should be seen only by its sender and recipients.

✔ **Authenticity:** As a recipient, you should know that e-mail comes from the sender, not from someone claiming to be the sender. As a sender, your e-mail should go only to the recipient (or recipients), not to someone claiming to be the recipient.

✔ **Integrity:** No unauthorized person should be able to modify an e-mail message.

This chapter is full of tips for securing e-mail. You find how to secure your e-mail client and secure your server, host, and network. If you use a browser client to read your mail, please check Chapter 11 for secure browsing tips.

Common Sense: The Most Important Tool in Your Security Arsenal

Everyone has common sense (unless you hear Candace's mother talk about her). The problem is that all of us occasionally forget our common sense or believe that we can put off something simple until we have more time. Because you obviously have lots of common sense, you probably already abide by the following advice, but just in case you need a reminder:

- ✔ **Keep your usernames and passwords secure.** Don't reveal them even (especially?) to Bill Gates.

- ✔ **Be diligent about installing security updates.** Most operating systems warn you when they publish updates. Figure 14-1 shows how Ubuntu Linux informs you that updates are waiting.

- ✔ **Be suspicious.** Be wary of anything or anyone unknown who wants access to your network or computer.

This is a true story. Marshall's sister took her computer to a well-known store with excellent references to be repaired. When she got it back, it had a different hard drive, smaller capacity, different manufacturer, and no data. Luckily, she tested her computer right away, found that her data was gone, went back to the store, and they returned her drive. Maybe it was some kind of silly mistake. We'll never know. We're not saying that computer repair people are dishonest — Marshall does a lot of computer diagnostics and performance upgrades for people who trust him but are strangers. Just be careful.

You can find more common sense and best practice tips for security in Chapter 20.

Figure 14-1:
This Ubuntu Linux computer needs its software updated.

> **Software updates available**
> Click on the notification icon to show the available updates.

Being Aware of Possible Attacks

Before you can decide which security tools will work for your e-mail environment, knowing what can possibly happen is important.

Even while this book is being printed, someone with too much time on his hands may be inventing a new kind of attack in addition to the threats listed in the following sections.

Phishing

Phishing e-mail tries to get you to go to some bogus Web site that looks official. A couple of years ago, Candace got an e-mail that looked like it came from her bank. The URL looked like her bank's, and the logo was the same, but the content was smelly. It asked her to confirm her personal information. She contacted the bank before replying to the phishy e-mail.

Another aspect of phishing is to report a problem and offer to fix it. One of these scams is to notify you that you have a serious security or performance problem and if you run their free program, all will be fixed. Some of these sites are legitimate, and after they give you a security or performance report, they offer to sell you a legitimate, safe product to fix your problems. When malicious sites "fix" the problem, they download all kinds of malware.

See Chapter 12 for information about a new phishing attack — spear-phishing.

Popping up and under

Pop-ups are a form of online advertising on the Web to put you on mailing lists and lure you to Web sites, where groups can collect more information about you. They come up automatically and are usually written in JavaScript. (See Chapter 11 about the languages of the Web.) Before the advent of pop-up blockers, your entire desktop could become covered with ads. The truly foul pop-ups kept returning faster than you could delete them until your desktop was covered with the same ad many times over.

Pop-under advertisements open under your active window. You see them only when you close the window. Sometimes you need to close all windows before you see the pop-under. As people got wise to pop-ups, they immediately closed them, defeating the purpose of the adverts. The idea behind pop-unders is to catch your undivided attention when you close your browser window.

Getting spied on

Cybersnoops sometimes eavesdrop on postal mail to look for all sorts of confidential information.

Imagine that you're having a wonderful time in Tahiti, but you run out of money. What do you do? Send a letter to Mum, asking for money. This letter moves from the post office in Tahiti to Australia to Singapore to Bombay to Cairo and finally reaches good old Mum in Dublin. Suppose that in each post office, an employee steams open and reads your mail. How rude! You think "If only I'd e-mailed to Mum instead, so no one would have known I was in debt." The problem is that e-mail messages are passed in plain text, so people can read your e-mail too unless you've protected it.

Keyloggers — spyware for good or evil?

Keyloggers record every keystroke you type. You can find software keyloggers or hardware appliances that do keylogging:

✔ *Software keyloggers* that you install on someone's computer are the most well known. These programs use very little memory or CPU, so they're unnoticeable. They can e-mail or FTP to the spy the file containing the keystrokes. Someone can install a keylogger on your computer if they can gain access when you go to lunch or a meeting, or they can download keyloggers inside an innocent-seeming e-mail or instant message. Your security products should be able to catch many malicious downloads.

Tip: When you get up from your computer to take a break, remember to lock your computer with a password screen. It takes only a minute for someone to set up a keylogger or any other program that you don't want.

✔ *Hardware keylogging appliances* are small devices that usually go on the back of your computer. They're hard to spot because of their size and colors. Keylogger hardware can also sit inside your computer, next to the keyboard port or inside the keyboard itself. These devices are physically invisible and don't usually show up as a device in Windows control panels.

Keylogging for good has a couple of purposes:

✔ As a parent, if you feel that your children are unsafe in cyberspace, or that cyberspace is unsafe from your children, you can record all their activities, including e-mail, with keyloggers. Parents debate with each other their children's right to privacy, and they also debate it with their children. (We're not getting into the middle of that discussion. We had to wrestle with that one ourselves.) Decide what you need to do. The tools are out there. Just search for the term *keyloggers* to find dozens of products, many of them free.

✔ Keylogging makes an effective training aid. When Candace teaches computer classes, she sets up a keylogger on herself and transmits her keystrokes to all the computers in the room so that attendees can see every keystroke in a demonstration.

Keylogging for evil has one purpose: To spy on and steal information, such as e-mail messages containing credit card numbers, bank account information, usernames, passwords, industrial secrets, and anything else you consider private. Keyloggers e-mail or FTP back to the spy a file containing keystrokes.

If you're concerned about being keylogged, you can find antikeylogger programs. We haven't tested their effectiveness.

Your mail message goes through more computers than just yours and your recipient's. Take a look at Chapter 13, especially the section about store and forward to read how mail can be stored briefly and forwarded through several computers on its way to its destination. A hacker doesn't even have to be good to snoop on your mail. All the busybody has to do to intercept passing mail messages is use a *packet sniffer,* which is a program that network administrators use to record and analyze network traffic — but the bad guys use them, too. Dozens of free packet sniffers are available on the Internet. Packet sniffers capture data from packets as they travel over a network. That data may be clear text, usernames, passwords, and confidential information, such as medical records and industrial secrets.

Spyware programs may put you at risk for identity theft or fraud. Programs scan systems and monitor activity, relaying the information to other computers.

Meeting malware

Software on your computer that you didn't intentionally install and that's running against your wishes and your interests is *malware*. It includes

- ✔ **Virus:** Usually arrives in an e-mail attachment. If you forward the e-mail, you unknowingly pass along the virus. A virus can affect individual computers or the entire network.

- ✔ **Worm:** A virus subtype that jumps from one computer to another on its own.

- ✔ **Trojan horse:** Seemingly innocent but secretly provides a way into your computer or network. Most Trojan horse programs create a way (a "back door") into your computer that you're not aware of. Cybersnoops set up back doors to access your private data or control your computer remotely.

- ✔ **Spyware:** Another favorite of cybersnoops that, unknown to you, tracks your online activities. Spyware may not be destructive to your computer and network, but they're destructive to you personally. The purpose of spyware is to steal personal information from you. Spyware can do something simple, such as monitor the Web sites you visit and use the information for market research and ads. At the other extreme, spyware can monitor every keystroke you type and collect all your private information.

- ✔ **Adware:** An annoying form of malware that displays advertisements. Sometimes, adware appears in Web sites to subsidize the cost of free applications, such as e-mail providers and game software. That's why adware doesn't exactly qualify as malware. It's in a special category: *annoying*ware.

Bombing

Bombing happens when nasty people continually send the same message to your e-mail address. This doesn't mean that someone who accidentally sends you the same message twice is a mad bomber. However, if someone sends you 200 copies of the same message, you can safely assume it's not an innocent mistake. Sometimes, bombing is targeted at your machine and not at you specifically. In either case, the damage has been done. The purpose of bombing is to slow down or fill up your computer and network.

If you believe you've been bombed, you must notify your ISP and security agencies so that they can track down the bomber. Here are a couple of important agencies to notify:

- ✔ **Computer Emergency Response Team (CERT):** In addition to acting on security intrusions, CERT maintains a list of notices of security problems and possible solutions. You can find the CERT Coordination Center incident reporting form at `www.cert.org/tech_tips/incident_reporting.html`.

- ✔ **Internet Crime Compliance Center (IC3):** You can find the IC3 reporting form at `www.ic3.gov/complaint/default.aspx`.

- ✔ **U.S. Federal Bureau of Investigation (FBI):** Notify the agency's National Computer Crime Squad in Washington, D.C.: `www.tscm.com/compcrim.html`; 202-324-9164; or `nccs-sf@fbi.gov`.

- ✔ **Other international organizations:** For example, many nations maintain their own CERTs. Wikipedia (`www.wikipedia.com`) maintains a list of international CERTs at

  ```
  http://en.wikipedia.org/wiki/Computer_Emergency_Response_Team#Other_
                          countries
  ```

Have you got anything without spam? Spam, spam, spam!

When someone sends junk mail to many (hundreds and more) users, they're *spamming,* which is a variation of bombing. You can easily become an accidental spammer: If you click your e-mail program's Reply All button and send a reply to a worldwide distribution list, you're a spammer. You might also be quite an embarrassed spammer if your message is confidential to one person and is sent out to everyone. Spamming has become less of a problem because e-mail clients have improved their spam protection, but it still happens. Any message from a stranger asking for money is almost always spam.

If you go on vacation and set up an automatic mail responder program, be careful not to let the information wind up in the hands of spammers. You might set up your autoresponder message to read, "I'm out of the office on vacation for ten days." This message goes out to all mailing list messages you receive, including those of spammers. Thieves have used autoresponder information to rob houses.

Spoofing

Spoofing happens when you receive e-mail from a fake address. If spoofing doesn't seem like it could be a major problem for you, think about this: Suppose that you receive e-mail from a system administrator telling you that you should immediately change your password to a new, administrator-defined password for security reasons. Most people comply because the system administrator knows best, right? Imagine the consequences, however, if a spoofer sent this e-mail, faking the system administrator's e-mail address, to all users of a network. All of a sudden, the spoofer knows everyone's passwords and has access to private and potentially sensitive or secret data.

Spoofing is possible because plain-vanilla SMTP (Simple Mail Transfer Protocol) doesn't have authentication capabilities. Without authentication features, SMTP can't be sure that incoming mail is from the address it says it is. Chapter 12 gives a brief description of authentication. In Chapter 21, we explain authentication in more detail. If your mail server allows connections to the SMTP port, anyone with a little knowledge of the internal workings of SMTP can telnet to that port and send you e-mail that appears to be from a spoofed address. Besides connecting to the SMTP port of a site, a user can send spoofed e-mail by modifying Web browser interfaces.

Plain-vanilla SMTP has a flavorful extension that allows an SMTP client to exchange authentication with the mail server. This service adds another part of the TCP/IP suite, Simple Authentication and Security Layer (SASL) for SMTP. SASL is a way to add authentication support to connection-based protocols. (See Chapters 2 and 8 for information about connection-based and connectionless protocols.) Although the title of the RFC (4954) is "SMTP Service Extension for Authentication," most of the time you see it as SMTP-AUTH.

You use SMTP-AUTH with your MTA, such as postfix or sendmail. With SMTP-AUTH installed, the mail client needs to go through one more step: Log in to the MTA mail server as part of sending mail. Servers that support SMTP-AUTH can require clients to use this additional step, to verify the authenticity of their identity.

Finding Out Whether You're a Victim

If your machine or network suddenly slows way down, or if your disk space mysteriously disappears, you may have been hacked. When you suspect hacking is the reason for your computer and network problems, start running down the problem by doing the following:

✔ **Check your log files for security events.** Whatever your operating system, you do run some kind of event logging, don't you? Operating systems usually have built-in logging functions.

> ✔ **Run a thorough antivirus scan of your entire computer.** Sure, it may take a while to run, but it's vital that you leave no stone unturned.
>
> ✔ **Run a thorough antispyware scan of your entire computer.** This process may also take a while, but it's still vital. Think of it as wearing a belt and suspenders to ensure that your pants don't fall down.

As you gain more experience in using the tools and investigating malware, you enhance your instincts about which tools to run when and in which order.

Playing Hide-and-Seek with Your E-Mail Address

A good way to protect your identity is to conceal your e-mail address from public sites. For example, if you want to visit a Web site that requires you to register but you regard registering as an invasion of your privacy and you're not interested in ever receiving e-mail from it, you can use a throwaway address. The Web site www.bugmenot.com (shown in Figure 14-2) is especially useful for this purpose.

When you visit the site, you search for the site that's forcing you to register. BugMeNot keeps a list of valid usernames and passwords that work with popular Web sites. Volunteers have spent time creating these usernames and passwords for those of us who like to remain private. It's all completely legal, at least in the United States.

Figure 14-2:
BugMeNot helps protect your privacy by keeping your e-mail address unlisted.

Layering Security

By now you're familiar with the TCP/IP layer cake of protocols, services, and applications. Now you're about to meet the security "onion," with layers of security that this chapter peels off and inspects one by one (see Figure 14-3).

If one layer of security is good, more are better.

After you know the possible threats to your personal information and computer and network safety, you can start to protect yourself. The following sections give you the lowdown on five layers of protection.

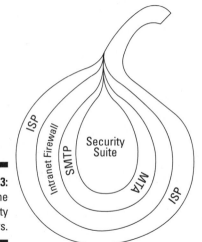

Figure 14-3:
Peeling the
security
layers.

Layer 1: Letting your ISP protect your network

A good firewall is your first layer of defense, like a moat around a castle, much as you can see in Figure 14-4. If your intranet is your castle, no matter how large or small, you defend it with a series of walls. Firewall protection starts at your ISP — Security Layer 1. It's useful to check with your ISP to see which firewalls they install on their servers and check out the features of those firewalls.

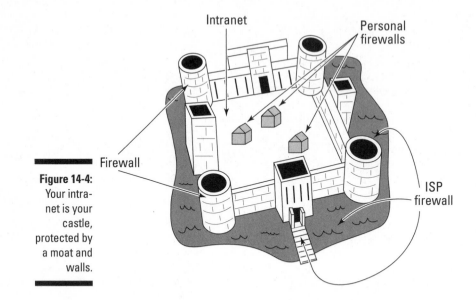

Intranet

Personal firewalls

Firewall

ISP firewall

Figure 14-4:
Your intra-
net is your
castle,
protected by
a moat and
walls.

Layer 2: Building your own walls

Don't stop with your ISP. Be sure to use firewalls to protect your home and office networks. Firewalls protect your network from unsafe incoming traffic and protect other networks from any dangerous outgoing traffic from your network, regardless of whether it's unintentional or malicious. Most routers have built-in firewalls. Way over in Chapter 5, Figure 5-1 illustrates an intranet with two subnets that are protected by a multipurpose router. Be sure that yours does. Otherwise, buy a firewall appliance — the sole purpose of this dedicated hardware and software system is to protect a network.

Here's the lowdown on using firewalls to protect your network and personal computer:

- ✔ **Protect your network.** If you receive mail from people outside your network, be sure that a firewall protects your network. Most routers, including routers for small office/home office (SOHO) environments, include a firewall. For example, if you don't want anything from Snoopers.com to penetrate your net, put your net behind a firewall. The firewall can then block out all Snoopers.com messages. See Chapter 12 for a quick intro to firewalls. If you're interested in more details about firewalls, Chapter 20 is for you. Refer to Figure 14-4 to see an intranet protected by a combination router/firewall.

✔ **Protect your personal computer.** You can also install a personal firewall on an individual computer. Recent Windows operating systems include the Microsoft Windows Personal Firewall. Ubuntu Linux has Firestarter. Other Linux and Unix distributions, as well as Mac OS X, include built-in personal firewalls. If your operating system has no personal firewall, you have a wide choice that you can download for free.

If you use a firewall from a security suite, such as Norton Internet Security or ZoneAlarm Pro, don't — we repeat, do *not* — also use Windows personal firewall. The firewall speaks to TCP/IP. Two firewalls will confuse your network protocols. However, if you're going mobile and using your notebook computer at a Wi-Fi hot spot, you have no real protection. Then it's time to turn on your personal firewall.

On Mac OS X, if you run a Web, mail, and DNS server on the same machine (and then you should think about using dedicated computers for each server), you need to enable ports 80 (Web), 25 and 110 (mail), and 53 (DNS). You can set the ports under Firewall Preferences: Choose Systems Preferences➪Sharing Panel➪Firewall tab➪Firewall Preferences. Figure 14-5 shows what the Firewall Preferences window looks like.

If you forget to enable the Web, mail, and DNS ports explicitly, your Mac personal firewall blocks incoming information for those services.

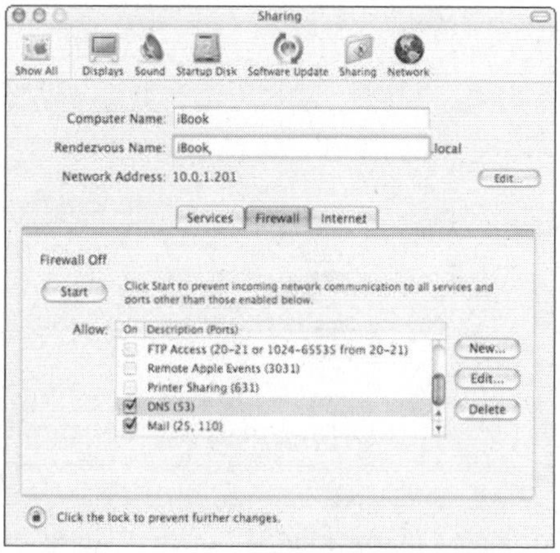

Figure 14-5:
You need
to do a little
extra work
to set up
the Mac OS
X personal
firewall.

Layer 3: Securing e-mail on the server side

After you set up your firewalls to protect your entire network, it's time to secure your servers. Thankfully, modern e-mail clients have lots of security features built in and turned on so that end users who don't want to do anything other than read and send mail are still protected. It's not so easy with servers. The life of a network administrator is never dull — almost always chaotic, but never dull. If you're a network administrator or security specialist, it's your responsibility to protect your organization's mail servers. If you're in a small office, your mail server is most likely at your ISP's, and its job is to protect the mail servers.

Killing spam with SpamAssassin

SpamAssassin (try saying it three times fast) is free open source software that runs on your mail server and identifies spam before it gets to you. The Web page www.spamassassin.apache.org/downloads.cgi provides links for downloading SpamAssassin. The program tests each message against a long set of rules that specify which kinds of messages might be spam. You can also write your own, custom rules for SpamAssassin. After testing a message, SpamAssassin gives the message a numeric score. You want to see low scores (0 and lower) on your messages. The higher the score, the higher the possibility that your e-mail is spam, and you shouldn't open it. SpamAssassin doesn't do anything to the message other than score it. It's up to you to decide how to handle the spam. Most e-mail clients have ways for you to deal with it.

Mac OS X Server (Leopard) includes SpamAssassin. It runs on Linux, Unix, Mac OS X, and Microsoft Windows (32-bit Windows only).

Installing SpamAssassin on Windows is complicated. You can find step-by-step instructions for downloading the required software and installing SpamAssassin at http://wiki.apache.org/spamassassin/InstallingOnWindows.

Shoring up SMTP with central e-mail servers

Mail transfer agent (MTA) software uses various TCP/IP mail protocols including SMTP, POP3, and IMAP4. SMTP is especially vulnerable.

You can keep to a minimum the number of computers vulnerable to SMTP-based attacks by using only a few centralized e-mail servers, depending on the size of your organization.

Allow SMTP connections that come from outside your firewall to go only to those few central e-mail servers. This policy protects the other computers on your network. If your site gets spammed or bombed, you have to clean up the central e-mail servers, but the rest of your networked computers will be okay.

Take a look at Figure 14-6. An SMTP connection from an MTA somewhere on the Internet, transporting an e-mail message to Marshall, is blocked by the firewall from going directly to his actual e-mail server, Neptunium. Instead, the connection is diverted to his organization's central mail server sitting in a demilitarized zone (DMZ). Chapter 20 describes a DMZ setup.

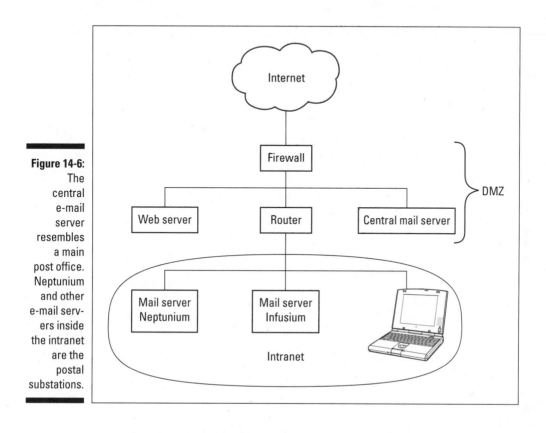

The central e-mail server runs an MTA that accepts mail on behalf of all the organization's internal mail servers and also maintains a directory of users within the corporate intranet. The directory can be something as simple as a list of e-mail aliases, including mwilensky@example.com, which really means marshall_wilensky@us.example.com or something as compli-cated as a corporate-wide database that works with the LDAP protocol. Because of the directory, when you send mail to Marshall, you never need to know exactly which computer is serving his mail — how convenient! The mail message passes through the firewall to the central mail server and is for-warded through the router to the MTA on Neptunium, which serves up mail to lots of users at Marshall's company. Neptunium notifies Marshall that he has new mail, which he finally reads with the MUA, described in depth in Chapter 13.

Making sure your MTA serves up security

In the trusting, friendly past, the essential service that an MTA performed was to route e-mail. Today, if moving mail is the main course, your MTA needs to serve up security as a side dish while it moves mail. Be sure that your MTA can provide security services such as the following (for a more complete explanation of these concepts, see Chapter 21):

- ✔ **SMTP authentication:** Proves that incoming mail is coming from the server that the mail says it's coming from — no spoofing allowed

- ✔ **E-mail encryption with Pretty Good Privacy (PGP):** Encodes e-mail messages so that only you and the recipient can read them

- ✔ **Software add–ons and updates:** Keeps your mail free from viruses and spam

- ✔ **A log of incoming traffic:** Used by the network administrator to track down potential bombers, spammers, and spoofers

Layer 4: Securing e-mail on the client side

Everyone, whether end user, corporate officer, network administrator, or even Bill Gates can and should be sure that they use their e-mail client (MUA) or browser securely.

If you use the tips and techniques in the following sections and teach them to others, you can gain some comfort about the confidentiality, authenticity, and integrity of your e-mail. But always stay alert and at least a little suspicious. Just because you're paranoid doesn't mean that some hacker isn't trying to break into your e-mail. Getting into your e-mail gives a hacker a chance to go beyond your e-mail and into your computer and network.

Don't think that using S/MIME for security can completely protect you.

Taking advantage of built-in e-mail client security

When e-mail clients include their own security functions, you've added another layer of security. We use the Mozilla Thunderbird e-mail client as an example of comprehensive security checking. Most e-mail clients include some level of built-in security, although Thunderbird and Chrome are exceptionally thorough.

One neat Thunderbird features is the use of add-ons (extensions). Programmers and organizations other than Mozilla write code for Thunderbird that can be downloaded and added to the Thunderbird e-mail client.

If your e-mail address needs to appear in public, such as on a Web page, you can use a popular method of disguising an address by substituting the word *at* for the @ sign; for example, `emilydatexample.com` for `emilyd@example.com`. If you want to fool spam harvesters, you can create an image of your e-mail address and put it on a Web page.

Terminology tips

In the e-mail terminology mix, remember these guidelines:

✔ Your MTA (also known as your mail server) software — such as postfix, sendmail, or Microsoft Exchange Server — communicates with other MTAs to get your mail to wherever you want it to go.

✔ SMTP is the protocol that MTAs use to communicate with each other. Although you sometimes hear people refer to "SMTP servers," technically, there's no such thing. SMTP is a protocol and only a protocol. When you hear or read about SMTP servers, the reference probably should be to an MTA.

✔ POP3 and IMAP4 are retrieval client/server software programs. After your destination MTA receives a message for you, it passes the message off to POP3 or IMAP4 for delivery to your mailbox.

✔ You send and read and manage your e-mail with whatever you choose — either an e-mail client or a Web browser.

Are we being too picky? Maybe, but at least everyone who's reading this book is on the same page, terminologically speaking.

Stalling spoofing

Be suspicious of your e-mail messages. You can never be sure that an e-mail message came from the person it says it's from. Anyone who wants to send fraudulent e-mail messages can change the name of her computer and domain — and even her username. When the message goes through, SMTP doesn't verify the username, the computer name, or even the sender's e-mail address. It just passes the message through with the counterfeit information. Figure 14-7 shows the SMTP dialogue between the sending and receiving computers.

One way to protect yourself from spoofing is to accept e-mail only from sites that authenticate data with digital certificates. However, you may find this method too restrictive, especially at home. One of our sisters, for example, doesn't have a digital certificate, and we want to read e-mail from her. Another way to guard against spoofing is to require strong authentication measures, such as running Kerberos, a security protocol, a service, and an application described in Chapter 21. You can also set up your router to filter messages from unknown addresses. In addition, most complete security suites automatically block any attempted connections that seem suspect.

For more information about spoofing, see RFC 4953, "Defending TCP against Spoofing Attacks."

```
% mail -iv mwilensky@lotus.com
Subject: file to put on floopy
~rtools.txt
"tools.txt" 623/34384
.
Cc: leiden
leiden... Sent
mwilensky@lotus.com... Connecting to crd.lotus.com. (smtp)...
mwilensky@lotus.com... Connecting to lotus.com. (smtp)...
220 lotus.com Sendmail 4.1/SMI-4.10801.1994 ready at Wed, 31 May 95 09:49:27 EDT
>>> HELO max.tiac.net───────────── SMTP trusts that you are who you say you are.
250 lotus.com Hello max.tiac.net, pleased to meet you
>>> MAIL From:<leiden@max.tiac.net>
250 <leiden@max.tiac.net>... Sender ok──────── SMTP doesn't ask to see your ID.
>>> RCPT To:<mwilensky@lotus.com>
250 <mwilensky@lotus.com>... Recipient ok
>>> DATA
354 Enter mail, end with "." on a line by itself
>>> .
250 Mail accepted
mwilensky@lotus.com... Sent (Mail accepted)
Closing connection to lotus.com.
>>> QUIT
221 lotus.com delivering mail
You have mail in /usr/spool/mail/leiden
%
```

Figure 14-7:
The receiving SMTP computer believes what the sending computer tells it.

Phaking out phishing

Thunderbird protects you from phishing by displaying a message when an e-mail is potentially phishing. Thunderbird also warns you when you click on a link that seems to be taking you to a different URL than the one in the link.

Thunderbird's Sender Verification Anti-Phishing Extension reports, in most cases, whether the domain shown in the From header is truly the sender's domain. Thunderbird adds a sender verification line at the top of the e-mail message saying whether the sender is confirmed or that the "sender does not appear to be legitimate." Google Chrome displays a similar message: "This is probably not the site you are looking for!" The message is intended to be a tool to identify phishing and spoofing to prevent fraudulent e-mails that are trying to steal sensitive, private data.

You are one of the best e-mail security defenders that exist. Follow these tips and exercise caution when you read your e-mail:

- ✔ Be suspicious of e-mail messages asking for confidential information.

- ✔ Confirm the authenticity of a suspicious request before responding by e-mail.

- ✔ Never click any links in e-mail. Surf to the link directly.

- ✔ When you hover the mouse over a link, make sure that the text of the link and the address on the status bar are the same.

Suppressing spam

The Thunderbird spam-prevention tools, or junk mail *filters,* work with your e-mail provider's spam filters to give you double protection. Every time you mark a message as spam, Thunderbird learns from it and improves its filtering from the new information you provide.

You can protect against spam on your own in addition to using tools:

✔ If you suspect that an e-mail is spam, delete it without reading or responding.

✔ Disable your e-mail client's preview pane and read your e-mail in Plain Text mode.

Getting rid of pop-ups and banner ads

The Thunderbird add-on Adblock Plus gets rid of pop-ups and banner advertisements. Use a tool such as this one to supplement the pop-up blocker in your computer's security suite. You do have a comprehensive security suite, don't you? Some of the most well-known and popular include Norton, MacAfee, ZoneAlarm, and Kaspersky. The cost for all of them is reasonable, and you can find free security suites to download from the Web. Just be sure, as in any download, that it's from a respectable site.

Protecting against malware

Remote images are a sneaky place for sneaky hackers to hide viruses and for spammers and phishers who are trying to grab your e-mail address to look. Thunderbird has a blocking feature to protect against possible virus threats, and it's turned on by default. The feature blocks images from sources not in your address book. You can always change this option. Thunderbird sends you an alert at the top of any mail message whenever it blocks images. If the images are from a reliable site and you believe them to be clean, click Show Images.

Here are some tips for avoiding damage from malware:

✔ Open e-mail attachments only from senders you trust.

✔ Before you open an e-mail attachment, scan it with antivirus software. You can set up most antivirus software to scan attachments automatically.

✔ Delete all unwanted messages without opening them.

✔ If you're not sure about a message, some e-mail clients let you check it out before opening it. Read the Help file for your specific client.

✔ When reading Gmail in the Google Chrome browser, before opening a message, right-click it and choose Inspect Element so that you can, without opening the message, read the text embedded in the HTML. If you see anything suspicious, delete the mail.

✔ If your client has a preview window, don't use it, because the client opens the e-mail automatically.

Layer 5: Suitely extending e-mail security

A complete suite of security tools protects not only your e-mail but also your computer and network. The combination of a security suite and a safe e-mail client or browser work together to keep your e-mail secure. If you use a security suite, make sure it includes the following items to protect your e-mail:

- ✔ Firewall
- ✔ Antispam
- ✔ Antivirus or anti-malware
- ✔ Antiphishing
- ✔ Spyware protection
- ✔ Event logging

Using Secure Mail Clients and Servers

This section is about POP or IMAP layered over Secure Sockets Layer (SSL) or Transport Layer Security (TLS) to add security to your e-mail retrieval and to e-mail servers. Don't get all excited: It's *much* easier than it sounds.

In your e-mail client, all you have to do is click buttons that select POP3 or IMAP4. You can see how to do that in Chapter 13. Then you need to take one extra step: Click either SSL or TLS and you're done. Voilà! You added extra security to your e-mail client.

SSL and *TLS* are cryptographic protocols that provide security over the Internet by encrypting network connections. In the TCP/IP layer cake, TLS encrypts at the transport layer. SSL sits on top of TCP and encrypts at the application layer.

IMAP4rev1 is the official name for Secure IMAP. You may also see IMAP4rev1/ Secure IMAP as IMAPS or IMAPs.

Secure POP or IMAP layered over SSL or TLS encrypts the session between your mail client and server when you retrieve your mail. Earlier in this chapter, in the example where your mother e-mailed you that she was sending you money, you don't use a secure protocol to retrieve your mail. Your mail came over the network in plain text, making it easy for even a wannabe hacker with a packet sniffer to eavesdrop on your mail. To prevent that ugly situation, you need to use a secure POP or IMAP client. Secure POP and IMAP clients also ensure that your e-mail password is encrypted.

You can configure either an IMAP mail retrieval client or a POP mail retriever client to use either SSL or TLS when you connect to a server that's SSL or TLS enabled. Apple Mail, Outlook Express, Mozilla Thunderbird, Mulberry, mutt, Netscape Communicator, and Pine are some of the e-mail clients that let you run your IMAP4 or POP3 client over SSL or TLS.

Secure IMAP and Secure POP3 clients work only with secure servers.

Setting up a secure IMAP or POP client

Setting up a secure e-mail client involves just a few steps. The setup is basically the same for all e-mail clients that support POP or IMAP over TLS or SSL. In the following example, we use the Mozilla Thunderbird e-mail client. Thunderbird is available for all operating systems. Depending on your particular e-mail client, the dialog boxes and buttons will look a little different, but you add the same information as you see in Figures 14-8 and 14-9.

Follow these steps to set up a secure IMAP or POP client in Thunderbird:

1. **Ask your ISP or network administrator for the name of your secure IMAP or POP server.**

2. **Open Thunderbird and choose Edit⇨Account Settings for your username.** If you have an existing account, proceed to Step 5. If you need an account, continue straight ahead.

   If you don't have a Thunderbird account, click New Account and answer the wizard's questions. On the Server Information screen, shown in Figure 14-8, do the following:

   • Select POP or IMAP for your mail delivery protocol.

   • Type your incoming mail server's domain name, as shown in the figure.

3. **Highlight your account name in the left pane.**

4. **Choose Edit⇨Properties.**

5. **Select the Server Settings line in the left pane, just under your account name (see Figure 14-9), and look for the Security Settings section on the right.**

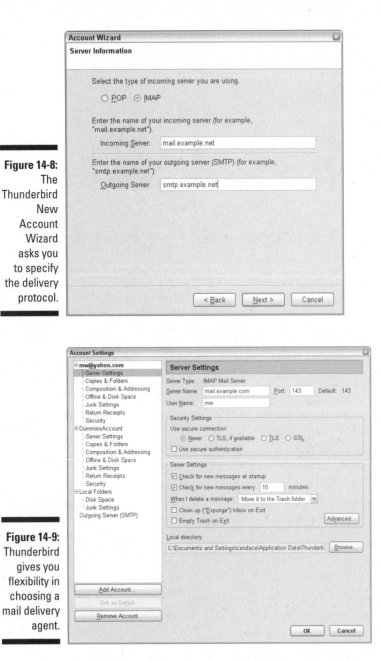

Figure 14-8:
The
Thunderbird
New
Account
Wizard
asks you
to specify
the delivery
protocol.

Figure 14-9:
Thunderbird
gives you
flexibility in
choosing a
mail delivery
agent.

6. Select either the TLS or SSL option, depending on your preference.

In the figure, Marshall is about to change Never to TLS for his account.

7. **Click OK.**

   At this point, you have secured the communication between your MUA and MTA.

TLS and SSL provide the same kind of security. The main difference is that TLS is on the Internet standards track and SSL was developed by Netscape.

Setting up a secure mail server

After setting security for your client, you may need to enable the same security for SMTP unless it's already been done. In the user pane on the left side of the Account Settings dialog box, click Outgoing Server (SMTP). Figure 14-10 shows the secure SMTP settings. SMTP is set to run under the username Marshall. It uses TLS, if possible, over port 25. When Marshall set up the properties for SMTP, the wizard also prompted him for the password for SMTP, although it's never displayed.

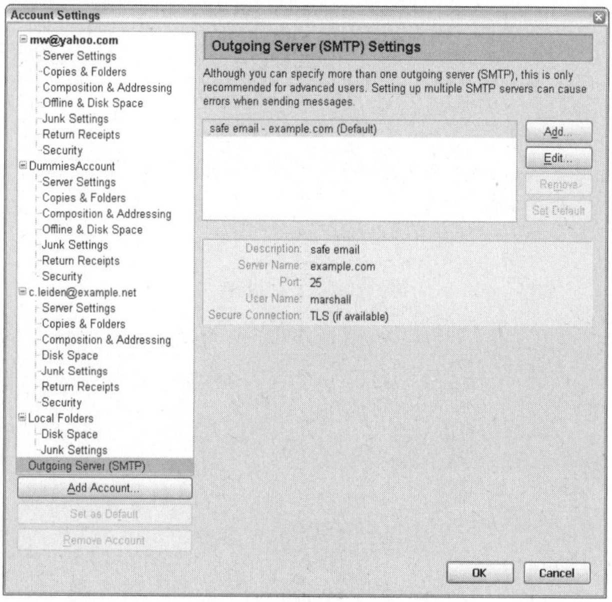

Figure 14-10: Be sure that the SMTP protocol is set to use the same delivery agent as the client.

Encrypting e-mail

E-mail encryption is easy and free. Pretty Good Privacy (PGP) encrypts e-mail to stop cyberthieves from stealing credit card numbers and information that can be used to commit identity theft.

Putting on PGP for encryption

Suppose that Sarah wants to send her sister, Emily, an e-mail about the mysterious, scary stranger who lives next door. This neighbor knows all the tricks, so he piggybacks on Sarah's Wi-Fi network and tries to hack whatever he can find. Of course, Sarah doesn't want Mr. Mystery to read the message she's sending to Emily. No problem: Emily uses PGP so that she has a pair of keys. In the encryption world, a *key* is just a string of letters and numbers, as shown in Figure 14-11. Emily's *public key* is available to everyone. She has made her public key available on her Web site for anyone who wants to send her encrypted e-mail messages. Emily's other key is a *private key*, which no one else has.

So Sarah looks up Emily's public key. She composes a message stating that her neighbor is weird and encrypts it with that public key. Without her pair of keys, the scary neighbor would be able to read Sarah's e-mail in plain text. Next, Sarah sends her message to Emily. In transit, that message looks like gobbledy-gook. Sarah's strange neighbor can't read her message, not even with a packet sniffer. He can't read the message because it's *encrypted* — it's in code.

You might wonder, after the e-mail is encrypted, how Emily will be able to read it. The answer is that, when Emily receives Sarah's message, Emily's private key decrypts it. Then Emily can read all about Sarah's neighbor in pretty good privacy (PGP).

The relationship between the keys is simple: Whatever one key of your pair encrypts, the other key decrypts.

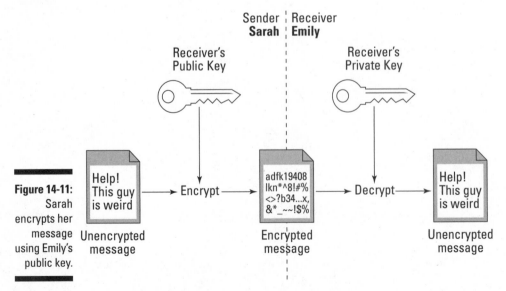

Figure 14-11: Sarah encrypts her message using Emily's public key.

Creating PGP keys

You set up PGP in a few simple steps. The following steps use the Thunderbird e-mail client as an example:

1. **From the Thunderbird main menu, choose Tools⇨Addons⇨Get Extensions.**

2. **Search for the string *openpgp* in the Privacy and Security section, shown in Figure 14-12.**

   You can also scroll through a list of add-ons rather than search the *openpgp* string.

3. **Download the EnigMail extension to provide OpenPGP message encryption and authentication for Thunderbird.**

   Refer to Figure 14-12 to see EnigMail listed in the Privacy and Security category for Thunderbird add-ons.

4. **Choose Tools⇨Install EnigMail. You're prompted for the file you downloaded in Step 3, as shown in Figure 14-13. Either double-click the filename or click Open.**

Figure 14-12:
Find the
OpenPGP
add-on.

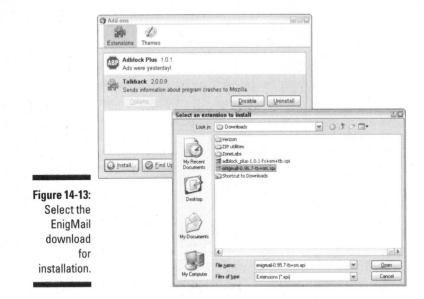

Figure 14-13:
Select the
EnigMail
download
for
installation.

5. **Click Install Now.**

   Notice that the main menu displays a new choice: OpenPGP, shown in
   Figure 14-14.

6. **Set your preferences and click Key Management. Key Management
   guides you through the remaining steps.**

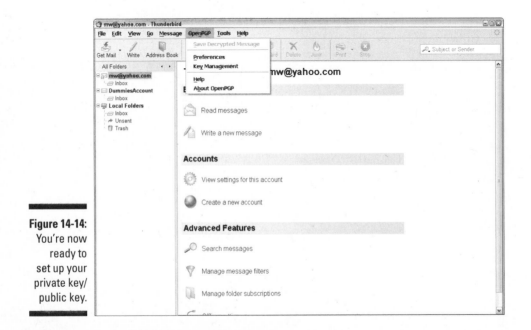

Figure 14-14:
You're now
ready to
set up your
private key/
public key.

Chapter 15

Beyond E-Mail: Social Networking and Online Communities

*T*hese days, whenever you want to communicate with other people, you have many options, but two major factors affect your choices: time and place.

Figure 15-1 shows you many ways to overcome the challenges of time and space. Plus, you can communicate *one-to-one,* one person to another person (1:1); *one-to-many* (1:n), one person to many people; *many-to-one* (n:1), many people to one person; and *many-to-many* (n:m), many people to many people.

Because we're all busy people with lots of communicating to do, this chapter doesn't detail all these solutions. Although TCP/IP makes them all possible, many of them use protocols that are covered in other chapters. Still, you should understand what's out there, and that's what this chapter is about.

You often have the best chance of communicating with someone if you stick with e-mail. The standards are terrific, and interoperability is amazingly high. When all else fails, e-mail it! (Chapter 13 gives you all the details about e-mail.)

	Same Time (synchronous)	**Different Times** (asynchronous)
Same Place (local)	Face-to-face conversations, passing notes, sign language	Paper notes, bulletin board flyers
Different Places (remote)	Telephoning, texting, instant messaging, voice/video chat, e-meetings and e-learning, virtual worlds	Postal mail, fax, e-mail, blog, wiki, Web sites

Figure 15-1:
Where, when, and how can you talk with someone?

Thumbing to Talk About

In addition to making voice calls, mobile (cell) phone users can send and receive text messages by using one of these two protocols:

- ✔ **SMS (Short Message Service):** Text-only
- ✔ **MMS (Multimedia Messaging Service):** Can include text, pictures, audio, and video

Exchanging messages with others is called *texting* or *text messaging*. Texting isn't the same as chatting, which is covered in the next section. Text messages move from phone to phone through the service provider's network (or providers' networks). People can also send e-mail messages to mobile phones. In that case, Simple Mail Transfer Protocol (SMTP; see Chapter 13) delivers the message to a gateway that converts the message and delivers it using SMS.

Typing a text message on a mobile phone is also called *thumbing* because it's natural to use only those fingers on the standard 12-key keypad. To spell words, you have to press keys multiple times *(multitap)* or learn a predictive text system (such as T9) that guesses which word you might be spelling. If you're not paying attention to the guesses, you might send words you didn't intend. Correcting an incorrect prediction requires more key presses. (If you thumb too much, you might get the repetitive strain injury known as Blackberry thumb, named in honor of Research In Motion smartphones, despite the fact that they use only small QWERTY keyboards.)

Smartphones that can access the Internet gain two protocols:

- ✔ **PAP (Push Access Protocol):** Also known as WAP (Wireless Application Protocol), push technology allows applications to send *(push)* information to a wide variety of recipients.

- ✔ **SMPP (Short Message Peer-to-Peer protocol):** SMPP provides flexible communications for transferring short messages.

As a user, you cannot tell which of the available protocols (if in fact there's more than one) is used to deliver messages.

Choosing a Communication Method

Long before the existence of mobile phones with their texting features and even before the creation of personal computers, certain software let two people exchange messages by typing on their computers. At first, both users had to be logged on to the same computer or bulletin board system because the software didn't recognize networks. That enhancement came pretty quickly, though. The first programs had names such as phone and talk, but the solution eventually became known as *online chat* and *instant messaging* (or IMing).

Chatting expanded to allow more than two people to participate in virtual telephone calls or to gather in *chat rooms*. As the number of Internet users and Internet service providers (ISPs) skyrocketed over the years, so did the number of chat clients and protocols.

Although huge differences exist in implementations and features, all IM products include these essential concepts:

- ✔ You have a unique *online identity* — a username or nickname.

- ✔ You have a *presence status* such as Online (and available to chat), Offline (or not running the client software), Busy (but interruptible for chatting), Away (from the computer), Do Not Disturb, or other values.

- ✔ You can maintain a list of other peoples' unique identities and see their presence status.

When your presence status changes — either automatically or because you update it manually — a *presence protocol* distributes the updated status to the people who have you on their buddy lists. An *instant message protocol* moves the messages from the senders to their buddies fast enough that they can hold conversations. Some of the combined instant messaging and presence protocols are covered in the following sections.

All instant messaging systems must address three security concerns:

- ✔ **Spam:** A "buddy" annoys you by sending too many or inappropriate instant messages.

- ✔ **Spoofing:** A "buddy" pretends to be someone else.

- ✔ **Stalking:** A "buddy" monitors your presence status to keep track of where you are and what you're doing.

Getting together with IRC

One of the oldest chat protocols for TCP/IP is Internet Relay Chat (IRC). Like its many eventual competitors, IRC provides one-to-one chats and multiuser conversations in chat rooms (though IRC calls them *channels*). IRC makes it easy to create a new chat room quickly for an impromptu gathering.

Dozens of IRC clients are available, including chatzilla, ircle, ircll, Miranda IM, mIRC, Pidgin, Trillian, and XChat. Most are free. Many are available for multiple operating systems, and some are for just one. Many clients support additional protocols.

Jabbering with XMPP

The Jabber protocol, which became XMPP (Extensible Messaging and Presence Protocol), is the heart of Google Talk, iChat, and other clients. Some, but not all, of the clients support other IM protocols. For example, iChat supports AIM in addition to Apple's own Bonjour protocol (formerly named Rendezvous) and MobileMe (formerly .Mac and iTools). Some clients are available for multiple operating systems. Most are free. Although dozens of chat protocols exist, most of them are proprietary, developed privately by a vendor. Only IRC and XMPP (Jabber) are part of the TCP/IP stack of protocols.

AIMing for an OSCAR

OSCAR (Open System for CommunicAtion in Realtime) is a hugely popular proprietary protocol and is the protocol used by AOL Instant Messenger (AIM) and ICQ (sounds like "I seek you"). AIM was one of the first instant messaging clients to use a proprietary protocol. AIM and ICQ clients are free.

Feeding Your Craving for News

For nearly 30 years, people all over the world have been communicating by way of *Usenet news* (also known as *netnews*). They post articles to a set of globally distributed *newsgroups*.

As of this writing, more than 120,000 newsgroups exist. Each one is a forum about a particular topic. Anyone can post an article stating an opinion, asking for information, answering a question, or doing anything else.

Newsgroup names look like the part of an e-mail address after the @ sign, but it's just a coincidence. Their names put them into hierarchical categories. The top-level categories are listed in Table 15-1.

Table 15-1	Top-Level Newsgroup Categories
Category	*Description*
comp.*	Computer related
humanities.*	Humanities topics
misc.*	Miscellaneous topics
news.*	Usenet news related
rec.*	Recreation and entertainment topics
sci.*	Science related
soc.*	Social discussions
talk.*	Controversial topics with no obvious category
alt.*	Alternative newsgroups, with fewer rules

Each subsequent part of the newsgroup's name is separated by a period and becomes a little more specific. For example, `rec.arts.tv.soaps` is devoted to soap operas on television.

The servers that store the articles use the Network News Transfer Protocol (NNTP) to copy articles from server to server and from server to newsreader client. Note that the terms *news server* and *NNTP server* mean the same thing.

Getting Even More Social

Many proprietary social networking and online communities live on the Internet, but are not part of the TCP/IP stack. Here's a taste and some examples:

- **Blog (Web log) sites:** LiveJournal, TypePad, Windows Live Spaces, and WordPress.com

- **Microblog services:** Twitter

- **Services sites:** Doodle.com, Meetup.com, SurveyMonkey.com

- **Social bookmarking and tagging services:** Delicious (formerly del.icio.us), Digg, StumbleUpon

- **Social networking sites:** Classmates.com, Facebook, LinkedIn, MyLife.com (formerly Reunion.com), MySpace, Twitter

- **Virtual worlds:** MMOGs (Massively Multiplayer Online Games), MMORPGs (Massively Multiplayer Online Role-Playing Games), MUDs (Multi-User Dungeons), Second Life

- **Vlog (video log) and shared content sites:** Flickr, Kodak Gallery, Shutterfly, Snapfish, YouTube

- **Wikis and document management systems:** Javapedia, Lostpedia, Wikipedia, Wookieepedia

Few, if any, of these sites have their own protocols. Most are simply Web applications built on common parts of TCP/IP.

Part IV
Even More TCP/IP Applications and Services

The 5th Wave   By Rich Tennant

"Hey-here's a company that develops short memorable domain names for new businesses. It's listed at www.CompanyThatDevelopsShort-MemorableDomainNamesForNewBusinesses.com."

In this part . . .

The chapters in Part IV delve into more applications, services, and protocols related to mobile IP, voice, and sharing files, printers, and CPU cycles.

Few people who use a computer go anywhere without a mobile device or two (or more), whether it's a big laptop, a tiny netbook, a smartphone, a PDA, or another device. The Internet Engineering Task Force (IETF) has worked to make special versions of IP, Mobile IP v4 and v6, to enable mobile devices to work across the Internet. Chapter 16 addresses mobile networking concerns in general and Mobile IP in particular.

To recognize that everyone wants to save money, Chapter 17 presents the Voice over IP (VoIP) set of protocols as a way to save on telephone bills or do away with telephone bills (and telephones) altogether. You also find plenty of security tips in Chapter 17 so that you can protect the privacy of your computer calls.

The rest of Part IV talks about sharing: sharing file and print services (Chapter 18) and compute services (Chapter 19). These last two chapters expand on the general client/server concepts we present in Chapter 3 by relating those concepts to specialized file, print, and computing clients and servers.

Chapter 16

Mobile IP — the Moveable Feast

. . . .

In This Chapter

▶ Chasing after the protocols in this chapter: Mobile IP, Mobile IPv4, Mobile IPv6

▶ Understanding how to get mobile

▶ Staying secure while on the go

. . . .

As a cellphone (mobile phone) user, you know that you can move around while you're on a call. Whether you're walking down the street or riding in a car, your mobile phone stays connected to the cellular network and your call continues as you move from one cell to another. Please don't talk and drive!

If you pay your cellphone service provider for a data plan, you have the same freedom of movement while you are surfing the Web from your Internet-capable smart phone. The routing is handled by the provider's Data Link layer.

In a perfect world, you could do the exact same thing whenever you're connected to the Internet, from any device. The world isn't perfect — yet — but we're getting there.

This chapter describes how the protocols Mobile IP v4 and v6, or simply Mobile IP, and some new protocol additions to Mobile IPv6, make mobile computing across the Internet workable. In addition, the chapter also cautions about security risks in mobile computing and lists ways to protect your mobile communications.

Going Mobile

You have great Internet access at your office and in your home, but what happens when you and your laptop (with its wireless NIC) move around? For this discussion, there are three different kinds of mobility:

- **Portability:** You can carry your (powered-down) laptop from your home to your office and back but it's not connected to any network during the move. This is portability but not true mobility, because you have to reboot or reconfigure to get an updated IP address each time you shift locations.

- **Local area mobility:** Within the reach of a wireless network, you can stay on the network as you move around — from the bedroom to the living room or from your office to a conference room for a meeting.

- **Pervasive mobility:** Can you stay on the network during the entire trip from Boston to New York? It depends! Some airlines, train companies, and bus services provide Internet access. What is possible when you're riding in a car? (Quite a lot — but please don't compute and drive!)

Understanding How Mobile IP Works

Normally, when you move to another location, you need to get a new IP address. One way to avoid this is wireless broadband, which we describe in Chapter 7. Another is *Mobile IP*. As you might guess from its name, Mobile IP enhances the IP protocol at the Internet layer of the TCP/IP protocol stack. It does this without touching the other layers so your numeric IP address stays the same. Additional routing capabilities come into play.

The functionality of Mobile IP is similar to the way the postal service forwards your mail when you go to your vacation house. You notify the post office staff of your temporary new address and then they capture the mail that comes to your old address, paste new address labels over the old address, and forward the mail to your current location.

With Mobile IP, whenever you take your computer away from your *home network* —not the one in your house, the one specified by its permanent IP *home address* —it becomes a *mobile node* (MN) supported by a *home agent* (HA) and a *foreign agent* (FA) as shown in Figure 16-1.

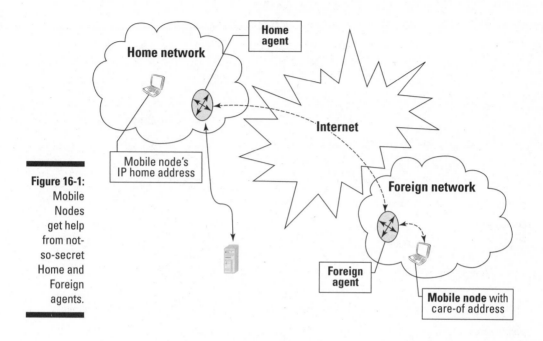

Figure 16-1:
Mobile
Nodes
get help
from not-
so-secret
Home and
Foreign
agents.

Here's an overview of the steps involved when using Mobile IP:

1. You connect your mobile node to a foreign network and get an IP address to use while you're there.

   In most cases, this *care-of address* (CoA) is the foreign agent's own IP address. Foreign agents are usually smart routers; they provide a kind of network address translation (NAT). In other cases, the foreign agent supplies the care-of address via a kind of DHCP (Dynamic Host Control Protocol).

2. The foreign agent updates its *visitor list* that includes visiting mobile nodes' home addresses, their home agent addresses, and their MAC addresses. (Keep in mind that a foreign network can be hosting mobile nodes from more than one home network.)

3. The mobile node registers the care-of address with its home agent. In most cases, it asks the foreign agent for help, as shown in Figure 16-2.

4. The home agent updates its *mobility binding table*. Home agents are usually smart routers, too, and every one maintains a mobility binding table that includes mobile nodes' home addresses and their current care-of addresses. (Keep in mind that every mobile node could be attached to a different foreign network.)

5. All the messages to your mobile node continue to use its home address. They are intercepted by the home agent and relayed to your mobile node, thanks to its care-of address.

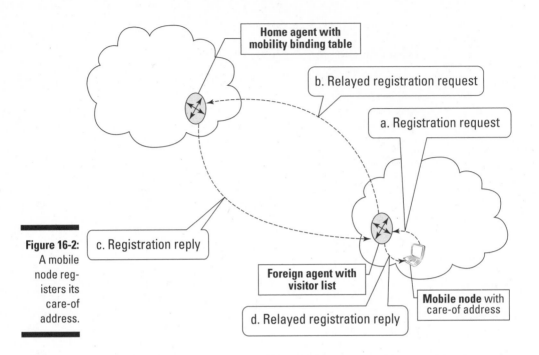

Figure 16-2:
A mobile node registers its care-of address.

6. Messages from your mobile node typically go directly to the destination computers rather than back through the home agent. (The foreign agent may be your mobile node's default router.)

7. If you take your mobile node to a different foreign network, it registers the new care-of address with the home agent and things continue.

8. When you and your mobile node return to your home network, it deregisters its care-of address.

Yes, there's some additional overhead from the indirect routing of your incoming messages, but it's a small price to pay for the mobility. Only your home agent and mobile node know that special routing is taking place; other computers are unaware that your node has gone mobile.

Sailing into the Future: Potential Mobile IPv6 Enhancements

With IPv6, going mobile is much easier — mobility support and routing optimizations are built in rather than bolted on. Every router that's capable of handling IPv6 traffic can act as a home agent; foreign agents aren't needed. Care-of addresses are more visible so messages from other computers come directly to your computer without going through your home agent first. Result: Elimination of the home agent as a bottleneck or single point of failure.

Before most of us can reap the benefits of IPv6, more of its infrastructure and Mobile IPv6 capabilities have to be deployed. In the meantime, more research happens every day to improve mobility. Keeps your eyes peeled for enhancements like these:

- ✔ HMIPv6 (Hierarchical Mobile IPv6 Mobility Management), with its Mobility Anchor Points (MAPs), is designed to reduce the number of messages a mobile node must send to update its care-of address.

- ✔ NEMO (Network Mobility) deals with moving whole networks rather than just individual nodes.

- ✔ PMIP (Proxy Mobile IP IPv6, sometimes called network-based mobility management) does not require any changes to the mobile nodes! Mobile Access Gateways (MAGs) and Local Mobility Anchors (LMAs) discover the arrivals and departures of mobile nodes, and collaborate to handle the nodes' routing needs.

Mobilizing Security

Security is even more vital when computers are moving all over the Internet. With Mobile IP, home agents must accept updates only from their mobile nodes, and they must protect those mobile nodes' IP home addresses and care-of addresses from theft.

Understanding the risks

Mobile devices typically use wireless networking technology. Wireless communication (see Chapter 7) is less secure than wired communication, because transmissions are more easily intercepted as they float through the air (radio waves) than if they go through wires and cables. It's also easier for malicious users to disrupt the operation of wireless devices than wired devices.

The security risks for Mobile IP occur because of the possibility of the registration system being hacked. Also, packets are forwarded across the unsecure Internet. The major security risks are

- ✔ **False care-of addresses**: Bogus care-of addresses registered to trick the home agent into sending packets to the bad guys instead of to the legitimate mobile nodes.

- ✔ **Registration interference:** Hacking the registration process to cause the data intended for a mobile device to be diverted to the wrong device — for example, diverting a message to your smartphone to someone else's netbook.

Using basic techniques to protect your mobile devices

The Mobile IP developers have kept security at the forefront of their work because mobile devices are usually wireless and therefore subject to the same security vulnerabilities as those described in Chapter 7. An important security measure built into the Mobile IP protocol is the authentication of the messages exchanged during the registration process. The goal of this authentication is to prevent unauthorized devices from intercepting data by fooling an agent into handling a registration improperly. Additionally, the Mobile IP standard requires all devices to support authentication.

Although all Mobile IP devices support registration authentication, the standard does not support data authentication or encryption. As with wireless security, authentication, tunneling, encryption, and time stamps ensure that only your organization's mobile nodes are allowed to talk to the home agent. One way to ensure that your mobile nodes' communications are secure is to use a Mobile Virtual Private Network (MVPN).

A Virtual Private Network (VPN) based on IPsec (see Chapter 21) and SSL (see Chapter 11) protocols provides a high level of security by using authentication and encryption to protect networks from unauthorized users by transmitting data through a private tunnel that goes through the very public Internet.

Sending mobile communications through Mobile Virtual Private Networks (MVPNs) provides the same authentication and encryption used in traditional data VPNs. MVPNs are designed for specific mobile computing issues, especially wireless security.

Chapter 17

Saving Money with VoIP (Voice Over Internet Protocol)

. . . .

In This Chapter

▶ Protocols in this chapter: IP, UDP, RTP, RTCP, SIP, SRTP, SRTCP, MGCP, H.323

▶ Understanding what VoIP is

▶ Getting the VoIP hardware and software

▶ Examining the five steps to making or receiving VoIP calls

▶ Looking at how VoIP packets move through the layers

▶ Preventing security attacks on VoIP calls

. . . .

*A*s far as TCP/IP is concerned, there's no difference between types of data; that is, text, binary, video, and voice are just plain data. Because TCP/IP sees voice and video as just data, you can transmit more than e-mail and files over the Internet. You can make and receive phone calls and video-conferences across the Internet, with no telephone company involved. VoIP, pronounced "voyp," stands for Voice over Internet Protocol, or Voice over IP.

Some other names for VoIP include broadband phone, broadband telephony, Internet telephony, IP telephony, and VOBB (voice over broadband). We call it VoIP in this book.

Getting the Scoop on VoIP

People usually think of VoIP as Internet voice conversations. That's true, but VoIP can use *any* TCP/IP network for voice conversations. Employees can call each other over the corporate network even if the network doesn't connect to the Internet.

In a traditional telephone call, your voice travels over your phone company's land lines and undersea cables. Your phone company's land lines inter-operate with other phone companies' lines all over the world to make global calling possible.

VoIP calls replace land lines with a connection to a network, bypassing the telephone company and its fees. VoIP may or may not use a telephone. (By the way, your network connection should be broadband, or else you'll think VoIP stinks. For more information on why a fast connection is needed, see the later section "Step 3: Make the call.")

VoIP protocols convert the sound of your voice into packets and send the packets across the network, just as any data is packetized and sent. Another difference between a VoIP call and a "regular" call is how your call shares (or doesn't share) circuits.

Think of a circuit as pipe between you and the person you're calling. VoIP packets share the pipe with lots of other packets from different sources, such as other VoIP calls, mail messages, file transfers, and Web browsing. That's the beauty of packetizing: Packets from different applications can become all jumbled on the Internet and then be reassembled on the other side. On the other hand, in a traditional telephone call, the pipe opens and stays open for your call only. Nothing else can share that circuit. The way VoIP packets share the pipe makes VoIP calls much less expensive than the regular tele-phone service.

Getting Started Using VoIP

You don't have to be a network guru to set up VoIP and start saving money. The easiest setup is to plug your analog terminal adaptor (ATA) into your broadband device (cable modem, for example) and then plug your phone into the ATA. You're ready to go. Of course, you could decide on something trickier, such as using VoIP on a wireless network with mobile devices.

You can get "VoIPed" in five easy steps.

Step 1: Get broadband

To make VoIP calls, you need a high-speed network connection. If the person you're calling will receive the call on a computer, that person also needs a broadband connection.

Step 2: Decide how to call

Decide how you want to call:

- ✔ From your computer to another computer
- ✔ From your computer to someone's phone
- ✔ From your phone to another phone

Calling from computer to computer

The simplest VoIP connection is from computer to computer. You need a computer with a sound card, a set of headphones, a microphone, and some VoIP software, such as Skype. Many VoIP software packages are free downloads and allow you to connect to any computer running that same software. Skype-to-Skype calls are free. The entire conversation happens completely on the network. Skype is only one of several VoIP software packages.

If you want to download free Skype, browse to `www.skype.com`. Skype is quite versatile in the number of systems it supports: Windows, Mac OS X, Linux, Windows Mobile, Wi-Fi phones, Cordless phones, Skypephone, and Nokia N800/N810 Skype on PSPiPhone. If you don't see your phone model or operating system in this list, check the Skype home page. Support for new devices will continue to appear after this book is published.

VoIP software also lets you send instant messages (IM) and make free video calls. As long as the connection is Skype-to-Skype, you can also make long distance and international calls. You pay a monthly fee for calls to telephones, either wired or mobile.

We use Skype as our VoIP example, but whichever VoIP software you choose, the basic principles are the same, although costs may vary.

Calling from computer to phone

To make a computer-to-phone connection, you don't need anything more than you do for making a computer-to-computer call. Only you need an Internet connection. Only you need VoIP software. Your party on the other end can use any regular landline phone or mobile phone. The VoIP data jumps off the Internet to connect to the phone company's landlines. This type of call isn't usually free, but it's much cheaper than your telephone company's charges.

Calling from phone to phone

To make a phone to phone connection, you have two choices:

> ✓ **Use a regular phone plugged into an ATA.** Plug the ATA into your broadband modem.
>
> ✓ **Use an IP phone (or SIP phone or softphone or VoIP phone).** Plug the IP phone directly into your broadband connection, as shown in Figure 17-1. A standard phone can make calls to and receive calls from an IP phone.

When you make a VoIP call, an ATA converts the analog signal of your voice into digital data. The ATA can be a separate box that plugs into your phone and into your broadband modem (refer to Figure 17-1), or it can be built into an IP phone. If you're using a computer to make calls, the ATA function is built into the VoIP software.

The ATA divides the analog voice signal into packets and shrinks the packets to reduce the amount of data to send. A coder/decoder, or CODEC, compresses the voice data.

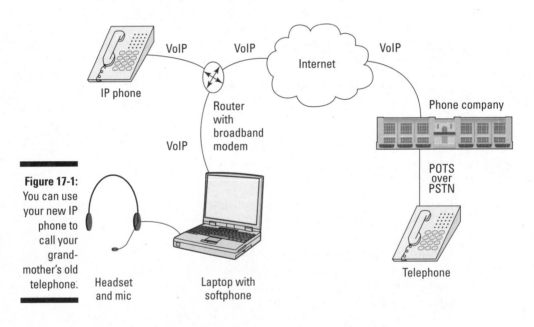

Figure 17-1:
You can use your new IP phone to call your grand-mother's old telephone.

Step 3: Make the call

After your voice has been converted to digital and compressed, it can travel across the Internet. Besides containing the voice data, the packets also carry IP addresses of the sender and receiver and the packet's position sequence in the data stream. Real-Time Transport Protocol (RTP) chooses to carry the packets over UDP rather than TCP, so RTP must resequence the packets.

Real-Time Control Protocol (RTCP) works with RTP and sends control information about the RTP transmission. (See "Trekking the Protocols from RTP to H.323," later in this chapter.)

Because RTP sends the packets over unreliable UDP, some packets might be dropped. Even so, the stream usually has enough data in it to make the conversation audible and understandable. This potential packet loss is the reason you need a fast Internet connection. The number of packets dropped depends on the speed of your Internet and the distance the packets must travel.

Step 4: Convert the bits back into voice (with VoIP software)

Before voice data packets can be returned to human speech, they must be put back into order and converted back to analog. In a computer-to-computer call, the receiver's VoIP software takes care of this process. If you're calling someone on a regular landline phone, the voice data stream leaves the Internet through a VoIP gateway and goes to a regular telephone line.

Step 5: Converse

After your phone call has traveled over the Internet, and possibly through a VoIP gateway onto the public switched telephone network (PSTN), it reaches the person you're calling, and you can start talking! Amazingly, all this analog and digital converting, packetizing, and gatewaying takes only a few seconds.

There's good news

Usually, if you're talking to a person who's using a regular phone, she doesn't know that it's a VoIP call. The voice quality is much the same (and sometimes better) than a regular landline call. And, it's much cheaper!

There's bad news

If your Internet connection is slow, you may lose too many voice packets along the way. Remember that UDP is connectionless. It doesn't care about lost packets, and there are consequences:

- Voices break up
- Words seem to get lost
- A delay occurs between talking and listening

Yo-Yo Dieting: Understanding How VoIP Packets Move through the Layers

When you make a call, your voice is digitized and packetized. The packets start their journey at the application layer and move down the TCP/IP layer cake. Those layers are quite "fattening." Figure 2-4 (earlier in the book) follows a packet as it gains weight and then diets.

As the packet moves down through the layers, it puts on more weight, as described in this list:

- **Application:** Special protocols at this layer ensure the quality and deliverability of VoIP packets.

- **Transport:** Both TCP and UDP can transport packets. VoIP uses UDP (the connectionless protocol) to transport VoIP packets. The VoIP packet swallows a UDP header.

- **Internet:** The packets gain more weight by adding the IP addresses of the sender and receiver. Every VoIP device acting as a VoIP phone gets an IP address, just like every other host on a network.

- **Data Link:** The packets have MAC addresses of the NIC added, and the packet is mighty plump at this point.

- **Physical:** This layer converts all packets to electrical signals or radio waves (for wireless) to send the packets over the network to the receiver's set of layers.

Now the voice packets are on the receiver's set of layers and move from the bottom up. The chubby little packet starts to lose weight as it makes its way up through the layers. As the packets move up through each layer, header and address information is stripped off until the packet is positively skinny. When the packet reaches the application layer, the receiver hears your voice.

Trekking the Protocols from RTP to H.323

VoIP isn't just one protocol. It's a collection of protocols that do all the work in Steps 3, 4, and 5 in the earlier section "Getting Started Using VoIP." The various VoIP protocols convert, transport, and route voice across TCP/IP networks.

Video and multimedia work like voice does. The analog data (the home movies of your new triplets, for example) is digitized and broken into millions of packets, they pass through the TCP/IP layered stack, and the packets are reassembled and reconverted so that Mom and Dad can see the new grandkids. The protocols involved in making VoIP a reality include protocols from the TCP/IP stack and protocols from an international communications standards group.

Talking the talk with the TCP/IP stack and more

VoIP depends on IP and UDP to carry the other protocols in this list. For information on IP and UDP, please flip through Chapter 2. Besides IP and UDP, the protocols include:

✔ **RTP (Real-Time Transport Protocol):** Sits on top of UDP and carries voice and multimedia.

✔ **RTCP (Real-Time Control Protocol):** Remember how packets "gain weight" as they move down the TCP/IP layers? RTCP is a protocol that helps RTP run more efficiently by compressing the packet's weight gain. RTCP's compression helps keep voice packets flowing on slow network links. RTCP packets carry data (the payload) such as

- *The caller's and the receiver's names and e-mail addresses*

- *Statistics about the quality of service (QoS), including lost packets and noisy calls, especially if the call is from computer to a traditional landline phone*

✔ **SIP (Session Initiation Protocol):** SIP, pronounced like the word that means to drink, is an IP telephony signaling protocol for VoIP calls. SIP is responsible for connecting, monitoring, and disconnecting VoIP sessions. Sometimes IM uses an extended version of SIP. SIP might be used in other applications, such as online games, streaming video, teleconferencing, and videoconferencing. SIP is much simpler than H.323, another telephony protocol (discussed in the next section). Also, because SIP is text based, the process of debugging problems is uncomplicated. The messages are human readable.

✔ **MGCP (Master Gateway Control Protocol):** A *gateway* allows communication between unlike architectures, such as different devices in a telecommunications network. The MGCP makes it possible for a computer to make a VoIP call across the Internet to the phone company's PSTN. You've heard it before: People like names, computers like numbers. Well, here's a variation: telephones like numbers, computers like numbers — just not the same kind of numbers. The gateway maps a phone number to an IP address. When your call is between a computer and a telephone, the MGCP takes care of moving and converting the data from one form (computer) to another (PSTN).

Ingesting VoIP standards from the ITU

H.323, a "packet-based multimedia communications systems," is another part of the VoIP collection, although it isn't part of the TCP/IP stack. The H.323 standard comes from the International Telecommunication Union (ITU), which is an international telecommunications standards body. H.323 is a set of guidelines for electronic whiteboarding, real-time voice, and videoconferencing. H.323 has more features than SIP, but SIP is simpler. You get to choose one or the other based on your needs and your energy level.

Vomiting and Other Vicious VoIP Vices

Almost everyone knows that it's possible to wiretap, or *bug,* regular and mobile phone conversations. You can also bug VoIP calls. Most of the well-known dangers for data security exist for VoIP security as well.

- ✔ **Eavesdropping with vomit:** VoIP gives nasty hackers a whole new playground. Cybercriminals can eavesdrop on your calls by stealing VoIP packets. In the corporate world, VoIP hacking might grab industrial secrets or even the KFC secret recipe. Vomit (rhymes with "comet") stands for Voice Over Misconfigured Internet Telephones, a freely available program for eavesdropping on VoIP calls. VOMIT enables VoIP eavesdropping by stealing your VoIP data. Then VOMIT converts VoIP conversations into a wave file that the criminal can play by using an ordinary computer sound card. Even worse, you might find your conversation posted on the Web.

- ✔ **Vishing:** Vishing is the VoIP equivalent of phishing, in which messages seem to come from an official site. See Chapter 12 for a description. Vishing does the same thing, except that it falsifies the caller ID.

- ✔ **Voicing DDoS:** A voice DDoS (distributed denial-of-service) attack bombards your SIP server and clogs your VoIP calling system. You know that you have a DDoS strike when all lines are busy or calls keep getting dropped.

Securing Your Calls from VoIP Violation

Because VoIP is vulnerable to many of the same security assaults as regular data, most VoIP security protections mirror the same protections you find in regular data networks.

You, too, can be a secret agent

Intelligence agencies such as the CIA, MI5, and MI6 have been scrambling their regular phone calls for decades. You've seen it in the movies: "Mr. Bond, are you sure this line is secure?" "Of course, M, what would you expect?"

Using built-encryption

When James Bond uses a scrambler for his phone calls, the calls are encrypted. Chapter 12 explains encryption, and Chapter 21 goes into technical detail. Many VoIP developers have built encryption into their software. Skype, for example, has optional built-in encryption. If someone VOMITs on your VoIP call, they can't decipher the scrambled sounds.

Jamming with new protocols

The Internet Engineering Task Force, or IETF (see Chapter 1 for a reminder), has put a couple of "new" protocols on the standards track. Remember that the thorough IETF standards procedure grinds slowly through time, so the first of these new RFCs came out in 2004 RFC 3711, "The Secure Real-time Transport Protocol (SRTP)." The RFC was updated in 2009 but still hasn't graduated to full standard, although it will eventually.

The Secure Real-Time Transfer Protocol (SRTP) is an extension to RTP to protect VoiP and multimedia traffic. The goals of SRTP are to

- ✔ Protect the confidentiality of VoIP data with encryption.
- ✔ Protect the integrity of VoIP data with authentication.

Secure RTCP (SRTCP) extends the same security for RTCP as SRTP does for RTP. SRTP and SRTCP work together the same way that RTP and RTPC do.

When you look for VoIP software, look for companies that have incorporated SRTP and SRTCP into their products. Browse to www.voip-info.org for a list of devices and software clients that use SRTP.

Authenticating VoIP-ers

In a data network, authentication ensures that people are who they say they are. You also use authentication (see Chapter 12) on VoIP callers to keep callers from pretending to be someone else. ("Who's calling?" "Bond. James Bond." "Do you have any proof of identity?") In addition to encryption, SRTP and SRTCP include strong authentication.

Keeping voice attacks separate from data

You don't want VoIP attacks to spread to your data, and you don't want data attacks to spread to your calling network.

Because an organization can easily have multiple LANs, it makes sense to separate the voice traffic on its own LAN and run the data traffic on its own LAN. This separation technique is especially useful if you're attacked by a DDoS. If your data LAN is crashed by a DDoS, your voice and media applications are unaffected. The reverse is true if your voice/media LAN is hit with a DDoS assault. The downside of this approach is that it requires more administration.

Defending with firewalls

A firewall is your first line of defense and can filter out packets from unfriendly IP addresses. Be sure to use VoIP-aware firewalls.

Testing Your VoIP Security

When you first start using VoIP, you may want to test your devices and software for security holes. Periodically, a good practice is to repeat the test to ensure that no one or nothing has hacked your VoIP system.

You can find VoIP security-testing tools available on the Web. You can download the SIP Proxy VoIP security-testing tool from the SourceForge project at `www.sourceforge.net`. Call hijacking occurs when an attacker spoofs an SIP response and steals your call, so SIP testing is a good place to start checking the security of your VoIP system.

You can test your VoIP configuration by eavesdropping on SIP traffic. You can also use predefined tests or make your own, custom tests to find weak spots in VoIP devices.

Chapter 18

File and Print Sharing Services

● ●

● ●

*B*efore TCP/IP and widespread networking, you used *sneakernet* to share files. After copying them from the local computer onto diskettes or magnetic tape (reels or cartridges), you then used your trusty athletic shoes to run them over to the remote computer. Sneakernet lives on; although, today you use USB memory keys, DVDs, and portable disk drives. In an update of a famous saying, "Never underestimate the bandwidth of an SUV full of disk drives."

This chapter covers resource sharing protocols, services, and applications in the TCP/IP stack.

Defining Basic File Sharing Terms

This chapter gives you the lowdown on sharing files on remote computers over a network. However, before we get into a detailed discussion, you need to know some basic file sharing terms:

> ✔ A *file server* is the software running on a computer that controls access to sharable disk space and files. We often call the computer a file server.
>
> ✔ Shared disk spaces from Microsoft Windows are called *shares*.
>
> ✔ Shared disk spaces from Linux and Unix are called *exported file systems*.

✔ When you copy a file from your computer to a remote computer, you *upload* it. Uploading is sending the file.

✔ When you copy a file from a remote computer to your computer, you *download* it. Downloading is receiving the file.

✔ When you listen to an Internet radio station or watch a YouTube video, you don't get to keep a copy of the content. The server that sends the content is *streaming* it to your media player. You're receiving the streaming media (audio or audio/video), but you can't save it. If you **can** keep a copy:

  • You're downloading it, or

  • It wasn't being streamed, or

  • You have a cool media recorder that you need to tell us about ASAP!

Be sure to virus-scan every file you transfer, whether you're uploading or downloading.

Using FTP to Copy Files

FTP is a protocol, a service, and an application. You use FTP (File Transfer Protocol) to copy files to and from a remote computer. (Keep in mind that the computer you're using is the *local computer*. The *remote computer* is the other one, farther away from you.) You use the FTP client application to connect to a remote computer that provides the FTP service. The FTP protocol comes into play whenever you ask the application to transfer files.

In the following sections, you find out how FTP works, what an FTP client is and how to choose one, how to upload and download files, and how to secure file transfers.

Understanding how FTP works

You use an *FTP client* (technically, *FTP client software)* to connect to an *FTP server* — a computer that's running FTP server software — to upload or download files using FTP. Confused yet? That's because, while FTP formally means the File Transfer Protocol, people tend to refer to any part of the file transfer process using the three letters *F T P.* In fact, many people use FTP as a verb: "Would you please FTP that file for me?"

Some FTP clients have GUIs (graphical user interfaces) while others provide only command line interfaces; some cost money while many are free; and some are available for multiple operating systems while others are made for only one.

Like the clients, some FTP servers have GUIs while others don't; some cost money while others are free; and some are available for multiple operating systems while others are made for only one.

With FTP, you don't have to worry about which operating systems run on the client and server computers because they all have TCP/IP. Wait; that's not 100 percent true. Sometimes you do have to worry a tiny bit. Keep reading, and we'll explain it.

This ability to upload and download between computers running different operating systems is one of the best things about FTP. For example, suppose your computer runs Windows Vista, a client operating system, but you need to upload to and/or download from a Linux system. No problem! Launch an FTP client, connect to the Linux system with your Linux username and password, and then move files to your heart's content. It works because the Linux system is very likely to have an FTP server running. But what do you do if your computer runs Linux and you need to upload to and/or download from a Windows Vista system? You have two choices:

 ✔ Install FTP *server* software on Vista. (This makes sense if you have to transfer files often.)

 ✔ Sit at the Vista system and download and upload from there instead.

Each version of Windows (including Windows 7, Vista, XP, Server 2008, and Server 2003) includes command line FTP *client* software. None of the desktop versions includes FTP server software, but the server versions do, if you install Microsoft IIS (Internet Information Services). There are also many free and commercial FTP server products that can run on any version of Windows.

Each release of Mac OS X includes GUI FTP client software. Mac OS X Server includes FTP server software. The various distributions of Linux and Unix include both FTP client and server software.

Using anonymous FTP to get good stuff

The Internet has many public FTP servers, known as *anonymous FTP sites* or *anonymous FTP archives.* When you connect to them, enter **anonymous** as the username and your e-mail address as the password.

All anonymous FTP sites store files that you can download for free. Some have software; others hold graphics, music, and movies; and still others contain weird and wonderful things. Companies, universities, and numerous other do-gooders provide the sites.

Make sure that you run a firewall and strong antimalware software so that any file you download is scanned before it's loaded on your computer.

Although all anonymous FTP sites are publicly readable, very few are publicly writeable. You can connect to any of them and download all the files you want, but only rarely can you upload files. (If you provide an anonymous FTP site, be sure to protect your site so that some scoundrel doesn't fill it up by uploading objectionable or even illegal content.) In addition, some organizations have private FTP sites that don't accept the username *anonymous*. If you're given a username and password to allow you to use the archive, be sure to keep them secret.

Choosing your FTP client

You have many choices in FTP client software, and these choices fit into three types:

- ✔ **Browser:** You may not know this, but you can browse to an FTP site using a URL such as `ftp://ftp.ietf.org`. Note the leading `ftp://` rather than the usual `http://` or `https://`.

- ✔ **Command line:** You can use the old, reliable text-mode client software, which is simply called FTP. It's free and built in to almost every operating system. There are also free, shareware, and commercial products. You have to type some commands, but this is the fastest way to download or upload a large group of files.

- ✔ **Graphical program:** You can use FTP client software that has a graphical user interface (GUI). There are dozens to pick from — some are freeware or shareware while others are commercial. Most, including FileZilla and FireFTP, provide two panes so that you can see the files on your local computer and the remote computer at the same time. Then you can just drag the files from one computer and drop them onto the other.

Transferring the files

In general terms, here's how to download files with all three types of FTP client (browser, command line, and graphical):

1. **Start your FTP client.**

   • *Browser:* Launch your favorite browser.

   • *Command line:* At a command prompt, type **ftp**.

   • *Graphical:* Launch your favorite graphical FTP client.

2. **Connect to the remote computer that has the files you want.**

   Many organizations link their Web sites and anonymous FTP sites, simplifying how they store things and how you get the stuff you want.

   - *Browser:* Surf to the FTP server (for example, `ftp://ftp.ietf.org`).
   - *Command line:* At the `ftp>` prompt, enter the `open` command with the name of the FTP server. (For example, type **open ftp.ietf.org**.)
   - *Graphical:* Connect to the FTP server (for example, `ftp.ietf.org`).

3. **Tell the remote computer your username and password.**

   - *Browser:* The browser automatically sends *anonymous* as the username and your e-mail address as the password.
   - *Command line:* At the `User` prompt, type **anonymous** and press Enter. At the `Password` prompt, type your e-mail address. When you type the password, nothing appears. That's for security. If you have your own account on the remote computer, type that username and password.
   - *Graphical:* Like a browser, the graphical FTP client automatically sends `anonymous` as the username and your e-mail address as the password.

4. **Locate the files you want.**

   - *Browser:* Click through the directory structure until you find the files you want, but don't click them yet!
   - *Command line:* Navigate through the directory structure until you find the files you want. At the `ftp>` prompt, use the `cd` and `dir` commands. For example, type **dir** and press Enter to see the list of directories and files. Type **cd** and the name of a directory (for example, **cd pub**). Repeat as needed.
   - *Graphical:* In the pane for the remote computer, double-click through the directory structure until you find the files you want, but don't double-click the files yet! The FileZilla graphical FTP client displays your local files (those on your computer) in the left panes and the files you're accessing on the remote FTP server in the right panes.

     On most anonymous FTP sites, the good stuff is in or below the subdirectory named `pub`, which is short for public.

5. **Transfer the files.**

   - *Browser:* Scroll down (or search) the page until you find a file you want. Don't click it! If you do, the browser displays it rather than downloads it. Instead, right-click (Control-click on Mac OS X) and choose Save As from the context-sensitive menu that appears. (In Internet Explorer, it's Save Target As. In Firefox, it's Save Link As.) Choose a destination directory and click Save. Repeat Steps 4 and 5 for other files.

- *Command line:* At the `ftp>` prompt, use the `get` command once for each file (for example, `get filename`). If you don't want to have to wait for each download to finish before you start the next, there's a better way. Use the `prompt` command so you don't have to confirm each download, and then use the `mget` command (for example, `mget example1.txt example2.txt example3.txt`) — without commas! You can also use commands with wildcards (for example, `mget example*.txt`).

Be sure to type the filenames exactly as you see them, case included. The files `example.txt`, `EXAMPLE.TXT`, and `Example.txt` are all the same to Windows. But to Linux and Unix, they're three different files!

- *Graphical:* Find the files in the pane for the remote computer, highlight the ones you want to download, and drag them to the other pane. Repeat Steps 4 and 5 as needed.

6. **Quit the FTP client when you're done.**

- *Browser:* Close the browser (or surf somewhere else).

- *Command line:* Use the `bye` command or the `quit` command. (Some command line FTP clients also provide an `exit` command.)

- *Graphical:* Close the FTP client.

In general terms, you upload files in almost the same way, except in how you transfer the files. Just use the instructions that follow to replace Step 5 in the preceding list.

- **Browser:** You can't simply upload files to a Web site by reversing the download steps. The Web site must provide an application with a file upload control.

- **Command line:** At the `ftp>` prompt, use the `put` command once for each file (for example, `put filename`). If you don't want to have to wait for each upload to finish before you start the next, there's a better way. Use the `prompt` command so you don't have to confirm each upload, and then use the `mput` command (for example, `mput example1.txt example2.txt example3.txt`) — without commas!

Be sure to type the filenames exactly as you see them, including case. The files `example.txt`, `EXAMPLE.TXT`, and `Example.txt` are all the same to Windows. But to Linux and Unix, they are three different files!

- **Graphical:** Find the files in the pane for the local computer, highlight the ones you want to upload, and drag them to the other pane. Repeat Step 4 (from the preceding list) and this step as needed.

Securing FTP file transfers

The FTP protocol, service, and software present a security risk because user-names, passwords, and the data go across the network in clear text. There are no security provisions, so you should avoid standard FTP unless you're working on a secured intranet. Other protocols with this security flaw include telnet, SMTP (Simple Mail Transfer Protocol), and other protocols that predate the design of SSL (Secure Sockets Layer) and TLS (Transport Layer Security).

If you use the FTP protocol, you can secure your file transfers in the following ways:

- ✔ Use standard FTP after establishing a VPN (virtual private network) tunnel to the remote network.

- ✔ Use FTP over SSH (Secure Shell Protocol) — also known as Secure FTP — that is, using standard FTP after establishing an SSH connection to the remote computer. Note that SSH version 2 (SSHv2 or SSH2) is a much, much better choice than version 1 (SSHv1 or SSH1) because it has better security and more capabilities.

- ✔ Use SFTP (SSH File Transfer Protocol), an enhanced version of SCP (Secure Copy Protocol); note that SFTP and FTP are separate protocols. See the upcoming section "Using rcp or scp to Copy Files."

- ✔ Use FTPS (FTP over SSL/TLS) — also known as FTP Secure and FTP-SSL. An FTPS server needs a public key certificate signed by a certificate authority.

- ✔ Use FTP with Advanced Encryption Security (AES) protocol, the newest, strongest encryption standard. Chapter 21 describes AES and lists where to find an FTP/AES client. If you search the Web for *aes ftp,* you find more than three pages of FTP/AES clients.

In all cases, remember that the capabilities of the client and the server must match. A client that speaks SFTP (but not FTPS) won't work with a server that speaks FTPS (but not SFTP). So your best bet is to use the smartest client you can find and afford — the one that supports the most protocols.

If you're a server administrator, here are some tips to help you provide your users with secure file transfer services.

- ✔ The best security option is not providing an FTP server at all if you don't really need to!

- ✔ Deploy the most secure FTP server software you can find. Convince management of the risks so they pay for a commercial product, if that's the best choice.

- ✔ Enable security features and monitor the server for violations.

- ✔ Configure the FTP server software so that it doesn't announce its product identification (name and version number).

- ✔ Limit the usernames that are allowed to access the server.

- ✔ Limit the number of failed login attempts since miscreants often try to guess passwords through this side door as opposed to direct logins.

- ✔ If possible, limit the IP addresses from which users can access the server.

- ✔ If you must provide an anonymous FTP server be very careful, especially if you allow uploading! Provide specific users with write-only access to specific, personalized folders.

Using rcp or scp to Copy Files

The main alternatives to FTP on Linux and Unix include *rcp* (remote copy) and *scp* (secure copy) applications. The `rcp` and `scp` clients extend the standard cp (copy) command so that you can copy files between computers. Be patient, the difference between `rcp` and `scp` is coming up shortly.

There are three ways to use `rcp` (or `scp`).

- ✔ Upload a file from your computer to a remote computer.

- ✔ Download a file from a remote computer to your computer.

- ✔ Copy a file from one remote computer to another (third-party copy).

Trust is essential for copying files with `rcp`. When you interact with the remote computer, it may prompt you for a username and password. It doesn't prompt you if the remote computer trusts you and the computer from which you're connecting. When two computers are set up to trust each other, all the user accounts on one computer that have matching account names and passwords on the other computer can use `rlogin` (remote login, discussed in Chapters 6 and 19) and `rcp` without being asked for a username and password.

Trust isn't automatically reciprocal. Just because computer A trusts computer B (and some or all of computer B's users), it doesn't mean that computer B trusts computer A (and its users). Nevertheless, trust is commonly defined in both directions. This definition and mechanism of trust come from Unix and are present in Linux and Mac OS X, but not in Windows, which has its own trust relationships in workgroups and Active Directory domains.

By the way, there's no such thing as anonymous `rcp`.

The protocol that `rcp` uses (RCP, the Remote Copy Protocol) contains the same security risk as FTP because usernames, passwords, and data go across the network in clear text. There are no security provisions, so you should avoid rcp unless you're working on a secured intranet.

Your security options include the following:

✔ Using an `scp` client, which encrypts the communication after it uses SSH (the Secure Shell Protocol) to authenticate the user to the remote computer (or computers).

✔ Using an `sftp` client (available only with SSHv2).

Remember that SSH version 2 (SSHv2 or SSH2) is a much, much better choice than version 1 (SSHv1 or SSH1) because it has better security and more capabilities.

Sharing Network File Systems

If you find that you (or your users) spend a lot of time copying files across your intranet, you're using twice the disk space. And, if you update any files, you have to be careful to copy those updates back. Otherwise, your files will be out of sync. There is an easier way! You need to share disk space instead.

In the following sections, we give you the lowdown on sharing network file systems in different operating systems.

Nifty file sharing with NFS (Network File System)

The Network File System version 4 (NFS4) is a distributed file system protocol that runs over UDP and IP and is available for all major operating systems. It runs in a client/server environment that allows computers to share disk space and users to see their files from multiple computers without having to copy the files to those computers. In the NFS environment, computers that have disk space they're willing to share are *NFS servers,* and computers borrowing disk space are *NFS clients*. Any computer can be

✔ Either an NFS server or an NFS client

✔ Both an NFS server and an NFS client, simultaneously

Some of the most outstanding benefits of using NFS include the ones described in this list:

- **Transparent operation:** You can't tell the difference between local disk space and shared disk space. When you access a file, you have no idea whether your file is on your own local host or on a remote host on the other side of the world. You can work at any NFS client on the network and still have access to the files stored on the NFS server. They follow you from computer to computer. A file is a file is a file, no matter where you're logged on. With NFS, your home directory may not be located on your computer. And, because file access via NFS is transparent, you may not even realize it.

- **Interoperability:** Because the operating systems for the servers don't have to match the operating systems of the clients, you can use any type of client, including Microsoft Windows and Mac, to access files stored on a Linux or Unix or Mac server.

- **Availability:** If your computer is unavailable, you can use any other computer on the network to access your files. With NFS, your files are available even when your computer isn't. It doesn't matter if you use a computer that runs a different operating system than your regular one. With NFS, you can access your files on any operating system.

The NFS disk sharing service is extremely valuable to

- **Users:** They can access much more disk space.

- **System administrators:** They can more easily provide disk space to users and more easily back up users' files.

- **All users:** They don't have to worry about keeping track of multiple copies of the same file on multiple computers. Regardless of how many computers you access, NFS stores only one copy of your file in its central repository.

NFS was originally developed for Unix by Sun Microsystems, Inc. (also the creator of NIS). The technical specifications are easy to find, and the source code has been licensed to almost every operating system vendor and to the third-party TCP/IP vendors. Specifications and source code are important, and anyone, including you, can write your own version of an NFS client or server.

Solving the buried file update problem with NFSv4

Some operating systems have file systems with *locking features* (also called *concurrency control*) to avoid the problem of buried updates. In the following example, two imaginary users show how concurrency control and locking work:

✔ The first user, Emily, accesses the data and gets a lock on it, which prevents other users from updating the data.

✔ When Emily is finished, the next user, Sarah, gets the lock and is assured of seeing Emily's update before making her own updates.

✔ Without effective locking procedures, Sarah could be writing to the dinner order file at the same time as Emily. Suppose that Emily orders their dinner — a pizza with pineapple topping. If Sarah doesn't know that Emily already ordered dinner, Sarah might order a pizza with mushrooms, thereby "burying" Emily's update. When the mushroom pizza arrives, Emily will be disappointed and confused: "I'm sure I ordered pineapple."

The potential for buried updates is rare, but it does exist in NFS3, which many organizations still use. The best solution to the buried update problem is to upgrade to NFSv4, which manages file locking. NFSv4 lock management leases a lock on the file. During the lease, the server doesn't grant conflicting access to any other clients. For example, when Emily opens a file for update, NFS locks the file. If Sarah tries to update the file while Emily's lease is current, Sarah sees a message that the file is unavailable for update. She has to wait until Emily is done with the file and the lease has expired. When Sarah is allowed to update the dinner order file, she sees that Emily already ordered dinner and that pineapple is a topping. If both Sarah and Emily are only reading the file, no lock conflict occurs, because there's no conflicting access — that is, Emily's read doesn't get in the way of Sarah's read.

Examining the mount Protocol

The *mount* protocol allows an NFS server to hand out remote access privileges to a restricted set of clients that the administrator selects. Behind the scenes, the protocol performs any operating-system-specific functions that allow the connecting of remote directory trees to different local file systems, such as

✔ Looking up server path names

✔ Validating users' identities

✔ Checking access permissions

The mount protocol allows NFS clients entry into a remote file system. Before NFS clients can access remote directories and files, the system administrator mounts remote directories. The technical term for this process is *NFS mounting*. The files appear as local to users, even though the files exist physically on a remote computer. Here's an example of the Unix and Linux mount command:

```
mount nfsserver.example.com:/projectx /projectx
```

Automounting

Enter the *automounter* — an enhancement to the mount protocol. Consider this: The user, Selena, usually doesn't sign on to the charliet computer; only occasionally does she need to see her files there. Keeping that in mind, you don't want to have Selena's files always mounted on charliet.

Whenever file systems are available, the possibility of a security vulnerability always exists. You also don't want to be at Selena's beck and call to mount the files on charliet whenever Selena decides that she needs them. You are, after all, a busy person.

The automounter automatically mounts the disk space you need, when you need it. This process is known as *dynamic mounting*. The automounter is quite fast — you don't normally notice the delay in preparing the disk space. But even if you do, the benefit is worth the tiny performance penalty.

The automounter is not only a security precaution but also a handy option for system administrators who manage file systems that are inactive for large lengths of time. The automounter keeps a timer for each of the mounted disk spaces so that it knows when people stop using files. When a timer expires, the automounter dismounts the disk space. When you need the disk space again, the automounter remounts it.

In NFSv4, mount is no longer needed; the file system tasks that mount performs are part of NFSv4 operations.

Configuring an NFS Server

An NFS server needs to know which directories to make available to users on remote hosts. On most Linux distributions and Unix versions, the `/etc/exports` file holds this information. In the following Linux example, NFS shares two directories. To configure an NFS server, follow these steps:

1. **Edit the** `/etc/exports` **file:**

   • List directories to be exported (made publicly available).

   • List any access options and any restrictions.

2. **Edit the** `/etc/netgroup` **file to list groups named in** `/etc/exports`.

3. **Start the** `rpc.mountd` **and** `rpc.nfsd` **daemon programs.**

You can perform these steps in command mode or use a graphical interface, such as GNOME. The example in the following section uses command mode.

Step 1: Edit the exports file

The exports file needs one line per directory to be public. Each line includes the directory to export, the name of one or more hosts, and any options and restrictions. Each field should be separated by spaces or tabs, as shown in the following `exports` file:

```
/usr/share/man/man1            (ro,squash_uid=0)
/usr/share/man/man8    dodo    (ro,squash_uid=0)
```

The first line of the file, the files in the `man1` subdirectory (under `/usr/share/man`), is to be made public. Because no host is listed, the files are available to everyone on the local intranet. The `ro` option indicates that the files are available for read-only access. The `squash_uid=0` part is a security option that specifies requests from remote user IDs 0 should come in with the permissions of the Nobody account (an anonymous account). In effect, we have squashed the permissions of certain users.

The second line of the exports file makes the `man8` subdirectory and its files available to users on the host, `dodo`. Users from other hosts on the network cannot share `man8` files. We added the first line of the file with the graphical Webmin system administration program. We used a text editor to add the second line. Either method works.

Other ways to specify who has access include listing these elements:

- **An entire domain:** The asterisk (*) wildcard stands for every host, as in

  ```
  *.cardinalconsulting.com
  ```

- **A group of users listed in the /etc/group file:** Use the at (@) sign to mean *group*. The following entry allows access to everyone listed in the programmers group:

  ```
  @programmers
  ```

Step 2: Update the netgroup file

The NFS server uses the `/etc/netgroup` file if the exports file grants access to any groups. You need this file only to grant access to individuals and groups of users. Each line of the file lists a group name optionally followed by host, user, and domain names. The format of an entry in the netgroup file is

```
group (hostname, username, domainname)
```

A comma in any position means to grant access for all, as shown in these examples:

```
programmers (,marshall,)
managers
```

The first line says that, in the programmers group, from any host, `marshall` has access from any domain. The second line says that all members of the managers group have access from anywhere. The groups named in the `/etc/netgroup` file must correspond to the groups named in the `/etc/groups` file. The system administrator adds entries to `/etc/groups` when adding accounts.

Step 3: Start the daemons

After you configure the files, you must start two daemons (server programs):

- ✔ **rpc.mountd:** When the system administrator mounts an NFS file system, this daemon verifies that the file system is in `/etc/exports`. If the file system isn't listed, the daemon sends an error message to the system administrator.

- ✔ **rpc.nfsd:** This NFS server allows users to access NFS-mounted file systems.

Both these daemons usually start automatically whenever the system boots, and they stop automatically at shutdown time. To check whether the NFS daemons are running, use the ps command combined with the grep command to search the system for running daemons:

```
# ps -elf | grep nfsd
# ps -elf | grep mountd
```

You can also start and stop the daemons manually by using the nfs command. The nfs command is in the directory path `/etc/rc.d/init.d/nfs`. To start NFS manually, type the following line:

```
# /etc/rc.d/init.d/nfs start
```

Don't type the pound sign (#). It's the system prompt that shows you're either logged on as root, the system administrator, or another privileged user.

To stop NFS manually, type the following line:

```
# /etc/rc.d/init.d/nfs stop
```

Windows Server 2008 includes Services for NFS. The three main components of Services for NFS are User Name Mapping, Server for NFS, and Client for NFS.

Configuring an NFS Client

NFS servers share file systems. NFS clients need to know which file systems they can access. To configure NFS on the client side, you edit the `/etc/fstab` file. Fstab stands for *file system table*. When your computer boots, it looks in the `fstab` file to see which file systems should be mounted automatically.

To configure an NFS client, follow these steps:

1. **Create a local directory on your hard drive to link to the remote directory. This local directory is a *mount point*. Create the directory by using the File Manager or the mkdir command. Substitute your directory for the one shown here:**

   ```
   #mkdir /home/SharedHelp
   ```

   Don't put any other files or directories into your new mount point. You can't use them.

2. **Edit the `/etc/fstab` file, adding a line for each NFS mount point you're creating:**

   - *Field 1:* The name of the device (disk partition) that stores the file system.

   - *Field 2:* The name of the empty directory that's the mount point.

   - *Field 3:* The file system type, NFS.

   - *Field 4:* Options. Most default options work well. If the fourth column is blank, the file system uses all the defaults. Changing some of the default options can result in better NFS performance — see the later section "Picking Up Some NFS Performance Tips." The following `fstab` file lists two NFS file systems.

   ```
   selenas:/usr/share/man /usr/share/man nfs ro,wsize=8192,rsize=8192 1 2
   charliet:/usr/selena /usr/selena nfs noauto 1 2
   ```

   The preceding file, from a Linux system, lists more than the NFS file systems. It shows all the file systems to mount. The fourth column lists special file system options, such as `ro` (read only). The `noauto` option says not to use the automounter. The last two columns (if present) represent Linux settings for backup and file system checks.

3. **Mount the file system manually to make it available immediately. Use the options `-a -t nfs` so that all nfs file systems will be mounted.**

   A sample mount command for Linux, Unix, and Mac OS X is

   ```
   mount -a -t nfs
   ```

If you ever need to stop a running NFS file system, use the umount command followed by the mount point name:

```
umount /home/SharedHelp
```

Picking Up Some NFS Performance Tips

This section helps system administrators set up NFS for high performance. The NFS client/server environment is quite flexible, in that any computer can play the role of client and server simultaneously. But system administrators should think about the trade-offs between flexibility and performance when they're setting up servers.

Hardware tips

Use fast disks for frequently accessed files. For example, if the most frequently used file is your inventory file, you should place it on a fast disk on the most powerful computer for quick retrieval.

Speaking of hardware, you also need to consider network hardware. You know that NFS clients access files across the network, such as cables, packets traveling across wires, network controllers, and maybe even items such as gateways and routers.

The quality and robustness of the hardware you use has a major effect on NFS performance. If the network interface card inside your computer is old and slow, don't expect to see files as quickly as your neighbor who has the latest and greatest interface card. If some of the hardware on your intranet is cheap and unreliable, the NFS server may not always be up and running, which means that your files (and lots of other people's) aren't available.

The good news is that you can solve performance and availability problems with reliable, redundant hardware and software, where you keep an identical copy (a *mirror*) of your NFS server. When it comes to network hardware and server and file availability, you get what you pay for.

Mirroring your NFS server means that performance improves because two computers are sharing file serving duties. Mirroring reduces availability problems because if either server crashes or breaks down, the other one handles all file serving requests. Things may slow down until the crashed computer is running again, but everyone can still see the files they need. Mirroring a hardware-software combination such as an NFS server is called *no single point of failure*. If either the hardware or the software fails, another copy takes over without interrupting the users' work.

Server tips

For best performance, dedicate a computer to be an NFS server and limit the other services provided by that computer. Everyone's files are stored on the NFS server, and users' computers become clients that access the files on the server. A dedicated NFS server also makes it easier for you to back up everyone's files because all files are on one computer. You can and should dedicate as many servers as you need. You're not limited to just one.

Client tips

In the `/etc/fstab` file, do not use the default values (1024) for the options wsize and rsize. Setting these options to 8192 improves NFS efficiency. The options stand for the number of bytes the server reads (rsize) and writes (wsize) in one operation. Consider changing the default value for retry. The default is `retry=10000` — 10,000 minutes. (You do the math — that's nearly a week.) If a mount command fails, NFS continues trying to mount the file system for `retry` minutes. If a file system or disk is broken, you can save a great deal of system resources if the mount command gives up after a couple of hours or so — 120 minutes, if our math is correct.

Weighing performance against security

Someone working on a large project, such as editing a large document, can reduce network traffic (and, therefore, work faster) by logging on to the server to work on the file locally.

However, as the system administrator, you shouldn't allow users to log on directly to the server unless your network bandwidth is too saturated to handle the NFS traffic. In that case, you should be looking at ways to upgrade your network, such as using faster routers and faster NICs.

Getting NFS Security Tips

If you're still using NFSv3, use NFSv4 as soon as you can. To secure NFS files, you need to

- **Protect the files:** File system security helps you do this.

- **Protect the server from unauthorized access:** The `exports` file helps you do this. It lists the file systems you're willing to share across NFS.

- **Use Secure NFS:** Available for all major operating systems.

To protect your files and server, try these strategies:

- ✔ Use the file system protection that's available on your server.
- ✔ Generally restrict permission for NFS files to read-only.
- ✔ Be cautious about allowing write access.
- ✔ Be selective about the hosts you allow to access your NFS files.

    An NFS server has a file named `exports` that lists the hosts which can access the NFS files on that server.

- ✔ Don't leave your file system open to access by everyone on the Internet.

Secure NFS works differently depending on your network configuration. You can use Secure NFS or run NFS under Kerberos, a strict security system described in Chapter 21. If your network is set up as a Kerberos realm, you can configure NFS to use authenticated and encrypted connections. See Chapter 12 for reminders about authentication and encryption.

Inside the guts of NFS is the client/server programming technique *Remote Procedure Calls (RPCs)*. You don't see RPCs, and you don't really need to know about them except to know about the *Secure RPC* version. If you're concerned about NFS security, try to buy an NFS implementation that uses Secure RPC. NFS plus Secure RPC equals Secure NFS — imagine that! Secure NFS prevents the bad guys from *address spoofing,* or fooling your NFS server into thinking that they originate from a legitimate address. The most secure form of Secure NFS uses AES encryption to authenticate hosts involved in Remote Procedure Call (RPC) transactions. NFS uses RPC to communicate requests between hosts. Secure NFS prevents attackers from spoofing RPC requests by encrypting the time stamp in the RPC requests.

Sharing Files Off the Stack

You have other file sharing options in addition to the TCP/IP standards. Although these options aren't part of the TCP/IP stack, they use some TCP/IP protocols to communicate across a network. Being an application on the stack and using TCP/IP are different methods — Internet standard versus nonstandard. Samba and Microsoft Windows network shares are examples of popular file sharing alternatives to the TCP/IP applications.

Using Windows network shares

In Microsoft terminology, a *network share* is a resource such as a file, folder, or printer that has been made sharable with other users on the network.

Under Microsoft Windows clients, file sharing and print sharing are enabled and disabled together. You can't separate them, though you can control individually which disk partitions and printers are (or aren't) shared.

On the server side, you share folders and drives with networked clients, change the properties to shared, and give the share a meaningful name. By default, the share name is the shared drive or folder location. You may want to set permissions allowing everyone or specific users or user groups to be able to connect and access the share and set access permissions. To serve a share, follow these steps:

- From Explorer, right-click the drive or folder you want to share and choose Sharing and Security➪Share This Folder.
- Fill in the share name, the number of users to allow, and any permissions you want to set.
- Click OK when you're done.

On the client side, you connect to the share or shares you want to access. From Explorer, choose Tools➪Map Network Drive. A wizard appears and helps you connect to a shared drive or folder. Answer the wizard's questions to connect and access the share.

Windows Vista simplifies some setup tasks, though Microsoft made some changes that can be irritating when adding these operating systems to an environment of computers running mostly Windows XP. The default workgroup name changes from MSHOME to WORKGROUP, the default network folder changes from Shared Documents to Public, and you must be sure to set the Network Location to Private. (If you choose Public, file sharing is turned off.)

Windows 7 introduces the new feature HomeGroup, which is designed to make setup easy, though it isn't available to other versions of Windows.

For more flexibility in file and print sharing, Samba software is similar to NFS.

Using Samba to share file and print services

Samba is a popular file and print sharing software that uses TCP/IP to communicate among servers and clients. It allows Unix, Linux, and Mac OS X hosts to be a client or a server of Microsoft Windows network shares.

The goal of NFS and Samba is the same — to allow clients to share files from a network server. Both NFS and Samba use client/server architecture. Both have clients and servers on almost every operating system. The big difference is that although NFS is a TCP/IP application, protocol, and service, no RFCs describe how Samba should work.

Samba is free, open source software (www.opensource.org) that provides both file and print services to clients on all major operating systems, including the numerous versions of the Microsoft Windows operating system. Samba is freely available under the GNU General Public License. Although Samba uses TCP/IP protocols and services for communication, it isn't part of the TCP/IP stack. Samba implements the Microsoft SMB (Server Message Block) protocol so that computers running Mac OS X, Linux, and Unix can participate in Windows file and print sharing. The environment is sometimes also referred to as CIFS (Common Internet File System). The administrator (possibly you) chooses which directories are available as Windows shares. Users cannot tell the difference between shares provided by way of Samba and those coming from a computer running Windows.

Working with Network Print Services

Another resource that TCP/IP network (and Internet) users share is the printer and print server software. A *print server* is software, such as the LPD (Line Printer Daemon) application, that allows multiple clients to share a single printer.

As an end user, all you have to do is type your operating system's print command in a terminal window or choose File⇨Print from your computer's menu. All you need to know is where the printer is located so that you can retrieve your output. (You can stop reading about printing now, unless you have an inquiring mind.)

This section is about using standard print protocols that are part of the TCP/IP stack. Using these standard protocols, you can share a printer in Marshall's kitchen with networked computers in Beijing and Mayberry. Even the oldest printing implementations allow print sharing.

You have a choice of two print sharing options:

> ✔ **A computer-attached printer:** Connected to the computer by either cable or wireless. The attached computer functions as the print server services all print requests from other computers. When multiple clients connect to a single computer running services for print sharing, the best practice is to dedicate that computer to printing. Printing uses system resources — such as CPU, memory, I/O, and disk space — for

each print request. If the print server computer is used for applications other than printing (in any network other than a SOHO; see Chapter 7), all applications on the print server slow down.

✔ **A network attached printer:** Directly attached to the network, eliminating the need for a computer to provide resources for print sharing. Not every printer, especially in the SOHO environment, is capable of connecting directly to a network.

The technical definition of *print server* is software providing print services, but remember that most people are referring to a computer when they use the term *print server.*

The TCP/IP protocol stack includes print sharing protocols, services, and applications. The TCP/IP stack includes three important print protocols:

✔ Line Printer Daemon (LPD), dating from 1993

✔ Line Printer Remote (LPR), dating from 1999

✔ Internet Printing Protocol (IPP), with work begun in 1993 and continuing to the present

LPD and LPR are older protocols that work primarily with Unix, Linux, and Mac OS X, although Microsoft Windows Server operating systems have LPD services built-in for printing interoperability with Unix and Linux. LPD and LPR have limitations, such as lack of security and weak support for interoperating with Microsoft operating systems. Because of these limitations, the IETF Printer Working Group drafted a new printing protocol, IPP. Most current network printer models build in IPP support as well as traditional LPR/LPD.

Valuing IPP features

IPP adds security to Internet printing and lets you connect and print to any IPP-enabled printer as long as you know that printer's URL or its IP address. If you can use a browser, you can print without knowing any special print commands or menus. The URL of an IPP-compatible device usually begins with ipp:// rather than http://.

IPP depends on other TCP/IP protocols. IPP depends on SSL or TLS to make printing much more secure than it has been with the older protocols LPD and LPR. By using SSL or TLS, IPP can provide authentication and encryption without doing the work. In addition, IPP sends print jobs over HTTP, allowing a Web browser to be the interface for IPP printing.

Chapter 2 describes most of the major TCP/IP protocols, including the protocols that IPP uses, such as SSL, TLS, and HTTP.

IPP consists of two components:

- ✔ **Management:** Setting up a printer and using a Web browser to view printer status and set properties
- ✔ **Internet printing:** Printing and viewing print job status by connecting to the printer's URL

In order for users to print using IPP, they need a Web browser and IPP client software running on their computers. The client software, which is hidden from the user, is usually part of the operating system unless it's an ancient operating system, such as Microsoft Windows 95.

If you're running a client operating system that doesn't support IPP, you can find downloadable clients for free on the Internet. Your search engine returns various choices.

Before you set up an IPP print server, you must meet these requirements:

- ✔ **The printer hardware must be IPP enabled.** It must support IPP. Most newer printers are IPP enabled.
- ✔ **The print server must have a valid IP address.** For printing by way of the Internet, the IP address must be global (allocated by your ISP) rather than local on your LAN.
- ✔ **Your intranet's firewall must not block the IPP port.** It's Port 631 over TCP.

CUPS, or Common Unix Print System, is the default printing system for most Linux distributions, Unix operating systems, and Mac OS X. You can, optionally, use CUPS on Microsoft Windows.

Setting up Windows Server 2008 print servers over IPP

To install an IPP print server for Windows Server operating systems, you must first define a role. The concept of server roles is specific to Microsoft Windows Server operating systems, to allow the administrator to configure services by using the Configure Your Server Wizard. The following steps describe the process of installing the Print Server role:

1. Run Server Manager and select Add Roles in the left pane. The Add Roles Wizard is launched automatically.

2. Click Next on the Welcome screen, if one appears. Select Print Services and click Next. When the wizard displays an informational message, click Next again to display Select Role Services.

3. Select Print Server to install print server software and the Print Management console.

4. To select Internet printing, create an Internet Information Services (IIS) hosted Web site. IPP uses a Web interface for managing printers, connecting, and printing to shared printers. The default URL for the Web site is `http://servername/Printers`, where `servername` is the name of the server running the print services.

5. (Optional) Selecting LPD Service installs the TCP/IP Line Printer Daemon Service (LPDSV) so that computers using LPD and LPR UNIX can print by using the Windows Server 2008 print server. This setting also opens a port in Windows Firewall to allow network print jobs to pass through the firewall to the print server.

6. To add a printer, from the Start menu, choose All Programs⇨ Administrative Tools⇨Print Management. Choose Print Servers from the list in the left pane. Right-click the local or remote print server for the new printer and choose Add Printer to display the Network Printer Installation Wizard. Select Search for Network Printers and click Next. The wizard scans your network for printers and lists each printer by name and IP address. Select the printer you want to configure and click Next. Then follow the wizard's instructions for setting printer properties.

Windows XP doesn't use roles, so you must run the proprietary Microsoft Internet Information Services (IIS) before setting up a print server to use IPP.

Printing with the Common Unix Print System (CUPS)

CUPS (Common Unix Printing System) is an application for printing and managing printers that enables Unix, Linux, and Mac OS X print clients to run over IPP (Internet Printing Protocol). If you're using Samba file sharing, CUPS includes access to Windows users and printers. CUPS software runs behind the scenes when you print. Suppose that you're using a graphical interface and you open a file to read. If you want to print, simply do the usual: Choose File⇨Print. You have no indication that CUPS is managing the print job.

The first time someone prints, CUPS creates a *queue* for that printer to track the status of the printer, such as out of paper, offline, or printing. Every time you print something, CUPS creates a *job* that contains the queue for your printer, the name of the document you're printing, and page descriptions. When your print job finishes, CUPS removes the job from the queue and moves on to the next one in the queue.

Each operating system has different menus and commands for setting up printing, but the basic steps are the same for all operating systems: Click through your system menus until you see a Print menu. Some systems open a wizard, and you follow its steps. Other systems step you through more menus. For example, on Ubuntu Linux v9.04, to set up CUPS printing so that the system can use the IPP protocol, you open Printer Manager: Choose System➪Administration➪Printing. Under Global Settings, choose Share Printers.

Mac OS X uses CUPS by default, with or without Samba, for printing and print sharing. Apple also provides Bonjour software (it's available for Windows too), which discovers sharable network resources, including file servers and printers, and announces their existence by way of broadcast messages on the local network.

Chapter 19

Sharing Compute Power

In This Chapter

▶ Protocols in this chapter: telnet, rlogin, rsh, ssh, vnc

▶ Using another computer's power

▶ Working via remote access

▶ Clustering and volunteering

*I*s your computer working too hard? Is it hungry for power? (Whose computer isn't at some time or other?) Well, don't worry. Thanks to TCP/IP protocols, applications, and services, you can connect to other computers and use *their* power. Some of those capabilities are evident in Chapter 18 — file and print sharing — and so are their security issues. In this chapter, we show you how to use remote access, clusters, and more. But (no surprise here) you still have security issues to watch out for.

Sharing Network Resources

The computers on your network are often shared resources. A *compute server* is a computer that's been set up specifically to share its CPU power. To distribute that power in an organized way, many businesses set up compute servers for you to use. A compute server is a powerful computer that's configured especially for use by many users.

In this chapter, you discover how to take advantage of shared resources, but remember that computer etiquette requires — and network security demands — that you always have permission to do so. If you go after resources from networks and computers without permission, don't be surprised if you find yourself in trouble with law enforcement agencies.

Not every computer can be a compute server. Some operating systems can't provide this service — others are set up so they don't. Unless you take special steps — installing and configuring extra software — your desktop or laptop computer won't provide compute services for network users. It's designed to be used by only one person at a time. (Why do you think they're called *personal* computers?)

Stealing cycles — and not Harleys

In the earlier, friendlier days of networking, sharing compute power was often called "cycle stealing" because a CPU cycle is a tick of the computer clock. By the way, a computer clock ticks millions of times faster than the alarm clock next to your bed. In those trusting days, the term, cycle stealing, meant something more like "cycle borrowing," and people generally didn't use anyone else's computer power without permission. In today's less friendly Internet atmosphere, cycle stealing really means stealing. Network administrators usually secure computers so that unauthorized people can't steal cycles (use a compute server without permission). Anyone who manages to steal CPU cycles is a hacker.

Multiuser operating systems — such as Linux, Unix, Windows Server 2008, Mac OS X Server, and others — are designed to be used by more than one person at a time and are capable of providing shared resources. The system managers must decide which services are, and are not, available.

One of the biggest benefits of taking advantage of shared resources is that the other computers can have different operating systems or different applications from those you have on your computer. In effect, the operating system you're working on doesn't matter. The operating system you want to share doesn't matter. TCP/IP protocols make all necessary operating system to operating system compatibility completely invisible to you.

Accessing Remote Computers

Sometimes the easiest way to take advantage of a shared resource is to sit down at the compute server itself. That works if the computer is nearby, or if the server is installed at a desirable vacation spot. Because that's not usually the case, many people turn to applications such as telnet, `rlogin`, or `rsh`, which are described in the following sections.

Regardless of how convenient it might be, you might need special permission to sit at the compute server because many large servers are in locked computer rooms for physical security.

Using a telnet client

Telnet actually predates the TCP/IP protocol suite. It was adopted as part of the TCP/IP stack almost as soon as the stack came into existence. Telnet client software connects to telnet server software and passes data using the telnet protocol. Yes, this is another case where you can't tell exactly what someone means when they say "telnet" — because it's a protocol, a client, *and* a service.

Some telnet clients have GUIs (graphical user interfaces); others provide only command-line interfaces. Some cost money; most are free. Some are available for multiple operating systems; others are made for only one. In any case, a telnet client provides a terminal emulator that lets you log in to a computer and use it interactively.

"Telnetting" to a computer running Microsoft Windows may not get you very much extra capability because you're limited to the things you can do in a Command Prompt window.

Before using telnet, you need to know two things:

 ✔ The name or the IP address of the computer to which you want to connect.
 ✔ A valid username and password for logging in to that computer.

If the other computer is not running a telnet service (because the system manager disabled it, for example), you can waste a lot of time troubleshooting the connection failures.

"R" you ready for more remote access?

An alternative to telnet is *rlogin,* which comes with most Linux and Unix distributions. The `rlogin` software is part of the *r utilities,* a group of network utilities developed at the University of California at Berkeley for accessing other computers. The utilities in the group all start with the letter *r.* Although they provide the same kind of functionality, telnet and `rlogin` were implemented by separate groups of people, and each works differently behind the scenes to accomplish the same thing.

Executing commands with rsh and rexec

Sometimes you need to connect to another computer and work interactively to perform a variety of tasks, as with `rlogin` or telnet. At other times, you have just one thing to accomplish. The r utilities (from the University of California at Berkeley) include *rsh* (remote shell). With `rsh`, you can tell the other computer to execute one command. On some versions of Linux and Unix the command is named *remsh* (still remote shell) so it doesn't interfere with a different `rsh` command, the restricted shell.

Trust is essential for `rlogin` and `rsh`. When you log in to the other computer, you may or may not be prompted for a username and password. You aren't prompted if the remote computer trusts you and the computer from which you're connecting. When two computers are set up to trust each other, all the user accounts on one computer that have matching account names and passwords on the other computer can use `rlogin` and `rsh` without being asked for a username and password.

Trust isn't automatically reciprocal. Just because computer A trusts computer B (and some or all of computer B's users), it doesn't mean that computer B trusts computer A (and its users). Nevertheless, trust is commonly defined in both directions. This definition and mechanism of trust come from Unix and are present in Linux and Mac OS X, but not in Windows which has its own trust relationships in workgroups and Active Directory domains.

There's another `r` application, *rexec* (remote execution). It's like `rsh` in function but uses different server software and, before it attempts to execute your command, `rexec` always prompts you for a username and password. Your password is encrypted before it is sent to the other computer.

Although `rsh` is quicker because it doesn't involve thorough logon processing, `rexec` is more secure because it does. Take your pick.

Securing Remote Access Sessions

Telnet, `rlogin`, and `rsh` all contain security risks because usernames, passwords, and the data go across the network in clear text. There are no security provisions, so you should avoid these protocols, applications, and services unless you're working on a secured intranet. Other protocols with this security flaw include FTP, SMTP, and other protocols that pre-date the design of SSL (Secure Sockets Layer) and TLS (Transport Layer Security).

Your security options include

- ✔ Using standard telnet, `rlogin`, or `rsh` only after establishing a VPN (Virtual Private Network) tunnel to the remote network.
- ✔ Using SSH (Secure Shell Protocol) client and server software.

SSH version 2 (SSHv2 or SSH2) is a much, much better choice than version 1 (SSHv1 or SSH1) because it has better security and more capabilities.

See Chapter 20 for more information about telnet security holes and why you should disable the telnet service.

The capabilities of the client and the server must match. A secure client and secure server work together to guarantee that your username and password as well as your data cannot be stolen or interfered with. Your best bet is to use the smartest client and server software you can find and afford — the ones that support the latest protocols.

Many programs provide both telnet and rlogin clients and support the Secure Shell (SSH1 and SSH2) protocol. There's even an SSH2 client for BlackBerry smartphones!

Taking Control of Remote Desktops

Telnet, rlogin, and friends are great tools, but they cannot help you run graphical applications on the other computer. For that, you need a screen sharing application — one that gives you remote control of the computer.

All remote control clients have GUIs (graphical user interfaces); some cost money while many are free; and some are available for multiple operating systems while others are made for only one. The Linux and Unix operating systems use the X Window System, which has built-in capabilities for remote access and remote control.

Apple licenses Apple Remote Desktop for Mac OS X. Microsoft includes Remote Desktop Connection in Windows. Both of these proprietary applications use TCP/IP for network communication, but neither application is part of the TCP/IP stack, as the X Window System.

For multiple-operating-system environments, you can't beat VNC (Virtual Network Computing) software. VNC client software connects to VNC server software using the RFB (remote frame buffer) protocol. (Ha-ha! You were expecting us to say "the VNC protocol," weren't you?) After you supply a username and/or password, VNC shows you the same GUI you would see if you were sitting at the other computer. Typing on your keyboard and moving your mouse control the other computer exactly as its own would. You can download VNC software, including a free edition, from www.realvnc.com.

Your client and the server software must match; you may need to use multiple products. For example, you can't use Microsoft's Remote Desktop Connection to control a computer that's running Linux unless you install a VNC server on the Linux machine and a matching VNC client on the Windows machine.

Your best bet is to use the smartest client and server software you can find and afford — the ones that include security and that are available for multiple operating systems.

Sharing Clustered Resources

A *cluster* is a group of computers that are linked together, managed together, and work together. In some respects, a cluster seems to be a single computer though this image depends a lot on how and why the cluster was assembled. The computers in a cluster are called *nodes*.

IPv6 uses the term *node* to mean computer or host. Although clustering uses the same term, clusters do not have to be connected by IPv6.

Computers are clustered to provide one or more of these features:

- ✔ **High availability:** The goal here is improving the uptime of their services and making sure that some nodes are always available.
- ✔ **Load balancing:** Computers in the cluster share the work load that none of them can handle on their own.
- ✔ **Supercomputing:** Pooling the clustered machines' computing power makes more ambitious tasks possible.

We discuss these features in detail in the following sections.

Clustering for high availability

In an HA (High Availability) cluster, if a node has a software or hardware problem, the service that node provides is started on another node via a process called *failover*. Users of the service may or may not notice that a failover has taken place.

In a common two-node HA cluster, one computer (let's call it SystemA) actively provides a service (let's call it Service1) and another (SystemB) waits idly until something goes wrong. This is called an *active/passive* configuration. Because an active/passive configuration essentially "wastes" the backup computer, many of these clusters are set to run another essential service (Service 2) on SystemB and keep SystemA as the backup for that service. Both SystemA and SystemB have to be powerful enough to run both Service1 *and* Service2 in the event there's a problem on either computer.

An application running on an HA cluster probably won't run any faster than it would on a single, dedicated computer. But it is nearly 100% available.

Clustering for load balancing

As the number of services and nodes in a cluster grow, the configuration and management of active/passive pairings gets complicated. In a load-balancing cluster, the computers and services function in an *active/active* configuration. Typically, the nodes all run the same services in a cooperative fashion (which may require services that are *cluster-aware*). Popular Web sites are often run on load-balancing clusters. Incoming Web requests are distributed to the nodes "fairly," ideally taking into account the performance of the node rather than just dealing out the requests in a round-robin manner.

An application running on a load-balancing cluster can handle more work, although any element of that workload probably won't reach completion any faster than it would it in a tamer environment.

Clustering for supercomputing

In an HPC (High-Performance Computing) cluster, the nodes often work together on just one intense application — such as simulations for weather forecasting, computational fluid dynamics, medical research, and more. HPC is sometimes called High-Productivity Computing; similar challenges are HTC (High-Throughput Computing) and MTC (Many-Task Computing). The idea is consistent for all these names: To pool computing resources so you can tackle big, complex tasks.

Each of these styles is better for some applications than others — and each has a different measure of success:

- ✔ HPC measures results in calculations per second because while they may need huge amounts of computing power, they usually don't take very long to generate (on the order of seconds or minutes).

- ✔ HTC measures how many results were calculated during the time period (say, a month, a year, and so on).

- ✔ MTC, a cross between HPC and HTC, measures how many results were calculated and how quickly.

Clusters of all kinds depend on TCP/IP but the details of their designs, implementations, and management do not.

Sharing Compute Power with Grid and Volunteer Computing

Grid computing and its sibling *volunteer computing* are similar to clusters. Both link computers together to form large pools of computing resources but the nodes in a grid are separately managed, and may be located anywhere in the world.

Grid computing

An organization chooses to deploy a grid to tackle problems it chooses. Acting on this intention has three practical requirements:

- The installation and configuration of the client software must be well managed.
- There can be no choice about participating; everybody has to.
- The computers and their results must be trustworthy.

Volunteer computing

With volunteer computing, individuals freely choose

- Whether to contribute to projects.
- Which client software to install and configure.
- Which projects they want to help with.
- When and how to let the client software run.
- When to stop volunteering.

Because the client software generates public statistics, there are often competitive feelings at work. ("My computers generate more results than yours! Nyah-nyah!") Sometimes this leads mischievous people to cheat to improve their results. Volunteers' computers sometimes generate bad results, too.

BOINC (Berkeley Open Infrastructure for Network Computing) is one of the best-known grid-computing and volunteer-computing client applications. It is free, open-source software. It's used in over 75 projects, in categories such as

- Biology and Medicine
- Mathematics, Computing, and Game Theory
- Astronomy, Physics, and Chemistry
- Earth Sciences

Part V
Network Troubleshooting and Security

"We take network security here very seriously."

In this part . . .

Part V is dedicated to TCP/IP protocols, services, and applications that help you maintain a secure, trouble-free network. Because reality can give you a sharp kick when it comes to network security, the chapters in Part V give you tips and techniques for finding and fixing network and security problems.

Chapter 20 goes beyond the minimum security introduction in Chapter 12 to describe some additional forms of malware. The chapter shows you how to use TCP/IP applications, such as syslog and netstat, to uncover and diagnose security incursions. Chapter 21 continues with more advanced security protocols and applications, such as the IPSec group of protocols and Kerberos, the strictest and most secure (and most complicated) security guardian in the TCP/IP stack.

Chapter 22 walks you step by step through solving an Internet connectivity problem, using basic TCP/IP tools and applications available on every operating system that runs a TCP/IP stack. Finally, Chapter 22 describes how complete Network Management Systems (NMS), based on the Simple Network Management Protocol (SNMP), help network administrators collect, collate, and report on network usage so that minor difficulties can be corrected before they become major problems.

Chapter 20

Staying with Security Protocols

. . . .

In This Chapter

▶ Protocols in this chapter: TCP, UDP, FTP, HTTP, ICMP, telnet

▶ Involving all users in TCP/IP security

▶ Prescribing preventive medicine to prevent security contagion

▶ Recognizing advanced malware infection

▶ Diagnosing network contagions

▶ Using the netstat, ps, and syslog tools to diagnose network ailments

▶ Looking through Microsoft proprietary logs

. . . .

*B*eing connected to a network, especially the Internet, comes with security risks. Is it worth it? For most people and organizations, the answer is yes, but a few important precautions are usually necessary. Security topics are spread throughout this book in several chapters, especially Chapters 12 and 14. Chapter 12 introduces a minimum of security concepts and terminology, including the worst that can happen to your computer and network, and points you to some tools to avoid those attacks. Both chapters introduce encryption and authentication. This chapter builds on Chapters 12 and 14 by going into more detail about security protocols.

This entire chapter is about security, so you don't see another Security icon after this one. Just imagine that you see one of these icons on every paragraph.

Before you even think about securing network protocols and services, you must secure the computers (and their users) on the network. As classic wisdom says, "A chain is only as strong as its weakest link." Often a single computer or its user is the weakest link — and a major entry point for crackers to sneak on to your network.

RFC 4949, "Internet Security Glossary" (also known as FYI 36), is the place to go when you need definitions of security terms. The RFC Editor (www. rfc-editor.org) is the official site for all RFCs and tutorials about the RFC process.

Determining Who Is Responsible for Network Security

Who is responsible for network security? The answer is *everyone:*

- ✔ **You:** You're responsible, whatever your role is.
- ✔ **All users:** They must not reveal their passwords to anyone.
- ✔ **Security administrators:** Also known as the network police, they set and enforce security policies for any network ranging from a small building to a worldwide enterprise.
- ✔ **System administrators:** They configure and monitor the services.
- ✔ **Network administrators:** They manage the network connections.

Don't practice *security by obscurity;* that is, don't assume that users are stupid. Some users are smarter than your assumptions; others make the most amazing mistakes.

Here's an example: You configure your organization's anonymous FTP server so that it's publicly writeable and assume that no one will find out simply because you don't announce the change. You're attempting to practice security by obscurity.

The bottom line: Assume nothing about trust. Exhort all users to be vigilant about security. Be proactive. If you're a system, network, or security administrator, publish security procedures for your organization and monitor users to ensure that they follow all your recommended security practices.

Following the Forensic Trail: Examining the Steps for Securing Your Network

Whether you're keeping an individual host secured or an entire network, they require the same procedures:

1. Practice preventive medicine. (See the following section, "Step 1: Prescribing Preventive Medicine for Security.")

2. Observe symptoms. (See the later section, "Step 2: Observing Symptoms of Malware Infection" and Chapter 12.)

3. Use diagnostic tools to validate observations and find hidden ailments. (See the later section "Step 3: Diagnosing Security Ailments with netstat and Logging.")

TIP

Antivirus behind the scenes

Antivirus software consists of two parts:

- ✔ **The signature database:** A set of files listing known viruses and how they behave. The scanning engine knows what (files, folders, zip archives) to scan.

- ✔ **The scanning engine:** An engine that compares your files to the viruses in the signature database, alerts you to any findings, and either quarantines or deletes the virus.

Unfortunately, new viruses appear in cyberspace all the time. Antivirus vendors update their signature files and let you know that updates are available. Most commercial antivirus software programs automatically update your signature files.

If you don't keep current on antivirus updates, your antivirus scans lose their effectiveness.

Sometimes the scanning engine needs updating. If one part of the antivirus software, the scanning engine, for example, is obsolete and the other part (the signature database) is current, your antivirus software doesn't work correctly, but usually you don't find out until it's too late — your computer is infected. It can seem to be working fine one minute and when you come back from lunch, be completely trashed if one part of the software isn't up to date.

To be as immune as possible, you must ban viruses at every possible entry point to your network — that is, you need to be sure that all hosts and servers on the network run antivirus software. Again, a network's weakest link is the unprotected host or its naïve user.

4. Report major diseases to your country's disease control center (Computer Emergency Readiness Team, or CERT); see Chapters 14 and 24.

5. Cure or quarantine. (Read this chapter.)

Step 1: Prescribing Preventive Medicine for Security

Your best security tool is common sense. We know we don't need to tell *you* that: *You* need to tell everyone else that.

Network security involves everything and everyone:

- ✔ **Users:** The people who use computers and who use the network. They may range from major technocrats to naïve users. By the way, those major technocrats are often the most careless about security because they know better, but they're usually in a hurry.

✔ **Hardware:** The computers and other devices on the network, especially mobile devices. Don't forget routers, cables, and other connection media. You may also have firewall appliances for firewalls and proxies.

✔ **Operating systems:** The security features, such as user accounts and passwords.

✔ **Software:** The applications themselves.

✔ **File systems:** The mechanisms for protecting directories and files.

✔ **Training and education:** Teaches users what you expect of them and the right way to do things.

✔ **Rules and regulations:** Includes punishments for breaking the rules. We know someone who was fired from a top secret facility and he didn't even break the rules. He just played a practical joke that looked like he broke the rules. On the other hand, Candace once completely disregarded the network police and their rules. They didn't exactly punish her — they made her one of them.

✔ **Physical security:** Includes locks on computer room doors and security cables for laptops.

So, given the whole internetworking picture, from one user on a single computer to the whole kit and kaboodle of overall network design, here's a list of common sense best practices. Following these suggestions is more important than installing any fancy network security hardware and software:

✔ **Limit physical access to clients and servers.** In other words, try to keep your servers in locked rooms only available to administrators. If possible, make sure that strangers can't wander around the office area, looking at individual hosts and trying to see which ones might be unprotected.

✔ **Use a firewall to protect your connections to the Internet**. Ensure that every computer runs some sort of personal firewall. Make sure that a firewall guards your entire network.

✔ **Protect your laptops and personal computers**. Here are some suggestions:

- *Use passwords that are hard to crack.* Change them regularly.

- *Use locks on your laptops.* You can buy screen locks and physical locks.

- *Use secure backups on every machine in your network.* Then store the backups off-site. If you work for a large company, it probably uses a commercial offsite storage company. If you run your own small business, the commercial facilities may be too expensive. Get a safety deposit box. Ask a reliable friend or relative to hold on to a copy of your backups.

Do not ever store your backups in your car. If you think that no one is careless enough to do that, guess again. (If you're reading this chapter, you know someone who tried it.)

- *Use file permissions everywhere.* If you're the system administrator, make sure that everyone uses file and folder permissions. As we say elsewhere, careless users can be the weak link in your security system.

- *Install patches and upgrades as soon as they become available.* Most operating systems and applications automatically let you know when updates are available. Operating system updates, especially, include security fixes.

Chapter 14 also lists a few more common sense security practices, especially for e-mail.

Step 2: Observing Symptoms of Malware Infection

Chapter 12 describes the most common attacks against networks and tools, such as antimalware software, that identify and prevent damage. (*Malware* refers to malevolent programs such as viruses, worms, and phishing.) In Step 2 on the forensic trail, you determine whether your computer might be infected by some sort of malware. To do that, observe any differences in how your system and network normally run. Here are some symptoms to look for:

- ✔ **Slow computer:** Your computer starts running so slowly that it's crawling. Slow motion is a common symptom of malware penetration. However, you might have other reasons for slow performance, including a hard disk that needs defragmenting, a computer that's memory poor, or a network controller that's overworked.

- ✔ **Unexplained problems with programs:** Programs, including your operating system, mysteriously start or stop automatically.

- ✔ **Sluggish network access:** An e-mail virus often mails hundreds or more copies of itself, and that extra traffic can cause your network performance to become obviously slower.

- ✔ **Strain on hard drive:** Your hard drives or storage area networks seem to be working overtime.

- ✔ **Sudden appearance of new toolbars, links, or favorites:** This type of annoyance is specifically a symptom of spyware.

✔ **Mysteriously changing default settings:** Your settings, such as home page, media player, or search program, change without your consent. Irritations such as these are also symptoms of spyware.

✔ **Redirected URL:** You type a URL, but a different Web site opens without notice. Again, you're probably a victim of spyware.

Some spyware doesn't show symptoms. It's loaded on your computer to collect information about you and your computer. Hopefully, you're running antispyware software to prevent spyware from secretly being loaded.

Yes, licensing agreements seem to go on forever, and at times you probably skip them entirely, but beware of certain site agreements. When you visit Web sites that offer free downloads, read the license agreement carefully and look for clauses where you agree to accept advertising and pop-up ads. Also, think carefully about allowing the software to send information back to the free program's manufacturer.

No matter how well you think you protect your network, stuff happens, and even trusted sources can cause grief. In addition to the ongoing Microsoft struggle with security vulnerabilities, in 2009 not even the reliable software giants are infallible. Google Android and Adobe PDF Reader security vulnerabilities introduced security problems in thousands of computers and networks.

Uncovering more contagions

But, wait! There's more. As if the list of malware in Chapter 12 isn't enough, we describe a couple more network ogres that often spawn the malware you may have encountered in that chapter.

Some other, more complex attacks not listed in Chapter 12 include

✔ Port attacks

✔ DDoS

✔ Botnets

✔ Rootkits

Plowing through port scanning

All hosts on a network run services that are identified by port numbers. Table 4-5, in Chapter 4, lists some common services and their port numbers.

Port scanning is a popular way for attackers to seek services that are vulnerable to break-ins. More than 6,000 defined ports are available, although port numbers 0 through 1023 are the standards for system services or for programs that privileged users are running. If attackers can exploit a port, they can potentially gain control of a server.

Port scanning doesn't damage a host or network. It leads an attacker to find which ports and services are the most susceptible to damage.

Here are a few other key points to know about port scanning:

✔ A port scan sends a message to each port. Because connection-oriented TCP ports always give a response, most hackers prefer those to UDP ports. The kind of response TCP returns aims at the ports that can be probed for weaknesses.

✔ For every service (such as HTTP, FTP, or telnet) that a host or server runs, at least one port is open for that service. Services must be disabled, and therefore their open ports, to reduce port scan weaknesses.

✔ A hacker doesn't have to be a programmer to run port scanning software. Programs such as SAINT are available for free on the Internet.

✔ Like packet sniffers, port scanning software can also be used for good. Network administrators frequently scan the ports on their networks to find areas where they need to shore up security.

You can't completely prevent port scans, but when you see a port being scanned, you can see the IP address of the scanner and set up your firewall to block that address in the future.

The free online service ShieldsUP!, from Gibson Research Corp. (www.grc.com), probes ports on computers running various operating systems to see what information you left public. The Common Ports option tests TCP connections to common ports and services, such as FTP, telnet, finger, HTTP, and POP3. The results can be stealth, closed, or open:

✔ **Stealth:** The most secure result — outsiders can't even *see* your ports. This result is the one you want for all ports (see Figure 20-1).

✔ **Closed:** The port is visible to outsiders, but they can't use it. Because you're giving intruders information about your system, however, system privacy could be better.

✔ **Open:** Not a good result. Not only are your ports visible, but they're also available for break-ins.

The Port Probe from ShieldsUp! also provides a text summary, as shown in Figure 20-2.

This Shields Up! textual summary may be printed or marked and copied for subsequent pasting into any other application.

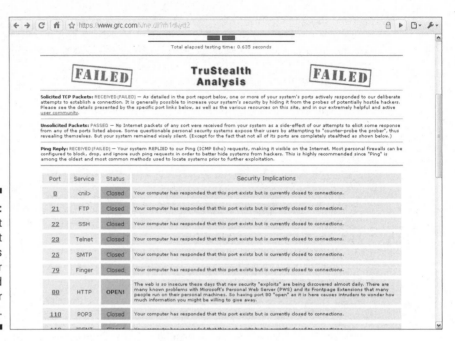

Figure 20-1:
The result
is okay, but
ports on this
computer
could
be better
protected.

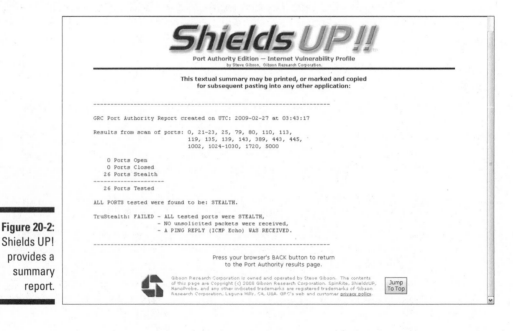

Figure 20-2:
Shields UP!
provides a
summary
report.

Revisiting some of the nastiest DDoS attacks

The first DDoS attacks appeared in 1999. In early 2000, a major DDoS took down Web sites such as Amazon, CNN, eBay, and Yahoo! for several hours. Even worse, in 2002, a well-coordinated DDoS crippled 9 of the 13 root servers with a ping flood. (See Chapter 10 for a description of root servers.) The ping program uses the ICMP protocol and appears throughout this book, including Chapters 9 and 22. This particular DDoS assault sent more than 150,000 ICMP (Internet Control Message Protocol) messages per second to the root servers. Because the root-level DNS servers do caching, the attack lasted about a half-hour. Nonetheless, traffic on the Internet was disturbed from the top down.

We've said this before: For the best level of security, turn off any services (daemons) you don't need.

If the computer you test is a Web server, you need the HTTP daemon/service, although you can hide the port. If the computer isn't a Web server, disable the HTTP service. You don't need a Web server to browse the Web; you need only a Web client — that is, a browser.

Despairing of distributed denial of service (DDoS)

A *distributed denial-of-service (DDoS)* attack is one where multitudes of messages attack a single target — host or network. The flood of incoming messages ultimately puts too many demands on system and network resources (memory, CPU, number of connections allowed). When that happens, the targeted system hangs or shuts down, becoming unavailable.

A cracker can set up a DDoS attack in a few simple steps. We don't give you a detailed list because we don't want to turn our readers to the Dark Side. (The cyber-evildoers already know how to do it.)

The following steps give you a general idea of how a DDoS works to bring down a single host or an entire network so that you know what to look for if your network or computer hangs for no apparent reason.

1. Run automated programs to find vulnerable hosts on networks that connect to the Internet. (You can find the programs for free on the Internet or build your own.)

2. When the programs find a vulnerable host, they crack the host and install a DDoS Trojan. That Trojan turns the affected host into a zombie.

3. A master controller server program launches the attack against the target — a single host or an entire network as big as the Internet.

Popular tools for launching such DDoS attacks are easily available on the Internet. Hundreds or even thousands of zombie hosts used in the attack send massive amounts of network traffic, which swamps TCP resources. TCP is too busy dealing with the DDoS requests to handle legitimate network requests. The network is unavailable, as shown in Figure 20-3.

Check out the article at `www.sans.org/dosstep/index.php` for advice on defending against DDoS.

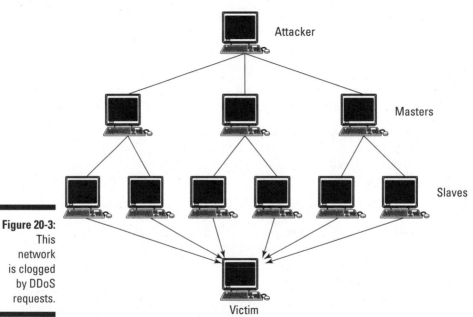

Figure 20-3:
This
network
is clogged
by DDoS
requests.

Banishing big, bad botnets

Bots (from robots), also known as *zombies,* are programs that wander a network — usually, the Internet — and perform repetitive actions, such as posting messages to multiple newsgroups or searching for news or prices. Don't they sound harmless?

At the time this book was written, ISPs said that bots are the biggest threat facing network availability and security.

A *botnet* is a collection of bots that run automatically. Botnets are famous for giant spamming attacks, running enormous phishing systems, perpetrating fraud, and launching DDoS (distributed denial-of-service) attacks. In other words, botnets make entire networks unavailable by clogging them with multiple assaults.

Botnets are also known as *zombie armies* because the owners of the computers in the botnet may be unaware that they're part of an army of spammers and virus passers. Computer Emergency Readiness Team (CERT) has documented botnets with over 100,000 computers in the army.

The best way to ensure that your computer is never drafted into a zombie army is to use standard first-line security techniques, such as

- ✔ Antivirus
- ✔ Antispyware
- ✔ Antimalware
- ✔ Firewalls
- ✔ Software updates and patches

Many botnets use Internet Relay Chat, or IRC, servers as botnet controllers (the generals of the army). It's a good reason not to allow chatting.

Raging over rootkits

A *rootkit* is a set of programs that let crackers steal administrator (root) access to a computer or a network. The first step is usually for a cracker to steal regular user access, by either sneaking in through a known security hole or cracking a password. After the next step, when the cybercrook installs the rootkit, the evildoer can hide the intrusion and gain privileged administrator access to the computer and, possibly, to other machines on the network, depending on which services are running.

Run only the services you need. Especially try not to run telnet and FTP because those services provide the front door to password cracking.

Rootkits hide in seemingly trustworthy sources: a downloaded program or a CD or DVD. Depending on the programs a rootkit includes, it can perform a variety of dishonest activities, such as

- ✔ Install spyware.
- ✔ Collect keystrokes.
- ✔ Build a "back door" into the system for the hacker's later use.
- ✔ Delete or edit log files to escape detection.
- ✔ Attack other computers on the network.

Some operating systems, such as Mac OS X and Ubuntu Linux, disable the root (administrator) password by default. The whole idea of a rootkit is to gain root access, and that's hard to do when the root account has no password. Mac OS X also has a package, OS X Rootkit Hunter, which provides protection against rootkits.

Pay attention to warnings!

Security messages come from all sorts of places: browsers, applications, the operating system, TCP/IP. The first figure below is from the Google Chrome browser. It's hard to miss: It fills the screen with an attention-getting red background. You can immediately run back to safety or explore the reason for the warning by clicking the Safe Browsing diagnostic link. The second figure shows the details that match the warning for the previous figure.

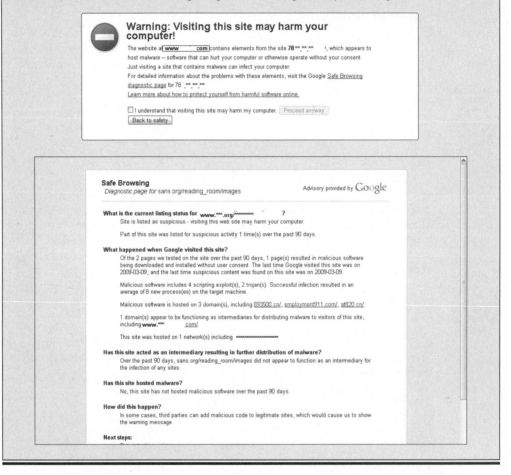

harden-environment package detects the installation of rootkits. For more information about harden-environment, browse to `www.debian.org/doc/manuals/securing-debian-howto`.

Step 3: Diagnosing Security Ailments with netstat, ps, and Logging

Step 3 on the forensic trail is to use diagnostic tools to investigate your observations from Step 2 and to find hidden ailments. Numerous tools are available from vendors such as Loriot SNMP Network Management, which you can find out about in Chapter 22. You can download more tools for free on the Internet. This chapter uses diagnostic tools that are built into the operating systems — no purchasing, no downloading.

Monitoring network use with ps

The ps command on Mac OS X and Linux/Unix and any version of Windows that can run the Powershell shows process information, including the network daemons that implement TCP/IP services. For example, when you disable the rwho daemon, use ps to prove that it's no longer running.

Ps-ing with Linux, Unix, Mac OS X

Figure 20-4 shows ps output from a Unix host with lots of network processes. If you followed the troubleshooting steps in this chapter and a network service, such as HTTP or FTP, still isn't working, ps is where you start. Use ps to see whether the problem service is running. Look in the far right COMMAND column for the service.

TIP

Don't get so mired in the trees that you don't see the forest. Even though the ps command puts out a lot of information, you're interested in the network processes.

You can identify network services by looking for the name of the service followed by the letter *d,* for daemon. For example, in Figure 20-4, you can see telnet running. This isn't the network service — it's someone running the telnet application. Look a little farther down the ps output and you see telnetd. That's the telnet service. Another clue for distinguishing a service from an application comes in the first column, labeled USER. Services run under the privileged username, root (the administrative user). Applications run under a username such as sylvan or ellend.

```
$ ps auwx                                                    Neat! The
USER      PID %CPU %MEM   VSZ  RSS TT  STAT STARTED  TIME COMMAND        rwho
leiden  20113  3.0  0.0   348  172 p3  R+   3:06PM   0:00.04 ps auwx     daemon is
root       65  0.0  0.0  1160  992 ??  Ss   Thu12PM  1:31.58 named       running.
root       68  0.0  0.0    52  108 ??  Ss   Thu12PM  0:08.83 rwhod ─┐
root       70  0.0  0.0    60  108 ??  Is   Thu12PM  0:00.09 portmap  │
root       76  0.0  0.0    56   16 ??  S    Thu12PM  5:13.29 nfsiod 4  Users
root       77  0.0  0.0    56   16 ??  I    Thu12PM  1:47.96 nfsiod 4  might
root       78  0.0  0.0    56   16 ??  I    Thu12PM  0:48.53 nfsiod 4  come in
root       79  0.0  0.0    56   16 ??  I    Thu12PM  0:20.84 nfsiod 4  via
root       80  0.0  0.0   444  132 ??  Ss   Thu12PM  0:39.04 sendmail:  rlogin.
accepting connections (sendmail)                                       /
root       83  0.0  0.0    76  100 ??  Ss   Thu12PM  0:17.39 inetd     /
root    22947  0.0  0.0    96   72 ??  I    10:28PM  0:00.48 rlogind  /
patt    22948  0.0  0.0   468   76 p1  Is+  10:28PM  0:00.53 -bash (bash)
WiseGuy 27152  0.0  0.0   312   72 r6  I+   12:36AM  0:01.55 ncftp ──Looks
root     5542  0.0  0.0    96   88 ??  I    8:26AM   0:23.60 rlogind  like a
sylvan   6137  0.0  0.0   148  112 r0  I+   8:36AM   0:30.77 telnet   version
netcom.com                                                            of ftp.
anmary   6792  0.0  0.0   568  476 p6  S+   8:52AM   0:35.11 irc (irc-2.6)
root     7004  0.0  0.0    84   88 ??  S    8:58AM   0:38.18 rlogind
root    15491  0.0  0.0   120  172 ??  I    1:00PM   0:00.35 telnetd
Bryant  16380  0.0  0.0   452  480 p2  S+   1:23PM   0:21.04 irc (irc-2.6)
root    16444  0.0  0.0    84  196 ??  S    1:26PM   0:15.52 rlogind
ellend  16534  0.0  0.0   156  260 q0  S+   1:29PM   0:07.03 telnet
realms.dorsai.org 1501    They're both using IRC to chat, but probably not to each other. ─┘
root    16936  0.0  0.0   120  200 ??  I    1:41PM   0:03.15 telnetd
shepherd 17449 0.0  0.0  2940  372 qc  I+   1:53PM   0:18.34 tin
ellend  17573  0.0  0.0   156  260 q0  T    1:56PM   0:00.47 telnet main.com
4444
root    17891  0.0  0.0    28  196 ??  S    2:05PM   0:00.46 comsat
deepwatr 18126 0.0  0.0  5408  592 s3  I+   2:11PM   1:08.44 trn       Someone's
root    18127  0.0  0.0    96  216 ??  I    2:12PM   0:04.62 rlogind   using
shift   18943  0.0  0.0   276  372 p7  S+   2:34PM   0:02.70 ftp       telnet.
rdf     19827  0.0  0.0   152  260 s8  I+   2:58PM   0:00.13 mail
batsoid@xx.netcom.com
root    19833  0.0  0.0   484  168 ??  I    2:58PM   0:00.06 sendmail:
server relay3.UU.NET cmd read (sendmail)
whitehed 20008 0.0  0.0   224  556 ??  S    3:03PM   0:00.40 ftpd:  Someone's
dip27n8.drc.com: whitehd: RETR pgp262.zip\r\n (ftpd)                   getting a file
root    20033  0.0  0.0    28  232 ??  S    3:03PM   0:00.07 ntalkd via FTP.
mlspeake 20060 0.0  0.0   440  356 pf  I+   3:04PM   0:00.42 gopher ──┘
```

Figure 20-4:
Using ps, you find that this computer has several TCP/IP services running.

Ps-ing with Microsoft Windows

The Windows Powershell program lets you run 130 commands, many of which are Unix-like. You start the Powershell application, as shown in Figure 20-5, and type **ps**, as shown in Figure 20-6. Although the command is the same as in other operating systems, you can see that the output is different.

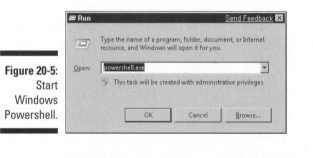

Figure 20-5:
Start
Windows
Powershell.

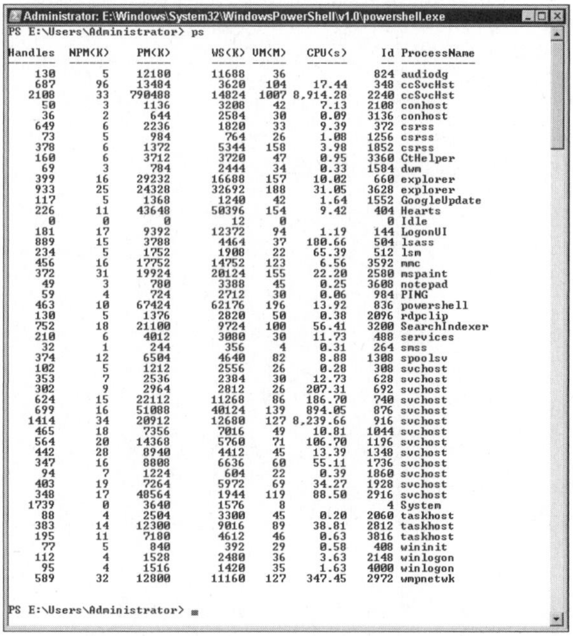

Figure 20-6:
Use
Windows
Powershell
to execute
the ps
command.

Nosing around with netstat

Some of the most important aspects of network security are running only the services you need, knowing which services are running at any given time, and determining which connections and services are available.

The netstat command gives you a quick overview of your network, including all available network connections, open ports, and services that may make your host vulnerable to attack. You can find the netstat command on most operating systems. It has been a part of TCP/IP on Linux and Unix practically forever (in the Internet space-time continuum).

The netstat command is newer to Microsoft Windows, however. You can use it starting with Windows XP Professional.

Another use for netstat

Netstat captures network performance statistics, such as packet traffic for important protocols, packet loss, and other packet information. To generate performance statistics, use the –s command option.

```
C:\Documents and Settings\candace>netstat -s

IPv4 Statistics

  Packets Received                   = 620516640
  Received Header Errors             = 0
  Received Address Errors            = 23790
  Datagrams Forwarded                = 0
  Unknown Protocols Received         = 0
  Received Packets Discarded         = 5986
---------- edited ----------------

IPv6 Statistics

  Packets Received                   = 69
  Received Header Errors             = 0
  Received Address Errors            = 0

---------- edited ----------------

TCPv4 Statistics
---------- edited ----------------
```

Using the netstat command on Unix, Linux, Mac OS X

When you examine netstat output, you may have to do some digging to find all network services that are running. Two daemons, inetd and xinetd, which start automatically whenever the computer boots, are responsible for starting and stopping other network services. These daemons are themselves network services that act as parents to other network services, by hiding specific network service names under their umbrella:

- ✔ **inetd:** The Internet daemon on Unix, Linux, and Mac OS X listens on standard ports, waiting to activate idle TCP/IP services such as FTP, POP3, or telnet whenever TCP or UDP requests them to run. Inetd is often called the Internet superserver.

- ✔ **xinetd:** The eXtended InterNET Daemon, a more secure version of inetd, can run on most Unix and Linux systems. Like inetd, xinetd manages the starting and stopping of idle TCP/IP services.

If a service such as telnet is available but not active, some tools show only the inetd or xinetd processes and not the services they run. In the following example, telnet is running, but the commonly used ps command, which shows processes recognizes only telnet's parent, inetd:

```
$ ps ax
  520 ?              Ss           0:00 /usr/sbin/inetd
```

If you run netstat on the same system, you see telnet sitting idle and ready for a connection:

```
$ netstat -a
tcp     0     0     *:telnet     *:*     LISTEN
```

It's important to see these idle services because you may not want their ports open, listening, and probe-able. The telnet service, especially, is a big security hole, and most systems should never run it.

Analyzing netstat output for security

The netstat command collects reams of output. Luckily, netstat comes with a bunch of command options so that you can see just what you want. From a security point of view, netstat is a quick way to

- ✔ **Check the TCP and UDP ports in use on your computer.** Chapter 4 lists a few commonly used ports. After you use netstat to provide a list of ports in use, you can check to see whether all of them should be in use.

- ✔ **Look for unnecessary services.** The more services your computer runs, the greater the opportunity for hackers. For example, if you're not running a server program, such as a Web server, and netstat shows a Web server port open, shut down the service.

- ✔ **List all current connections.** All inbound and outbound connections between your computer and other computers are listed.

You get results about both open connections and listening ports by using the –a option, as in `netstat-a`.

Some services known for being security targets include the ones described in this list:

- ✔ **time**: Time services are insecure, but also useful. Only you know if your system needs them. The netstat output for the time service looks like this:

  ```
  tcp     0     0 *:time     *:*          LISTEN     1110/inetd
  ```

- ✔ **finger:** Another unsafe service, it gives out information about the users on your system and is easy to crack:

  ```
  tcp     0     0 *:finger      *:*     LISTEN     1110/inetd
  ```

✔ **portmap, rpc.statd:** You need this service only if you're using Solaris:

```
tcp        0        0 *:sunrpc          *:*        LISTEN    531/portmap
tcp        0        0 *:723             *:*        LISTEN    543/rpc.statd
```

✔ **telnet:** Please get rid of telnet and use a secure, encrypted protocol, such as SSH (Secure Shell Protocol). Otherwise, telnet sends usernames and passwords across the network in plain text — it's a cracker's dream:

```
tcp        0        0 *:telnet          *:*        LISTEN    1110/inetd
```

This is probably the least secure service you can run.

Using the GNOME graphical interface to netstat

If you prefer to point and click rather than type commands, a GUI (graphical user interface), such as GNOME on Linux and Unix, is for you. Figure 20-7 shows graphical netstat output generated by selecting the Netstat tab in the Network Tools window.

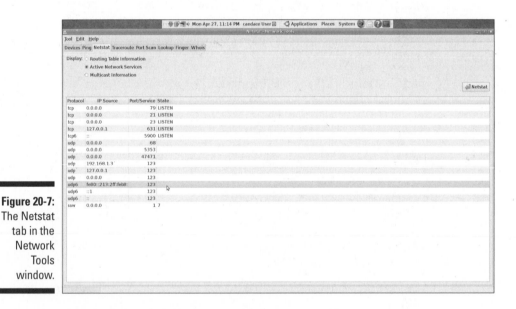

Figure 20-7:
The Netstat tab in the Network Tools window.

Using netstat on Microsoft Windows

Windows doesn't have a native Internet daemon (inetd), although if you really want one, you can download the Windows versions of inetd from the Internet. Instead, at system startup, the Windows process svchost.exe checks the services part of the Registry. Svchost builds a list of services to load. If you look at the process list in Windows Task Manager (you can see an excerpt in Figure 20-8), you see multiple instances of svchost.exe running at the same time.

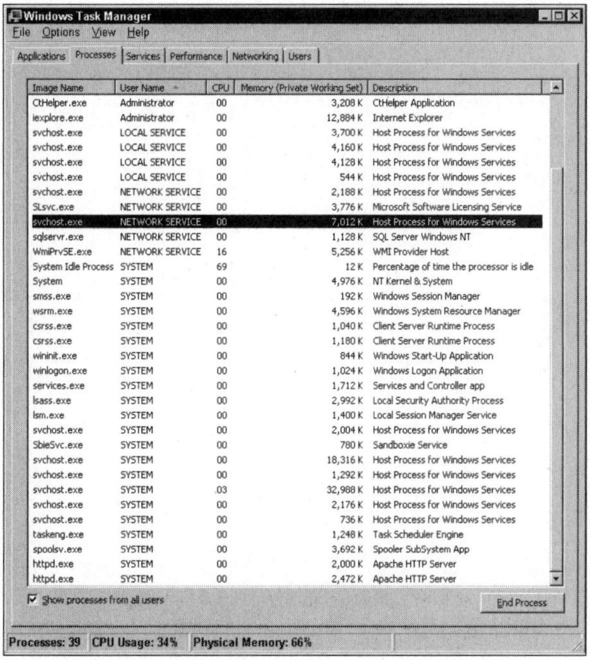

Figure 20-8:
So many
svchost
processes
— what
could they
possibly be
doing?

Like inetd, one svchost.exe session can manage a group of services. To find out which services are running under svchost, Windows has the tasklist command. Running tasklist with the /svc command option shows all services running on your computer. Here's an excerpt from the output:

```
C:\Documents and Settings\candace>tasklist/svc

Image Name                       PID Services
========================== ====== ===========
System Idle Process              0 N/A
System                           4 N/A
smss.exe                      1512 N/A
csrss.exe                     1568 N/A
winlogon.exe                  1596 N/A
services.exe                  1640 Eventlog, PlugPlay
ati2evxx.exe                  1864 Ati HotKey Poller
svchost.exe                   1884 DcomLaunch, TermService
svchost.exe                   1992 RpcSs
svchost.exe                    308 6to4, AudioSrv, BITS, Browser, CryptSvc,
                                   Dhcp, ERSvc, EventSystem,
                                   FastUserSwitchingCompatibility, helpsvc,
                                   lanmanserver, lanmanworkstation, Netman,
                                   Nla, RasMan, Schedule, seclogon, SENS,
                                   SharedAccess, ShellHWDetection, srservice,
                                   TapiSrv, Themes, TrkWks, w32time, winmgmt,
                                   wscsvc, wuauserv
```

```
svchost.exe                  356 WudfSvc
EvtEng.exe                   444 EvtEng
S24EvMon.exe                 500 S24EventMonitor
WLKEEPER.exe                 552 WLANKEEPER
svchost.exe                  816 Dnscache
svchost.exe                  916 LmHosts, RemoteRegistry, upnphost
aawservice.exe              1212 aawservice
spoolsv.exe                  292 Spooler
svchost.exe                  948 WebClient
GoogleUpdate.exe            1056 N/A
mDNSResponder.exe           1192 Bonjour Service
explorer.exe                1292 N/A
200 ehSched
svchost.exe                  576 HTTPFilter
issimsvc.exe                 940 ISSIMon
jqs.exe                     1424 JavaQuickStarterService
mdm.exe                     1532 MDM
NicConfigSvc.exe            2140 NICCONFIGSVC
```

If that list seems a bit long, well, it is. On a large server, the task list can stretch across several screens. So, if you're interested only in the services managed by svchost.exe, you can run the tasklist command with a filter (/FI) that shows only the svchost image name:

```
C:\Documents and Settings\candace>tasklist /svc /fi "imagename eq svchost.exe"

Image Name                     PID Services
========================== ====== ==================
svchost.exe                   1884 DcomLaunch, TermService
svchost.exe                   1992 RpcSs
svchost.exe                    308 6to4, AudioSrv, BITS, Browser, CryptSvc,
                                   Dhcp, ERSvc, EventSystem,
                                   FastUserSwitchingCompatibility, helpsvc,
                                   lanmanserver, lanmanworkstation, Netman,
                                   Nla, RasMan, Schedule, seclogon, SENS,
                                   SharedAccess, ShellHWDetection, srservice,
                                   TapiSrv, Themes, TrkWks, w32time, winmgmt,
                                   wscsvc, wuauserv
svchost.exe                    356 WudfSvc
svchost.exe                    816 Dnscache
svchost.exe                    916 LmHosts, RemoteRegistry, upnphost
svchost.exe                    948 WebClient
svchost.exe                    576 HTTPFilter
svchost.exe                   2668 SSDPSRV
svchost.exe                   5496 stisvc
```

Examining logs for symptoms of disease

Log files, log files, everywhere. Between security and operating system logs, you can find almost every kind of attempted and successful contamination. The good part about security and operating system event logs is that they capture a lot of data that tells you the condition of your network and its hosts. Alas, all those logs mean that you're left with a ton of data to look through.

Event logging can record almost everything that happens on your computer, although if you set up logging to do that, you'll never have enough time to analyze the data. Sometimes, event logging is called error logging, although event logging tracks far more than just errors. You can set up logging to record these elements:

- **System events:** Operating system actions, such as shutting down the system or starting a service. An operating system event logger automatically records failed (and optionally, successful) events. Not all system events are security events. For example, if the system crashes, investigate to see whether the cause was a security attack or a cable severing in a forklift incident.

- **Audit records:** Records in the security log. Auditing allows system administrators to configure Windows to document operating system activity in the Security Log Auditing. This is usually optional, and the system administrator decides whether to turn on auditing. Sometimes, because auditing uses CPU and memory resources, a system administrator chooses not to run auditing. Audit records contain security event information, such as

  - *Authentication attempts:* For example, a failed login attempt may be caused by a break-in or just a user who forgot a password.

  - *Changes in user accounts:* If new user accounts have appeared on your system without your knowledge, perhaps a malware application created a user account for its own, devious purposes.

  - *Changes in security policies:* The system, network, or security administrator should be the only person to set security policies.

Security software often writes information to operating system logs as well as to its own log. Logs are most helpful in investigating suspicious activity involving a particular host. For example, if your firewall detects an attack against a particular host, your next step in finding out more is to look into the host's log files to see who was logged in during the attack and whether the attack was successful. Most operating systems use the standard syslog protocol to create logs. Microsoft uses a proprietary logging facility, and you can purchase or download dozens of logging products.

Syslog-ing into the next generation

RFC 5424, The Syslog Protocol, also called *syslog-ng,* is an application, a service (syslogngd), and a protocol that collects event log messages.

Syslog: The next generation of nuts and bolts

Syslog is a client/server protocol in which the client is the *syslog sender* and the sender sends a text message to the *syslog receiver*. The receiver is also known as the syslogd, syslog daemon, or syslog server, and in every case you can change the name from syslog to syslogng. Syslog messages travel by default on UDP in clear text to unprotected files. Because log files are one of the most easily attacked parts of a system, syslog-ng has added options. You can tell it to carry the messages on TCP for more reliable delivery. UDP is fast, but you might lose a message — maybe even a critical one. Another syslog-ng option is to send the message wrapped in SSL (Secure Sockets Layer, a secure protocol; see Chapter 11). The SSL wrapper encrypts the messages so that no one can read them as they cross the network.

An *event* can be anything (even a formal wedding if it's broadcast on YouTube) from a successful login to someone breaking through your firewall, although most administrators configure syslog to collect security and network errors. You tell syslog which kinds of events to collect, filtering the messages that aren't important to you. What's not important to you may be a priority for another network, system, or security administrator. This flexibility is one of the benefits of using syslog.

This new syslog-ng (ng stands for *next generation*) protocol is the descendant of a more than 20-year-old syslog that ran mainly on Unix and Linux. It also runs on Mac OS X. Syslog-ng is a standard for forwarding event and log messages in any TCP/IP network, regardless of operating system. This new concept means that the IETF has worked out a single standard protocol that lets you integrate Windows, Mac, Linux, Unix, and what-have-you to log data into one central location. Figure 20-9 shows how a network of various hosts and devices sends all log messages to one log server.

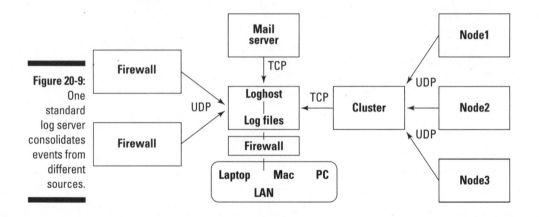

Figure 20-9:
One standard log server consolidates events from different sources.

Unix, Linux, and Mac OS X come supplied with the basic syslog daemon. The newer versions of those operating systems also come with syslog-ng. If your operating system doesn't include the syslog-ng daemon, you can download it for free from www.freshmeat.net/projects/syslog-ng/releases. At the time this book was written, syslog-ng was too new to be included in Microsoft Windows versions, but you can find syslog-ng daemons for Windows as freeware or shareware, and, of course, you can find vendors who are happy to sell you their versions.

Deciding what to log

The syslog.conf file lists the kinds of events you want to log and the action to take based on the event. The following excerpt from a syslog.conf file instructs the syslog daemon to log error messages from the operating system kernel; any line in the file beginning with the # character is a comment:

```
# Store all kernel messages in the kernel file.
# Mail critical and higher messages and higher ones
# to users Candace and root.
#
kern.*                          /var/adm/kernel
kern.crit                       @finlandia
```

The kernel is the heart of an operating system, controlling system resources and communications. You can see a kernel message occurring at 12:40:07 in Figure 20-11, later in this chapter.

Level numbers identify the severity of the event. Table 20-1 lists the level numbers and their severity. (May all your logs have only Level 6.)

Table 20-1	Syslog Error Levels and Their Severity
Level	**Severity**
0	Emergency (or, sometimes, Panic)
1	Alert
2	Critical
3	Error
4	Warning
5	Notice
6	Info
7	Debug

The following line, from a `syslog.conf` file, tells the syslog daemon to send all events, `*.alert` and more severe, to the user's root (the administrator) and candace.

```
*.alert                         root, candace
```

Each configuration line consists of two fields:

- ✔ **The selector field:** The types of events and severity levels to log.

- ✔ **The action field:** The action to take, which is written in shorthand. If the action field consists of usernames, the daemon should mail information about the event to the users in the action field. If the action is a filename, the daemon should write the event to the file. If the action is a hostname, such as @woodstock, forward the messages to the syslog daemon on the remote host. This action protects your logged events in case your local copies get lost, either by accident or by hacking.

Whenever you see an asterisk (*) in a field, it means *all*. The following `syslog.conf` excerpt says to send all events of info level or higher to a file, `/var/log/messages`:

```
*.info          /var/log/messages
```

The first line below from the syslog.conf file says that any event (*) of emergency level should be sent to every user on the system. The second line says to forward all emergency records to the syslog daemon on woodstock.home:

```
*.emerg         *
*.emerg         @woodstock.home
```

Locating the log files

You can tell syslog where the various log files should reside, or you can go with the operating system's default locations. Using the default syslog collection, Table 20-2 lists where Ubuntu Linux stores the text log files. You can read these files with your favorite Unix-type command or text editor.

Default file locations vary not only from operating system to operating system but also from version to version.

Table 20-2	Syslog Text Files
File Location	*File Contents*
`/var.log/boot`	Boot messages
`/var/log/auth.log`	Login and authentication logs

File Location	File Contents
/var/log/faillog	Failed logins
/var/log/daemon.log	Messages from running services that don't have their own logs, such as squid proxy
/var/log/mail.*	Log files from all mail servers
/var/log/apache2	Apache Web server logs

Viewing the logs

If the log files are text files and you're a whiz at writing scripts to sort and analyze them, go to it. Each syslog message has only three parts:

- ✔ The date and time
- ✔ The facility or program and the hostname or IP address of the source of the message (The most important facilities include auth, authpriv, cron, daemon, ftp, kern, lpr, mail, mark, news, syslog, and user.)
- ✔ The message itself

On the other hand, if you just want to check the logs with no fuss, no muss, the GNOME System Log Viewer is a graphical viewer for looking at and analyzing system logs. The System Log Viewer comes with a few functions that can help you manage your logs, including a calendar, log monitor, and log statistics display.

On Ubuntu Linux, choose System Menu➪Administration➪System Log to see a display such as the one shown in Figure 20-10. The left pane shows the separate files containing logged messages. Figure 20-10 shows evidence of someone trying to log in to root at 11:27 a.m., the privileged account (UserID 0), and failing. The figure shows that someone again attempted to break in at 12:40. Figure 20-11 shows the raw syslog text file that generates the graphic output. The syslog entry authentication error occurring at 12:40:11 matches the graphical output shown in Figure 20-10.

GNOME is a graphical interface to Linux and Unix. It doesn't matter which version of Linux or Unix you have; it's still the GNOME System Log Viewer.

Mac OS X users can download GNOME, but why download a graphical interface when you already have one? You can view log files under the console.

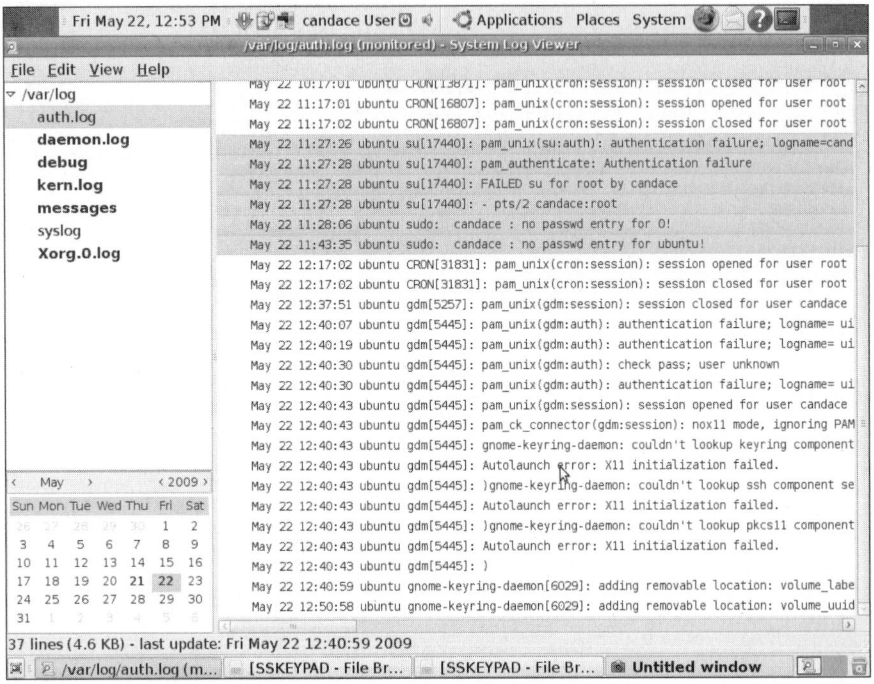

Figure 20-10:
No need for typing when you can point and click.

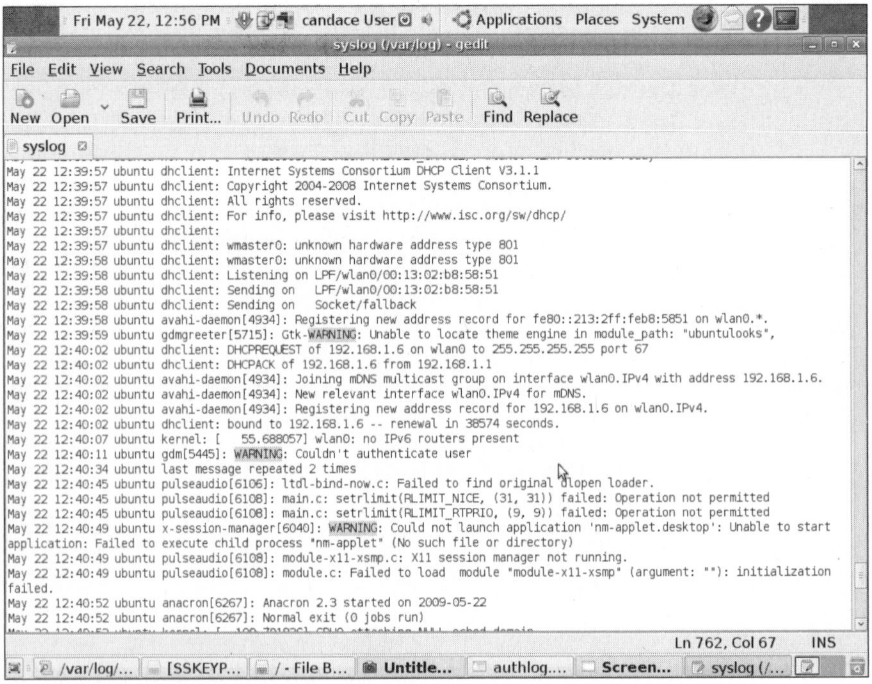

Figure 20-11:
Text syslog messages correlate with the graphic output.

Searching security logs for system illnesses

Security software logs contain computer- and network-security-related information. You're probably saying "Of course. That's obvious," and you're right, as far as that statement goes. However, operating system logs and application logs (such as the Apache Web Server log) also contain lots of security-related data.

You can find network and host security illnesses in log files created by

- **Antimalware software:** These log files record
    - The presence of malware on your system
    - Whether disinfection attempts are successful
    - Lists of quarantined files

- **Firewalls:** Firewall logs contain intrusion-detection and -prevention information, such as attempted or successful attacks and various forms of suspicious behavior (such as unusually high e-mail traffic or maybe a denial-of-service attack). When you install a firewall, you usually set up rules that determine what and who (users, Web sites, or IP addresses, for example) can pass through it. If you have a well-configured firewall system, the firewall log files tell you about attempts and, hopefully, that the firewall kept them out.

- **VPN and other remote access software:** VPN software (see Chapter 1) logs successful and failed login attempts, as well as the dates and times that each user connected and disconnected.

- **Web proxy servers:** Chapter 11 describes how Web proxies help performance and also add a layer of security between Web clients and servers. Web proxies often keep logs of all URLs that pass through them.

Microsoft Windows systems uses binary *event* logs that automatically overwrite themselves when they're full. The Windows event log consists of three logs: system log, security log, and application log. (Think of them as three syslog facilities.) Each log is stored in a separate file.

If you're a Windows XP user, be aware that Microsoft has completely redone event logging for Windows Server 2008, Windows 7, and Windows Vista. The newer versions of Windows store these elements:

- **Windows log:** Stores the logs that are available in older versions of Windows: the Application, Security, and System logs plus two new logs: Setup and ForwardedEvents.

✓ **Application log:** Stores events logged by application programs. A database program might record a file error in the application log, for example. Application developers decide which events to log, so one application might log events thoroughly while another one might expect you to guess what went wrong.

✓ **Security log:** Stores events such as successful and failed logins and the creating, opening, or deleting of files with or without permission. Just as with syslog, you can decide which events to record.

✓ **Setup log:** Stores events related to application configurations.

✓ **System log:** Stores Windows system component events, such as the failure of a driver to load during system startup.

One of the first things an attacker tries to do when penetrating your system is to copy and remove your log files or delete all records showing any hacking activity. Your logs may contain useful information about your system configuration and weaknesses as well as usernames and file locations. You can use two protections (after you set up a good firewall):

✓ Ensure that the log files are readable and writable only by the SYSTEM user.

✓ Forward a copy of your logs to another host.

Microsoft proprietary event logging

Although syslog is the Internet standard, Microsoft mainly uses a proprietary event-logging and -auditing system. The Microsoft Event Logger is a *hybrid*: It automatically audits system and application events. Most security tools write to binary-format event logs, which means that the computer can read the log files but you can't. You use an event viewer program, such as Microsoft Event Viewer, to read the security logs. After you set up security auditing, you can review the log files. For example, the Windows XP Pro Event Viewer displays various security violations and attempted break-ins.

One way to run the Microsoft Event Viewer is from the Start menu. Choose Start⇨Programs⇨Administrative Tools⇨Event Viewer. By default, the Event Viewer displays activity in three log files: Application, Security, and System. Double-click the log you want to view. The Event Viewer displays a list of events, including the date and time the event occurred and how serious the event is. If you want more details, double-click a single record in the list. Figure 20-12 shows a TCP/IP event from the system log — a computer connected to the network.

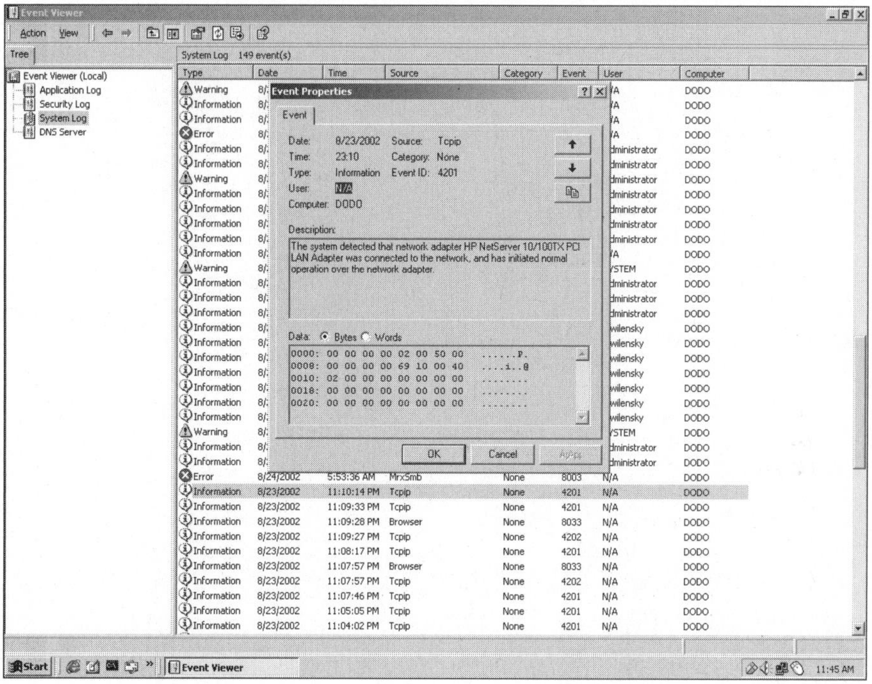

Figure 20-12:
Not all
events
are cause
for con-
cern — this
message
is informa-
tional.

Before you can see any security events in the Windows Event Viewer, you must enable security auditing. Follow these steps to turn on security logging (Figure 20-13 shows what's happening in Steps 1 through 4, and Figure 20-14 shows Steps 5 through 8):

1. **Choose Start⇨Run, type** mmc /a, **and then click OK.**

2. **On the Console menu, click Add/Remove Snap-In and then click Add.**

3. **Under Snap-In, click Group Policy and then click Add.**

4. **In the Select Group Policy Object dialog box, choose Local Computer, click Finish, click Close, and then click OK.**

5. **In the Local Computer Policy section, click Audit Policy.**

6. **In the details pane, highlight the attribute or event you want to audit.**

7. **Choose Action⇨Security.**

8. **In the Local Security Policy Setting dialog box, select the options you want and then click OK.**

Look in all three Microsoft log files to find information about break-ins and attempted break-ins.

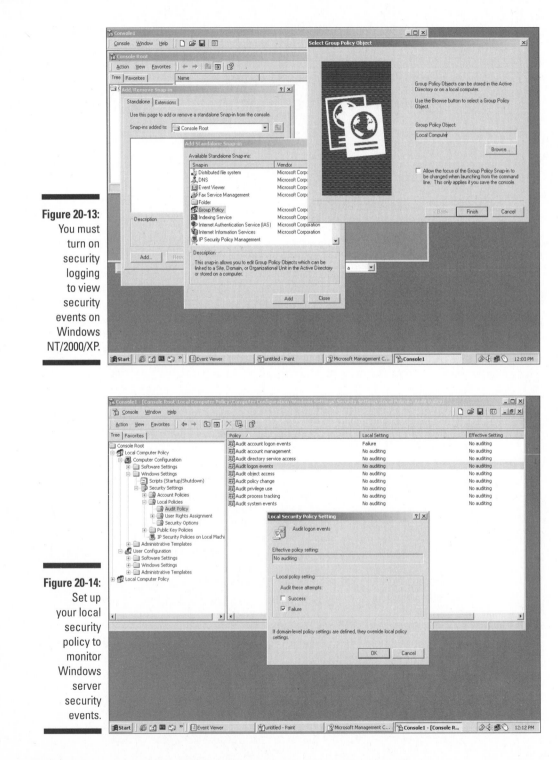

Figure 20-13:
You must
turn on
security
logging
to view
security
events on
Windows
NT/2000/XP.

Figure 20-14:
Set up
your local
security
policy to
monitor
Windows
server
security
events.

Chapter 21

Relishing More Meaty Security

. . . .

In This Chapter

▶ Protocols in this chapter: Kerberos, IPSec, NTP, IPv4, IPv6, AES, SSL, TLS

▶ Working with authentication and advanced authentication with AES

▶ Working with digital certificates and signatures

▶ Making authentication and encryption easier with IPSec

▶ Playing with Kerberos — woof!

. . . .

The Computer Emergency Response Team (CERT) has been collecting statistics on computer security since 1988, when it reported six incidents. CERT statistics include incidents such as denial-of-service (DoS) attacks, attacks by malicious insiders on intranets, and viruses and Trojan horses. One incident may involve one site or thousands of sites. CERT reported 3,734 incidents in 1998 and 43,136 in the first half of 2002. These statistics certainly raise security consciousness.

In the first three quarters of 2008, the organization cataloged 6,058 new vulnerabilities. Though CERT doesn't report statistics any more, it remains useful because it still identifies and addresses threats.

Visit www.cert.org/stats to see CERT historical incident statistics as well as links to other security information that CERT collects.

You snack on security all through this book — check out how many security icons are used! This whole chapter is about security, so rather than mark each paragraph with an icon, we use just the single icon at the beginning of this paragraph.

This chapter works with Chapters 12, 14, and 20 to provide guidelines and techniques for building secure systems and networks. The information in this chapter is aimed primarily at administrators.

Defining Encryption

At the bottom of the TCP/IP structure, in the physical and data link layers, you can encrypt the data on the wire. This technique is one of the most common security techniques used in communications. Encryption and some of the other terminology used for computer security come straight from the world of secret agents. Here are some definitions:

- ✔ **Cryptography:** The process of *encrypting* (scrambling) and *decrypting* (deciphering) messages in secret code. (We've seen some authors use the term *cryptology,* but as far as we know, that's the study of crypts.) Chapter 24 shows you how to take a virtual tour of the United States National Cryptologic Museum.

- ✔ **Encryption:** The process of scrambling a message into code to conceal its meaning. A common method of encryption is to use a pair of keys — a public key and a private key — to encode data so that only the person who is intended to see it can read it. When Marshall sends a message to Candace, for example, he encodes the message with Candace's public key. She decodes the message with her private key. Only Candace's private key can decode the message. No one can peek at what Marshall and Candace are saying.

- ✔ **Encryption key:** The essential piece of information — a word or number or combination — used in encrypting and decrypting a message, but it isn't the algorithm (process) used for encryption. You can just refer to "the key."

IPv6 is more flexible than IPv4 by allowing applications to encrypt an entire packet (maximum security) or just the data portion using various mathematical methods.

- ✔ **Public key/private key cryptography:** In the public key/private key coding process, an encryption key used to encrypt the message and another used to decrypt the message. A mathematical relationship exists between the two keys. The public and private keys are long prime numbers that are numerically related (factors of another, larger number). Possession of one isn't enough to translate the message because anything encrypted with one can only be decrypted by the other.

Every user gets a unique pair of keys — one key is made public, and the other is kept secret. Public keys are stored in common areas, mailed among users, and may even be printed in newspapers. A private key must be stored in a safe place and protected. Anyone can have your public key, but only you should have your private key. It works something like this: "You talkin' to me? I won't listen unless you encrypt the message by using my public key so that I know no one else is

> eavesdropping. Only my private key, which no one else has, can decrypt the message, so I know that no one else can read it. I don't care that lots of other people have my public key, because it can't be used to decrypt the message."

PGP, which stands for *Pretty Good Privacy,* is an exportable, public domain (free) software package for public key/private key cryptography. It's one of the most widely used privacy programs. PGP, which provides the technical underpinning for adding security to applications, encrypts and decrypts Internet e-mail. It can also be used for digital signatures. The best answers (plural!) to "Where can I get PGP?" are at `www.faqs.org/faqs/pgp-faq/where-is-PGP`. PGP is available for all the major operating systems. Some e-mail clients have PGP built in to them.

Advancing Encryption with Advanced Encryption Standard (AES)

Chapters 12 and 14 and the preceding section in this chapter describe encryption in various levels of detail. This section advances the level of technical detail surrounding encryption. Encrypting data is a set of intricate steps that use both the cipher and the technique used to apply the cipher to the data. The Advanced Encryption Standard (AES) replaces the 1977 Data Encryption Standard (DES), developed at IBM. AES was adopted in 2001 and is composed of the three block ciphers AES-128, AES-192, and AES-256. Here are some definitions to make the AES mumbojumbo clear:

- ✔ **Cipher:** The mathematical method used to encrypt data by transforming plain text into a scrambled set of data (cipher text). You can't read the encrypted text without a key to reverse the encryption. AES provides three secret-key sizes: 128 bits, 192 bits, and 256 bits. The larger the key size, the more bits there are to use in scrambling the data. On the other hand, the more bits there are, the more complex the process, which means slightly slower encryption and decryption. The United States government requires AES-192 or AES-256 to encrypt Top Secret documents.

- ✔ **Block:** A contiguous set of bits. The AES block size is 128 bits.

- ✔ **Block cipher:** The technique used to encrypt a block of data as a group to generate a block of cipher text of the same size rather than encrypt data one bit at a time. The transformation requires a secret key. AES requires that each block be encrypted differently so that breaking the code for one block doesn't decrypt the remaining data.

To use AES, you need protocols and standards that require AES and developers who build AES into programs such as the SmartFTP client (www. smartftp.com), PKZIP, SecureZIP, and WinZip. Some other AES-based implementations include the ones described in this list:

- **AES programming libraries for C, C++, C#/. NET, Java, and JavaScript:** Tools and routines for developers to build products, such as FTP, that implement AES

- **Security standards for Local Area Network communications:**

  - **IEEE 802.11i:** The extension to the IEEE 802.11 security standard for wireless networks. The WPA2 (see Chapter 7 for a description) wireless security protocol uses AES.

  - **G.hn:** The standard for next-generation home network technology. This standard specifies ways for building high-speed (as much as 1 gigabit/s) LANs using home wiring, such as power lines, phone lines, and coaxial cables. It requires AES-128 for encryption. The International Telecommunication Union (ITU-T) coordinates the development of the G.hn standard.

- **SSL (OpenSSL):** Secure Sockets Layer and Transport Level Security. See Chapter 11 for detailed information about SSL and TLS security. SSL or TLS connections that use AES ciphers provide extra strong encryption for applications such as online shopping and banking.

- **Hardware:** Routers, security appliances, hard drives, USB hard drives, and biometric devices

Peering into Authentication

In the middle of the layer cake, in the Internet and transport layers, is a security measure for the authentication of computer names and addresses that an application may use.

Authentication proves that you are who you say you are or that a server is what it says it is. Take a look (again, possibly) at the section in Chapter 12 about authenticating people to make sure they are who they say they are.

In TCP/IP, the process of authentication must be built into the applications. For example, an anonymous FTP server performs only basic authentication. To interact with the FTP server, you need an FTP client program, a user account name (anonymous), and a password (just your e-mail address). Username and password authentication is the easiest kind to crack; encrypting those items makes cracking them much more difficult. Certain applications, such as Lotus Notes, and electronic commerce Web sites use much more stringent authentication controls, such as digital certificates and digital signatures, which are described next.

Do you have any ID? A digital certificate will do

Just as your passport proves that you are who you say you are to an immigration official, network authentication proves that you are who you say you are to an application or a server. Sometimes, but not always, your passport is sufficient to allow you to enter a country. Some countries require a visa — an additional piece of identification — for security purposes: Network and computer security works the same way. Sometimes an application or server accepts your simple authentication by itself, and you're then allowed to access the application and server resources. Sometimes, however, the application or server requires additional electronic identification for security purposes. That "electronic visa" is a *digital certificate* that contains your encryption keys.

In real life, you have separate forms of identification for specific purposes: passport, driver's license, and employee ID, for example. For these identification papers to be trustworthy, they must come from recognized authorities, such as the government or your employer. On a network, you may need a separate digital certificate for each application or server you need to use. For these certificates to be trustworthy, they must come from a *Certification Authority* (CA), an organization that issues certificates. It's also called simply a *Certificate Authority.*

Your passport connects your identity (your photograph) with your identification (name, age, birthplace, citizenship). A *digital certificate* is an encrypted, password-protected file that connects the identity of a person or a server with its identification, including these items:

- The name of the certificate holder

- The private key for encryption and decryption and verifying the digital signature of a message sender by matching the sender's public key

- The name of the issuing CA; for example, VeriSign or RSA Certificate Services

- The length of the certificate's validity period

The CA digitally "signs" and guarantees the file (certificate).

Getting digital certificates

Your organization acts as its own CA when it issues the certificate you need in order to access intranet resources. The Internet has trusted third-party CAs that issue electronic IDs only after verifying the identities of the requesters. You can get a personal certificate to use with your Web browser or e-mail client by completing an application at VeriSign (`www.verisign.com`), Thawte (`www.thawte.com`), GlobalSign (`www.globalsign.net`), and others. Some applications and software programs are responsible for creating certificates. For example, when you're registered as a Lotus Notes user, you get a user ID that contains your certificate and public key/private key pair.

To get a signed digital certificate from a trusted third-party CA, follow these steps:

1. **Decide which kind of certificate you need:**

   - *Personal certificates* let you send and receive encrypted e-mail and digitally sign documents.

   - *Server certificates* enable 128-bit SSL encryption so that users have secure communication. Versions of server certificates exist for Web servers, wireless servers, and other purposes.

   - *Developer certificates* digitally shrink-wrap your applications and Web content so that an ActiveX control, a VBA file, a Java applet, a dynamic link library, a `.cab` or `.jar` file, an HTML page, or channel content is safe.

2. **Submit a request to a CA (a company that checks to see whether your server and organization are who they say they are).**

3. **Pay the service fee to defray their costs for verifying that all requesters are who they claim to be.**

Using digital certificates

Organizations on the Internet use digital certificates to establish mutual trust so that the participants can trust each other's identity during transactions, such as when they

- ✔ Make Internet credit card purchases

- ✔ Participate in Internet banking and investing

- ✔ Enroll in and check benefits with healthcare organizations

- ✔ Communicate between employees about private corporate information

The certificate request and validation protect you and your organization. A server certificate provides these protections:

- ✔ People who communicate with your server are sure that it truly belongs to your organization, not to an imposter's.

- ✔ Your e-commerce server is set up to conduct transactions on the Internet.

✔ Your Web server is able to establish secure SSL connections with Web browsers.

✔ Your e-mail server is able to establish secure connections with other e-mail servers and with e-mail clients by using S/MIME (Security-enhanced Multipurpose Internet Mail Extensions).

Checking your certificates

When you connect to a secure Web site, the Web server shows your browser a certificate to verify its identity — that you're browsing the real site and aren't a pretender. Your browser analyzes the address in the certificate, the certificate's expiration date, and its verifier to be sure that you're browsing securely.

You can examine the certificate your browser knows about. The menus and tabs for examining your browser's trove of certificates vary, but the general idea is the same. Figures 21-1 and 21-2 come from Google Chrome. Click the wrench icon in the upper-right corner of the browser and choose Options⇨Advanced. Select the Under the Hood tab, which shows your privacy selections, and then scroll down and click the Manage Certificates button. Figure 21-1 shows Marshall's personal certificate, and Figure 21-2 shows the list of trusted certificate authorities (CA).

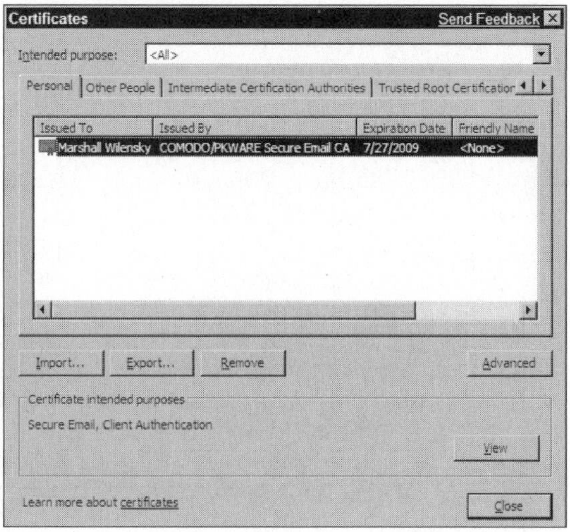

Figure 21-1: Marshall's personal certificate was issued by PKWare when he registered SecureZIP.

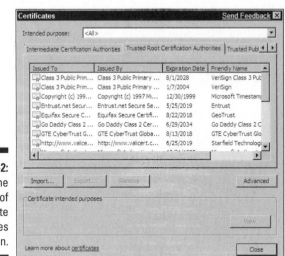

Figure 21-2:
And the
list of
Certificate
Authorities
goes on.

Coping with certificate problems

Not every Web site has a certificate. You may run into a Web site that has a
certificate that has expired. You really shouldn't trust anything without a
valid certificate, but practically speaking, sometimes you have to decide
whom and what you're willing to trust.

Suppose that no valid certificate exists

If the site has no valid digital signature, you can't be sure that the file you
want to download is from the legitimate site it claims to be from. You also
don't know whether the file has been tampered with (possibly by a virus). Be
safe and avoid opening the file unless you're certain who created it and you
know whether the file contents are safe to open.

If you're concerned about the security of an online shopping site, be sure
that you see HTTPS as the protocol in the URL. If the site has no digital certificate, look for security credentials from other organizations. For example,
look at the bottom of the Web page for the green TRUSTe logo. TRUSTe is
an independent, nonprofit, private organization that investigates Web site
privacy policies thoroughly. If a Web site "passes" the stringent tests, TRUSTe
bestows its Web Privacy Seal on the site. TRUSTe runs the world's largest
privacy seal program, having certified more than 2,000 Web sites. The Better
Business Bureau Online is another accreditation organization. Look for
the blue BBB Accredited Business Seal at the bottom of a Web page as an
indication that a Web site has had its credentials verified by the BBB.

Suppose that a certificate error occurs

Sometimes a problem may occur with a certificate or with the server's use of the certificate. If you encounter a certificate error, the certificate probably has expired. Your browser notifies you so that you can decide to continue or not access the site. If you go ahead, most browsers turn the address bar red or add another red signal to the page.

IPSec (IP Security Protocol): More Authentication

IPSec is a set of multiple protocols for securing remote access. RFC 2411, "IP Security Document Roadmap," describes how the multiple documents that explain the IPSec protocols are interrelated. If you're interested in IPSec, RFC 2411 helps you decide where to start reading. It explains what you can find in each IPSec RFC.

IPSec secures IP communications by authenticating and encrypting the data (payload) in each packet of a data stream.

IPSec is built in to IPv6 and optional for IPv4. IPSec is especially useful for setting up secure remote access to private intranets and for building VPNs (virtual private networks). A big advantage of IPsec is that the security doesn't require you to change anything, such as your IP address, on your computer.

IPSec provides two levels of security services:

✔ **Authentication Header (AH) — authenticating the sender of a network message:** The AH ensures that the message sender is the person that she claims to be and that the data wasn't changed during transmission. However, if the data is clear text, nothing guarantees that snoopers won't see it as it crosses the network.

✔ **Encapsulating Security Payload (ESP) — authenticating the sender and also encrypting the message:** ESP makes the data unreadable by snoopers.

IPSec information gets stuffed into the packet before the data and after the IP packet header. Because IPSec runs at the Internet layer of the TCP/IP layer cake, it can protect more traffic — everything that runs at layer 3 or higher. Running at a low layer means that applications need not be specifically designed to use IPSec. However, other frequently used security protocols and applications, such as SSL, SSL VPN, SSH, and TLS, run at layer 4, the transport layer. Applications that use upper-level protocols, such as TLS and SSL, need to implement authentication into the design of applications.

Kerberos — Guardian or Fiend?

Kerberos is an authentication service, application, and protocol. Project Athena at the Massachusetts Institute of Technology (MIT) was dedicated to researching very large computing environments (containing thousands of computers).

In Greek mythology, Kerberos was a three-headed dog with a dragon's tail and snakes wrapped around his neck; he guarded the entrance to Hades. If you got past Kerberos, you were in hell. Because of the complexity of Kerberos, some system and network administrators wonder whether that was MIT's intention.

The Kerberos master server — only one is in your secure network — provides an authentication service used for security in an Internet environment. The master server stores encrypted user account information. In a Kerberos environment, there's no local or domain password database.

A secure computing environment also needs coordinated time services so that all computers synchronize their ticket expirations properly. (Aha — that's a new piece of the pie: tickets. We tell you more about them shortly.) When Kerberos clients' and servers' clocks are out of sync, authentication can fail. Kerberos can use the Network Time Protocol (NTP) to keep time synchronized across the network.

Understanding Kerberos concepts

Kerberos authentication is based on a trusted third party that negotiates between a user and the service that user wants to access. Kerberos is the strictest network authentication protocol and application. Because it's so thorough and complex, it uses plenty of new terminology:

- ✔ **Single sign-on:** This central login point enables users to log in only once (single sign-on) to use network resources. A special central database, maintained by a Key Distribution Center (KDC), stores all authentication information for all clients.

- ✔ **Password safety:** In a Kerberos network, passwords never travel across the network.

✔ **Kerberos domain:** Provide authentication for all computers, users, and individual network services (daemons) participating in the domain.

A Kerberos domain is another type of domain you encounter on a network. It's different from a DNS domain (described in Chapter 10) and a Microsoft proprietary domain. It provides the ability to control which users and computers can use specific network services, such as HTTP or FTP.

✔ **Kerberos realm:** A unique area of control and management created when you install Kerberos. Computers and applications that join a Kerberos realm are *Kerberized.* Common practice labels your Kerberos realm with the same name as your DNS fully qualified domain name (FQDN). An FQDN — `examplecorp.com`, for example — is also the name of your Kerberos realm. This naming practice is optional, but it makes overall network management easier.

✔ **Principal:** Any user, computer, or service. You need to be registered with the server as a Kerberos principal.

✔ **Key Distribution Center (KDC):** The heart of Kerberos, consisting of three parts: a database listing principals, an authentication server, and the ticket-granting server, or TGS. Each realm must have at least one KDC. Two KDCs are safer than one. You don't want the KDC to be a single point of failure for your Kerberos realm.

✔ **Ticket:** Confirmation of the identity of two principals. One principal is a user, and the other is a service requested by the user. Tickets establish the encryption key for the authenticated session.

✔ **Ticket granting server (TGS):** The issuer of tickets to clients to use a service.

✔ **Ticket granting ticket (TGT):** A ticket that grants other tickets. The TGT is encrypted and embedded in the user's password and is known only to the user and the KDC.

Don't worry about knowing these definitions yet. Playing with it at Casino Kerberos clears up any murky terminology.

Playing at Casino Kerberos

Now we walk you through what happens when you're running under Kerberos. Meet Marshall, who likes to play roulette. The following minitable tells you what happens in the casino and then behind the scenes, in Kerberos:

At the Casino	In Kerberos
One fine day, Marshall knocks on the special door at the back of Casino Kerberos.	Marshall types his username at a Kerberos-enabled computer.
He asks the bouncer for permission to enter the secret inner casino.	His computer asks the Kerberos master server for a *ticket granting ticket,* which is permission to talk to the ticket-granting server.
The bouncer then asks Marshall for the casino password. Marshall gives the correct response and is allowed in.	Marshall's computer asks him for his password and uses it to verify the response from the Kerberos master server.
Marshall is happy. He goes to the cashier window to buy gaming chips. He has a choice: The casino games all require different chips, and the chips are valid for only a short time. When that time is up, his chips are worthless.	Marshall's computer sends a request to the ticket-granting server to request an *application service ticket,* which has a limited lifetime. In Red Hat Linux, the ticket has a default of eight hours.
Marshall is ready to play. He can now lose money at the casino game of his choice, as long as he uses the correct chips at the gaming table he chooses. If he wants to move to a different gaming table, he must have the correct chips or return to the cashier window to buy them.	Marshall's computer can now present the application service ticket to an application server as permission to use the service.
By the way, everyone in the casino speaks pig latin.	All communications between Marshall's computer and the Kerberos master server, between Marshall's computer and the ticket-granting server, and between Marshall's computer and the desired application are encrypted.
When all of this is in place and operating properly, Marshall can be sure that he's at the right table and that everyone else standing around the table is playing by the rules.	Marshall knows that he's talking to the computers and services he wants to talk to, and the computers and services can be sure that Marshall is who he says he is. Everybody's happy, right?

Training the dog — one step per head

Kerberos includes a framework, a set of command-line tools, the Kerberos management application, and a Kerberos logon authenticator. A system or network administrator has a lot of work to do before Kerberos is ready to protect a network. Follow these basic steps, which are necessary to configure (or *Kerberize*) the computers and applications on your network:

1. **Start the Kerberos server.**

   Attention, network administrators! Forget about sleep and regular meals until you finish this step. You have to install software, edit files, create a database, and insert records for people and computers.

2. **Register principals.**

   A *Kerberos principal* works like a regular computer account. The name of the principal looks like this:

   ```
   You choose this part@YOUR.REALM
   ```

   If you love chocolate, you probably love chocolate brownies frosted with more dark chocolate. If you love security, the idea of a Kerberos-encrypted principal is the frosting on the Kerberos security brownie. A principal looks something like an e-mail address, but the resemblance ends there. Kerberos knows just how to use it in a secure environment. You get to choose the part before the at-sign (@). A typical choice is your regular account name. The part after the @ is the name of the realm — it may look like your computer name, for convenience. Each principal is encrypted with a Kerberos master key so that not just anyone can examine it and it's stored in the Kerberos database. The principal includes the name and password and some technical stuff.

3. **Get programmers to Kerberize applications.**

   Kerberizing involves checking to see who is using the application, validating that user's identity, checking to make sure that the user has the right ticket, and getting the user the appropriate ticket.

Setting up a Kerberos server step by step

In this section, we describe the basic steps you need to follow to install and configure Kerberos server software on Linux or Unix. The following steps are specific to Red Hat Linux running the Gnome user interface (your flavor of operating system, such as Windows or Mac OS X, may vary slightly):

1. **Decide which computer will be your key distribution center (KDC).**
   The KDC network service distributes session tickets and temporary session keys to users and computers. The KDC computer usually runs the ticket granting server (TGS) and the authentication server (AS).

2. **Install these packages on the KDC:**

   - *krb5-libs:* Shared libraries

   - *krb5-server:* Kerberos server programs

   - *krb5-workstation:* Kerberos client programs

   - *gnome-kerberos:* GUI tools, including krb5 for managing tickets and gkadmin for managing realms

   Note: You need krb5-workstation on every client computer, too.

3. **Name your Kerberos realm (in UPPERCASE letters) and domain-to-realm mappings by editing the files** `/etc/krb5.conf` **and** `/var/kerberos/krb5kdc/kdc.conf`.

   Remember to enter DNS domain names and host names in lowercase letters. If you just need a simple configuration, change either

   - `EXAMPLE.COM` and `example.com` to your DNS domain name. Be sure to use the same case as the text you're replacing.

   - `kerberos.example.com` to the fully qualified domain name of your KDC.

4. **Create the Kerberos database that stores the keys for your realm by typing this command:**

   ```
   /usr/kerberos/sbin/kdb5_util create -s
   ```

5. **Control which principals have the right to administer the database by editing this file:**

   ```
   /var/kerberos/krb5kdc/kadm5.acl
   ```

   For the simple configuration, simply change `EXAMPLE.COM` to your DNS domain name in the line `*/admin@EXAMPLE.COM *`.

6. **Register a username as an administrator principal.**

   The following command registers user marshall as an administrator principal:

   ```
   /usr/kerberos/sbin/kadmin.local -q addprinc marshall/admin
   ```

7. **Enter these commands to start Kerberos:**

   ```
   krb5kdc start
   kadmin start
   krb524 start
   ```

8. **Add principals with your choice of the kadmin add_principal command or the gkadmin menu** Principal .. Add.

9. **Test your environment by entering these commands:**

   ```
   kinit
   klist
   kdestroy
   ```

   Your Kerberos server is running!

Setting up a Kerberos client step by step

In this section, we describe the basic steps you need to follow to install and configure Kerberos client software on Linux or Unix. The following steps are specific to Red Hat Linux running the Gnome user interface (your flavor of Linux/Unix may vary slightly):

1. **Install these packages on every client:**

   ```
   krb5-libs
   krb5-workstation
   ```

2. **Copy the** `/etc/krb5.conf` **file from the KDC.**

3. **Run kadmin and enter these commands (substitute the computer's fully qualified domain name for** *myhost.example.com*):

   ```
   add_principal -randkey host/myhost.example.com
   ktadd -k /etc/krb5.keytab host/myhost.example.com
   ```

4. **Using kadmin, add a host principal for the workstation.**

   The instance in this case is the hostname of the workstation. Because you never again need to type the password for this principal and you probably don't want to bother with coming up with a good password, you can use the -randkey option to the kadmin command addprinc to create the principal and assign it a random key.

5. **After you create the principal, run kadmin on the workstation and enter this ktadd command:**

   ```
   ktadd -k /etc/krb5.keytab host/blah.example.com
   ```

   This step extracts the keys for the workstation and installs them.

Setting up a Kerberos 5 client is less involved than setting up a server. You need to install, at minimum, the client packages and provide clients with a `krb5.conf` configuration file. Kerberized versions of `rsh` and `rlogin` also require some configuration changes.

You need to follow a few more steps in order to run Kerberized applications:

✔ Before a particular client in your realm can allow users to connect using Kerberized `rsh` and `rlogin`, that workstation must have the xinetd package installed and have its own host principal in the Kerberos database. The kshd and klogind server programs must have access to the keys for their service's principal.

✔ To use the Kerberized versions of `rsh` and `rlogin`, you need to run either ntsysv or chkconfig to enable eklogin, klogin, and kshell.

✔ To use Kerberized telnet, use ntsysv or chkconfig to enable ktelnet.

✔ If you want to provide FTP access as well, you must create and extract a key for a principal with a root of FTP and the instance set to the hostname of the FTP server. Then use ntsysv or chkconfig to enable gssftp or another Kerberized FTP application.

That's "all" you need to do to set up a simple Kerberos realm.

Chapter 22

Troubleshooting Connectivity and Performance Problems

....

In This Chapter

▶ Protocols in this chapter: ICMP, IP, DNS, SNMP, MIB

▶ Pinging every which way

▶ Finding DNS name server info with nslookup

▶ Stepping through a troubleshooting process

▶ Tracing the route of a packet from start to end

▶ Monitoring your network with a Network Management System (NMS)

....

*P*ing — pang — pung. Today we ping, yesterday we pang, and many times we have pung. In this chapter, we describe tools for basic connectivity troubleshooting and walk you through a troubleshooting exercise step by step. Depending on which operating system you run, you may be able to use additional tools for these information-gathering tasks. Most operating systems include their own tools, such as event loggers and graphical monitors, that track processes and display dozens of network utilization statistics. Other vendors sell tools with fancy extensions and user interfaces. You can also find freeware or shareware troubleshooting tools on the Internet. Ultimately, we find that the basic tools in this chapter provide almost all the troubleshooting capabilities you need.

When you start diagnosing network problems, the basic tools provided on all major operating systems are the practical places to start. This chapter describes how to keep it simple — at least at first — with a simple set of tools that work on all operating systems:

✔ ping, ping6 for IPv6 networks on Linux, Unix, and Mac OS X, and `ping -6` for ipv6 networks on Windows operating systems

✔ ipconfig/ifconfig

✔ traceroute (tracert for Microsoft Windows)

✔ nslookup

Finally, we glance at Simple Network Management Protocol (SNMP) and look at a network management system that uses SNMP for network monitoring and troubleshooting.

Before you start diagnosing network problems, be sure that your computer hardware, such as hard drives, memory, and NICs, is working. You can't find network problems from a computer that has its own problems.

Chasing Network Problems from End to End

Imagine that you tried unsuccessfully to browse a Web site or use a service on a remote host — maybe FTP — and you can't get there. There may be a dozen reasons why you can't do what you need to. A remote host may be unavailable because

✔ Your computer isn't properly configured for networking.

✔ Your NIC isn't working.

✔ The remote host is dead; that is, shut down, hung, doesn't exist any more.

✔ The network connection (yours or the remote host's) is dead, by either hardware or software.

✔ The network is so congested that it takes too long to get there. Requests time out.

✔ A router along the way isn't reachable.

✔ The system or network administrator has set up the firewall to keep you away from the site you want to access.

If you find your computer unusable or untrustworthy because of one of these obstacles, it's time to organize a troubleshooting strategy.

Getting Started with Ping

We introduce ping in Chapter 6 to check your own host's availability on the network. The ping command is the first troubleshooting command that most network administrators use when investigating network problems. Ping lets you find out whether a remote computer is available by using network "sonar" — the Internet Control Message Protocol (ICMP). Ping bounces an ICMP echo request message off a computer; if ICMP sends back an echo reply, the computer is alive — but not necessarily well.

ICMP (Internet Control Message Protocol) — the unsung hero

ICMP is the little known workhorse of the four core protocols in the TCP/IP suite: IP, ICMP, TCP, and IUDP. ICMP sits in the Internet layer along with IP and generates IP error messages. Some of these messages include packet loss, network congestion, unavailable services, and unreachable routers and hosts. In a perfect networking world without errors, ICMP could take a long, restful holiday. In the real world, poor old ICMP is always working hard and gets little recognition. By the way, the name ICMP refers to IPv4. ICMP also has an IPv6 version named — surprise! — ICMPv6.

 The ping command tests connectivity only to a host's NIC. It doesn't test whether the operating system, the TCP/IP configuration, or services are working.

Pinging away with lots of options

The ping command tells you whether a host is alive or dead. It also gives you a hint about network congestion and slow performance. When troubleshooting with ping, you may need to ping more than just one host. If ping doesn't return a response from the host you're trying to contact, it doesn't necessarily mean that the host isn't available. Maybe the router or a DNS server isn't available. If either of them is down, the remote host may be fine, but there may be no way to get to it.

Here are a few important points to remember about the ping command:

✔ You can ping to check the availability of a specific computer or domain.

✔ You can ping by name or IP address.

✔ You can use the ping command or use a graphical interface to ping.

In the example in Listing 22-1, ping contacts an IPv4 domain. The output is from a Microsoft Windows 7 computer. The time is the response time from the remote host. Hosts that are electronically close to you (that is, on faster connections with fewer hops) should have faster response times than hosts farther away, unless network congestion occurs on the route to the nearby host. If you suspect this type of congestion, run the traceroute command (which we describe in the section "Using traceroute (tracert) to find network problems," later in this chapter). Ping also displays summary statistics about packets sent, packets lost, and how long the ping round trip took. Ping is available on any system that runs TCP/IP.

In Listing 22-1, you can see that google.com is available and that no packets were lost. All is good. We bolded the four default Microsoft replies in the example.

Listing 22-1: Reach Out and Ping Someone from Windows 7

```
Microsoft Windows [Version 6.1.7000]
Copyright (c) 2006 Microsoft Corporation. All rights reserved.

E:\Users\Administrator>ping google.com

Pinging google.com [74.125.67.100] with 32 bytes of data:
Reply from 74.125.67.100: bytes=32 time=47ms TTL=237
Reply from 74.125.67.100: bytes=32 time=43ms TTL=237
Reply from 74.125.67.100: bytes=32 time=49ms TTL=237
Reply from 74.125.67.100: bytes=32 time=47ms TTL=237

Ping statistics for 74.125.67.100:
    Packets: Sent = 4, Received = 4, Lost = 0 (0% loss),
Approximate round trip times in milli-seconds:
    Minimum = 43ms, Maximum = 49ms, Average = 46ms
```

Microsoft has a dual stack — IPv4 and IPv6 — but because google.com is at IPv4, our Windows 7 knows to use its IPv4 stack. Listing 22-3 shows an example where Windows 7 pings another iPv6 site. When you look at that example, check out the difference in the address format.

Listing 22-2 shows the same ping on google.com, but check out the packet loss numbers, as indicated in bold. The network is probably congested. Remember that with TCP as the transport, when a packet is lost, it's retransmitted. It takes time to retransmit and put the packet back together. A slow connection with no packet loss often outperforms a high-speed connection with packet loss.

Listing 22-2: Network Congestion Causes Lost Packets

```
E:\Users\Administrator\candace>ping google.com

Pinging google.com [209.85.171.100] with 32 bytes of data:

Reply from 209.85.171.100: bytes=32 time=191ms TTL=232
Request timed out.
Reply from 209.85.171.100: bytes=32 time=204ms TTL=232
Reply from 209.85.171.100: bytes=32 time=126ms TTL=232

Ping statistics for 209.85.171.100:
    Packets: Sent = 4, Received = 3, Lost = 1 (25% loss),
Approximate round trip times in milli-seconds:
    Minimum = 126ms, Maximum = 204ms, Average = 173ms
```

Listing 22-3 shows the ping -6 command on an IPv6 network.

The example in Listing 22-3 is from a computer running Microsoft Windows 7. Although the other operating systems have a handy ping6 command, Windows systems do not. Instead, you use the regular ping command with the -6 option to indicate IPv6. Pinging Google's IPv6 site also shows packet loss.

Listing 22-3: Wow! The Addresses Are So Much Longer Than IPv4

```
E:\Users\Administrator>ping -6 ipv6.google.com

  Pinging ipv6.l.google.com [2001:4860:0:2001::68] with 32 bytes
  Request timed out.
  Reply from 2001:4860:0:2001::68: time=221ms
  Reply from 2001:4860:0:2001::68: time=221ms
  Reply from 2001:4860:0:2001::68: time=221ms
  Ping statistics for 2001:4860:0:2001::68:
     Packets: Sent = 4, Received = 3, Lost = 1 (25% loss),
  Approximate round trip times in milli-seconds:
     Minimum = 221ms, Maximum = 221ms, Average = 221ms
```

Did you notice that the IPv4 version of ping has TTL information and the IPv6 output does not? *TTL* means "time to live" — how long this packet should be allowed to survive before being discarded. TTL is measured not in time, but rather in hops from computer to computer across the network. IPv6 doesn't use TTL. It uses *Hlim* instead (hop limit). Although Hlim means about the same thing as TTL, it's a more accurate term.

And now, for "some-ping" completely different: Running ping graphically

To this point in the book, our ping examples are commands executed in a terminal window. If you're a point-and-click person who wants to avoid commands, you can use a graphical version of ping. Most operating systems kindly give you the option of pinging graphically or by command. Figure 22-1 shows a graphical way to use network tools, including ping.

GNOME (pronounced "guh-nome") is a graphical interface to Linux, Windows, Unix, and Mac OS X. So, although the Linux examples in this book use Ubuntu Linux with either a command line or the GNOME graphical interface, you can do the same thing on any operating system. GNOME is bundled into Linux and most versions of Unix. For Windows and Mac OS X, you can download GNOME from www.live.gnome.org/Dia/Download and live.gnome.org/GTK%2B/OSX.

The neat thing about GNOME is that you can just download pieces of it, such as certain applications. You don't have to set up the whole desktop on top of your Windows desktop.

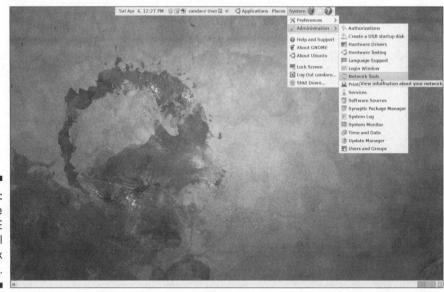

Figure 22-1:
Use the
GNOME
graphical
network
tools.

To run ping graphically, choose System⇨Administration⇨Network Tools (refer to Figure 22-1). Then click the Ping tab, shown in Figure 22-2.

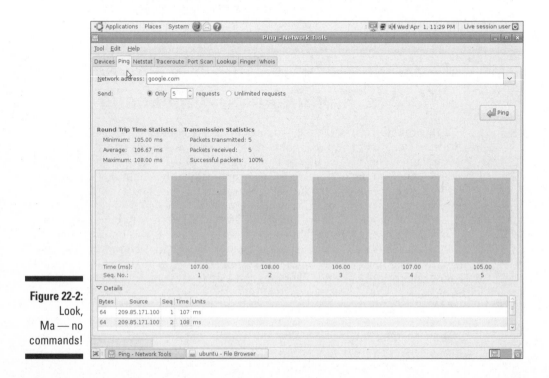

Figure 22-2:
Look,
Ma — no
commands!

Ping works a little differently on Microsoft Windows systems than on Linux, Unix, and Mac OS X. On non–Microsoft systems, ping returns replies until you stop them by pressing Ctrl+C. On Microsoft systems, ping replies four times by default and stops. You can use the `ping -n` command option to tell any system to reply a specific number of times. The following example delivers ten replies and stops:

```
ping -n 10
```

Death by ping

Sometimes your ping replies lead you to believe that a system is unreachable, as in the following example. In fact, you might be seeing a false negative. Some sites' routers block ICMP echo requests — ping, in other words — because of a denial-of-service (DoS) attack called "the Ping of Death" that was prevalent in the late 1990s. Vendors and Open Source software distributions now have patched their operating systems to avoid the Ping of Death. Still, many Web sites block ICMP echo requests at their firewalls to prevent any future variations of this kind of attack. This example shows an attempted ping that might make you think that ibm.com is not available. However, IBM blocks ICMP echo requests, so the ping output is misleading.

```
Microsoft Windows XP [Version 5.1.2600]
(C) Copyright 1985-2001 Microsoft Corp.


C:\Documents and Settings\candace>ping ibm.com

Pinging ibm.com [129.42.18.103] with 32 bytes of data:

Request timed out.
Request timed out.
Request timed out.
Request timed out.

Ping statistics for 129.42.18.103:
    Packets: Sent = 4, Received = 0, Lost = 4 (100% loss),
```

Try again with the numeric IP address to ensure that it isn't a DNS problem.

```
C:\Documents and Settings\candace>ping 129.42.18.103

Pinging 129.42.18.103 with 32 bytes of data:

Request timed out.
Request timed out.
Request timed out.
Request timed out.

Ping statistics for 129.42.18.103:
    Packets: Sent = 4, Received = 0, Lost = 4 (100% loss),
```

The Ping of Death is also known as "long ICMP." Normally, ping is implemented as a tiny ICMP request that couldn't harm a flea. However, the Ping of Death sends a giant request (more than 64KB — 65,535) broken into fragments. This giant ICMP request overwhelms the remote computer, and the computer freezes or shuts down until someone reboots it. A lowlife villain can make an entire network unreachable by sending the Ping of Death to the network's router. Like all denial-of-service attacks, the Ping of Death doesn't damage a computer or network — it just makes its victim unusable.

Packet filtering on a router or firewall that blocks fragmented ICMP echo requests (ping messages) keeps your network safe from death by ping. Most network administrators want ICMP echo capabilities to debug network problems, whereas security administrators want to limit or prohibit these messages.

Diagnosing Problems Step by Step

After you know all about ping and its variations in different operating systems, you're ready to ping to diagnose network problems, by checking these items:

- ✔ Your local network configuration
- ✔ Your hardware
- ✔ Your router
- ✔ The DNS on both sides (yours and the remote's)
- ✔ Internet problems, such as outages

Windows Firewall might prevent a successful ping operation. You might need to configure a port exception for the ping to succeed.

The following sections walk you through a network troubleshooting process so that you can find exactly where a problem exists. Naturally, we start with ping.

Pinging yourself and others

Follow the same steps whether you're on an IPv4 or IPv6 network. The figures in this section use IPv4.

If you cannot successfully ping a host, the host may still be okay. Many firewalls ban requests from the ICMP protocol and the TCP/IP ports that ping uses. See the earlier section, "Death by ping," for more information.

Follow these steps to troubleshoot your network:

1. **Ping 127.0.0.1 (the numeric IP address of localhost).**

   Ping the numbers before the names to see whether the connections work and to circumvent the name lookup step.

   If the ping succeeds, proceed to the next step. If it fails, something is seriously wrong with your TCP/IP configuration. Here are some possible problems:

   a. TCP/IP is configured wrong on your workstation.

   b. You did not get a correctly leased DHCP from your DHCP server.

   c. The IP address you're using is already in use by another client.

2. **Ping localhost, as shown in Listing 22-4, to prove that your hosts file is available.**

   Pinging the name tests the name resolution and lookup.

   The example shown in Listing 22-4 is from a computer running Ubuntu Linux. Although the output may look a little different to Windows users, don't worry: The information is the same. Different operating systems like to put a little different spin on commands.

Listing 22-4: Ping Yourself — You're localhost

```
candace@ubuntu:~$ ping -n 5 localhost

PING localhost (127.0.0.1) 56(84) bytes of data.
64 bytes from localhost (127.0.0.1): icmp_seq=1 ttl=64 time=0.037 ms
64 bytes from localhost (127.0.0.1): icmp_seq=2 ttl=64 time=0.033 ms
64 bytes from localhost (127.0.0.1): icmp_seq=3 ttl=64 time=0.037 ms
64 bytes from localhost (127.0.0.1): icmp_seq=4 ttl=64 time=0.032 ms
64 bytes from localhost (127.0.0.1): icmp_seq=5 ttl=64 time=0.033 ms

        --- localhost ping statistics ---
        5 packets transmitted, 5 received, 0% packet loss, time 3998ms
        rtt min/avg/max/mdev = 0.032/0.034/0.037/0.005 ms
```

   If this ping fails, TCP/IP may not be able to resolve names into addresses.

3. **If Step 2 works, ping your own IP address because some operating systems cheat when you ping localhost.**

   The TCP/IP stack realizes that localhost is this computer, so it doesn't test your NIC. Pinging your own IP address involves more of the TCP/IP stack.

If you don't know your IP address, run `ipconfig/all` in Windows to find out. (Chapter 5 introduces ipconfig for Windows and ifconfig for all other operating systems.) In Linux and Unix, `ifconfig -a` gives you a lot of information, but not your IP address. Figure 22-3 shows some options for finding your IP address in Linux.

There's more than one way to do most things in Linux. If you don't like typing commands, use a graphical interface, such as GNOME, to find your IP address. Using the GNOME menu, choose System⇨ Administration⇨Network Tools. The Devices tab displays your IP address, as shown in Figure 22-4.

4. **Ping your hostname, not the whole FQDN, to be sure that your DNS resolver (see Chapter 10) understands how to translate your hostname into a numeric IP address.**

   If this step fails, you may have trouble with name lookups. If this step succeeds, you know that your resolver is working properly. Continue to the next step.

5. **Ping your FQDN to be sure that your DNS client is working.**

   At this point, you have proven that your computer's network configuration isn't the problem, not including whatever connection media you use.

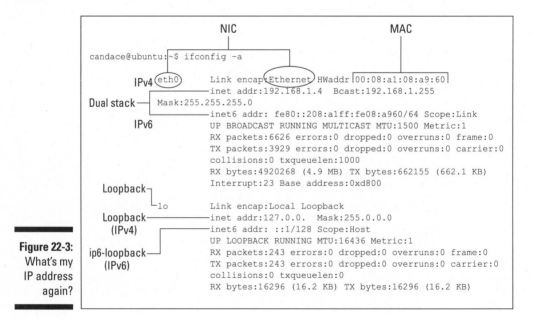

Figure 22-3: What's my IP address again?

6. **Ping your router to be sure that packets can travel on your LAN.**

   Don't know where your router is? On Windows, use ipconfig, as shown in Figure 22-5. Look in the output for *default gateway* — that's your router. On other operating systems, use the command `route -n` (for net) to show your router. If you're a non-Windows user, use the `route -n` command to find out your router's address (default gateway) and ping your router. You can see an example in Figure 22-6.

   If you can ping your router (the default gateway), your NIC is working. If it fails, check the status of your NIC and other connection media. You might be on a wireless LAN, but you still have connection media. If a cable is loose or disconnected, the packets can't reach the router. Repeat Step 6.

7. **If pinging your router succeeds, surf to your router and get *its* gateway address, which comes from your ISP's DHCP server.**

8. **Ping your router's gateway address to be sure that you can get to your ISP.**

```
C:\Documents and Settings\candace>ipconfig

Windows IP Configuration

Ethernet adapter Local Area Connection:

        Media State . . . . . . . . . . . : Media disconnected

Ethernet adapter Wireless Network Connection:

        Connection-specific DNS Suffix  . : home
        IP Address. . . . . . . . . . . . : 192.168.1.6
        Subnet Mask . . . . . . . . . . . : 255.255.255.0
        IP Address. . . . . . . . . . . . :
           fe80::213:2ff:feb8:5851%8
        Default Gateway . . . . . . . . . : 192.168.1.1
C:\Documents and Settings\candace>ping 192.168.1.1

Pinging 192.168.1.1 with 32 bytes of data:

Reply from 192.168.1.1: bytes=32 time=10ms TTL=64
Reply from 192.168.1.1: bytes=32 time=3ms TTL=64
Reply from 192.168.1.1: bytes=32 time=2ms TTL=64
Reply from 192.168.1.1: bytes=32 time=2ms TTL=64

Ping statistics for 192.168.1.1:
    Packets: Sent = 4, Received = 4, Lost = 0 (0% loss),
Approximate round trip times in milli-seconds:
    Minimum = 2ms, Maximum = 10ms, Average = 4ms
```

Ping

Figure 22-5:
Windows
users, find
out your
router's
address
(default
gateway)
and ping
your router.

```
candace@ubuntu:~$ route -n
Kernel IP routing table
Destination     Gateway         Genmask         Flags  Metric   Ref  Use Iface
192.168.1.0     0.0.0.0         255.255.255.0   U      0        0    0   wlan0
0.0.0.0         192.168.1.1     0.0.0.0         UG     0        0    0   wlan0
```

Router

Wireless NIC

Figure 22-6:
Non-
Windows
users, use
the route
−n com-
mand.

9. Ping your ISP's default gateway (router).

If this ping fails, call your ISP's customer service department. If you can't ping your ISP's gateway, your ISP cannot route traffic to the Internet.

10. **If your ISP's router ping is okay, bypass DNS by pinging the destination by its IP address. Substitute the destination address for the address shown in the earlier section "Death by ping."**

Although you know that DNS name resolution works on your localhost, you need to complete this step for two reasons. First, the name or address (or both) of the remote destination may be missing or incorrect on the DNS server. Second, the DNS server might not be reachable.

Later, in Step 12, if nslookup displays a different address, redo this step using that address.

11. **Try to reach your ISP's DNS server or servers by pinging them. (You can use** `ipconfig /all` **to find your DNS servers' IP addresses, too.)**

If the ping fails, either your DHCP server is giving you bad information or you configured DNS manually on your client and made a mistake. For example, when you created or edited your DNS database file, maybe you typed a number incorrectly. If so, your DNS server is sending incorrect information and you need to contact the administrator. If you're the server administrator, now you know that you made a mistake. Go fix those IP addresses now!

Now you know whether the DNS server is reachable, but you don't know whether it's working *properly*.

12. **Switch to the nslookup program (see the following section) to see whether the DNS service is running on the remote server.**

Using nslookup to query a name server

Nslookup is a built-in DNS tool, so it's available to any operating system, as long as the computer is running DNS. When you start nslookup (*ns* for name server and *lookup* for, well, lookup), you connect to a default name server — the same one your computer normally uses for DNS queries. Figure 22-7 shows how to use the server command to switch to your ISP's DNS server — remember to use ipconfig or ifconfig if you don't know the address of your DNS server.

Be careful as you enter nslookup commands. Any typographical error is treated as a request for DNS information. For example, if you want to set a timeout value but you type **sit timeout=5** rather than **set timeout=5**, nslookup asks the name server to find a computer named sit. If a computer named sit exists, you have information that you didn't want. If no computer is named sit, you see a message to that effect — still not what you want.

Figure 22-7:
For
inquiring
minds: The
command
`set`
`type=`
`any` returns
all available
information.

13. **Run nslookup to verify that the IP address from Step 10 is correct.**

Figure 22-7 shows an nslookup query for an IPv4 address, followed by an nslookup query for an IPv6 address. Notice that the lookup for the IPv6 address can reply non-authoritatively. If nslookup shows a different address, retry Step 10 with this new address:

```
C:\>nslookup ipv6.google.com
DNS request timed out.
    timeout was 2 seconds.
Server:  UnKnown
Address:  192.168.1.1

Non-authoritative answer:
Name:    ipv6.l.google.com
Address:  2001:4860:0:2001::68
Aliases:  ipv6.google.com
```

14. **If you know for a fact (you talked to the people at the remote host) that nslookup gave you the wrong IP address, add an entry to your localhosts file to override the DNS information. If you're in charge of the DNS server, edit the database file.**

At this point, you can be sure that the problem is on the Internet.

15. **Use traceroute or tracert (see the next section) to figure out how far a packet gets before running into the problem.**

Using traceroute (tracert) to find network problems

Traceroute (or *tracert,* in any version of Windows) is a program that helps you identify where problems exist on a network. When you ping a host, ping's ICMP packet may have to travel through dozens of routers to reach the remote host. Sometimes, your localhost and the remote host are working correctly but your ping fails. Your ping fails because one of the routers along the way is having problems.

Fortunately, you can use the traceroute or tracert command to diagnose where the problem occurs. Traceroute displays both the route that packets follow on their way to a destination and the time in milliseconds for each round-trip hop. Each place a packet goes through is a *hop*. Traceroute tests each hop along the way three times and displays, in milliseconds, the minimum, average, and maximum time for a round trip.

Listing 22-5 shows a successful tracert command. The first time, it fails. The second time (Listing 22-6), it succeeds. Notice that traceroute tries to show both the name and IP address of the router. When traceroute goes out onto the Internet, the router is a fully qualified domain name.

The tricky bit about analyzing traceroute output is to know what a slow response time is. For example, 220 milliseconds may be a long time between Boston and New York, but it's normal between Ottawa and Tokyo. Hops between local links should take no more than a few milliseconds.

16. **Run traceroute or tracert (as shown in Listing 22-5) to see whether packets make it to the destination.**

If the traceroute is successful, the problem is with the service on the remote computer. Perhaps that FTP service you're trying to use is stopped or hung or simply misconfigured. Maybe the firewall prevents you from using the service.

Most operating systems spell out the traceroute command. When using a Microsoft Windows operating system, you spell the command *tracert.*

Traceroute tests (such as in Listing 22-5) each hop along the way three times and displays the minimum, average, and maximum time for a round trip in milliseconds.

Listing 22-5: Traceroute Finds Slowdowns in Your Packet's Path

```
C:\Documents and Settings\candace>tracert google.com

Tracing route to google.com [209.85.171.100]
over a maximum of 30 hops:

 1     2 ms    <1 ms    <1 ms  Wireless_Broadband_Router.home [192.168.1.1]
 2    10 ms     7 ms     7 ms  L100.VFTTP-66.BSTNMA.verizon-gni.net [72.93.254.1]
 3    10 ms     7 ms     9 ms  P0-2.LCR-05.BSTNMA.verizon-gni.net [130.81.54.0]

 4    10 ms     9 ms     6 ms  so-7-2-0-0.BB-RTR1.BOS.verizon-gni.net [130.81.2
                                 9.172]
 5    19 ms    19 ms    17 ms  so-9-1-0-0.BB-RTR1.NY325.verizon-gni.net [130.81
                                 .19.70]
 6    20 ms    35 ms    19 ms  0.so-4-3-0.XL3.NYC4.ALTER.NET [152.63.10.25]
 7    24 ms    18 ms    19 ms  0.ge-4-2-0.BR3.NYC4.ALTER.NET [152.63.3.126]
 8    20 ms    17 ms    16 ms  204.255.173.54
 9    25 ms    17 ms    17 ms  vlan52.ebr2.NewYork2.Level3.net [4.69.138.254]
10    45 ms    37 ms    59 ms  ae-2-2.ebr1.Chicago1.Level3.net [4.69.132.65]
11    37 ms    34 ms    38 ms  ae-6.ebr1.Chicago2.Level3.net [4.69.140.190]
12    86 ms    72 ms    72 ms  ae-3.ebr2.Denver1.Level3.net [4.69.132.61]
13   101 ms   102 ms   158 ms  ae-2.ebr2.Seattle1.Level3.net [4.69.132.53]
14   100 ms    99 ms    99 ms  ae-21-52.car1.Seattle1.Level3.net [4.68.105.34]

15    98 ms    94 ms    94 ms  GOOGLE-INC.car1.Seattle1.Level3.net [4.79.104.74]
16    97 ms    96 ms    96 ms  209.85.249.32
17   104 ms   102 ms   101 ms  216.239.46.204
18   124 ms     *       187 ms  64.233.174.127
19   209 ms     *       145 ms  209.85.251.153
20   104 ms   165 ms   204 ms  74.125.31.6
21     *        *       106 ms  cg-in-f100.google.com [209.85.171.100]

Trace complete.
```

If you're concerned about the responses that timed out (*), you can use the -w command option, shown in Listing 22-6, to increase the wait timeout.

Listing 22-6: Use the -w Command Option to Increase the Wait Timeout

```
C:\Documents and Settings\candace>tracert -w 600   google.com

Tracing route to google.com [209.85.171.100]
over a maximum of 30 hops:

 1     1 ms     8 ms     4 ms  Wireless_Broadband_Router.home [192.168.1.1]
 2    11 ms     6 ms     8 ms  L100.VFTTP-66.BSTNMA.verizon-gni.net [72.93.254.1]
 3     6 ms     7 ms     7 ms  P0-2.LCR-05.BSTNMA.verizon-gni.net [130.81.54.0]
 4    11 ms     9 ms    18 ms  so-7-2-0-0.BB-RTR1.BOS.verizon-gni.net [130.81.2
                                 9.172]
```

```
 5    19 ms     20 ms    17 ms   so-9-1-0-0.BB-RTR1.NY325.verizon-gni.net [130.81
                                     .19.70]
 6    22 ms     17 ms    17 ms   0.so-4-3-0.XL3.NYC4.ALTER.NET [152.63.10.25]
 7    30 ms     17 ms    16 ms   0.ge-2-2-0.BR3.NYC4.ALTER.NET [152.63.3.130]
 8    20 ms     19 ms    19 ms   xe-10-2-0.edge2.NewYork2.level3.net [4.68.110.23
                                     3]
 9    20 ms     18 ms    18 ms   vlan52.ebr2.NewYork2.Level3.net [4.69.138.254]
10    38 ms     36 ms    35 ms   ae-2-2.ebr1.Chicago1.Level3.net [4.69.132.65]
11    38 ms     38 ms    36 ms   ae-6.ebr1.Chicago2.Level3.net [4.69.140.190]
12    75 ms     71 ms    75 ms   ae-3.ebr2.Denver1.Level3.net [4.69.132.61]
13   250 ms    154 ms    97 ms   ae-2.ebr2.Seattle1.Level3.net [4.69.132.53]
14   101 ms     96 ms    97 ms   ae-21-52.car1.Seattle1.Level3.net [4.68.105.34]

15    97 ms    158 ms    96 ms   GOOGLE-INC.car1.Seattle1.Level3.net [4.79.104.74]
16    96 ms     94 ms    95 ms   209.85.249.32
17   148 ms    101 ms   106 ms   216.239.46.204
18   124 ms    102 ms   102 ms   64.233.174.127
19   133 ms    205 ms   203 ms   209.85.251.149
20   225 ms    210 ms   199 ms   74.125.31.134
21   104 ms    102 ms   101 ms   cg-in-f100.google.com [209.85.171.100]

Trace complete.
```

If a trace ends with a series of timeouts and never reaches the destination, you found the host or network connection that's the obstacle.

The GNOME graphical interface has a visual traceroute network tool if you prefer point and click to typing commands. Figure 22-8 shows an excerpt from GNOME's traceroute tool on a Linux operating system.

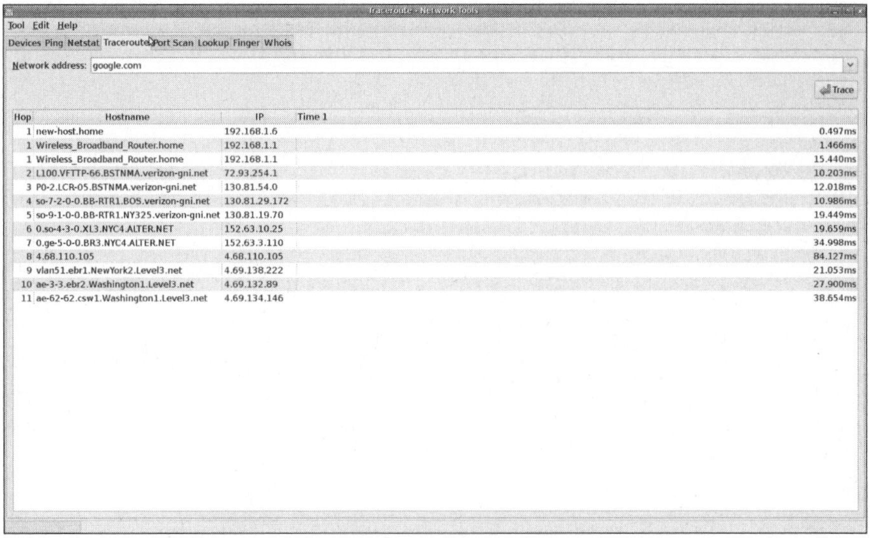

Figure 22-8: There's more than one way to trace a route.

17. **If you're running traceroute on a private intranet, you should let the administrator know where the problem is. If the problem is on the Internet, you can either contact the administrator where traceroute identified a blockage or wait for it to be fixed.**

Of course, if you've read this far, you're probably the administrator of the intranet. Aren't you relieved to know where to look on your network to solve the problem?

There's one exception to this step: A series of timeouts, like this one:

```
16   *   *   *    Request timed out.
```

usually means that the firewall at the destination is blocking ICMP requests. In other words, you reached the destination's firewall, and the firewall won't let the trace in. You can't find out anything else from here without contacting the system or network administrator at the last point in the trace.

Don't add all the times to find the total time to the traceroute destination. The time for the last hop is the total round-trip time.

Simplifying SNMP, the Simple Network Management Protocol

Earlier in this chapter, we give you tips about troubleshooting from single device to single device — for example, pinging from your host to your ISP or to a DNS server. Sometimes, you may need to look at all devices on your network as a whole. You can do this with the tools described earlier in this chapter. Just follow the steps on each machine in your network and collate the information.

It's easier said than done, right?

TCP/IP has the solution. SNMP is the protocol for collecting vast amounts of network usage and bandwidth statistics from a single device to a network of thousands of hosts.

Just barely describing how SNMP works

SNMP software consists of a manager and an agent (a *client,* in version 3) and a set of objects known as management information blocks, or MIBs. The manager and agent run SNMP over UDP. The *SNMP manager* collects network data by sending SNMP requests. Even on a small network, the amount of data

SNMP collects can seem massive. You can use the data to write reports and display graphs of SNMP data, such as devices connected to the network, network blockages, and alerts.

SNMP agents and clients run on every network device. Commercial products can poll your network and map all your devices in the network. The SNMP agent listens to requests coming from the SNMP manager and is located on the device to monitor.

Are you wondering why the *S* in SNMP stands for simple? Wait — there's more! MIBs organize the collected data into objects, such as the Internet object. Small elements are grouped into larger objects. Some of the small objects include power supplies, fans, files, processes, and buffers — and the list goes on almost forever. The RFC-Editor publishes more than 25 RFCs about MIBs. The RFCs publish the structures of each standard MIB so that everyone has access to the data to write reporting programs.

Using SMNP programming free

You can write amazingly sophisticated network monitoring programs and maybe receive a raise or a promotion or at least a pat on the back. But here's the thing: While you're spending all that time programming, who's taking care of the network?

To work smarter, get a network management system (NMS) that organizes the data and gives you lots of monitoring and reporting options. If you search for *SNMP network management* at www.google.com, you see lots of choices in commercial products and free products. The examples in this section come from the Loriot Pro V5 Network Management System, free edition, down-loadable from www.loriot.com. Several good products are available, but whatever you choose, your NMS should be able to map out your network or networks so that you know which devices you have and their IP addresses, as shown in Figure 22-9. After the NMS is installed, the wizard asks whether you want it to auto-discover which networks and devices you have or map out your network manually.

When you look at the map of the network, it's useful to be able to identify what kinds of devices participate in the network. Your NMS should be able to show you specifically (for example, a host and a router) which devices were running when your NMS collected the sample data. If a host is shut down for some reason, your network map shows you where to start troubleshooting.

Figure 22-9:
This organization has two small networks.

Although your NMS might have displays that look different from our examples, you should be able to point to and click icons to get the information you need to monitor and troubleshoot your network. Because SNMP collects so much data, an NMS gives you an amazing variety of reports to choose from. Take a look at Figure 22-10. When you right-click the router icon, you see a menu of actions to take. When you choose the Tools option, you find enough troubleshooting and reporting tools to keep you busy all year.

Finally, in addition to mapping your network and providing tools for reporting on the state of your network as a whole and on individual devices, your NMS should give you information about the MIBs. For even a small SOHO (small office/home office), the MIB tree can look like a 100-year-old oak tree with all its branches and leaves. Look at the tree and run away, or enjoy deciphering the MIBs, depending on how advanced a network administrator you are.

Did we say that the MIB tree can become quite big? Just look at the tree that our Loriot-brand NMS displays in Figure 22-11. This is a tree for one network with a single host and router.

A network management system makes monitoring and troubleshooting networks much easier than programming against raw SNMP data and requests. Your screens may vary from ours — in fact, we guarantee that they will. Networks are like snowflakes: No two (well almost no two) are alike. Just get a product that meets your needs, and monitor it.

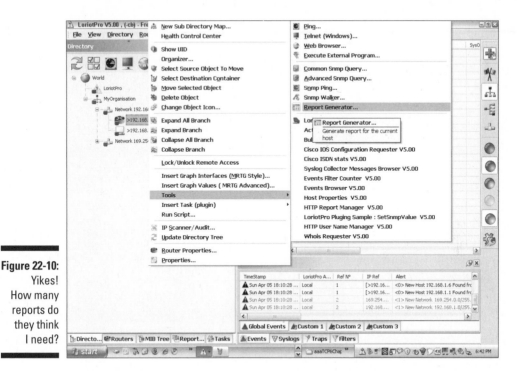

Figure 22-10:
Yikes!
How many
reports do
they think
I need?

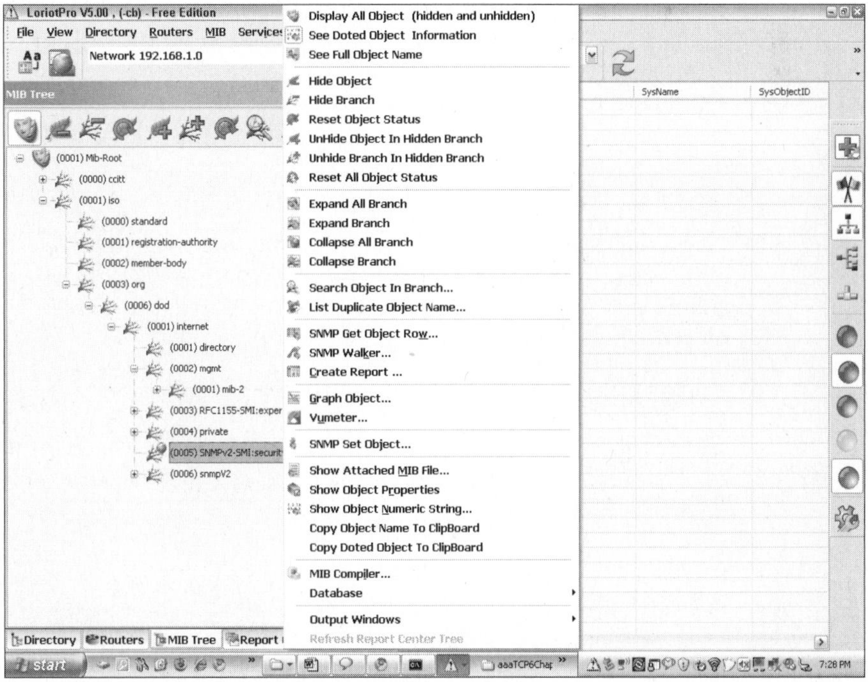

Figure 22-11:
Have mercy.
Do you
really need
that much
data? Only
the admin-
istrator
knows.

Part VI
The Part of Tens

The 5th Wave   By Rich Tennant

EXPERIMENTING WITH THE WIRELESS LASER BEAM NETWORK

"Okay — did you get that?"

In this part . . .

The chapters in this part of the book are TCP/IP nuggets. We even give you lots of ice to keep them fresh. If you're ready for some fun and new things to do, look at Chapter 23. If you need some recreation, have a snack of cola and candy and then try blowing something up! If you're the artistic type, we show you a site where you can create animated films in only four steps. When you're interested in making more serious movies, Chapter 24 directs you to some absorbing security videos.

If you're an armchair traveler, you can travel from one pole to the other by driving down a road made of ice and watching penguins and scientists. Chapter 23 helps you take language lessons before you go. Speaking of traveling, check out the Internet traffic report to see whether your packets will get jammed up on the Internet superhighway. If you want a trip that's not so wild, walk around (virtually) the U.S. government cryptologic museum to see the how and why of encryption and other computer artifacts.

When you're in a more serious mood, Chapter 24 points you to a useful Internet glossary to remind you what all the lingo and buzzwords mean and to keep you up to date on new jargon that appears in the TCP/IP-and-Internet world. You can also find quick security tips in this chapter and pointers that advise you where to go to keep up on the latest viruses, worms, Trojan horses, and other nasty intrusions. Parents have to be especially careful about the Internet goodies they let into their kids' computers. Chapter 24 is the place to find a guide for kids' online safety.

And, because we've salted cooking analogies throughout this book, Chapter 24 ends with a security cookbook.

As you work through Part VI, you may notice that "ten" doesn't always equal 10 — that's computer math for you. Are you talking decimal numbers or binary? Hex, maybe? In octal, 10 means 8; in binary, it means 2; in hexadecimal, it means 16. We reserve the right to count in whatever base we like!

Chapter 23

Ten More Uses for TCP/IP

*T*CP/IP makes it possible for you to travel the Internet and Web looking for technical information, such as security tips and locations for Internet congestion. The protocol stack also provides communications underpinnings so that you can have a little fun. This chapter lists almost ten serious and not so serious places you can visit, compliments of the TCP/IP protocol stack.

Find Internet Traffic Jams

Hopefully, most of the time your Web surfing is smooth sailing. (Yes, we're mixing our sports, but, hey, they're all water sports.) If you're having trouble reaching some sites, however, you may want to check out the Internet Traffic Report, which tells you if any geographic regions of the Internet are congested. For example, you can get an idea if the site in Europe you're trying to reach is impacted by high traffic. The map, updated every five minutes, is at www.internettrafficreport.com/main.htm.

The Traffic Report tracks the worldwide flow of Internet data around the world. You can see a map of the world that shows an index for each continent, except Africa and Antarctica. The current index is a number between zero and one hundred. The higher the index, the faster and more reliable the connections are.

If you're hungry for more, you can view graphs for each continent that show the average packet loss rate and response rate for each continent.

Take Language Lessons on Your Phone

Talking phrase books and dictionaries turn your smartphone into a talking translator. These phrase books use native speakers, so there's no confusion about accents. You can use your phone to order lunch in more than 40 countries without having to point to a menu and hope you get it right. LingvoSoft's Talking PhraseBooks act as more than audio dictionaries. You also get a multitude of commonly used phrases, so that when you travel, you don't need to look up nine or ten separate words to ask how to get to the metro. LingoSoft's Talking Hebrew PhraseBook contains more than 14,000 complete phrases, organized into 15 subjects.

Several vendors make language translators for those of you on the move. You can get translators for more than just phones. Providers make them for most mobile devices running Palm OS, Pocket PC, and Windows Mobile. If you just want to stay home and relax, don't worry; you can get lots of translation software for your PC or Mac. The CNET.com Web site reviews language translators and has several available for download. See their Web page at `http://download.cnet.com/mobile/language-software/3150-2279_4-0.html?tag=bc` for a list of translators for various languages.

Visit Antarctica (Armchair Traveler)

Communication satellites carry live images of the South Pole. You can watch live satellite coverage for about 11 hours and 15 minutes each day. Because the South Pole has six months of daylight and six months of darkness, the light gets too low from mid-September to mid-April for the camera to capture an image, so you see a still picture on the Web page during the dark months.

Our favorite Antarctic Web cam (`www.usap.gov/videoClipsAndMaps/spwebcam.cfm`) is at the Amundsen-Scott science station, which is part of the U.S. Antarctic Program Web site. In addition to the Web cam, you can watch videos, examine maps, and watch what's going on live at McMurdo Sound. The Web portal to all these goodies lives at `www.usap.gov`.

Check on the State of the Internet

Akamai Technologies publishes a quarterly report, "State of the Internet." Akamai is a huge server network provider all over the world, and it collects data from its global server network to report about network outages, attacks, hacks, and trends. In "The State of the Internet Q2 2008," Akamai lists the most attacked TCP/IP ports. The top four assaulted ports were Microsoft communication and programming ports. There is much to learn about dangers and trends at www.akamai.com/stateoftheinternet.

Akamai has an interesting little button labeled Visualizing the Internet on its technology page. Clicking this button lets you look at some neat information about Internet usage, such as all the online shopping that's happening while you're watching. As we write this chapter, we see that the United States, Central America, and Canada are listening to a lot of digital music, more than any other place in the world. The link to the technology page is at the top of Akamai's home page, www.akamai.com.

Create Animations Online

If you're bored and looking for something to do or if you want to take up a new hobby, try making animated movies, and e-mailing them to your friends. In a four-step process, you can create your own little movie:

1. Select a background.

2. Select objects.

3. Move the objects around as you record the movements.

4. Play back your animation.

You can get a lot more creative by drawing your own objects or importing them. If you're proud of your clips, you can embed them in a Web site or a blog.

FluxTime Studio, at www.fluxtime.com, even has a gallery so you can display your clips to the world. Only the demo portion of the site is free, but the cost to use the software for a year around $20, which includes Web space for storing your gems.

Test Your Computer's Security for Free

Gibson Research Corporation, www.grc.com, provides free and reputable security services. It's one of our favorites. The free online service ShieldsUP! probes computers running various Microsoft Windows operating systems from the Internet to see what information you've left public. There are two tests: Probing ports and LeakTest.

✔ **Probing ports for security levels:** Port testing tries to establish TCP connections to common ports and services, such as FTP, Telnet, Finger, HTTP, and POP3. The results can be stealth, closed, or open:

- *Stealth:* The stealth result is the most secure port type — outsiders can't even *see* your ports.

- *Closed:* The closed result means that the port is visible to outsiders, but they can't use it. Because you're giving intruders information about your system, however, a closed result does mean that system privacy could be better.

- *Open:* The open result isn't good. Not only are your ports visible, but they're also available for break-ins.

You can opt to have all your service ports tested, but be aware that there are more than 65,000 ports. Even if you're not using all ports (and you're probably not), a hacker could try to get in on one of the high-numbered ports.

✔ **Testing your firewall for outbound leaks:** LeakTest is a program that checks your firewall to see if anything nasty can leak out of it. LeakTest tries to make an outbound connection from your computer to the Grc. com server. LeakTest lets you know the effectiveness of your computer's personal firewall.

Watch Diet Coke and Mentos Explode

Is it an urban legend, or is it true that Diet Coke and Mentos candies explode when put together? And what about regular Coke and Mentos? Does that combination explode? If you want to see some big explosions, visit www. youtube.com/watch?v=hKoB0MHVBvM. KABOOM!

Ride in a Big Rig Over 350 Miles of Ice

People used to think the Internet superhighway was something amazing. Well, most of us have started to take the Internet for granted, but how about a 350-mile ice superhighway?

Up at the top of Canada, the geography is mostly deep lakes and permafrost. When the lakes freeze, an icy road across them is possible. When the ice is at least 16-inches deep, the road builders have one month to build the road. Truckers haul 10,000 loads of supplies to oil-searching camps in 60 days before the ice melts. Visit the Web site www.history.com to ride along with some of these brave (foolish?) truckers in 35 degrees below zero temperatures. Sadly not everyone survives. When the ice starts to thin out, trucks occasionally fall through the ice.

Chapter 24

Ten More Resources for Information about TCP/IP Security

*R*emember the old saying, "The Internet protects those who protect themselves"? Okay, you caught us. We made it up. As you work your way across the Internet and Web, try saying it over and over. Protect yourself. Protect your business. Protect your kids. This chapter provides a smorgasbord of tasty delights that protect you from being eaten alive by security breaches. And to give you a break from all your hard work, this chapter takes you to visit a museum and watch a video.

Security from A to Z

The Security Center at www.linuxsecurity.com is for everyone who needs to know about Internet security, not just for Linux lovers. It includes invaluable information about Internet security. The Security Dictionary defines just about every Internet security term. In addition to the Dictionary, the Security Center contains security tips, book reviews, and white papers such as these:

✔ "Wireless Security: Threats and Countermeasures"

✔ "Are Passwords Really Free? A Closer Look at the Hidden Costs of Password Security"

✔ "Wi-Fi Security: What Hackers Know That You Don't"

✔ "Establish Trust to Protect and Grow Your Online Business: Authentication and Encryption – The Cornerstones of Online Security"

If you want to get deep into technical details about TCP/IP security flaws and solutions, read the paper, "TCP/IP Security" by Chris Chambers, Justin Dolske, and Jayaraman Iyer from the Department of Computer and Information Science, Ohio State University, Columbus, Ohio. Find it here: www.linuxsecurity.com/resource_files/documentation/tcpip-security.html.

CERT-ainly Don't Forget the CERTs

CERTS are where you go to find the most recent and reliable news about security happenings around the world. Internet-savvy folks join the CERT (Computer Emergency Response Team) mailing lists and subscribe to RSS feeds. CERT keeps you up to date on the latest and newest security vulnerabilities; and shows you how to solve or work around such problems.

CERT also publishes tech tips and practices. This collection of documents gives you a leg up on designing and implementing security polices for your network. The U.S. government CERT (at www.us-cert.gov/) probably has the most comprehensive information, but numerous other countries maintain CERTS as well. Countries ranging from A to V, Argentina to Vietnam, have Web sites for their CERTS.

Take a Virtual Museum Tour

Interested in cryptology, the basis of encryption? When you take this tour (www.nsa.gov/about/cryptologic_heritage/museum/virtual_tour/index.shtml), you can visit any or all of the exhibits in the museum. Our favorite is the Computer Development exhibition, which has a Cray XMP-24 supercomputer, one of the first supercomputers.

Crime Stoppers' Cinema

One of Google's online video TechTalks, "Crime: The Real Internet Security Problem," presents some startling security ideas. Dr. Phillip Hallam-Baker, a leading designer of Internet security, sets out a comprehensive strategy for defeating the serious and growing problem of Internet crime. Consumer fraud, for example (in particular, phishing), keeps growing despite all the protections that are in place. Internet crime is big business. Dr. Hallam-Baker talks about how Internet users consider security a top priority. Despite that fact, Dr. Hallam-Baker explains that almost none of the security mechanisms developed to end Internet crime have worked effectively.

To watch and listen to Dr. Hallam-Baker's talk, visit the Web site, `video.google.com`, and use the search term "Internet Security." If you also search on "TCP/IP," you will find several more videos about Internet security and TCP/IP.

Speaking of video, don't forget `youtube.com`. Search for Internet security, and you'll find lots of useful videos.

YouTube may also have content that you find inappropriate and offensive. Just to be safe, keep your search parameters tight.

The TCP/IP Guide — Free and Online

Don't feel daunted by the size of the site for the TCP/IP Guide at, `www.tcpipguide.com`. Charles Kozierok, the author, has supplied a guide to the Guide. In addition to sections about all aspects of security protocols, this book is a comprehensive guide to all things TCP/IP from A to Z: addressing to zones.

Finding Podcasts about Internet Security

A *podcast* is a pre-recorded audio program that's listed on a Web site as available for download. You can listen as soon as you find a podcast you like, or you can download it and listen to it later on your computer or mobile devices. Although podcasting is associated most often with Apple's iPod MP3 players, you can listen to podcasts on any computer or mobile device. You can subscribe to RSS feeds of podcasts so that new podcasts can automatically be sent to you.

A good place to start finding podcasts about security is the Network Security Podcast at `mckeay.libsyn.com`. This site broadcasts weekly talks about Internet security. Some topics have included

✓ Cybercrime servers selling billions of dollars worth of stolen information, illicit services

✓ Fast-spreading phishing scam hits Gmail users

✓ Facebook

✓ The DNS Changer trojan starts its own internal DHCP server

✓ And dozens more podcasts . . .

If you spend all your time listening to security podcasts, another good source is the Cisco Security Podcast Series at

`cisco.com/en/US/solutions/ns170/sml_podcast.html`

Save the Children

"DIY: Parents' Guide to Online Safety" is a must-read article for parents:

```
www.cnet.com.au/software/security/0,239029558,240057410,00.htm
```

Your kids may know more than you do about computers and the Internet. Marshall and Candace are techie geeks, and yet their niece, Emily, had to teach Candace about chat. Even though kids have a lot of Internet know-how, they can be very naïve as well. Sadly, we speak from experience. "DIY: Parents' Guide to Online Safety" is filled with tips on how to protect kids from their own curiosity and from online predators. Not only is this an excellent article, but the authors also list products that help you restrict kids from certain sites and teach you how to find out exactly what your kids are doing, right down to every keystroke they type, if you feel that's necessary.

Besides this valuable article for parents and anyone concerned with children's online safety, CNET Australia, the source of the Parent's Guide, is filled with articles about security and reviews of security-software suites.

Microsoft TechNet Library

You might think that the Microsoft TechNet Library (`technet.microsoft.com/en-us/library`) is about all things Microsoft. Well, it is, but one of the main topics in the TechNet Library is "Security." If you use any recent Microsoft Windows operating system, you need to look at the security topics at TechNet. The only problem with TechNet is the sheer volume of information, and that you want to read all of it.

Security Cuisine

Sean Boran's IT Security Cookbook (`www.boran.com/security`) is another one of those sites that has more information than one person can take in with just one reading. But not to worry — the Cookbook is so well organized that you can find what interests you pretty quickly.

Index

• *J* •

• X •

• Z •